A COMPANION TO
BRITISH WILDLIFE

A COMPANION TO

BRITISH WILDLIFE

Foreword by Tony Soper

MARSHALL CAVENDISH

Contents

		page
FOREWORD		6
1	THE THAMES VALLEY	8
2	THE NEW FOREST	24
3	THE ISLE OF WIGHT	38
4	DARTMOOR	52
5	THE LIZARD	68
6	THE ISLES OF SCILLY	82
7	BRECKLAND	96
8	THE NORFOLK BROADS	110
9	THE PEAK DISTRICT	124
10	THE YORKSHIRE DALES	140
11	THE LAKE DISTRICT	156
12	THE WELSH HILLS	170
13	ANGLESEY	184
14	THE SCOTTISH HIGHLANDS	200
15	THE CAIRNGORMS	214
16	THE WESTERN ISLES	230
17	THE SHETLAND ISLANDS	244
18	THE ORKNEY ISLANDS	260
19	LOUGH NEAGH	274
20	THE REPUBLIC OF IRELAND	288
21	THE BURREN	302
INDEX		316
PICTURE CREDITS		320

This edition published 1992 by Bookmart Ltd Desford Road, Enderby, Leicester LE9 5AD

Original material © 1985-7 Marshall Cavendish Ltd
This arrangement © 1992 Marshall Cavendish Ltd

Prepared by Marshall Cavendish Books Ltd
119 Wardour Street, London W1V 3TD

Printed in Hong Kong

ISBN 1 85435 3926

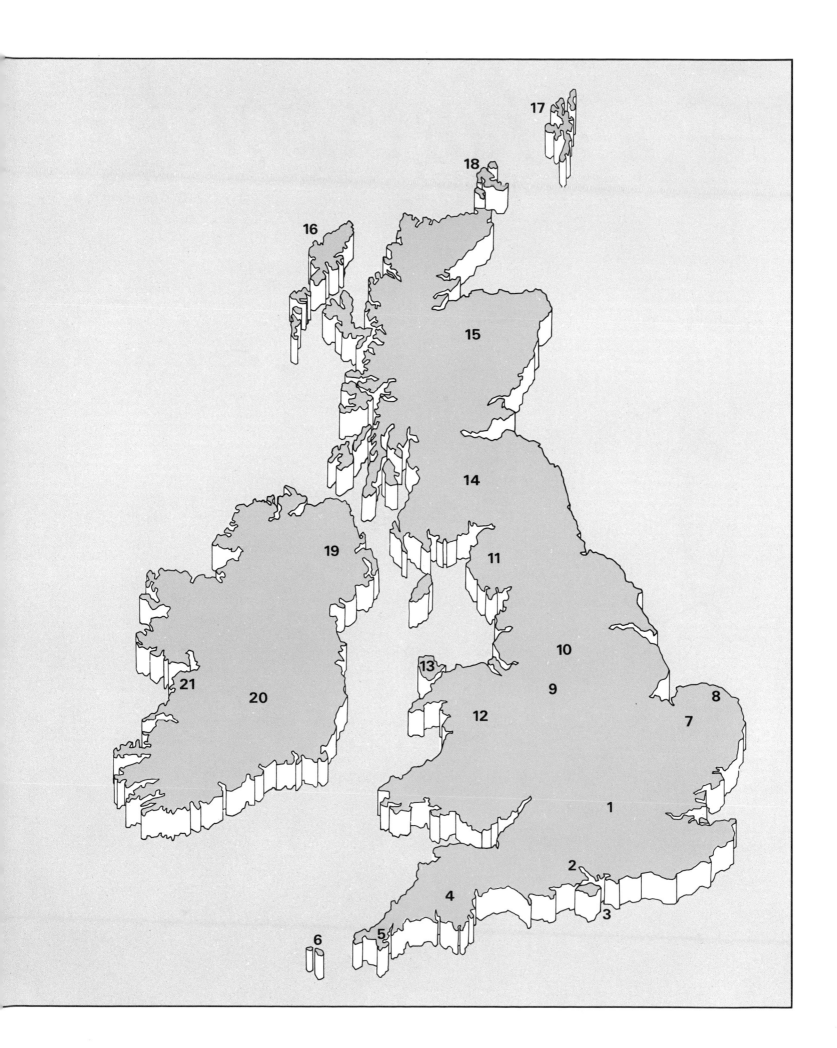

Foreword

One of the great pleasures of travelling the world in
search of wildlife comes when you get back home to Britain.
For no matter whether it's Manchester or Gatwick, Exeter
or Glasgow, Southampton or Harwich, you find yourself again
in a country which offers an astonishing diversity of
habitat within a small compass of land. Travel to far-away
places and you cross tracts of desert or open plains,
conifer forests or even swamp, for days on end. And jolly
exciting, too. But back home you can sample a quiver full
of different kinds of country comfortably inside twenty-
four hours. In a day's good walking, I can set out from
my front door in South Devon and tramp along an estuary,
over the clifftops, up a freshwater reedbed and marsh,
across cattle country and uphill to sheep country and
then wild open moorland, turning back to follow a stream
alive with dippers becoming a river flowing through broadleafed
woodland and taking me back home. A long day's hike, if
you like, but it proves the point. Britain is home to
a varied collection of plants and animals living in tolerable
harmony with people.

With well over fifty million people crowding into
a small island, human pressures on wildlife are intense.
You could correctly say that natural vegetation has been
practically eliminated from all but a few beleaguered
remnants of wilderness Britain – saltmarsh, cliffs and
mountain tops. But better to be positive and say that
wild plants and animals are quick to take advantage of
opportunities whenever and wherever they offer themselves. For
instance, lowland freshwater and marsh are diminishing
features, meriting special care, but gravel pits and sewage
works maintain a healthy population of wetland species.

The fertile lowlands of Britain, concentrated mainly
in the south and east, continually endure change from
farmers who seek to 'improve' their production as a
consequence of the extravagant use of artificial fertilizers. Yet
the pendulum is slowly swinging back to a husbandry which
tolerates wild corners and creates shelter belts and practises
soil conservation methods, all of which actively promote a

more healthy wild community. And, make no mistake, country which supports an abundance of wild plants and animals is an indicator of real health. We rely on wildlife not only for its leisure and aesthetic value, but for pollination and pest control and as agents of seed dispersal, to say nothing of its value as a primary food source.

Balancing the fertile lowlands of the south and east, the north and west enjoy an almost equal area of moorland and mountain, the last retreat of wilderness Britain. This is where golden eagles soar, holding sway over square miles of hunting country. And, though we may not see much of eagles in the south, we can soar, in spirit at least, with the buzzards hunting rabbits over the Dartmoor edge. with the buzzards hunting rabbits over Dartmoor. These upland places have a special value and demand their territorial rights.

Birdwatchers don't just tick off birds on a list, any more than bug-hunters or plant-watchers. One of the great joys of an interest in wild nature is the slow learning of the relationship between species and their habitat. Why is it that bitterns live in reed swamps and grouse up on the moor, moles in woodland and caterpillars on nettles? Because life exists in a whole complex of interwoven and ever-expanding circles of habitat, ecosystems within ecosystems, each subtly interacting with the rest.

This book explores carefully chosen examples of Britain's best and most productive wild country, and finds the plants and animals which are characteristic. Turn the pages and you can enjoy all shapes and sizes of a host of colourful plants and animals designed to exploit an enticing range of country – from the reed swamps of Norfolk by way of the legendary Isles of Scilly and up through the kite country of mid-Wales, the Dales and the Lakes to the Highlands and the Islands, then across to the magic of the Burren and the grandeur of Lough Neagh. We are fortunate to have this cornucopia practically at our doorstep. Go to these places and enjoy their wildlife to the full. But do please remember when you come home that the whole of Britain, not so long ago, rejoiced in places of this quality. And the happiest thought is that all is not lost. The principles of wildlife management and conservation may best be learned in these treasured places, but they may be practised in the most unlikely spots. The pleasures of improving urban and industrial habitats are slowly taking root. Join the growing band of active urban wildlife groups and see Britain bloom with a range of wild plants and animals in unexpected places!

Tony Soper

The Thames Valley

Fed by chuckling springs and lazy tributaries, the Thames meanders leisurely for over 200 miles from its source in Gloucestershire to its exit in the North Sea, growing from a quiet stream to a wide, wooded waterway much used by pleasureboats, and finally to a busy working river. The Thames has long been valued as a trade route and many early settlements grew up on its banks. In more recent times riverside towns caused major pollution, but a clear-up campaign in the 1960s means that once again it is a rich habitat for many species of fish, birds and flowers.

COTSWOLDS

OXFORD

THAMES HEAD

RIVERSIDE MEADOWS

CHILTERNS

GORING GAP

BERKSHIRE DOWNS

READING

The Thames – flowing through the country's heartland and its history – is the doyen of British rivers. Yet this famous waterway retains one secret: the origin of its name. When Julius Caesar referred to the river as the 'Tamesis' he was merely latinizing the vernacular version – phonetically 'Tems', probably pre-dating the Celts and possibly meaning 'dark'.

Rooted thus in antiquity, Old Father Thames would seem a suitable epithet – but only from the human viewpoint. In geological time, the river and its basin are relatively young, going back just 160 million years. The basin, saucer-shaped, lies on a bed of chalk which protrudes at the edges to form the Chilterns and the North Downs; the depression in-between – overlaid with clay, glacial gravels and alluvium – corresponds to the Thames and its valley.

CHANGING FORTUNES

The river's course across this lowland was definitively decided some 500,000 years ago when thrusting ice diverted the waters into their present channel. Glaciation had another direct effect on the river: freezing and melting of the great ice caps caused an alternating pattern of coastal emergence and submergence. When the sea level dropped, the Thames cut down, abandoning its old bed and leaving gravel terraces on either side – Hyde Park, in London, stands on one such terrace. But when water levels rose, silt swept in to form marshy flood plains in the lower reaches. During the final subsidence, at the end of the last Ice Age, 10,000 years ago, the North Sea broke through to the Channel, turning Britain into an island and giving the Thames an estuary of its own; until then, it had been a tributary of the Rhine.

From source – Trewsbury Mead near Cirencester – to mouth, today's Thames covers 215 miles and so ranks as Britain's second-longest river after the Severn. During its seaward journey the Thames is joined by 1500 miles of smaller rivers and streams which together create a drainage basin of almost 4000 square miles.

Some of the earliest traces of man in Britain are found in the Thames valley; ancient hunters and gatherers were followed by prehistoric farming communities who grazed stock on the chalk hillsides and cleared the trees below for cultivation. Then, in their turn, came Neoliths,

Iberians, Celts, Romans, Saxons, Danes, Normans . . . all attracted to the region by its prosperity and, in particular, to the river for its defence potential and transport role.

For 4000 years or more the Thames has functioned as a commercial highway. From distant Bronze Age beginnings – when skins, grain and flints were exchanged for imported copper and tin – trade and traffic steadily increased, turning the Thames into one of Britain's busiest thoroughfares. Travel was leisurely for both cargo and passenger traffic and journeys were often made slower by shallows and weirs erected by millers to concentrate water power (and to raise tolls), or by fisheries (often monasteries) to trap shoals of salmon, trout and eels.

Canal construction in the late 1700s boosted the river's fortunes – especially the Oxford Canal, which established a link with the

THAMES STORY
(above) From Thames Head on the edge of the Cotswolds, the Thames wends its way through lowland plains, to the gentle gorge of Goring Gap, where the chalk hills of the Berkshire Downs and the Chilterns meet. The river widens gradually towards London, which is built on a series of old river terraces, and finally empties into the North Sea, bordered by docks and the marshy flood plains of the lower reaches.

LONDON

RIVER TERRACES

RIVER TERRACES

NORTH DOWNS

Nature Walk

A variety of interesting landmarks, bridges and locks testify to the Thames' long history. Look for:

THAMES HEAD, at Trewsbury Mead, near Cirencester, where the source of the Thames is marked by a stone.

ST JOHN'S LOCK, Lechlade, the site of a statue of Father Thames and the first of 45 locks.

RADCOT BRIDGE, probably built in the 14th century and one of the two oldest bridges on the river.

ALBERT BRIDGE, London – elegant and delicate – a notice warns troops to break step when crossing.

FROM SMALL BEGINNINGS

In the upper reaches the Thames is little more than a stream which flows through water meadows bright with wild flowers. As it travels eastwards the river increases in volume, fed by numerous springs and tributaries until, at Teddington, the freshwater outflow meets incoming salt tides. For centuries exceptionally high tides have caused severe flooding along the river margins, but the Thames Barrier (left), built in 1982, now forms part of a modern flood defence system.

Midlands, and the Thames-and-Severn Canal, cutting through to the West. But within 50 years, railways had overtaken the Thames and its network and sabotaged their success. Since then, the Thames' role as a working river has declined – but its recreational use has increased: barges have been replaced by launches, dinghies, skiffs and canoes; towpath horses by anglers, ramblers and campers.

Throughout history, exploitation of the river has brought problems. One was congestion, another flooding, and a third pollution. By the 1850s, the Thames had degenerated into an open sewer and by the 1920s the water was so contaminated that no fish could survive below Fulham. However, a major clean-up programme begun in 1953 was so successful that 104 fish species now live in the tidal Thames.

Problems such as these have fallen to the lot of various agencies. Today, the river – apart from its port activities – is in the hands of the Thames Water Authority. In addition to the daily task of supplying 710 million gallons of clean water and treating 944 million gallons of sewage, the Authority is responsible for managing water resources in rivers and reservoirs; patrolling and maintaining the non-tidal Thames (above Teddington); providing leisure facilities; developing fisheries; protecting wildlife and preventing pollution.

The Authority is also concerned with flood control and, in 1986, inherited from the Greater London Council the Thames Barrier – a rising-sector gate built across the river at Woolwich in 1974-82. If danger threatens – usually when a 'surge' driven down the North Sea by storm-force winds coincides with a high spring tide – the gates swing up through 90° from their river-bed position to form a continuous steel wall. Other factors contributing to the flood menace – causing tide levels to rise in London by 30 inches (75cm) a century – are the gradual settlement of the city on its clay bed and the submergence of south-east England, which has been going on since the last Ice Age.

Thames-side Wildlife

The Thames is a varied river: flowers and insects enliven its upstream reaches, fish have returned to its London waters, and waders and wildfowl throng the broad estuary.

Some of the plants and animals of the Thames are confined to certain stretches, but the grey heron can be seen all along the river, from source to mouth. Even in the youngest reaches of the river it can find food, standing to attention in the shallow water, or wading slowly along, darting to take a fish from the water or a frog from the bank.

Among this herbage there may be a slight rustling, then a plop, as a water vole enters the stream. It is a vegetarian, eating the roots and stems of waterside plants. The smaller water shrew lives here, too, but it is rather different. A much shyer animal, it is a voracious little carnivore, hunting underwater for insects, small fish and frogs. As it swims below the surface the air bubbles trapped in its coat give it a shining, silvery appearance.

FLOWERS ALONG THE RIVER

The young river winds between banks of green. Water crowfoot trails in the flow, covered with white flowers. Bankside plants abound and often grow tall above the water. Stands of reedmace, sweet flag, common reed and the naturalized balsams provide an important habitat. Here the nymphs of hawker dragonflies and blue damselflies can climb to dry their wings, before taking to the air as adults to hunt the tiny insects which swarm over the surface of the water. The caterpillars of the elephant

hawk-moth feed on willowherbs by the water's edge. They will grow into delicate pink and green moths. They are equally impressive, though less elegant, as larvae, pulling back their heads when disturbed to shock a predator with the huge eye-spots on their backs.

Mayflies float over the warm summery waters, attracting swallows and martins to feed. When dusk falls, the birds are replaced by bats, which hunt the night-flying caddis flies. Daubenton's bat is particularly fond of hunting over water and has a characteristic swooping, skimming flight over the surface.

Swans glide along the river, and the anglers who fish the runs are taking increasing care of them, joining in to help save the noble birds from lead poisoning and injury from the line and weights discarded by careless anglers in the past.

Once there were many meadows and pastures by the Thames, often river-flooded in the winter, then cut for hay in the summer and grazed during autumn. Today few remain undrained. But along the upper reaches of the river there are still several places where the old meadow flowers may be seen. Here meadowsweet, lady's smock and adder's tongue fern grow, sometimes with the deep red heads of the greater burnet.

Sometimes, too, the heads of the mysterious snake's-head fritillary nod among the grasses.

MUTE SWANS
(left) Swans courting – the male, with his larger bill knob, is on the left. Swans were once found in large numbers on the Thames but have declined, partly due to lead poisoning from anglers' weights. Nevertheless, swan-upping still takes place each year when the Dyers' and Vintners' companies mark young swans.

One legend has it that each plant springs from a drop of the blood of a Dane killed in battle. It certainly can be a reddish flower, although some blooms are white, their papery petals drained of all colour. As ancient meadows have disappeared, so has the fritillary, but it is protected in most of its remaining havens, including the meadows of Magdalen College, Oxford.

Further downstream the Thames has another special flower, the Loddon lily, which is named after a tributary of the Thames at Reading. It flowers in relative safety on some of the Thames' islands, in waterlogged woody places. The flowering rush, too, is a Thames-side flower, and has been typical enough of the river's banks over the centuries to be known as

WILDLIFE OF THE THAMES VALLEY

Water drains off the chalk hills into the upstream reaches of the Thames. Waterbirds feed and breed on the river and its associated gravel pits. Some, such as the heron and kingfisher, prey on fish, particularly the small bleak. Waterside plants include sedges, bur-reed, willowherbs and purple loosestrife. Old meadows, where slow-worms glide between the stems and moles burrow underneath, are rich in flowers. Butterflies haunt them and the yellow wagtail nests here.

KEY TO SPECIES AND FEATURES

1 *Hobby*
2 *Chalk slopes*
3 *Cultivated farmland*
4 *Black poplars*
5 *Flooded gravel pit*
6 *Osiers*
7 *Mute swans*
8 *Kingfisher*
9 *Tufted ducks*
10 *Brown aeshna*
11 *Canada geese*
12 *Alders*
13 *Mallards*
14 *Bur-reed*
15 *Great willowherb*
16 *Purple loosestrife*
17 *Grey heron*
18 *Reed bed*
19 *Banded agrion*
20 *Molehills*
21 *Meadowsweet*
22 *Yellow wagtail*
23 *Bleak*
24 *Greater pond sedge*
25 *Unploughed meadow*
26 *Meadow buttercup*
27 *Pepper saxifrage*
28 *Woolly thistle*
29 *Bulrush wainscot moth*
30 *Tench*
31 *Slender tufted sedge*
32 *Female slow-worm*
33 *Green-winged orchid*
34 *Meadow brown*
35 *Yellow rattle*
36 *Meadow grasshopper*
37 *Adder's tongue fern*

the Pride of the Thames.

The islands appear as the river broadens. As London comes nearer they become refuges for wildlife. They are often overgrown with lank vegetation among the trees; small birds nest here and insects abound. One unusual occupant is the two-lipped door snail, an unpromising sounding creature, but a great rarity. It is rare enough for one of the Thames' islands to have been spared development partly on its account. It spends the day tucked down among the willow roots, climbing up after dark to crop the verdant plants near the water's edge.

THE CAPITAL'S RIVER

The Thames in London is imprisoned, as often as not, between walls of concrete. But the capital's river is far from bereft of wildlife. As the pleasure boats and the lines of refuse barges make their way to and fro, gulls wheel up from the mud exposed by the tide to follow the boats' wakes. Herring gulls, black-headed, black-backed and common gulls fly here. In addition to the flotsam they devour indiscriminately, they can also expect fish.

London's once-poisoned Thames has had a remarkable revitalization over the last few decades, as it has been progressively relieved of the ugly shadow of pollution. Since 1963 more than 100 species of freshwater and marine fish have been recorded, and even salmon are seen from time to time. The freshwater fish of the

upper reaches are all present in London. They include roach, dace, chub, carp, bream, perch and eels. Particularly frequent is that modestly-named fish the bleak, which is too small to interest most anglers.

As the tide affects the waters, the marine and estuarine fish appear – sprats, common gobies, whiting and the occasional bass. In the little tidal creeks which run into the river in east London and downstream, baby flatfish – often flounders – can sometimes be spotted.

As the Thames leaves London and flows on to meet the North Sea, it passes the reclaimed marshes of the north Kent and south Essex coasts. Cattle graze here, cropping close the

CADDIS FLY AT NIGHT
(right) Adult caddis flies are rarely seen, for most fly at night. The larvae, however, are easily found in all types of freshwater.

LARGE BARBEL
(above left) The Thames and its tributaries have long been a stronghold of the barbel. It has since been introduced to other rivers because of its qualities as a sporting fish, but is absent from Scotland and Ireland. It is a bottom-feeder – note the position of its mouth. The four fleshly barbels on its upper lip help it to locate food such as caddis larvae.

A BANKSIDE STAND OF HIMALAYAN BALSAM
*(left) Brought from the Himalayas in 1839, this
flower – it has white or purplish-pink blooms –
is commonest along river banks.*

Sands, brent geese occur in huge numbers late
in the year. As the Thames reaches the end of its
journey, red-breasted mergansers and scoters
dive for food in what has finally become the
North Sea.

From the green rippled stream of its headwat-
ers to the wide, grey waters passing through
London and beyond, the Thames has a fine
range of wildlife – the great natural history of a
great river.

MALE COMMON SCOTER
*(right) Less than 200 pairs of this sea duck
breed in Scotland and Ireland but wintering
birds can be seen in the Thames estuary.*

mixed sward behind the walls which keep the
river from the marshes. Many of the grazing
marshes are gone, lost to grain fields. Where
they remain they provide winter haunts for the
short-eared owl, which elegantly quarters the
grassland in search of small mammals. Some of
these owls also breed here.

In the autumn, huge numbers of waders and
wildfowl arrive on the marshes and their dykes.
Some are passing through but others will winter
here; they have done so in greater numbers as
the river has been cleaned up. Near to London,
the ubiquitous mallard and the tufted duck are
most frequent, and are often joined by pochard.
Further out, pintail and shelduck occur, while
wigeon, teal and shoveler flock here too.

All along the tidal stretches of the river,
scampering or strolling across the mud, are
waders. Ringed plover and redshank – which
also breed on the marshes – and numerous
dunlin and occasional flocks of ruff occur here.
Large numbers of lapwing congregate on the
grasslands beside the river. The waders are
particularly partial to the riverside silt lagoons,
which are regularly topped up with mud
dredged from the bed of the Thames.

Further out towards the sea, on the Maplin

NODDING BLOOMS OF SNAKE'S HEAD
*(right) The snake's head fritillary is a flower of
unploughed, damp meadows. Once common,
it is now scarce due to farming changes.*

15

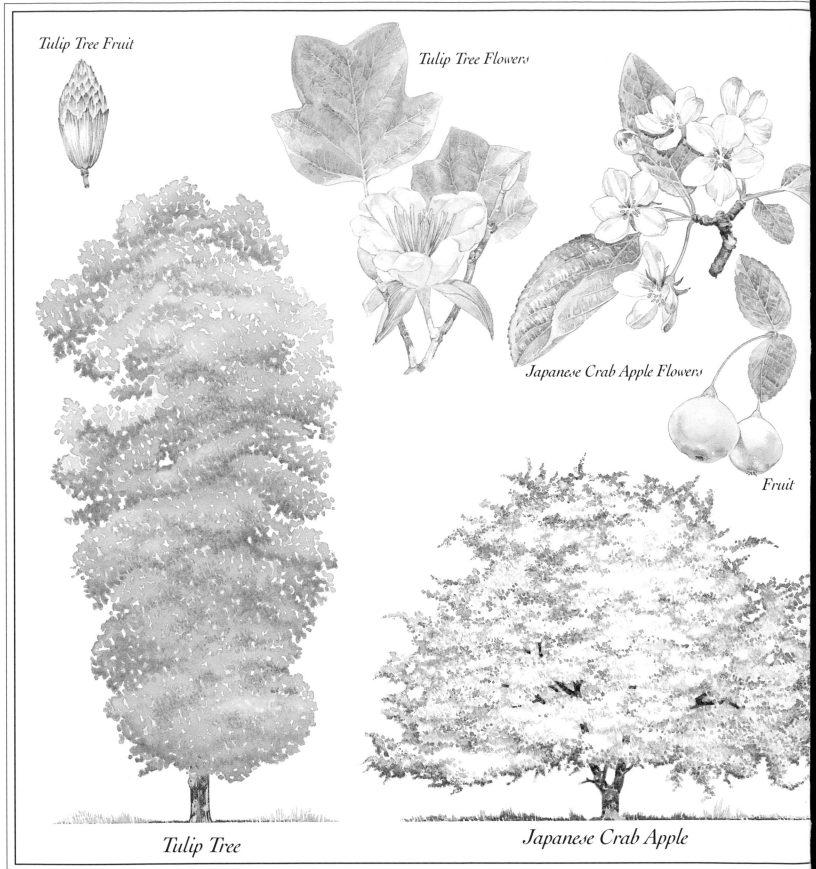

Tulip Tree Fruit

Tulip Tree Flowers

Japanese Crab Apple Flowers

Fruit

Tulip Tree

Japanese Crab Apple

TULIP TREE *(Liriodendron tulipifera)* Like magnolias, this tree has leaves and flowers with primitive characteristics. It was brought to British gardens in the 17th century, an introduction from eastern North America. Preferring rich, damp soil, they occasionally reach 150′ (45m) in Britain – less than their fullest height – and thrive best in southern and central England. The mature crown is tall and domed in outline. 4-lobed glossy leaves turn a deep gold in autumn. Greenish flowers June-July are followed by stiff, papery fruits.

JAPANESE CRAB APPLE *(Malus floribunda)* Frequently planted in parks, gardens and along streets for its masses of pink blossom, this is a neat tree about 20′ (6m), with a wide, shallow crown. Small, but very numerous flowers appear in May, and the toothed leaves are oval or lance-shaped, hairy below. In autumn, small yellow apples ripen – too sour to eat – they nevertheless provide food for birds. Introduced to Britain from Japan in 1862, it is hardy, thriving well on most soils throughout Britain, except upland areas and the North.

Ornamental Trees

Southern Magnolia Flowers

White Poplar Leaves

Male Catkin

Southern Magnolia

White Poplar

SOUTHERN MAGNOLIA *(Magnolia grandiflora)* Grows as a fairly tall tree 60-100′ (18-30m) in its homeland, southern United States, but reaches only 30′ or so here. Mostly raised from cuttings and often grown against walls in southern England and Ireland. The evergreen oval leaves are thick and glossy above, felted orange below. Set against this dark green foliage, the sweetly scented flowers stand out clearly, and at 8-10″ (20-25cm) across, present a lovely sight July-October. The 2″ (5cm) fruit is conelike in appearance.

WHITE POPLAR *(Populus alba)* Probably an early introduction, this poplar only reaches about 66′ (20m) here – frequently making a scrubby thicket. Young trees have pale bark, which darkens with age, becoming fissured, and an open crown often leaning slightly. Catkins open in March, well before the leaves – and almost all white poplars in Britain are females. Leaves may be small and roundish or larger and 5-lobed. Seen mainly in the South, it is often planted in parks, and tolerates the salt-spray of coastal areas.

17

Collared Dove

Marsh Warbler

COLLARED DOVE *(Streptopelia decaocto)* This 11″ (28cm) dove has spread across Europe and Britain at a truly impressive rate – from the first pair to nest here, in the mid-1950s, numbers increased to about 19,000 birds in 9 years! Now common and widespread, it frequents parks and gardens of suburban areas and villages, feeding on seeds and some green vegetables. Very flimsy, twiggy nests are built chiefly in trees, favouring dense conifers. Two white eggs are laid, sometimes four times a year. Call is the familiar *coo-COO-coo.*

MARSH WARBLER *(Acrocephalus palustris)* A rare summer visitor, with a quiet, secretive nature while nesting. It is very similar to the more common reed warbler, and there may be more than the estimated 100 or so pairs breeding here – mostly in Gloucestershire and Worcestershire. Marsh warblers are 5″ (13cm) long, greenish-brown above, and have pinkish legs, but it is their trilling, varied song that identifies them most easily. Nests are made in tall herbage near water, 4-5 blue-green eggs laid in June.

Jack Snipe

JACK SNIPE *(Lymnocryptes minimus)* Smaller and with a shorter bill than the snipe, its resident relative, the jack snipe is 8″ (20cm) long. It winters regularly here in small numbers, skulking in the herbage of marshes, water meadows and sewage farms. They feed on invertebrates and on some seeds, and will break cover only reluctantly, landing again after a short burst of flight. During icy conditions inland they move to coastal areas, seeking unfrozen ground in which to probe. Call is a strange thudding sound.

The Sparrow

The house sparrow has earned the nickname 'Cockney sparrer' from its association with man and his settlement. In contrast, its 'country cousin' – the tree sparrow – is a shy secretive, mainly woodland bird.

FAMILIAR HOUSE SPARROW *(above) Despite its familiarity, the house sparrow is often overlooked. A close view reveals a highly attractive little bird, boldly marked in shades of brown and grey. Contrary to popular belief it is not Britain's most common bird, being outnumbered by several other species, notably the starling and wren. The British population is estimated at about 10 million birds. The tree sparrow is much scarcer – about 250,000 pairs.*

In the early hours of the morning an energetic splashing, accompanied by a cheerful, boisterous chirruping, is heard from outside the window. The house sparrow is indulging in a favourite pastime – taking its early morning bath in a puddle of water in the garden.

Whether splashing in a bird bath, scooping hollows in a flower bed to dustbathe, ripping the petals off fresh yellow crocuses, or making a lot of noise in quarrelsome, courting groups on the lawn, the house sparrow draws attention to itself. It rarely invites the critical descriptions given to 'greedy starlings' or 'thieving magpies', yet few would list the house sparrow in their table of favourite birds.

There are two species of sparrow in Britain: the house and tree sparrow. Of the two, the chirpy 'Cockney sparrer' – the house sparrow – is by far the most familiar, with a natural ability to survive in the most diverse circumstances; but everywhere it chooses to inhabit is generally close to man. It has learned that such an associ-

ation affords two important advantages – relative freedom from predators and a ready food supply. Even in the country it likes the vicinity of a few houses or a farm, or at least a couple of barns. The lure of a few crumbs, and a likely nesting place safe under the eaves or inside a drainpipe, seems too strong to resist.

Although tree sparrows are occasionally seen in gardens, they are much more likely to be encountered in farmland, open woodland and orchards with plenty of large, old trees and tall hedges. Such habitats provide the holes in which they like to nest.

The dunnock popularly known as the 'hedge sparrow' is not a sparrow at all, but an accentor – a separate family altogether.

Both the British sparrows are streaky brown birds, small but stout. The house sparrow is the slightly larger of the two, at 5¾ inches (14.5cm), and male and female plumages are different. In spring, male birds have a narrow grey cap, pale cheeks, a black chin and a broad

band of reddish-brown through the eye. Females are a duller brown, light buff below, with no black or grey on the face, but instead, have a band of paler buff over each eye. Retaining these basic patterns, the plumages of house sparrows alter slightly with the seasons. The tree sparrow has a smaller, neater body and has just one basic plumage for both sexes. It can be distinguished from the house sparrow by its pale brown cap, white cheeks with a characteristic black spot in the centre, and a thin white ring around the neck.

House sparrows will nest in any sort of cavity, such as inside brickwork, behind a drainpipe, amongst Virginia creeper on a wall, or amongst ivy or hawthorn. The nest is a globular, untidy structure of loosely woven grasses and three to five slender, pale eggs — often with one of the clutch paler than the others — are laid from May onwards; there may be as many as three broods during the summer. The young fly at about 15 days old.

The tree sparrow is more dependent on holes in which to nest, and parkland, with small stands of oaks or limes, is particularly favoured although some will nest in a hole in a wall or barn, or in a thatched roof. Six eggs are normally laid in each of two clutches and these are smaller, darker and browner than those of a house sparrow. They hatch after two weeks and the young fly two weeks later.

The house sparrow may not be thought of as a likely symbol of fidelity. Flocks hundreds strong often gather, and fights between rival males are commonplace; in spring courtship displays are often seen. Males hop around disinterested hens, wings lowered and head and tail raised in a show of self-importance, accompanied by a lively, joyful song. Yet despite such displays and sociability, pairs are usually faithful to each other and to their nest site, for life.

Above all, the house sparrow should be

NESTING TREE SPARROW
(above) Tree sparrows tend to keep away from human habitation, preferring to nest in holes in old trees and walls.

better respected for its liveliness and cheery good humour. Unprotected by law, the target for catapults and airguns, prey of every domestic cat and unwanted scrounger at the bird table provided for more refined species, the sparrow persists and never takes offence; if we can only open our eyes to it, we will see a bird more deserving of our care and protection.

WARY BY NATURE
(left) Despite its apparent boldness and cheeky nature, the house sparrow is a shy bird, wary in its behaviour and will not tolerate a close approach. The sight of a human entering the garden may well cause it to beat a hasty retreat into the trees — whereas a robin, or even a blackbird, will often stay put or just step into the shade of the shrubbery.

KEY FACTS

IN FLIGHT the tree sparrow has a brown cap, black cheek spots and bib, white collar and pale buff underparts.

HOUSE SPARROW PLUMAGES change with the seasons from a rich chestnut in spring to a duller brown in winter.

THE EGGS of the house sparrow are white with grey blotches; the tree sparrow's are dark brown and smaller.

The Carp

Deep in the murky waters of our lowland lakes and rivers swims the stately but elusive carp. Only on balmy summer evenings is its impressive form seen near the surface as it rises to feed and bask.

SHADY CUSTOMER
Carp thrive in the warm waters of lakes and ponds and in slow-flowing rivers, growing up to 40lb (18kg) in seven or eight years where plant and insect life is plentiful. Like other forms of carp, the common carp (above) has a powerful body with a single dorsal fin, and is fast and wily – as many an angler can testify. Apart from its head, the common carp is covered with large shiny scales. Its colouring varies from a muddy grey to a striking golden yellow, while its strongly forked tail is often tinged with pink.

The summer sun pours down on a slow-moving, weedy river, warming the languid flow so that the water seems to slip between the banks like heat-thinned oil. The surface is unbroken, even by the stands of vegetation that have crept out from the margins with the season's advance. Then, just beyond the weeds, a dark shadow emerges cautiously from the depths, still, solid, unmoved by the current. The shadow hangs motionless, too vague to recognize, but through the murk, a ghostly white circle opens just below the surface, getting bigger, wider, until revealing itself as a huge opening mouth. The mouth delicately sips at some unseen morsel held in the surface film; a light swirl marks the spot and the water boils gently with a quiet 'ploop'. With the dying ripples the shadow drops away and is gone, scarcely betraying that a vast, 30-pound fish – a carp – is feeding and basking nearby.

Noted for their wilyness and shyness, wild carp are not often seen. Not for them the flamboyant, attention-drawing slash of a trout rising confidently to a fly. Instead, in keeping with their bulk and regal bearing, carp remain inscrutible, hidden, feeding discreetly and gliding quietly to the safety of the depths at the slightest disturbance.

A DOMESTICATED SPECIES

The carp is not native to our islands. The species originates from the deep, warm lakes and rivers of Asia, but was probably introduced here by the Romans, who, like many Asian and central European communities sited far from the sea, valued this freshwater fish for the table. Cultivated over the centuries, the elegant, slender wild carp was selectively bred to become the heavy, hump-backed, deep-bodied fish we know today. And our carp are the feral descendants of these 'domestic' fish.

When plants or animals are domesticated, several different varieties often develop and this has happened with the carp. Three types swim wild in Britain's warm lowland waters; the common, leather and mirror carp. The common carp is a magnificent fully scaled fish, resembling the original wild type except in size and shape – it has a fatter, deeper and humped body. The leather carp is similarly shaped but is unusual in being virtually scaleless. This characteristic was bred into the fish to make its preparation for the table easier. The mirror carp is an intermediate form of the former two – it has a patchy distribution of large scales and sometimes shows a well-defined line of scales along the lateral line. Although these forms are quite distinct, they all belong to the same species and can interbreed freely.

RIVER-BED SCAVENGER

Carp feed on both plant and animal material, mainly on the bottom. Here, they rootle in the mud and silt, sucking up mud and foodstuffs together and separating the goodness from the rest as it all passes through the body. Being naturally warm-water fish, carp are very sensitive to a drop in temperature and gradually stop feeding as the weather gets colder. They cease feeding at temperatures below 14°C, and in winter seek out the deepest, warmest waters, becoming inactive and sluggish in the process.

Temperature also has an effect on the carp's breeding behaviour, and not until the water has warmed to between 17-20°C in spring does it attempt to spawn. Then, the males develop tubercules (wart-like growths) on their heads and shoulders and gather with the females among the vegetation at the water's edge. Females lay enormous numbers of eggs – it has been calculated that the 15-pounder lays around two million – and these are fertilized by the males' 'milt', or sperm.

If temperatures remain suitably high, the eggs hatch after a few days. At first the emergent larvae depend upon the nourishment from their yolk sacs, but later begin to feed on plankton before graduating to tiny worms and insects. After about three months or so they resemble, at one inch long, miniature adults, and if they survive the perils of predation by a multitude of aquatic enemies they may eventually grow big enough to fear no water-bound enemy. Indeed, carp of over 40 pounds have been caught in Britain and they grow even bigger in mainland Europe and Asia. Carp are renowned for longevity too. They certainly survive for 20 years or more in the wild and have been known to reach 40 in captivity.

BOTTOM FEEDER
(above) Although carp live in groups, they are shy, secretive fish which spend much of their time feeding on the river or lake bottom. Their soft rubbery lips and lack of teeth belie a strong hard jaw, while the two short barbels on the upper lip house taste cells which search out tasty morsels from the silt and the sand.

AN IN-BUILT DETECTOR
(right) The mirror carp is the fastest growing and the largest of the three types of carp, and is immediately recognizable because of its exceptionally large scales. In some fish these are arranged in a well-defined band along the base of the dorsal fin – in which case the fish is known as a band carp. In others they follow the lateral line – present in all fish, but often less pronounced – where sensory cells detect pressure changes in the water. This enables the fish to navigate efficiently and also alerts it to unseen threats.

The New Forest

In today's terms the New Forest is misleadingly named, for it is neither new, nor completely wooded as we expect a forest to be. Nonetheless, it is a startlingly beautiful area presenting a landscape of contrasting and varied panoramas. In places, visitors can walk between giant old trees and tread wildwood paths where prehistoric man once strode; elsewhere, the land is open heath. Trees, in fact, only cover just under half the area of this, the biggest tract of 'wilderness' in lowland Britain, and the explanation lies in the New Forest's long history.

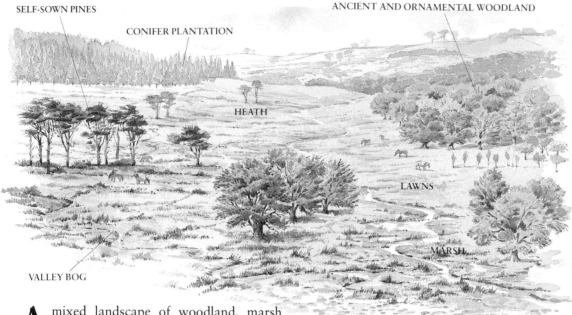

SELF-SOWN PINES

CONIFER PLANTATION

ANCIENT AND ORNAMENTAL WOODLAND

HEATH

LAWNS

MARSH

VALLEY BOG

THE NEW FOREST

THE FOREST LANDS
(left) Today's varied New Forest landscape reflects the mixed geology and chequered history of the area. Infertile open heath accounts for much of the Forest, with valley bog and marsh on low-lying ground where clay or a hard pan lies below the surface. Conifer plantations and old inclosures witness the Forest's role as a timber factory, while the 'Ancient and Ornamental Woodlands' represent some of Britain's finest deciduous forest.

A mixed landscape of woodland, marsh and open heath, the New Forest today accounts for some 145 square miles of Hampshire, stretching from Southampton in the east to Ringwood in the west, and from the Wiltshire border at its northern limit to the Solent in the south. The area lies within a shallow chalk basin which was gradually filled with sands, clays and gravels when a large river estuary covered the region. Rivers and streams have since cut shallow valleys down through the gravels to the clays, creating a variety of soils and conditions in the Forest.

The modern landscape of the New Forest has its origins in Norman times. In 1079 William the Conqueror designated the area the *Nova Foresta*. At that time the word 'forest' had a definite, strictly legal, meaning, as land set aside for the royal hunt. The ground was sometimes wooded, but as often not, and much of the New Forest would have been gorse-covered wasteland, with only a few sparse woodlands in the north.

THE FOREST TAKES SHAPE

From 1079 the New Forest became a place apart, with definite boundaries and a stringent system of Forest Law to protect the hunting ground. The peasants of the area were not permitted to enclose their holdings or otherwise interfere with the run of the deer. In recompense, they were given commoners' rights to graze their cattle and pigs in the Forest. Poaching, illegal fencing and farming were severely punished by the Forest courts.

Although new woodland was planted in Norman times, by the Middle Ages the appearance of the Forest was changing, as trees gradually disappeared from the scene. Trees felled for timber were not replaced – young saplings were eaten by deer and the domestic

AUTUMN HEATH
(right) Atop the infertile gravelly plateaux of the Forest lies heather and bracken-covered heathland with self-sown Scots pine and birch.

cattle, pigs and ponies of commoners with grazing rights.

The dearth of timber trees was a very serious problem. Wood was needed for many uses, not least for the naval ships which were built in local shipyards like Buckler's Hard. A series of Inclosure Acts, the first dating from as early as 1482, allowed land to be enclosed so that new woodland could be created. The Act of 1698 allowed the fencing of 6000 acres, but individual inclosures were reopened for grazing once the trees had become established, and other areas fenced, increasing the amount of

OPEN BEECHWOODS
(*right*) *Like oak, beech is one of the oldest trees found in the New Forest. Both were grown in inclosures from the Middle Ages, but many of these inclosures are now grazed, forming part of the Open Forest, and the trees appear as natural woodland. Beech trees form some of the most beautiful woods in the Forest, including Soarley Beeches and Berry Beeches. These woods provide a particularly colourful display in autumn, when the beech leaves turn golden brown.*

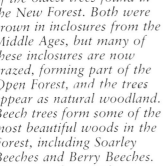

woodland by much more. The pollarding or lopping of trees for crops of branches was also banned, since this ruined their timber value.

Until the 18th century, Forest woodland, glades and timber inclosures were of deciduous hardwoods, mostly oak and beech. But in the 1770s softwood conifers were introduced and the oaks and beeches of some of the old inclosures gradually became part of the Open Forest. Their ragged descendants – some 250 years old – form the Ancient and Ornamental Woodlands, which are now a major feature of the Forest landscape.

The growing demand for timber and the declining interest in hunting resulted in the 1851 Deer Removal Act, which allowed deer to be killed and new inclosures set. Grazing pressure was reduced, and many young trees grew up beneath older inclosure giants. But the deer were by no means wiped out and the commoners resumed their grazing as soon as they could. Hence many of the older woodlands have two, and only two, ages of tree – a feature very noticable in some beech groves.

Since 1924 the Forestry Commission has managed the Forest and preserves a balance between timber resources – in the form of deciduous inclosures and modern conifer plantations – and conservation.

THE FOREST TODAY

Today's New Forest offers splendid and varied panoramas. The larger part is Open Forest, some 65,000 acres in all. This includes glorious reaches of heathland on the higher gravelly ground, such as that at Hampton Ridge, with scattered stately pines self-sown from conifer plantations nearby. The Ancient and Ornamental Woodlands, such as those of Marsh Ash Wood, also form part of the Open Forest, accounting for some 8000 acres.

Bogs are found in many of the valleys, whilst elsewhere clear pools abound and limpid streams bubble across their beds. Alongside many of these streams are flat 'lawns' – sheltered grassy areas where Forest ponies love to graze.

Across the Open Forest the deer and the animals of the commoners roam more or less at will. Thousands of day visitors travel across the Forest on new fenced roads and are lured to such places as the Rufus Stone, and the grassy peace of Lindford Bottom. The Forest is also a haven for wildlife enthusiasts, for it provides a home for many of Britain's rare species of birds, animals, insects, reptiles and plants.

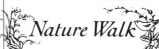

The New Forest abounds with folklore and interesting reminders of its past, like:

THE RUFUS STONE, marking the spot where Rufus (William II) was killed while hunting.

COMMONERS' BRANDS, compulsory on all animals grazing in the Forest.

BISHOP'S DYKE, said to represent the distance crawled by a Bishop of Winchester to define Church lands.

FORDINGBRIDGE, just beyond the western edge of the Forest, where a 14th century, seven-arched bridge crosses the Avon.

The Nature of the Forest

The New Forest's large patchwork of habitats – often changed by Man but rarely spoiled – harbours a wide variety of exceptional plants and animals, from hardy ponies to Britain's only cicada.

The New Forest is a place of colours: the million greens of spring, the purple heather draped across the hillsides, the steel-cold grey of the winter streams. Wherever and whenever you look, there are more colours to celebrate, a pattern of tints reflecting the variety of plants and animals that live here.

The Forest's habitats are not unique – it is their extent which is extraordinary. For mile after mile across the gently curved landscape, woods merge into heaths, heaths into mires, mires into streams, streams into lawns.

Inevitably, the Forest has a great range of wildlife: important populations of plants and animals rare elsewhere; plenty of familiar common species; and a few specialities such as the New Forest cicada.

This cicada was thought to be extinct earlier this century, but was rediscovered in the 1960s. It lives in the woods, where the eggs are laid on the small-leaved lime. The larvae burrow into the ground to live on the tree's root sap for several years. When the insects emerge for their brief weeks of adult life, they continue to drink sap – this time from the aerial parts of the tree.

LONG-ESTABLISHED WOODS

The woods are very variable, their composition influenced by soils, drainage, history and management. They are most often dominated by oaks and beeches, some of great size and considerable age, and are often bare of ground flora. Both native oaks – common and durmast – grow here, and they hybridize extensively. The oldest trees are often ancient pollards, with several 'trunks' growing together from a few feet above the ground. Younger trees around them have grown up straight-trunked, spreading their branches fully and, in summer, blocking light to the woodland floor.

Beneath the trees there is often only holly, its silver-grey bark contrasting with the sombre browns and shadows of the deep wood. Sometimes there are brambles and sometimes ferns, and on the trees themselves grow rich cloaks of mosses and lichens, including some, like the lichen *Parmelia dissecta*, which grow nowhere else in the British Isles.

The presence of trees of all ages, including those dead, fallen and rotting 'Old Men of the Woods', which are so often tidied away in modern woodlands, encourages a wide range of insects and other invertebrates. Perhaps the most spectacular of the many insects is the stag beetle, whose larvae spend their lives chewing through rotten wood before emerging to fly in the summer, often buzzing and clattering into houses, attracted to the light.

The rare wood cricket occurs in great numbers in the woods, filling the humid glades with its song of high summer. And the hornet occurs commonly, too, engendering fear when it is found by chance.

The Forest has many deer. A careful walk through the green shade is sometimes rewarded

MALE REDSTART
Its beak crammed with a crane-fly and caterpillars, the male is perched here waiting to feed the incubating female or their chicks. Redstarts occur throughout Britain but are very scarce in Ireland. The particular attraction of the New Forest is the old trees, especially oaks, which provide suitable nest-holes and foliage rich in insects and their larvae. Redstarts are summer visitors, arriving in April from Africa.

THE NEW FOREST'S VARIED WILDLIFE

The woodpeckers, stock dove and redstart nest in tree-holes: the sparrowhawk and rare honey buzzard and hobby nest in treetops. In areas fenced off from grazing deer and ponies the caterpillars of the silver-washed fritillary may find dog violets on which to feed; those of the white admiral may feed here on honeysuckle. Silver-studded blues and graylings occur on heaths. Old stumps can be riddled with holes bored by woodpeckers, or by beetle or goat moth larvae. Wetland areas are brightened in summer by sundews and bog asphodel and are enlivened by the ticking 'song' of the large marsh grasshopper.

KEY TO FEATURES AND SPECIES

1 Great spotted woodpecker
2 Female redstart
3 Stock dove
4 Ancient wood
5 Beech
6 Honey buzzard
7 Swallow
8 Hobby
9 Holly
10 Oak
11 Fallow deer
12 Sparrowhawk
13 Silver-washed fritillary
14 Roe deer
15 Conifer plantation
16 Willow scrub
17 Alders
18 Ponies
19 Leucobryam *moss*
20 White admiral
21 Bramble
22 Marsh
23 Tussock sedge
24 Cross-leaved heath
25 Nightjar
26 Dartford warbler
27 Wild balsam
28 Bog
29 Bog asphodel
30 Stag beetle
31 New Forest cicada
32 Gorse
33 Heather
34 Silver-studded blue
35 Scarce blue-tailed damselfly
36 Goat moth caterpillar
37 Wild gladiolus
38 Grayling
39 Dwarf gorse
40 Large marsh grasshopper
41 Heath
42 Sand lizard
43 Bog myrtle

where there is water – they are fine swimmers and they catch and eat frogs. A sizeable proportion of the national smooth snake population also occurs on the Forest's heaths.

The open skies above the heaths are the home of the hobby, which can be seen scything the air in its hunting flight. As well as catching small birds and mammals it sometimes takes dragonflies on the wing; the New Forest is rich in these insects, which thrive in its clean waters. The hobby breeds in the Forest, almost always selecting an old nest – often that of a crow.

Other heathland birds include stonechats, meadow pipits, nightjars and the rare and declining woodlark. A special sight is the Dartford warbler, popping its crested head up from a gorse bush for a burst of song before retiring again or moving to another clump.

by a view of one of the wild, secretive Forest herds. They are mostly fallow deer which are believed to be descended from those introduced by the Normans. They differ from park deer in changing their coats annually; in summer they are dappled roan, but the darker, colder days of winter see them in coats of dark, dull grey. They are shy and nervous: a careless movement and they are alert; one snapped twig and they are gone.

Many birds breed within the woods. The old trees attract redstarts, and other hole-nesters include nuthatches, spotted flycatchers and all the woodpeckers. The chaffinch is common everywhere, its metallic song rattling breezily at the woodland edge in spring.

HEATHLAND

From the woodlands, paths emerge onto the heaths. The tree cover was stripped from these places long ago, and the sandy, gravelly soil was leached by the rain, producing acid soils on which heather thrives with cross-leaved heath, petty whin and clumps of gorse.

In the sunny spots, adders soak up the warmth. They are not the only snakes here. Grass snakes haunt grassier places, especially

WILD GLADIOLUS
(above) This stunning rare flower is most likely to be seen in the New Forest or in Dorset. It grows in grassy or heathy areas, flowering in June and July. The crimson-purple petals are quite as attractive as those of the commoner garden gladioli.

HEALTHY LICHEN
(above right) The vigorous growth of this Parmelia *species of lichen reflects the clean, unpolluted air of the Forest. Here, it is growing on the trunk of a larch.*

NEW FOREST PONIES
(right) Ponies have roamed the area in semi-wild herds since Saxon times. Though their greatest enemy may once have been the wolf, today it is probably the motor car.

DARTFORD WARBLER
(above) This attractive, red-eyed warbler is one of the New Forest's specialities. It no longer breeds in Dartford, where it was first discovered and named, and the bulk of the 1000 or so breeding pairs occurs on the heaths of the New Forest and adjacent Dorset. The Dartford warbler suffers very badly in severe winters and less than 12 pairs bred in Britain after the winter of 1963, before the population recovered.

BUTCHER'S BROOM
(right) A tiny, red-berried evergreen shrub, butcher's broom grows only in the dry woods of southern England.

The glamorous green larvae of the Emperor moth – a member of the Silk moth family – can be found feeding on heather. The Forest is also one of the best places to see the silver-studded blue butterfly, clouds of which can be seen on some heathery slopes during summer.

Where the heaths slope down into valley bottoms, the ground underfoot gets wetter and softer, often becoming carpeted in sphagnum mosses. Here grow bog asphodel, marsh cinquefoil, great sundew and the fragile, greenish bog orchid.

In these very wet places, and by the ponds which the Forest has in abundance, grow a number of rare plants. Hampshire purslane, for example, which is unspectacular but nationally rare. And the scarce shore-weed, which is just

THE NEW FOREST CICADA
Britain has only one cicada and it seems to be confined to the New Forest. This adult has emerged from the soil in early summer.

on the edge of the water, and flowers only when exposed – it is wind-pollinated.

Perhaps the most delightful local plant is pillwort, a slender denizen of the water's edge. Looking just like a grass, it carpets damp places with its filigree leaves, which, on close inspection, can be seen to start their careers as tiny coiled watch-springs of green; pillwort is in fact a fern.

The ponds also hold such rarities as *Triops cancriformis*, a crustacean resembling a miniature king-crab, and in the clean-watered streams swim brook lampreys and stone loach.

FOREST LAWNS

The Forest ponies make a crucial contribution to another of the habitats, the lawns. Here the ponies graze the turf to a short, tight sward, which is speckled with wild flowers. In some years, the plaited spikes of the autumn lady's tresses orchid appear in abundance. The minute yellow gentian grows here, too, as does noble chamomile, the sweet scent of its crushed leaves giving it its richly-deserved name.

In some of the lawns there are seasonally flooded hollows, and in them grow two more of the Forest's specialities – lesser fleabane and pennyroyal mint. Both were widespread once, but as grassy areas have been drained, tidied and sanitized, so the plants have retreated.

It is on the edge of the lawns, just tucked into the bracken, that one of the Forest's brightest dashes of colour is found – the vermilion flowers of the wild gladiolus. It blooms almost nowhere else, and is a symbol and a reminder of the unique nature and very special identity of the New Forest.

Hampshire Purslane

Autumn Lady's Tresses

Long-leaved Lungwort

Lesser Fleabane

HAMPSHIRE PURSLANE
(*Ludwigia palustris*) A trailing 3-6″
(8-15cm) perennial aquatic,
growing as a native only in the New
Forest, although occasionally found
elsewhere as an aquarium castout.
The little greeny-red flowers are
borne singly during June and July.

AUTUMN LADY'S TRESSES
(*Spiranthes spiralis*) A slender 4-9″
(10-23cm) perennial, blooming in
August and September. Takes its
name from the spiral twist of
flowers, resembling a plait of hair.
Grows in short turf; local but
widespread except in the North.

LONG-LEAVED LUNGWORT
(*Pulmonaria longifolia*) Grows in
clayey woods and very local in
meadows in Dorset and Hampshire.
An 8-12″ (20-30cm) perennial, it
blooms from spring until early
summer, each flower is at first pink,
but later turns bright blue.

LESSER FLEABANE (*Pulicaria
vulgaris*) Once scattered through
the South and Midlands in winter
wet spots, this 1-10″ (3-25cm)
annual of late summer now grows
only in a handful of sites – the New
Forest is its stronghold. It grows on
village greens and on roadsides.

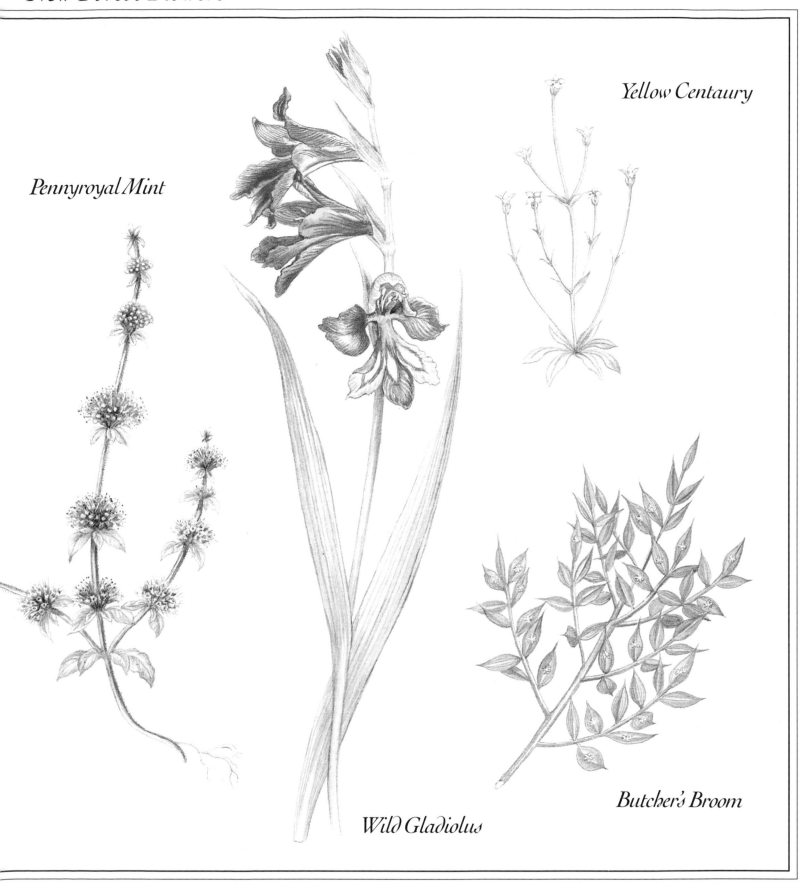

Pennyroyal Mint

Yellow Centaury

Wild Gladiolus

Butcher's Broom

PENNYROYAL MINT *(Mentha pulegium)* Long ago familiar to herbalists, and sold in bunches in London's markets, it is now a rarity, growing only in a few winter wet spots. A 3-12″ (8-30cm) annual; the late summer whorls of flowers are borne upon trailing stems.

WILD GLADIOLUS *(Gladiolus illyricus)* Smaller than the garden gladioli, but subtler and more elegant. Flowers beneath bracken during June and July in the New Forest and in a few nearby places. A stout 1-3′ (30-90″) perennial with flat leaves.

YELLOW CENTAURY *(Cicendia filiformis)* A miniature amongst our wild flowers – although it can reach 6″ (15cm), it is often as small as 1″ (3cm) tall. A rare and local annual, its flowers sparkle in damp sandy and peaty places in the South and West in late summer.

BUTCHER'S BROOM *(Ruscus aculeatus)* The 'leaves' are actually modified stems and the tiny flowers grow through the middle of them. Native in the South where it reaches 24″ (60cm). The flowers appear in spring, and are followed by red berries.

Turtle Dove

Goldcrest

TURTLE DOVE (*Streptopelia turtur*) The only migrant amongst our pigeons and doves, arriving in spring to breed in the South and Midlands. It leaves in late summer, having raised two or even three broods. A small dove, reaching 11″ (28cm), it has a soft, purring call.

Its diet consists of seeds, most especially those of fumitories — weeds of dry soils — which may account for the bird's scarcity in the damper North and West. The nest, a flimsy platform of twigs, is made in a tree or bush, and 2 glossy white eggs are laid.

GOLDCREST (*Regulus regulus*) A 3½″ (9cm) resident, very widespread and often common. When populations become very dense, it will colonize deciduous woods, but is more reliably found amongst conifers. A lively, tiny bird, it has a fittingly tiny call which

Honey Buzzard

is rhythmic. Vulnerable to cold weather, its numbers often crash after hard winters. A compact, rounded nest of moss and other soft materials is slung from the branches of a tree and two clutches of 7-10 pale, slightly spotted eggs are laid.

HONEY BUZZARD (*Pernis apivorus*) This 23″ (58cm) summer visitor, has its stronghold in the mixed woodlands of the New Forest; elsewhere it breeds regularly only in north Norfolk and in a few places in the Midlands and the North. It spends a lot of time on the ground, raiding grubs from the nests of wasps and bees – hence its name. It also eats other large insects, small birds and mammals and reptiles. The flight is floating and soaring, the call raucous. In the nest of sticks, built high in a tree, 1-3 reddish blotched eggs are laid.

The Honey Buzzard

One of Britain's rarest breeding birds, the honey buzzard has
an extraordinary diet for a bird of
prey – it feeds almost entirely on wasps, bees and their larvae.

ADULT HONEY BUZZARD
(above) *A summer visitor to
the south of Britain, the
honey buzzard is close in its
size and appearance to the
buzzard, with brown or grey-
brown plumage and barred
underparts, but with a longer
tail and narrower head.*

papery nest and rips apart the honeycomb to
devour the juicy wasp grubs inside. Eventually
satisfied, it takes off into the tree tops to preen
itself, well hidden amongst the foliage.

Today, this strange bird of prey is a rare sight
in Britain. Small numbers – usually less than a
dozen pairs each year – breed in the southern
half of the country, with their stronghold in the
New Forest. Although never common, the
honey buzzard was once more abundant and
widespread, preferring quiet areas of mature,
mainly deciduous woodland, with plentiful
open glades and rides. However, clearance of
large tracts of woodland which this shy bird
needs to survive and breed, and its unjust
persecution by gamekeepers or landowners and
by egg collectors, have helped to bring about its
virtual extinction as a British breeding bird.

A close look at a honey buzzard reveals
special adaptations for its unusual diet. In
contrast to the powerful flesh-tearing bills of a
sparrowhawk or golden eagle, its bill is narrow
and delicate, well adapted for tweezering wasp
and bee grubs out of their waxy brood cells.
Unlike the curved piercing talons which other
birds of prey use for subduing birds or mammals, the honey buzzard has blunt-clawed,
almost straight toes, like those of a hen, which
are ideally suited for digging out the soil. Also
unusual is that it spends a good deal of time on
the ground and can walk easily, unencumbered
by long curved talons.

In a woodland clearing, an angry buzzing
fills the air, emanating from a cloud of
wasps swarming frantically around their
nest beneath an old beech tree. The source of
their disturbance is one of our most unusual
birds in the act of taking its lunch. The bird is a
honey buzzard, and its diet consists mainly of
wasp and bee larvae. Furiously, it scrapes away
the soft soil to expose the heart of the insects'

SOARING HONEY BUZZARD
(right) *Although they mainly soar on migratory flights with wings outstretched and held flat, honey buzzards can also maintain a sustained wing flapping over large stretches of water. In winter, they migrate to Africa, often flying in large flocks.*

NEST WITH YOUNG
(below) *The honey buzzard's nest is small for its size — about a foot in diameter — and is built high in a tree, often near the edge of a wood. It is built from twigs and dead branches, with a leafy central cup inside.*

The honey buzzard scans the ground for prey from a high vantage point and will follow any passing worker wasps or bees returning to their nest. On locating the nest, it digs furiously, like a feathered terrier, sometimes excavating such a deep trench that it disappears from view. It may return daily for several days to finish off a large nest or group of nests and the wasps or bees are powerless to prevent the destruction.

Adult wasps are caught deftly in the bird's bill, and the hind parts of their bodies containing the sting are nipped off before being swallowed. As well as the wasp grubs and some of the adults, the bird also eats the comb.

Honey buzzards do sometimes supplement this diet with frogs, lizards, other insects (such as ant pupae) and the occasional small bird or mammal, but they rely on wasps and unless they can find enough nests they cannot live and breed. A family of honey buzzards may eat a prodigious quantity of wasp grubs in a season — as many as 90,000, according to one estimate.

Arriving at their British breeding sites in late May, after wintering in Africa, honey buzzards soon begin their courtship display, soaring together and plunging up and down in a dramatic series of swoops and climbs. The male may stall as the top of a climb, then raise his wings several times vertically over his back, quivering them, before diving to repeat the performance.

SECOND HAND NEST

The nest is built high up in a tree, and often an old nest of a crow or buzzard is used as a base. The male does most of the work of gathering the nest material, while his mate is the chief architect, constructing the nest from leafy twigs, interwoven with a few dead branches.

Normally silent birds, a pair of honey buzzards may become more vocal during the nesting period, when they utter high-pitched *kuwee-ee-eew* calls. The male may also make a curious clicking noise that has been likened to the sound of a stick held against the spokes of a spinning bicycle wheel, and calls like the spitting of cats have also been recorded.

Once the female has laid her two (occasionally one or three) handsomely patterned eggs, however, the birds are generally quiet and secretive. The male takes an unusually large share of the task of incubation, and the pair alternate shifts through day and night.

Although both eggs usually hatch, the younger and weaker of the two chicks often dies, and may even be killed by its larger sibling. Both parents brood and feed their young although the male does most of the hunting. When almost four weeks old, the young are able to remove wasp grubs from a nest by themselves. By six weeks of age, they make their first shaky flights and in a further ten days or so will start preparing for their mid-September migration back to Africa.

The Isle of Wight

Just off the south coast of England lies the 155-square-mile island of Wight. Once a part of the mainland, it became separated when rising seas cut off this 'tail' of land only 10,000 years ago. At the western extremity of the island a spectacular series of stacks, known as the Needles, bears witness to the eternal retreat of the land in the face of the violent sea. Other parts of the coast, too, are unstable and great tracts of cliff have slumped into the water. Inland, though, is a different picture – a picture of peaceful, pastoral lowland and down.

COWES

THE SOLENT

RYDE

SALT MARSH

RIVER MEDINA

ALUM BAY

DOWNLAND

NEWPORT

THE NEEDLES

CHALK RIDGE

SOUTHERN DOWNS

CHINES

SLUMPED UNDERCLIFF

THE ISLE OF WIGHT

COUNTRY IN MINIATURE
(left) For its size, the Isle of Wight exhibits a wide range of scenic features. The 60-mile coastline comprises towering cliffs, sheltered bays, narrow chines and, on the north coast, mudflats and salt-marshes. Inland, the undulating lowlands of the north and south are separated by rolling chalk downs. The warm climate ensures a long agricultural growing season.

Nestling some three or four miles off the Hampshire coast, the Isle of Wight measures 23 miles at its broadest point – from the Needles in the west to Bembridge Foreland in the east – and just 13 miles from Cowes in the north to St Catherine's Point in the south. Today a diamond-shaped island with an area considerably smaller than that of Greater London, the Isle of Wight was once joined to both mainland Britain and the European continent. Then, some 10,000 years ago, the sea level changed and the English Channel was formed. At roughly the same time the sea broke through the continuous chalk ridge which ran from the Purbeck Downs (in present-day Dorset) to the eastern-most point of the island, creating the Solent – a narrow strait which now separates the Isle of Wight from the south coast of England.

SCENIC VARIETY

Despite its small size, the island boasts a very varied geology, which is reflected in its diverse landscape. Like most of southern England, the island is composed entirely of sedimentary rocks. But the dominant rock is chalk, which runs in an east-west ridge across the whole width of the island, culminating in the dramatic white sea cliffs for which the island is famous. Culver Cliff in the east reaches nearly 400 feet (130m), and at the western extremity are the Needles – a series of stacks, which are one of Britain's best-known coastal features.

Inland, the chalk ridge forms undulating downland where thin soils support short turf interspersed with patches of gorse and brambles. The chalk downs divide the island into two distinct regions. To the north irregular lowlands are dotted with copses (mainly oak and hazel) and larger areas of woodland. The soils are poorly drained and, in places, quite acidic. To the south of the spine lies the 'bowl' of the

Nature Walk

When visiting the Isle of Wight, look out for these famous sights:

THE NEEDLES — spectacular 100' high chalk stacks sculpted by the sea.

CARISBROOKE CASTLE — one of the finest in Britain and the prison of King Charles I.

OSBORNE HOUSE — Victoria and Albert's favourite home and the death-place of the long-reigning queen.

ROMAN MOSAICS — some of the country's finest can be found in the Roman Villa at Brading, near Sandown.

ALUM BAY
(above) The bay is named after the deposits of alum (sulphate of aluminium) which were mined here as long as 300 years ago. It is renowned for the number of different coloured sands which make up both its steep cliffs and its beaches.

CHALK DOWNS
(left) Inland, the Isle is composed of soft rolling downland, akin to the chalk downs of southern England. Here, at the eastern end of the chalk ridge that runs virtually the full width of the island, the landscape presents a predominantly pastoral view, revealing evidence of a thriving dairy industry in this northern part of the island.

island — a fertile region of lush pastures, fields and wooded ridges.

South of the 'bowl' and forming the southern-most tip of the island are the Southern Downs — at 770 feet (235m) or so, the highest ground on the Isle of Wight. In the north they are indented by numerous deep valleys which, like those of the central downlands, are often dry.

On the coastal margin of the Southern Downs is the undercliff, where steep wooded slopes are backed by vertical scarps up to 200 feet (60m) high. Here porous chalk and greensand overlie beds of clay, which water cannot easily penetrate. The resulting cliff springs and the seaward dip of the strata make the land very unstable. Major landslips occurred in 1810 and 1818 and subsequent shifting and settling has caused great damage to houses and roads. Elsewhere on the south coast small streams have cut their way through the cliffs to produce narrow ravines or chines (from the Anglo Saxon word *cine* or fissure). Each has its own character: Shanklin Chine is richly vegetated with trees and ferns, while at Blackgang stark rock faces drop some 400 feet (130m) to the sea.

The Isle of Wight's equitable climate favours the tourist industry and agriculture — the two most important sectors of the island's economy. 75 per cent of the land is under agricultural management: the ill-drained lowlands of the north support a thriving dairy industry, while the more fertile soils of the south are given over to cereals and fruit and vegetable crops.

Today, much of the Isle of Wight's country-side and coast is overseen by local and national conservation bodies, including the Archeological Society, the National Trust and the Nature Conservancy Council. Their involvement helps to maintain a balance between the demands of modern tourism and agriculture and the long-term protection of the diverse habitats which support the island's very varied flora and fauna.

Island Life

**From its precipitous chalk cliffs and rolling downs to its marshy estuaries
and sandy beaches, the Isle of Wight provides a varied home to a
great diversity of wildlife – including the rare Glanville fritillary.**

Early December on Afton Down, over-looking the Isle of Wight's south coast. The light is dazzling, the view breathtaking, as one looks west along Tennyson Down to the chalk cliffs and the sea.

Jackdaws wheel above the cliff edge, and the air is filled with the amorous calls of herring gulls. Once populated by choughs and peregrines, the cliffs still support thriving colonies of fulmars, kittiwakes and great black-backed gulls.

Even in mid-winter on the cliffs one can still see the mauve, scented flowers of hoary stock, which is rare in the wild though common in gardens. Growing by it is sea beet, with its crinkly, rich green leaves. In summer the bright blooms of yellow-horned poppy are joined by the less showy flowers of white horehound and rock samphire.

The cliffs are also home to the island's most famous insect – the Glanville fritillary, a handsome, bright orange-brown butterfly with black markings. In Britain it is found only in this locality and the Channel Islands, though on the Continent it is quite common.

BLACK-TAILED GODWIT *(left) Less than 100 pairs breed in Britain and this species is most commonly seen in winter. It feeds in small flocks around our coasts, using its long bill to probe for crustaceans, molluscs and marine worms. The bird shown here is in winter plumage. Its black tail is one feature which distinguishes it from the bar-tailed godwit.*

The great bulge of chalk that makes up the downs has a rich flora but, because of its proximity to the sea and the exposed position, the plants of these maritime downs tend to be much smaller than normal. Betony, small scabious and wild carrot all grow only a couple of inches high. The only true dwarf species, however, is the pink-flowered dwarf centaury.

Soft mounds of old ant-hills litter the downland slopes. In summer they are covered with colourful clumps of rock rose, thyme, trefoil and carline thistle. The flowers provide sources of nectar for butterflies such as the adonis and small blue. The latter, the smallest British butterfly, is dark brown; only the males have a hint of blue. The caterpillars of both butterflies are tended by ants for the sweet secretions which exudes from their tenth body segment.

THE SOUTHERN CLIFFS

All along the south coast are chines, sheltered gullies leading to the sea. On their damp flanks grow ferns and flowering plants. Notable among these is golden saxifrage, a delicate plant that grows profusely along Blackgang chine.

At St Catherine's Point, the southernmost tip of the island, the boulders are blotched with orange, green and grey marine lichens. This is an excellent place to watch the passage of seabirds – eastwards in the spring and westwards in the autumn. It is not unusual to see gannets

WILDLIFE OF THE ISLAND

The island's downs are home to chalk-loving plants such as the vetches, orchids and yellow-wort. Many of the flowers in the short, wind-pruned turf, such as stemless thistle and harebell, are low-growing because of the strong onshore winds. The flowers attract butterflies. The small blue lays its eggs on kidney vetch. The dark green fritillary is a butterfly of exposed grassy slopes. The clouded yellow is a migrant which likes clovers and trefoils. The Glanville fritillary haunts the undercliff, living close to the cliff-nesting guillemots, cormorants and gulls.

fishing, and Arctic skuas and sheerwaters flying past.

The six miles of undercliff from St Catherine's Point to Luccombe provide the naturalist with a special treat – boulder-strewn woodland with such rarities as Italian cuckoo pint and green-flowered helleborine. Irish ivy festoons the trees, and a fascinating variety of ferns and mosses abound.

The soft chalk and crumbling sandstone cliffs provide a rich, sheltered habitat for solitary bees and wasps. A notable insect here is *Philanthus*, a bee-killing wasp more common in the sandy lanes of Provence. Another Provencal insect also found on the island is the great green bush-cricket, an elegant, carnivorous insect that feeds on smaller bush-crickets and grasshoppers.

KEY TO THE SPECIES

1 *Herring gull*
2 *Skylark*
3 *Jay*
4 *Fox*
5 *Long-eared bat*
6 *Dark green fritillary*
7 *Gorse*
8 *Blackthorn*
9 *Badger*
10 *Privet*
11 *Traveller's joy*
12 *Great black-backed gull*
13 *Cormorants*
14 *Anthills*
15 *Bumble bee* Bombus jonellus
16 *Pyramidal orchid*
17 *Early purple orchid*
18 *Clouded yellow*
19 *Guillemots*
20 *Glanville fritillary*
21 *Common lizard*
22 *Harebells*
23 *Clustered bellflower*
24 *Yellow-wort*
25 *Mignonette*
26 *Stinking iris*
27 *Ribwort plantain*
28 *Kidney vetch*
29 *Small blue*
30 *Stemless thistle*
31 *Wild madder*
32 *Yellow horned poppy*

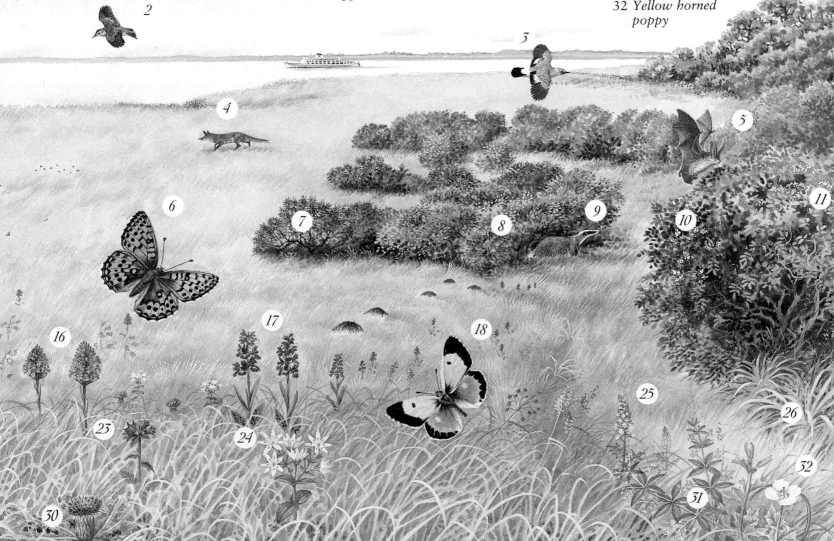

A DRAMATIC SPIDER
(left) Argiope bruennichi *is found in Britain only on England's south coast – the rest of the population occurs on the Continent. The female (shown here) is the most brightly coloured of the sexes: the male is drab brown and slimmer. The female spins a large (1' diameter) orb-web close to the ground. The 'smoke-trail' in the web (known as a stabilamentum) reinforces the web and is particularly characteristic of this species. Adult female spiders can be seen from August until October.*

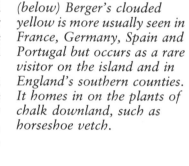

Ventnor and its surroundings are especially sheltered, cut off from cold northerly and easterly winds. The balmy Mediterranean feel of the place is enhanced by the sight of lizards scampering up and down the walls of houses and hotels. These are not common lizards, but wall lizards, introduced to the island at the turn of the century. Scattered colonies now survive in and around Ventnor.

More recently (in the 1960s) the South African clawed toad was also introduced, to pools created by landslips at Brook, also on the south coast.

ON THE SHELVING SHORE

The rocky shore at Foreland is a good place in winter to watch purple sandpipers feeding close to the water's edge, advancing and retreating with the tide. The shelving rock pavements are rich in seaweeds, molluscs and tube worms.

On the island's north-west coast, the creeks and marshes of Newtown Nature Reserve pro- vide an excellent spot for wintering waders and wildfowl. Redshanks, black-tailed godwits and curlews wade through the swirling channels or probe the mudflats for invertebrates and are joined by the occasional greenshank and spotted redshank.

Teal dabble in the creeks, wigeon graze on nearby fields and brent geese gather on the mudflats, uttering low, croaking calls as they feed. Breeding birds, such as the reed bunting, shelduck, ringed plover and black-headed gull, can all be seen here in winter.

To the north and west there are small patches of heath where nightjars and adders occur. Here, too, one can come across a somewhat monstrous showy spider, *Argiope bruennichi*.

STINKING IRIS: FRUIT AND FLOWER
(below) This plant grows on chalky soils. The alternative name 'roast beef plant' better describes the smell of its crushed leaves.

RARE MIGRANT
(below) Berger's clouded yellow is more usually seen in France, Germany, Spain and Portugal but occurs as a rare visitor on the island and in England's southern counties. It homes in on the plants of chalk downland, such as horseshoe vetch.

THREE GULLS
(left) A female great black-backed gull with two fledglings (she lays 2-3 eggs). Very few of these gulls breed on England's south and east coasts but the offshore chalk stacks of the Isle of Wight provide ideal nest sites. The largest of our gulls, it preys on other seabirds and also takes fish, molluscs and carrion.

The boldly marked female may be seen perched on her web in a sunny spot.

What remains of the original woodland lies to the north of the chalk ridge, on heavier clay soils. Parkhurst Forest, which is mainly planted with conifers, has some oak and beech woodland with wild service trees and holly. The open woodland rides are flanked in parts with a form of lungwort, a hairy plant with blue-purple flowers pollinated by bumble bees. Stinking iris is most noticeable in autumn, when its seed capsules burst open to reveal bright orange-scarlet berries. In the spring many of the island's

woods are clothed with wild daffodils, which flower as early as February.

MISSING SPECIES

The island is an important sanctuary for the red squirrel, which is quite common, though seldom seen unless you are about early. Evidence may come from a pile of half-eaten cones, or the sighting of a winter drey. The grey squirrel has never managed to gain a footing on the island. Nor, surprisingly enough, have such woodland birds as tawny owl, nuthatch, redstart and wood warbler, which are all common on the mainland.

Despite these absent species, the Isle of Wight is a gem of a place for the naturalist because of its variety of habitats well served by footpaths.

WALL LIZARD
(above) This species is commonly found in Italy, other parts of southern Europe and as far east as northern Asia. It is not native to Britain but is imported as a pet. Small colonies have established themselves — there are, for instance, two colonies on railway bridges in London. The wall lizard on the Isle of Wight may be descended from pets that escaped or they may have been deliberately introduced.

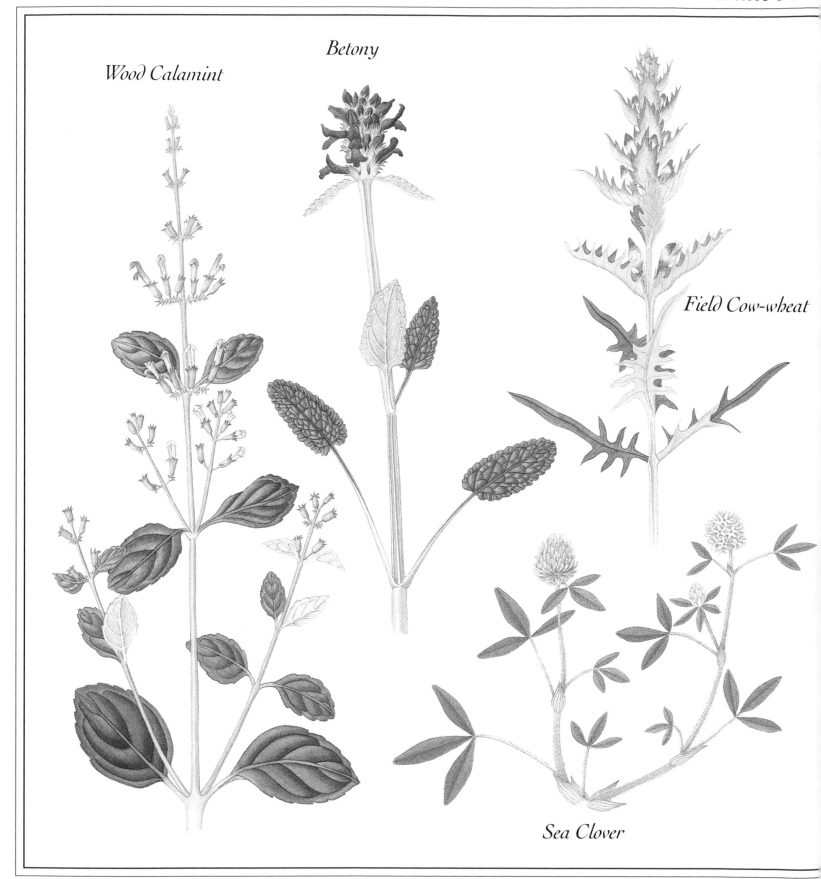

Wood Calamint

Betony

Field Cow-wheat

Sea Clover

WOOD CALAMINT (*Calamintha sylvatica* ssp. *sylvatica*) 12-24″ (30-60cm) tall, this hairy perennial is known to occur in one locality on the Isle of Wight, growing on a chalky bank. The leaves are large and coarsely toothed; blotch-lipped flowers are seen July to September.

BETONY (*Stachys officinalis*) Sparsely hairy, this perennial has erect, square stems to 24″ (60cm) and well-spaced leaves with rounded teeth. Tubular flowers are seen in June to September. Widespread and common in rough grassland, England and Wales.

FIELD COW-WHEAT (*Melampyrum arvense*) A very rare, protected annual weed of chalky arable fields, it occurs only in southern England. Erect 8-24″ (20-60cm) stems bear lance-shaped leaves and pink, hooded flowers, June-September.

SEA CLOVER (*Trifolium squamosum*) A rare annual of short coastal turf, found locally around south and east England and south Wales. Up to 16″ (40cm) tall, its leaves are divided into 3 pointed leaflets, and round heads of flowers open June-August.

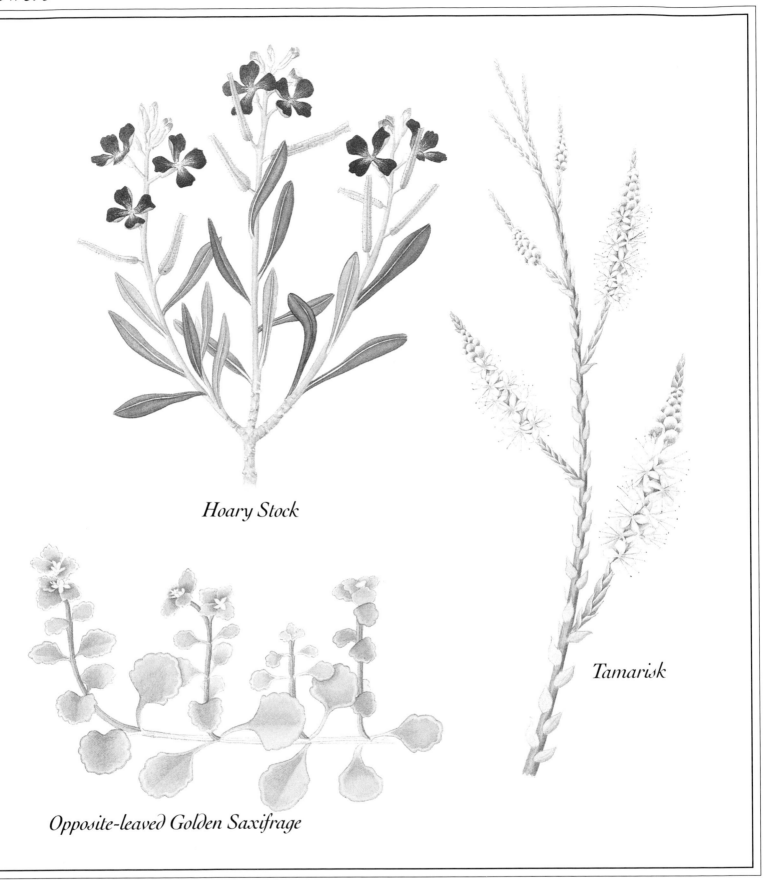

Hoary Stock

Tamarisk

Opposite-leaved Golden Saxifrage

HOARY STOCK (*Matthiola incana*) This rare plant is found only on the chalky sea cliffs of south England, where it makes erect shrubby clumps to 31″ (78cm). Leaves, stems and seed pods are hairy, and the flowers, seen May-July, may be red, purple or white.

OPPOSITE-LEAVED GOLDEN SAXIFRAGE (*Chrysosplenium oppositifolium*) Locally plentiful on wet woodland floors through much of Britain, this 2-6″ (5-15cm) perennial may carpet large areas. Shiny leaves are round, and heads of green flowers open April-July.

TAMARISK (*Tamarix gallica*) Tiny, overlapping blue-green leaves give this 3-10′ (1-3m) shrub a frail feathery appearance – but it survives the winds and salt-spray of the sandy coasts of south England where it is widespread. Dense flowerspikes open July-September.

Summer

Spotted Redshank

Winter

SPOTTED REDSHANK (*Tringa erythropus*) A migratory bird, this 12″ (30cm) wader is seen in southern Britain and south Ireland, over-wintering on freshwater marshes, sewage farms, saltmarshes and sea shores. Here they occur singly or in small groups, picking out tiny crustaceans and molluscs from mud and wet vegetation. Long-legged and with a long, dark slender bill, its winter plumage is greyish, in clear contrast to the handsome white-speckled black of spring migrants in breeding plumage. Call is a *tchoo-wit*.

Little Gull

Winter

Summer

Curlew Sandpiper

CURLEW SANDPIPER *(Calidris ferruginea)* This 7″ (18cm) wader is an occasional bird of passage – and it is mainly immature birds that are seen here. They arrive in late summer and may sometimes occur in small flocks of up to 20, resting and feeding before continuing their journey south. Saltmarshes, sewage farms, mudflats and reservoirs are all likely sites. Similar to the dunlin in winter but with a more upright posture and a longer, curved bill, the curlew sandpiper has a splendid red-brown breeding plumage. The call is a clear, fluid whistle.

LITTLE GULL *(Larus minutus)* A neat bird with rounded wings and a buoyant, tern-like flight. At only 11″ (28cm), it is Britain's smallest gull. An autumn and winter visitor, it is seen regularly in small numbers and occasionally in small flocks over eastern Britain and the offshore waters. Best identified by its small size and dark, blackish underwings. Only in breeding plumage is the black hood seen. Though mostly maritime in winter, they may frequent weedy lakes and marshes, feeding on tiny fish, molluscs and insects.

The Glanville Fritillary

The Glanville fritillary flutters and glides amongst the brightly
coloured flowers of the chalk cliffs and warm grassy slopes of
the Isle of Wight coast – the last haunt of this butterfly in Britain.

Gliding smoothly on its rich brown wings, the Glanville fritillary resembles a drifting leaf as it skims low over the cliff-top turf. Then it lands to sample the nectar of one of the numerous coastal flowers, and as it closes its wings the delicate patterning of its pale undersides is revealed.

The Isle of Wight is now the only British haunt of the beautiful Glanville fritillary. The butterfly was first discovered on the island in 1824, but it had been known on the mainland long before that and had been named after Lady Eleanor Glanville, a keen collector of butterflies in the 18th century. But the Glanville fritillary has long since ceased to be a permanent resident of mainland Britain, probably as a result of the development of its coastal habitat. It is a butterfly of rough hillsides and other places where its foodplant – ribwort plantain – flourishes. Ribwort plantain is a pioneer plant that rapidly colonizes fresh earth but then gradually dies out in the face of competition from grasses and other taller plants. At the western end of the Isle of Wight, where the cliffs of sand and clay are continually slipping and exposing new surfaces, both the ribwort and the butterfly are most common.

DISTINGUISHING MARKS

Although there are several similar species on the Continent, the Glanville fritillary is easily distinguished from other British fritillaries by the row of black dots close to the margin on the underside of the hind wing. There are also some black dots under the tip of the forewing. The upperside is very similar to that of the heath fritillary, but can be recognized by the clear row of black dots in orange circles near the edge of the hind wing.

The adults fly from late May to early July and

ISLAND BEAUTY
Once common in parts of mainland Britain, the beautiful Glanville fritillary is now only found on the Isle of Wight, where it is at the northern limit of its European range. Although its markings are similar to those of other British fritillaries, it can be distinguished by the row of black dots in orange circles near the edge of the upper hind wing.

maintain fairly discrete colonies, the largest of which are on the undercliffs and in the steep valleys or chines running down to the shore. The butterflies fly quite strongly, however, and commonly disport themselves around the cliff-tops, alternating fast flapping flight with long, graceful glides. Some individuals move right away from their original colonies and start up new ones elsewhere on the island or even on neighbouring parts of the mainland, although these new colonies are usually short-lived because few habitats can support the successive stands of plantain needed by the larvae.

After mating, the females lay their oval yellow eggs in large batches on the undersides of young ribwort plantain leaves. Warmth is an important factor in egg-laying, and the butter-flies rarely use plants growing on north-facing slopes. There may be as many as 200 eggs in a single batch, and when they hatch about three weeks later the dense clusters of spiky black caterpillars launch a massive attack on the plantain leaves. They also spend a lot of time basking on silken sheets which they spin over the leaves, and in the densest colonies they turn

WINTER NEST
(right) In winter, family groups of young larvae hibernate in a silken web woven amongst the leaves of the ribwort plantain. The nests are usually located on warm, south-facing slopes which mitigate against damp, while the web itself prevents desiccation by the sea winds or the sun.

SUMMER COURTSHIP
(below) Mating takes place in May or June. The male butterflies emerge first and disperse over the habitat ready to pounce on the females as soon as their wings have spread. Females are slightly larger than the males, with an average wing span of 47mm as opposed to the males' 41mm.

the vegetation black. Relatively few caterpillars are taken by birds, because of their spiky coats, but parasites take a heavy toll.

As autumn approaches, the caterpillars of each family group congregate even more densely and spin a conspicuous hibernation nest amongst the grasses. The dense silken nest protects the caterpillars from the drying winds and prevents desiccation. But damp must also be avoided, as this would allow fatal moulds to spread through the sleeping colony during the winter months.

SPRING AWAKENING

The caterpillars wake to feed again in the spring and, as they approach maturity, they begin to separate. Each has a shiny brown head at this stage, but its dark, spiky body could easily be mistaken for a young plantain flower head as it rests on the edge of a leaf. During April or early May the caterpillar reaches full size and hangs upside down from a grass stalk or from the underside of a rock or stone to turn into a purplish-grey chrysalis. The new adult emerges about three weeks later.

Although the Glanville fritillary is one of our rarest butterflies, with only about a dozen permanent colonies in recent years, its future on the Isle of Wight does not appear to be seriously threatened. Numbers fluctuate a great deal as some areas of plantain become overgrown and others develop, but on balance the population remains fairly constant. Because of the unstable nature of its habitat, much of which belongs to the National Trust, the area is unlikely to be developed and, as long as the climate does not change too much, the butterfly should continue to flourish in this little corner of England.

Dartmoor

The largest tract of open country in southern England, Dartmoor comprises 365 square miles of high heather, bracken-covered moorland and bleak, inhospitable bog. It is a granite landscape – a desolate rolling plateau punctuated by sinister weathered outcrops which pierce the high ground and rise in the north to over 2000 feet. In contrast, the edge of the moor is marked by steep-sided gorges and lush wooded combes, where rivers tumbling from the uplands flow towards the neatly hedged, fertile farmland of the surrounding Devon countryside.

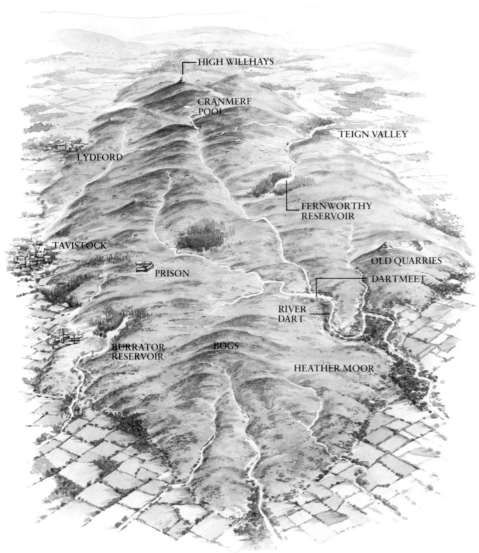

A VARIED LANDSCAPE

A great rolling granite plateau at the heart of south Devon, Dartmoor slopes southwards from High Willhays — at 2038 feet the highest point — in the north. The inhospitable bogs of the high ground give way to dry, heather-covered moorland where prehistoric remains and recent farms and quarries testify to man's long involvement on the moor. At the edge of the plateau deep wooded valleys guide rivers to the gentle patchwork of the 'in-country'.

(203cm) of rainfall a year), conspires against all but the hardiest of plants.

Where the ground remains sodden, boggy mires occur. An extensive bog stretches around Cranmere Pool in the north, covering the high watershed which lies between Teignhead, Fur Tor and Cut Hill. Other mires lie to the south. Bleak and exposed, they are bedded on peat up to 12 feet (3.5m) thick, which make treacherous walking country. Where the ground is drier, heather and bilberry grow and it is this 'dry moor' which is so admired by visitors.

At the heart of the granite country lies the 'Forest of Dartmoor'. Once a royal hunting preserve (and still belonging to the Duchy of Cornwall), it is now an open wilderness which gradually merges with the open common moorland grazings and the 'in-country' – a patchwork landscape of walled fields and narrow lanes on the edge of the moor. Here the Teign and other rivers cut deep, wooded valleys on their way to the lower farmlands which surround Dartmoor.

Today's villages lie along the 'in-country', but high on the moor innumerable prehistoric

Dartmoor is a magnificent expanse of granite moorland rising steeply from the lush green fields and wooded valleys of Devon. A sloping plateau with two distinct elevations to the north and south, the moor represents the weathered remains of a huge mass of granite which was forced up from within the earth some 300 million years ago, intruding into the overlying sedimentary rocks. Subsequent erosion of these softer rocks exposed the harder granite as a high plateau. This in turn has been eroded to give a rolling landscape of smooth slopes and valleys dissected by small chuckling streams. The highest ground lies to the north-west, where High Willhays rises to 2038 feet (621m) and nearby Yes Tor reaches 2030 feet (618m).

The tors are a famous feature of Dartmoor. There are more than 170 of these outcrops of hard rock scattered over the landscape, many of them weathered into fantastic shapes. At their feet and strewn across many of the slopes lie clitters — haphazard jumbles of frost-fractured boulders — the first stage in the breakdown of the granite. In time, the rock weathers to a poor acid soil and this, in conjunction with the bleak winters and wet climate (more than 80 inches

BLEAK MOORLAND
(right) High on the moor lie large expanses of blanket bog. Once covered in forest, little now grows in the acid peat soil: vegetation consists of mosses, lichens, purple moor grass and sedge.

remains testify to ancient settlement there. Other relics date from later periods, like the granite waymarks and stone-built homes of medieval farmers and tin miners. First mined in the 12th century, tin became a major industry during the Middle Ages, and mining continued until the price fell in the 1920s. Granite and china clay are still quarried on the fringes of the moor.

Until this century Dartmoor remained a remote fastness, scarcely touched by the outside world. The landscape had changed little since early times when grazing on the moor first began, creating the open ground we know today. Only patches of ancient woodland, like Wistman's Wood, tell of a different landscape in prehistoric times.

CAREFUL MANAGEMENT

It was to protect the unique character of the moor that Dartmoor was proclaimed a National Park in 1951. By this time more and more interests were making increased demands on the landscape: expanding population centres had necessitated reservoirs such as Fernworthy, dammed in the bog country; the forestry commission had planted acres of conifers to improve the nation's timber resources and the Ministry of Defence had appropriated 27,000 acres of land as a training ground. In addition to these are the continuing pressures of tourism and leisure, and the ancient rights of the local 'commoners' to graze their stock and fire the heather. Only by achieving a balance between all these interests can the Park Authority achieve its aim of protecting this magnificent wilderness for future generations.

RAVINES AND GORGES
(above) Fourteen rivers rise in Dartmoor's upland bogs. Initially small, burbling streams, they leave the plateau as powerful torrents and gouge deep gorges in the softer rock. On the west of the moor, the River Lyd roars down a typical, thickly wooded valley to the White Lady Falls. Here it tumbles 110 feet into the Lydford Gorge – a 1½ mile long ravine carved from the rock some 450,000 years ago.

Nature Walk

Dartmoor has a wealth of intriguing natural landforms and man-made remains, such as:

BOWERMAN'S NOSE, a famous tor with a human form, said to be a hunter turned to stone by witches.

GRANITE TRAMWAYS, built to transport quarried granite from Haytor Down to the Teign valley.

LOGAN STONES, huge granite boulders which rock on their axis, surrounded by myth and mystery.

GRIMSPOUND, a Bronze Age settlement which comprises 24 hut circles enclosed within an impressive granite boundary wall.

On Rocky Dartmoor

Dartmoor's habitats, from bog and moor to wooded valleys and farmland, hold exciting upland birds, herds of deer, unusual flowers and some captivating songsters.

The habitats of this 'last great southern wilderness' are arranged in a huge inverted figure-of-eight. Around two large centres of blanket bog – totalling 30,000 acres (12,000 hectares) – lie the long gentle slopes of wet heath, steeper ones of dry heath, and then the boulder-strewn plateau edge crowned by tors. These form the moorland area. Whitewater streams, forming valley bogs high up, radiate from the twin centres in steep-sided, oak-wooded valleys. Farm fields, reservoirs and plantations complete the habitat picture.

UP ON THE MOORS

The loneliness of the vast moors, bleak and misty on most days, is intensified by the calls of curlew and lapwing, and the croak of a raven. There are few animal and plant species – but the grass-and-heather 'desert' is broken by features that attract wildlife. The isolated thorn is a nest site for the crow; each sallow thicket carries its reed bunting; and the biggest boulder is a vantage point for predator and prey. The same rock may have a perching buzzard one day, and red grouse the next.

Telegraph poles act as observation posts from which kestrels and buzzards watch for prey. Cuckoos swaying on the telephone wires track the flight paths of meadow pipits back to their nests, so that they can follow when the coast is clear and lay an unwanted egg. Pipits and whinchats sing from the wires, while ring ouzels perform their fluty song from the top of the poles.

Ring ouzels are found in territories with stone ruins, or abandoned quarry faces. Wheatears, too, need rock piles with holes and crevices, and Dartmoor's tors, clitters (boulder fields) and walls provide one of the bird's densest strongholds in England and Wales.

BIRDS OF THE BOG

Nesting waders are confined to the bogs. The extensive valley bogs hold curlews and maybe a lapwing or two in early summer. At the heart of the blanket bog a tiny population of dunlin and golden plover hang on in the face of increasing human rambling. The plovers are breeding here at their most southerly site. Game-bird chicks, like those of the red grouse, are about early in the season, and hen harriers have recently lingered over them longer than the normal passage bird would. Breeding merlins have not been found for some time.

In spring and autumn more birds of prey pass through and flocks of golden plover are a common sight then, wheeling round the grassier moors. Hen harriers have taken to over-wintering recently, and there is at least one communal ground roost in tall heather.

Buzzard, heron and raven – the biggest breeding birds – nest at the edges of the moorland, mostly in trees. Ravens may lay eggs as early as January, so as to feed their chicks on the lambing afterbirth 'crop'; herons nest in April; and buzzards are late nesters – still fledging in July.

PIED FLYCATCHER
Perched here at its nest hole, this cock pied flycatcher has brought a beakful of insects for the nestlings. These birds are summer visitors, arriving from Africa in May and departing in August. They have a particular fondness for river valleys in hilly districts, nesting in alders, birch and sessile oaks. The western oakwoods are ideal, with a good supply of both nest holes and caterpillars.

WILDLIFE ON DARTMOOR

Crows, kestrels and buzzards nest in the woods but can be seen from the high moors to the river valleys. Wheatears are abundant where there are stone crevices for nesting, and skylarks are widespread. Stonechats nest at the base of gorse bushes, while snipe favour boggy moorland, and grouse prefer dry heather. Ponies are the most obvious mammal but the less visible fox is common. Otters, though, are rare. Adders hunt voles, mice and the occasional frog, while lizards stick to insects such as grasshoppers and beetles. Boggy areas are enlivened by the flowers of bog asphodel and butterwort. The fox moth lays her eggs on heather and bilberry whose flowers attract bumble bees and honey bees.

KEY TO FEATURES AND SPECIES

1 Tor
2 Buzzard
3 Carrion crow
4 Eroded peat
5 Kestrel
6 Oakwood
7 Fox
8 Dartmoor ponies
9 Snipe
10 Cotton grass
11 Red grouse
12 Hazel
13 Holly
14 Alder
15 Green hairstreak

16 Pale butterwort
17 Bog asphodel
18 Cock stonechat
19 Otters
20 Hard fern
21 Wheatear at nest
22 Mat grass
23 Skylark on nest
24 Bristle-leaved bent grass
25 Bracken
26 Plume moth
27 Tormentil
28 Adder
29 Honey bees

30 Meadow grasshopper
31 Common lizard
32 Common tiger beetle
33 Bilberry
34 Bumble bee
35 Heather
36 Fox moth

The greatest variety of species occurs where moorland meets valley oakwood. Here, redstart and siskin nip out and back for a change of diet. Increasing numbers of red deer and fallow may do the same, and so will many a fox and badger, though both also breed out in the deeper moorland. Badgers, as everywhere in Devon, inhabit the woods and fields in good numbers. Their tracks, latrines and setts punctuate any walk. Surprisingly for such large animals, both badgers and deer are prospering on intensively used Dartmoor. Stoats and weasels thrive on voles, mice and the growing numbers of rabbits. Hares, on the other hand, seem to be thinning out.

MOORLAND INSECTS AND PLANTS

The moors are not rich in insect species but there are notable ones present, such as the emperor moth. Flying by day in June and July, it produces hefty bright green caterpillars that feed on heather until late August. St Mark's flies swarm around tors in late May, and large numbers of crane-flies emerge in September. Heather beetles produce rust-coloured patches of dead heather, that stand out when the undamaged plants are flowering in August and September.

The heathers – ling, cross-leaved heath and bell heather – all flower at the end of summer, and are joined by the inconspicuous dodder, and the bright golden flowers of western furze. This furze is a low, cushioned plant of the Dartmoor hillsides, not to be confused with the long, leggy bushes of gorse which flower all year. The grazed turf between the bushes is starred with yellow tormentil and blue milkwort – both of which have long flowering seasons.

Most of the early summer colour is to be found in damper places. Water forget-me-not follows bog bean in the wettest mires, while bog asphodel and marsh St John's wort provide yellow spikes in June. On the blanket bog,

cotton grasses sprout their fluffy white heads in mid-summer. Dartmoor's rarest flower is the inconspicuous pale butterwort, an elegant southern cousin of the 'common' version from further north.

Within the woods, bluebells get their flowering over while sunshine can still reach the forest floor. After that, greater woodrush and enchanter's nightshade almost alone vie with the ferns and mosses, so typical of damp south-western woodland. Flourishing in the clean air, vigorous lichens coat twigs, bark and rock faces. Flowers grow on many of the large boulders, and those in the rivers are submerged so briefly in the winter that woodrush and small sallows cling on.

IN RIVERS AND RESERVOIRS

River-bed rocks are spotted with the tell-tale droppings of dippers and grey wagtails, and signs of otters can be found on a few streams.

Dragonflies and damselflies abound in high summer and pond skaters throng each still backwater, snapping up terrestrial froghoppers that have mistakenly landed in the water. Now and then, brown trout take the skater, as a variation to their diet of caddis fly, stonefly and mayfly larvae and adults. Salmon still spawn in all the Dartmoor rivers, and spawning beds appear to be extending.

WISTMAN'S WOOD
(below) Growing near the natural tree line, the oaks of this small, ancient wood are noted for their luxuriant ferns, mosses and lichens. Liverworts grow beneath them.

ADDER BASKING
(below) Adders occur almost throughout Dartmoor, from the moors to the farmland and woods, but are commonest on dry heaths.

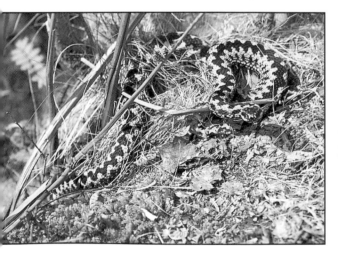

ROWAN BERRIES
(left) This most
striking of upland
trees is bright with
flowers in spring and
heavy with berries in
autumn. Ring ouzels
feed up on the berries
before migrating, and
redwings and fieldfares
re-fuel on arrival from
Scandinavia.

GOLDEN PLOVERS
(right) Two fluffy
chicks, dappled black
and gold, nestle up to
their handsome parent.
Able to run shortly
after hatching, the
chicks soon find much
of their own food.

HAIRY FOX MOTH CATERPILLAR
(below) Feeding on a wide range of plants –
including bramble, heather, heaths and bilberry
– this caterpillar can be found in many parts of
Dartmoor. The caterpillars appear in late July.
In spring male moths fly by day and night but
females are active only at night.

DARTMOOR PONIES
(above) These three ponies
show the range of usual
Dartmoor colours, though
dark brown is also common.
Their thick coats are retained
for most of the year. Few
ponies are pure-bred, as
other stallions, particularly
Shetlands, have been turned
out on Dartmoor. Each
stallion controls a wild herd
of up to 30 mares and foals
which keep to an established
territory. The ponies are hardy
enough to weather the winter.

Reservoirs also carry trout, which cormorant
and goosander will pause to sample in winter.
Reservoirs are usually accompanied by plantations, which, while they displace moorland
species, add new ones of their own. There
would not be siskins and redpolls, crossbills
or grasshopper warblers within Dartmoor were
it not for the acres of conifers planted in
the 1930s.

Wrapped around the upland woods and
moors is a landscape of walled fields and copses,
granite farmsteads and villages. From here daily
squadrons of swifts, swallows and martins fly
out in summer to hawk over the high moors.
Roaming buzzards, the jinking sparrowhawk
and hovering kestrels may travel in the opposite

direction from their nests to hunt the fields.
Ravens and crows scavenge here, often more
easily than out on the moor. Deer bound out
of the kale fields at first light, badgers stumble
home before dawn, and the foxes slink to
raid the contents of village dustbins as they do
in the suburbs.

Summer warblers swell the farmscape's
chorus, pied flycatchers add their simple tune
to the high oakwood and nightingales enrich
the lowest thicket. Woodlarks still patrol the
field and moorland boundary in two places,
but their beautifully lilting song, the finest
symphony of all, and commonplace until the
mid 1960s, is the worthy reward of a long, hard
search.

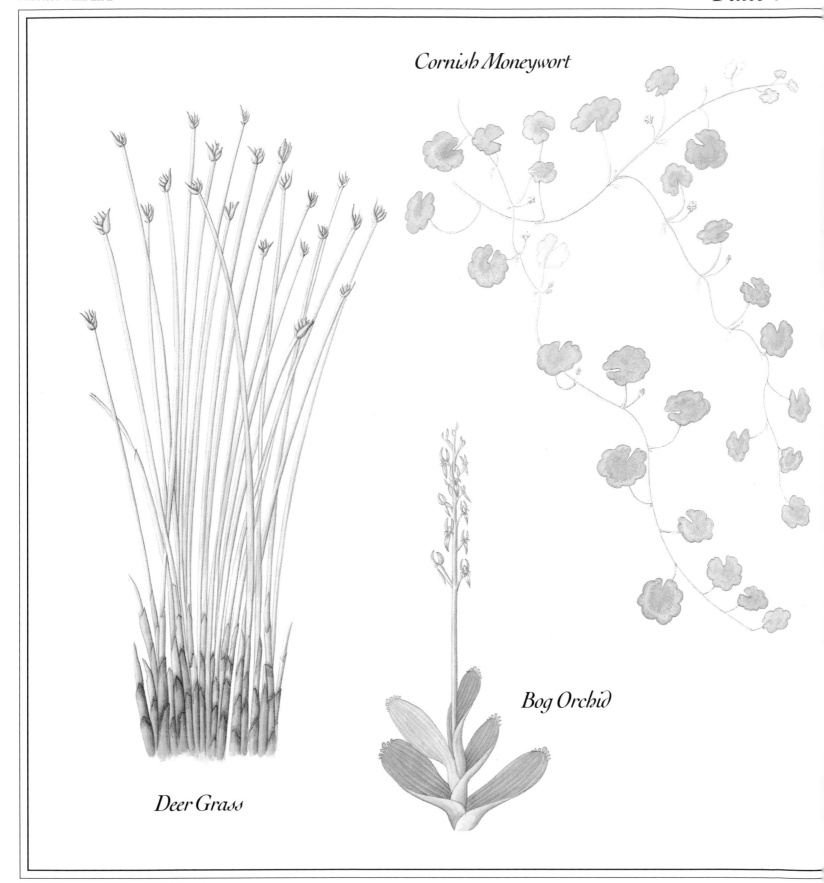

Cornish Moneywort

Bog Orchid

Deer Grass

DEER GRASS *(Scirpus cespitosus)* Dense tufts of this 2-14″ (5-35cm) perennial are locally very abundant on moorlands and wet boggy areas throughout Britain. Spikelets of flowers are borne at the top of a smooth round stem in May and June, 3-angled nutlets ripen by August.

BOG ORCHID *(Hammarbya paludosa)* A rare orchid 1-5″ (3-12cm), with green flowers open July-September. It is found only among sphagnum, in scattered, wet acid bogs of north and west Britain. Small concave leaves clasp the stem and have tiny buds all round the edge.

CORNISH MONEYWORT *(Sibthorpia europaea)* Limited to wet acid rocks and soil in shade, this low-growing hairy perennial is local in south-west England, very rare elsewhere. Creeping stems have lobed, kidney shaped leaves on stalks to 1″ (2.5cm) and flowers July-October.

Moorland Plants

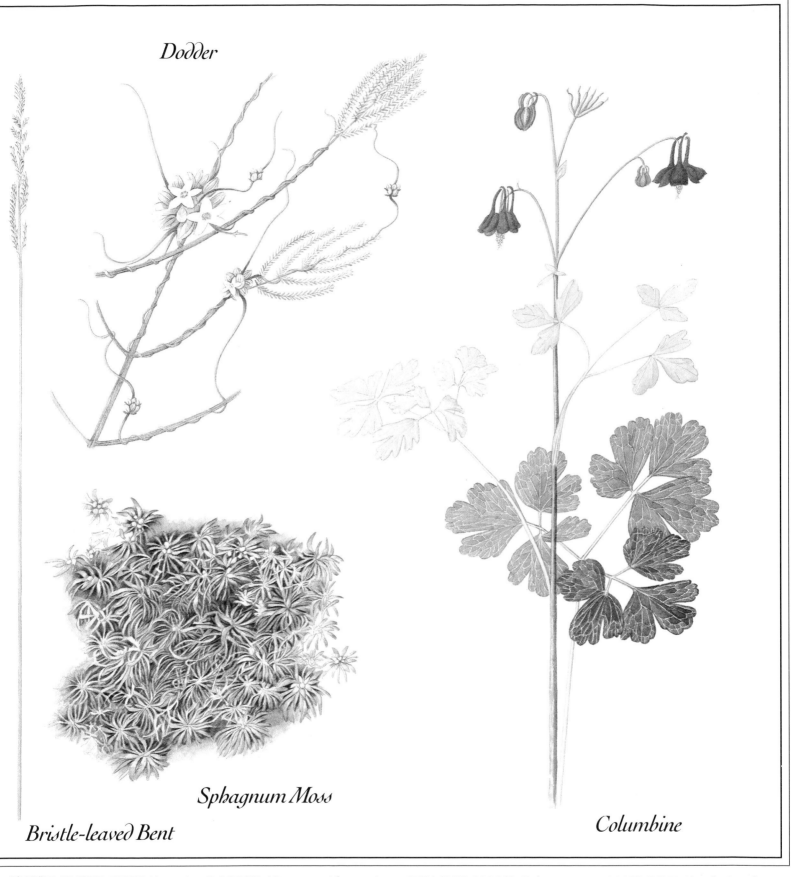

Dodder

Sphagnum Moss

Bristle-leaved Bent

Columbine

BRISTLE-LEAVED BENT *(Agrostis setacea)* A perennial grass with fine, bristle-like leaves, growing as a turf or in dense tufts. Stems 4-24″ (10-60cm) bear narrow heads of flowers, June-July. It is often abundant on dry heaths and sandy soils, mostly in the South-west.

DODDER *(Cuscuta epithymum)* Gorse and heather bushes can be smothered by the thin, twining red stems of this parasitic annual. Leaves are reduced to tiny scales, and heads of tightly packed flowers are seen July-September. Locally common in the South, scattered elsewhere.

SPHAGNUM MOSS *(Sphagnum palustre)* Common by streams and in waterlogged woodlands, this variety is easily spotted – it is whitish, tinged pink and bright green. Forked stems to 10″ (25cm) bear the topmost branches in a dense cluster, with tiny hooded leaves.

COLUMBINE *(Aquilegia vulgaris)* Familiar in gardens, the columbine is also a native perennial of shady glades, growing locally on limy soils except in the far north. Stems 12-36″ (30-90cm) branch, and bear nodding flowers May to July. Leaves are divided into lobed leaflets.

61

Cirl Bunting

Female

Male

CIRL BUNTING (*Emberiza cirlus*)
This 6½" (16.5cm) resident occurs
in Wales and southern England. It is
an uncommon bird of hedge and open
woodland. The males are distinctive,
with yellow, black and green
markings, females and immature
birds are dull and streaked brown.

Generally rather secretive, their
presence is announced by the loud
metallic call of the cock defending
his territory while the hen builds a
compact nest. Often double or treble
brooded, 2-5 greeny-blue eggs with
black lines are laid from May. They
eat seeds, berries and some insects.

FIRECREST (*Regulus ignicapillus*)
At 3½" (9cm) this is our smallest
bird, along with the goldcrest. It is
known as a winter visitor to southern
England, though a few pairs breed
here. The conspicuous white
eyestripe and generally clearer,
brighter plumage distinguish it from

Female

Whinchat

Firecrest

Male

the similar goldcrest. Both occur in woodland, firecrests also frequenting scrub of bramble and gorse. They feed entirely on insects. A fragile nest of moss is lined with feathers and secured to twigs with cobwebs. 7-11 pinkish, speckled eggs are laid in May. Call is a repeated *zit-zit-zit*.

WHINCHAT *(Saxicola rubetra)* A summer visitor, this 5" (12.5cm) bird breeds here in open country with sparse shrubs or small trees. Widespread throughout Britain, it is most common in north England and Scotland, scattered and local in the South. The cock bird is brighter

than the well-camouflaged hen, with white eyestripe and black cheek and wing patches. The alarm call and short song are given from the bush-tops. 5-7 pale blue, flecked eggs are laid May-June in a nest hidden in tussocks or other vegetation at ground level. They feed on insects.

The Buzzard

Soaring and gliding in warm updraughts of air on broad wings, the buzzard, our largest common bird of prey, finds its strongholds on our western moors and wooded valleys.

A ringing, mewing 'pee-ow' draws the moorland ramblers' eyes high above to focus on a dark speck in the sky, hanging on the wind. Gliding overhead, the bird looks like a small eagle; but it is a buzzard, one of our most majestic birds of prey.

On warm days throughout the year, especially in springtime, buzzards love to soar on the up-draughts of air that rise from the land. This behaviour appears to be indulged in for sheer pleasure, for the sky is home to these masterful fliers. Relying on their broad, outstretched wings to give lift on the rising air currents, buzzards spend hours at a time wheeling and gliding effortlessly, the feathers at their wing tips spread wide like great fingers. In spring and summer they are usually seen soaring during the middle of the day when the warmth of the sun on the land creates the strongest updraughts of air.

Despite its large size and impressive appearance, with a 4 feet (1.2m) wingspan, the buzzard is not quite the bold predator that its looks suggest. It feeds mainly on small mammals – especially rabbits, rats, voles and mice – young, injured or sickly birds, lizards, snakes, frogs and toads, and also takes many insects and

LOOKOUT POST
(left) Buzzards are commonly seen perching on posts, telegraph poles, rocks or in trees. Such sites give a good vantage point from which the bird can scan its surroundings for prey. When perching, its compact build, short rounded head, thick neck and upright stance can clearly be seen.

earthworms; it is not above eating carrion.

The buzzard is, however, a versatile predator, with four distinctive hunting styles. It spends long periods of time perched patiently in a tree or on a fence post, rock or telegraph pole, scanning the ground beneath for the slightest evidence of a meal. On spotting prey, it drops down on half-closed wings and sinks its talons into the victim.

Sometimes, the buzzard makes use of air currents in hunting. Although unable to hover in still air like kestrels, on their fast-beating wings it can ride almost without motion on updraughts of air on gently fanned wings.

At other times, the buzzard will quarter the ground methodically, repeatedly flying across a patch of land. It will also walk about on the ground when searching for insects or earthworms.

In spring – and also in autumn – buzzards defend their territories, which average 600 acres (225 hectares) on Dartmoor. If neighbouring males meet at the edge of a territory, they may show their antagonism by performing impressive

wool. The female decorates the interior with fresh leafy green branches to provide a soft bed for her eggs. Favourite nest sites are in the fork of a tall tree and on a cliff or quarry ledge.

The eggs, usually three, are laid in April or early May. Both birds incubate them for about five weeks, the female taking the greater share of the task. The chicks are covered with greyish or pale brownish down, and remain in the nest for seven or eight weeks. For the first few days,

HUNGRY YOUNG
(above) Feeding the
demanding chicks is a
full-time task and
both parents must
hunt to provide
enough food. Young
buzzards soon starve
when prey is scarce.

SWIFT ATTACKER
(left) After planning
its tactics from above,
the buzzard swoops
down on prey; small
mammals are favourite
targets, but amphibians,
insects and earth-
worms are also taken.

the female stays with the chicks, while the male brings food, but soon the demands of the hungry offspring force both adults into the hunt. The chicks grow fast, and learn to fly after about 30 days and can hunt for themselves around two weeks later.

Buzzards are very much birds of western Britain, with their greatest numbers in the West Country and Wales, and many in the New Forest, the Lake District and Scotland.

DECLINE AND RECOVERY

In 1800, however, the buzzard was found virtually throughout the British Isles, but by 1865 it had been all but exterminated in the midland and eastern counties of England and most of Ireland due largely to extensive persecution, especially by gamekeepers. The decline continued at an alarming rate until, by 1900, the buzzard clung on only in the wilder parts of the west of England, Wales and western Scotland.

Fortunately, following World War 1 and the subsequent changes in society which saw many large game estates divided up and fewer game-keepers controlling them, the buzzard made a dramatic recovery. Regaining some of its former range – despite a setback between 1952 and 1955 when myxomatosis decimated the rabbit population (one of its chief source of prey) – numbers slowly built up and today almost 10,000 pairs of this handsome bird of prey breed in Britain every year.

IN FLIGHT when gliding, the wings are held flat, or slightly upturned, with the tips directed backwards. When soaring, the wings are raised, held forward and widely outstretched, with the tips turned up and the tail broadly fanned. The flight is slow and strong, with laboured, gentle beats.

THE EGGS are white with variable brown blotches. One clutch of 3-4 eggs is laid in a large nest of sticks, leaves and grass.

diving displays. They also demonstrate their right to possession of their patch by soaring and by occupying conspicuous perches at the boundaries of their territories.

As the first days of spring unlock the rolling moorland from the icy grip of winter, pairs of buzzards soar together over their territories, calling loudly and demonstrating their ardour by diving at each other. After pairing (sometimes for life) they build a large nest, up to 3 feet (1m) across, of stout sticks and heather, crudely lined with dry grass and sometimes also with sheep's

The Grass Snake

The largest and most common of Britain's three species of snake, the grass snake is the only one not to give birth to live young. Instead it lays up to 40 leathery white eggs which hatch in late summer.

Folded into the high moor between dark mats of heather, a shock of bright green moss skirts a ring of boggy pools. In one the water heaves and starts to boil as the banded, olive coils of a grass snake slide into view. Flickering its forked tongue, the snake parts the vegetation with its wedge-shaped head as its bright unblinking eyes strain to detect the slightest movement. Finding no trace of prey, the snake abandons its search, and with sinuous ease winds off back across the water, disappearing into a clump of rushes.

Encounters such as these, with Britain's largest and most numerous snake, are surprisingly common. Widespread in England and Wales, though rare in Scotland and absent from Ireland, the grass snake prefers moist lowland areas and may often be seen sunning itself on the bank of a stream or swimming sinuously across a shallow pond.

Grass snakes will prey on lizards, nestling birds, mice and voles, but newts, tadpoles and frogs form the bulk of their diet. The grass snake tracks its prey by scent, for despite its unblinking, glassy stare, its eyes are not well developed and only much use for detecting movement. But with each flick of its forked tongue the snake literally tastes the air for traces of its next meal.

Lacking the venom of the adder, or the constricting coils of the smooth snake, the grass snake relies on stealth and a lighting quick strike to catch its prey. Once a frog or newt is in its grasp, the snake dislocates its lower jaw and then slowly inches first the upper and then the lower jaw over its victim until it is swallowed whole, often appearing as a conspicuous bulge in the snake's elastic and muscular tube-like body.

Wherever possible, the snake catches its prey head first. This minimizes the risk of the biter

being bitten and makes the prey easier to swallow. Most victims then quickly drown in the snake's copious saliva, before the digestive juices get to work.

Because the snake squanders none of its energy on keeping warm, a large meal can last it a week. But being cold blooded does have its disadvantages. In order to become active enough to hunt, the grass snake must first raise its body temperature – which it does by sunbathing.

WARMING UP FOR ACTION

On a midsummer's morning when the dawn temperature is above the critical 15°C, the grass snake will be active soon after sunrise, catching any unwary frog or newt and then sunbathing until the sun becomes too fierce around noon, when it will slither into the shade. But in cooler weather it must spend longer periods basking before it is fit for the chase. This reliance on the sun means that by the end of September it is forced to seek out a sheltered hideaway, such as an old rabbit burrow, where it can hibernate beyond the reach of winter frosts.

When the balmy fingers of spring reach down

SNAKE IN THE GRASS
(left) Black bars on its
olive flanks and a collar of
black and yellow make the
harmless grass snake easy to
distinguish from its
venomous cousin, the adder.

FACE TO FACE
(below) Frogs are the
principal diet of grass snakes,
but toads are occasionally
taken. As a defensive ploy,
this one has puffed itself up
in the hope it will escape the
grass snake's cavernous jaws.

OPENING TIME
(above) The young snakes
hatch in August or
September, 6-10 weeks after
the sticky white, leathery
eggs are laid. Feeding on the
yolk, the young snake grows
to about six inches in length
before ripping through the
soft shell with a sharp 'egg
tooth' on its snout.

IN THE SWIM
(left) An expert swimmer, the
grass snake hunts for
tadpoles, newts and frogs
in the shallows.

into the snake's lair to wake it from its winter's sleep, the snake emerges slothfully, and for the next week or two will spend every opportunity sunbathing. Once fully revived, the urge to mate drives the males off on the trail of the females which exude a powerful scent. Once a suitable mate is found the two snakes will bask together, sometimes for days on end. Eventually the male will become aroused and begin sliding over and around the female. Flicking his tongue over her skin and thrusting his head into her coils he will attempt to make her unwind so that they can lie side by side and mate. After mating, the pair may remain together for some time, but over the six week mating period from April to May, each snake may have several partners.

In mid-June the female starts looking for somewhere to lay her eggs. A compost heap, where the warmth generated by the rotting vegetation will nurture the sticky white, leathery eggs, is ideal. Young females may lay as few as 10 eggs, older ones up to 40. But because ideal nest sites are few and far between, many females often lay in the same place – leading to a mass hatch and stories of plagues of snakes.

The young snakes are six inches long when they hatch but grow quickly, shedding their skin for the first of many moults when they are two or three weeks old. In their first year they will grow five inches, adding a further four inches in their second. By their third year the male grass snakes will be around 20 inches long and sexually mature. Females mature in their fourth year when they will be about 26 inches long. Growth then slows, and, once mature, the snake will start thickening rather than lengthening. An average female grows to 30 inches and a male to 26 inches.

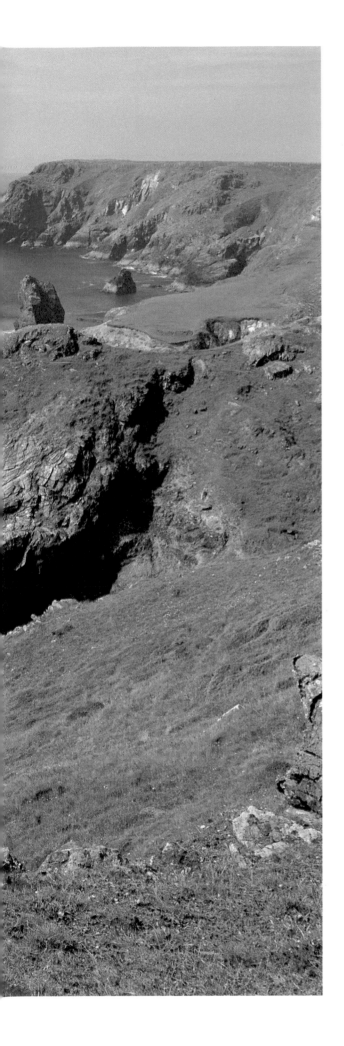

The Lizard

The southernmost point of mainland Britain, the Lizard is famed for its spectacular coastline and picturesque fishing villages set in sheltered coves, its magnificent cliffs and treacherous offshore reefs. At twilight it seems a remote and eerie place, the true home of ancient Celtic legends. Gulls scream through the frequent sea mists like echoes of the drowned lured to their deaths by the wreckers of old. But sunshine transforms the scene, and the headland shows itself as a natural garden, where geological chance allows myriad flowers to flourish.

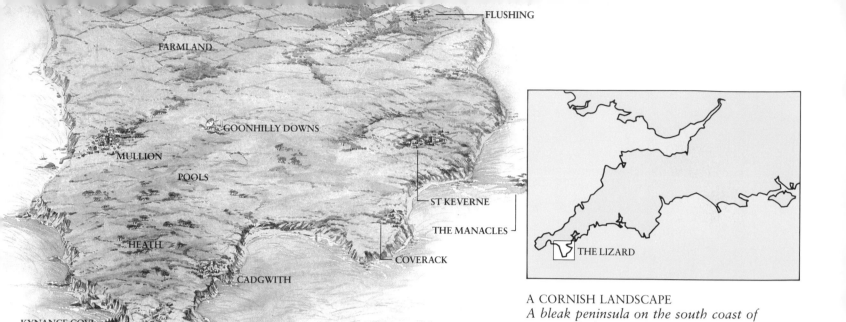

FLUSHING

FARMLAND

GOONHILLY DOWNS

MULLION

POOLS

ST KEVERNE

THE MANACLES

HEATH

COVERACK

CADGWITH

KYNANCE COVE

HIGH SERPENTINE CLIFFS

LIZARD POINT

THE LIZARD

A CORNISH LANDSCAPE
A bleak peninsula on the south coast of Cornwall, the Lizard is renowned for its treacherous coastline and spectacular cliff scenery. But it also has a gentler face, much loved by visitors – meandering lanes, small sandy coves and picture-postcard villages.

The Lizard Peninsula lies on the south coast of Cornwall – a level plateau which rises 200 to 300 feet (60-90m) above the sea and reaches even further south than Land's End. On the west coast magnificent tall cliffs take the full force of the Atlantic waves, giving welcome shelter to the numerous small harbours and sandy coves which lie to the east.

The Lizard has a remote feel to it. The long tongue of the Helford River stretches deep into its eastern side, almost isolating the promontary from the rest of Cornwall. The area is thought to take its name not from the lizards which can be found basking on its sunny heaths, but from an old Celtic word for outcast. However, the Lizard is more than just another storm-racked and legend-haunted Cornish headland. The rock of its southerly half gives it a character unique in Britain.

AN UNUSUAL CLIFFSCAPE

This rock is serpentine – one of the oldest in Cornwall, dating from perhaps more than 570 million years ago. It can be seen forming the rugged cliffs which back the idyllic Kynance Cove, Mullion and Coverack and appears in a marvellous range of colours, from rich greens to reddish purples and browns. Through the rock run veins of white, yellow or black, which give it the appearance of a reptile's skin and hence the name serpentine. 24 different kinds of serpentine are recognized. Once quarried on a large scale as a local building stone for walls, farmsteads and village houses, serpentine was also exported throughout Britain for decorative use, especially in Victorian times. Today it is fashioned into tourist souvenirs. But serpentine is not the only rock which occurs on the Lizard. In some areas a granite-like gabbro surfaces, littering the plateau with large boulders. Elsewhere schist rock is found.

If away from the sea this flat, heath-covered plateau seems scenically dull, this is more than compensated by the rich plant life. Chemically, serpentine is an alkaline rock which weathers to give a rich soil that supports huge numbers of different flowers. Indeed the Reverend Charles Johns, a local headmaster and a fine Victorian naturalist, claimed that he could cover no less than 12 different species wherever he placed his hat on the ground. Amongst the Lizard's abundant flora are several rarities, found nowhere else in Britain.

SEASIDE SETTLEMENT
(below) The sheltered east coast is the site of numerous small harbours where small boats still fish for lobster, crab and mackerel. In Cadgwith, shown here, as elsewhere on the Lizard, many of the houses are built from locally quarried serpentine.

ON THE HEATH
High above the rugged cliffs the plateau is rich in flora. Gorse gilds much of it in early summer, Cornish heath (above) following in August.

On grey days, however, the brilliance of this natural flower garden is dimmed. When the mists creep in from the sea, ghost and memory seem to roam. Exposed and isolated, the Lizard has been both a natural goal for storm-damaged vessels, and a terrible hazard. Over the centuries its rugged coastline has taken a heavy toll in shipping. The mile-square cluster of offshore rocks called The Manacles have a particularly forbidding reputation. In January 1809 they foundered two ships simultaneously — one setting out from Falmouth and the other returning. St Keverne church, whose spire is such a landmark across the flat plateau, has more than 400 shipwreck victims in its graveyard.

It is no surprise that the lighthouse on Lizard Point is notable. Built in 1752, its original light was produced by two coal fires. Today's electric beam is visible for 21 miles, making it one of Britain's brightest. Shipping still plies in and out of nearby Falmouth or passes en route for Plymouth, while colourful fishing boats add to the allure of Mullion and other small harbours.

With their dramatic cliffs, beautiful clear water and attractive beaches at low tide, Kynance and other coves are tourist magnets, attracting thousands of visitors each year who literally wear away the turf on the clifftop paths. However, major path restoration has been undertaken by the National Trust, while the botanically rich plateau heaths are now in the care of the Cornish Trust for Nature Conservation and other bodies. The magnificent cliffscapes — some of the finest in Britain — together with the unexpected diversity of plant life and the numerous sea birds all combine to make the Lizard a valuable British habitat.

Nature Walk

The Lizard landscape has many interesting man-made features, old and new, such as:

LANDEWEDNACK CHURCH — the most southerly church in mainland Britain. It is made from dark serpentine blocks alternated with pale granite ones for strength.

GOONHILLY DOWNS satellite communications station, where giant dish ariels beam inter-continental communications to satellites which boost the signal and relay it back to earth.

PILCHARD CELLARS — where pilchards were once pressed and dried in vast numbers for export.

On Lizard Point

Mild winters make the windswept heaths and rugged cliffs of the Lizard a haven for many rare and delicate wild flowers, while in summer numerous migrating birds drop in and sharks may be seen offshore.

Swept by southwesterly gales and battered by Atlantic breakers, Britain's most southerly point might seem an unpromising place for plant or animal life. But the heathlands and cliffs of this Cornish promontory are a haven for many rare plants, and a staging post for thousands of birds on their annual migration.

All over the Lizard, from the high inland plateau down to the cliff edge, Cornish heath grows in abundance, forming dense mats that hug the ground. Unlike most heathers, Cornish heath is no lover of acid soil and thrives here on the alkaline soil that forms over the Lizard's ancient serpentine rocks. Apart from a tiny patch in County Fermanagh in Northern Ireland, this is the only place in the British Isles where it can be seen, blooming pink and purple from July to September.

Mixed in with Cornish heath are low thickets of gorse, whose bright yellow flowers brighten the landscape in almost every month of the year. In this treeless landscape, Cornish heath and gorse thickets offer almost the only shelter to the Lizard's land birds. But here wrens are happy to hop mouse-like among the gorse stems, probing for small insects, emerging only occasionally for a short flutter to the next feeding spot or to take up a prominent perch for an ostentatious vocal performance. Stonechats, too, find shelter among the gorse and heath thickets of the Lizard, and like wrens, can often be seen perching upright above the undergrowth, bobbing and ducking their heads and scolding intruders with their distinctive *wheet-chak-chak* call.

VISITING BIRDS

In spring and autumn, the Lizard's resident populations of wrens, stonechats and yellowhammers are joined by waves of migrants, most pausing here only briefly. From March to the end of April, willow warblers, whitethroats, chiffchafs, sedge warblers, redstarts, nightingales and many other species may be spotted in the low vegetation of the cliff-top as they recover from their long flights. In autumn, a spell of bad weather – fog or strong headwinds – discourages the birds from setting out across the sea again, and they can often be seen skulking in the bushes or flitting about restlessly, waiting for the right moment to move on.

Bad weather frequently plays havoc with birds' navigation, and as a result, quite unexpected species may turn up 'by mistake'. If there is a particularly strong system of depressions stretching across the Atlantic, North American birds may be swept out to sea on the eastern seaboard and carried eastwards to Britain and Ireland by strong tailwinds in little more than two days. Many end up on the Lizard, an early landfall, and almost every year some North American species are recorded here, the most common ones being waders, thrushes and warblers.

The coastal heathland is also an ideal habitat for some of Britain's reptiles. In this open landscape, any sunshine quickly heats up the ground, enabling reptiles to stay warm and active. Adders are common, but secretive, and unlikely to be seen except when basking in the early morning sun. A sudden rustling of dry stems and leaves in the summer undergrowth is more likely to be a much faster-moving reptile, the common lizard. Adders feed on the voles, mice and shrews that live on the heathland, while the lizards concentrate on a variety of insects, but especially young grasshoppers, which hatch out

CORNISH HEATH (*left*)
Found nowhere else in mainland Britain, Cornish heath grows on the Lizard in abundance, and in high summer great carpets of its pink and purple blooms cover the heaths from Goonhilly Downs to the sea. Unlike most heathers, Cornish heath thrives on alkaline soils.

WILDLIFE OF THE LIZARD

Above the gorse and heather clad heath, the harsh cry of a great black-backed gull is met by the more restrained tchack of a jackdaw. Down below, a prowling badger approaches a boggy pool alive with newts and frogs. On a sun-warmed rock a lizard basks and is stalked by an adder. All about there is a colourful jumble of daisies, violets, fig and squill that spills over the craggy cliffs which provide a refuge for kittiwakes, fulmars and guillemots.

KEY TO THE SPECIES

1 Cormorant
2 Great black-backed gull
3 Heather
4 By-the-wind-sailor
5 Badger
6 Purple moor grass
7 Jackdaw
8 Bog rush
9 Palmate newt
10 Frog

11 Gorse
12 Pale butterwort
13 Juniper
14 Cornish Heath
15 Kittiwake
16 Common blue
17 Four-spotted chaser dragonfly
18 Guillemot
19 Fulmar
20 Lichen
21 Spring squill

22 Adder
23 Chives
24 Hottentot fig
25 Common lizard
26 Navelwort
27 Wolf spider
28 Ox-eye daisy
29 Dwarf bettony
30 Bloody-nosed beetle
31 Wild thyme
32 Dog violet

AUTUMN SQUILL
(above) One of the Lizard's many rare flowers, autumn squill adorns the cliff-top grass with its purple blooms.

NIGHT SONGSTER
(left) On quiet May nights, the song of the nightingale can often be heard bubbling out of dense thickets of bramble and gorse. A shy bird, the nightingale nests deep in the undergrowth and is rarely seen from the time it arrives in April to the time it leaves late in summer.

NEWLY HATCHED SHARK
(below) Called mermaid's purses, the egg capsules of the nurse hound – Europe's commonest shark – are often washed up on the shores of the Lizard.

in large numbers each spring.

Down by the cliff edge, the Cornish heath and gorse give way to turf, and another of the Lizard's special wildflower habitats begins. Here, a number of botanical rarities can be found, including the beautiful autumn squill, a delicate flower rather like a small bluebell, but with upturned star-like flowers of an exquisite pinkish-blue.

ON THE CLIFF-TOP

The cliff-top turf is kept trim by rabbits, and also by hares, which may stray there from the heathland higher up. Among the grassblades are all the familiar plants of cliff-tops, such as kidney vetch and birdsfoot trefoil, but alongside these are more of the Lizard's rarities. Two kinds of clover found nowhere else on the British mainland, upright clover and twin-flowered clover, grow here. So also do the rare hairy greenweed and a unique variation of dyer's greenweed, both members of the pea family. In high summer, dyer's greenweed sends forth brilliant yellow blooms and, as long ago as the 14th century, its flowering stems were used for dye, mixed with blue woad to make kensal green – hence the name.

Despite its exposure to wind and rain, the Lizard does not experience extreme cold. The warm waters of the Gulf stream ensure that frost is a rarity, and as a result, plants brought to the British Isles from warmer parts of the world have been able to establish themselves where

boulders and gullies give protection from the wind. Alongside the native rock plants such as samphire, thrift and sea campion, the Hottentot fig, a native of desert South Africa, can be seen, often trailing down the serpentine. The Hottentot fig is a succulent, with thick fleshy leaves, and its brilliant crimson or yellow flowers, shaped like large daisies, only open in strong sunshine. Where rocky outcrops give protection from the wind, South American wild fuschia has managed to establish itself, its slender, crimson flowers hanging like rain drops among dark, luxuriant leaves.

Below these outcrops, where streams have cut gullies running down to the sea, grows the exotic looking royal fern, a magnificent plant that was all but exterminated by 'nature lovers' during the passion for fern-growing in Victorian times. A native British fern, despite its appearance, the royal fern has unusual spores. Whereas most other ferns simply produce their spores on the undersides of the leaves, royal fern has special spore-producing stems that look almost like a spike of brown flowers. It may be from ferns such as this, with specialized parts for reproduction, that the flowering plants of today have evolved.

Towering above the gully that shelters the royal fern are cliffs of serpentine that tumble haphazardly into the sea below. Here, gulls, fulmars and jackdaws nest in abundance, while above the surf and spray at the cliff's edge, even in the middle of winter, shag and cormorant may be visible, as after each dive for fish they must sit afterwards to dry their wings. The reason for this is disputed, however, as their plumage is as waterproof as that of any waterbird. Even in light rain, they can be seen, standing motionless on platforms of rock with their wings held open, presenting a forlorn picture.

BOTTLING SEALS

Out in the water just beyond the cliff, grey seals sometimes appear, bobbing upright in the water or resting with just their heads above water, a habit known as 'bottling'. On a windless day, the seal's snort can be heard as it fills its lungs, before diving, leaving just a tell-tale circle of ripples on the surface of the calm and glassy sea.

Cornwall has a tradition of shark-fishing, and from the cliff-top it is occasionally possible to spot sharks in the distance. Despite their fearsome reputation, the sharks around the Lizard coast present little danger to man. The largest of them, the basking shark, feeds entirely on plankton, scooping up planktonic organisms with its gaping mouth and sieving them out with its gills.

ADDER AND YOUNG
(below) Late in summer, a female and new-born young bask on a patch of sun-warmed gravel amid the coastal heath of the Lizard.

MALE STONECHAT
(above) The stonechat owes its name to its call which sounds like two pebbles being knocked together. This call, along with its distinctive headbobbing, makes the stonechat easy to identify as it flits among the gorse.

BUSH CRICKET
(left) Britain's largest bush cricket, the 1⅝" (42mm) long great green, is restricted to the warm south of England where it inhabits dense thickets of gorse.

Upright Clover

Dyers Greenweed

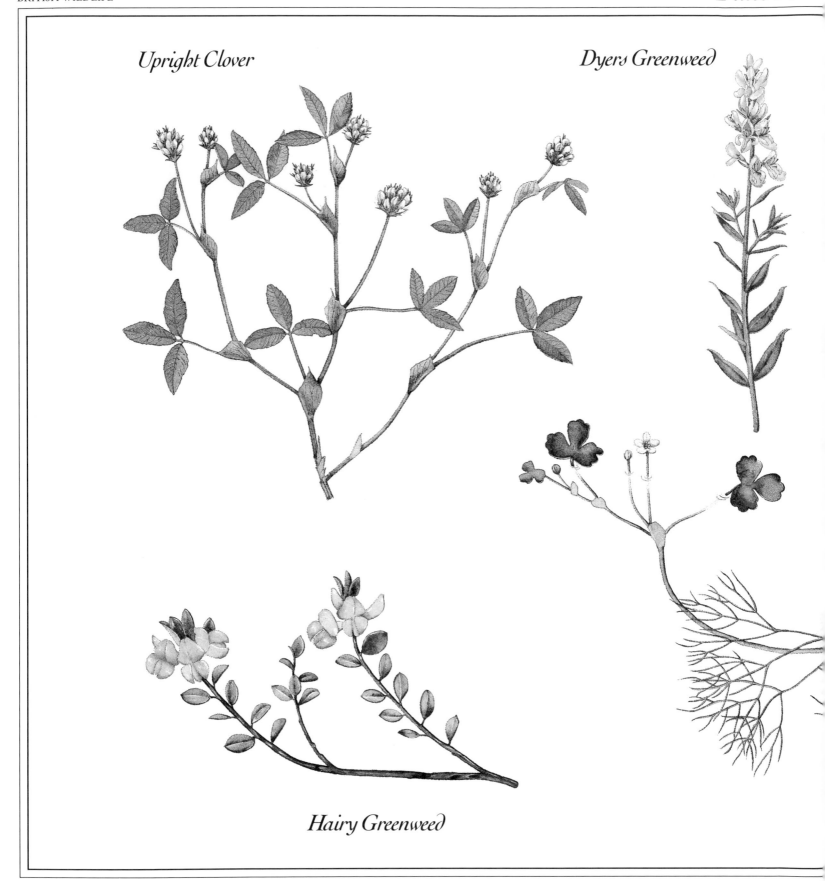

Hairy Greenweed

UPRIGHT CLOVER (*Trifolium strictum*) Grows only in grassy spots on the Lizard and in the Channel Isles and, like several of the Lizard's specialities, is typically a plant of the warmer parts of Europe. An erect 2-6″ (5-15cm) June flowering hairless annual.

HAIRY GREENWEED (*Genista pilosa*) A hairy little perennial shrub of a few dry and sandy places, mainly near the sea in the South and West. Blooms in May and June and the flowers are followed by silkily hairy pods. The stiff, much-branched stems reach 16″ (40cm).

DYER'S GREENWEED (*Genista tinctoria*) A rather local 8-24″ (20-60cm) perennial shrub of rough grassland, it was once widely used in dyeing. Summer flowering, usually with hairless pods: a prostrate form, with partly hairy pods, occurs near the Lizard.

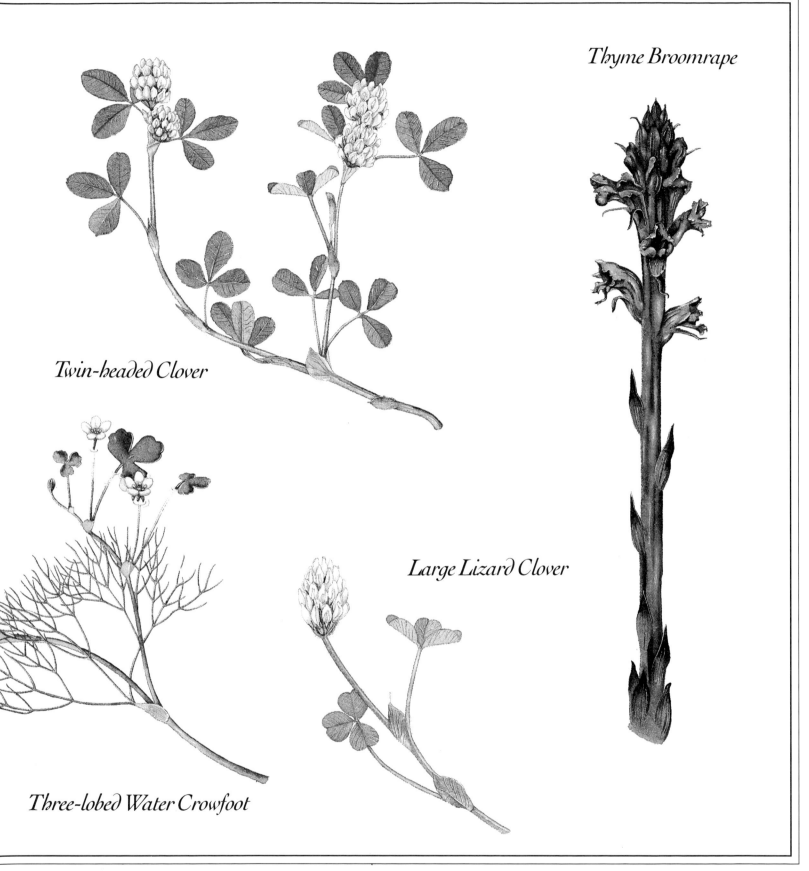

Thyme Broomrape

Twin-headed Clover

Three-lobed Water Crowfoot

Large Lizard Clover

THREE-LOBED WATER CROWFOOT (*Ranunculus tripartitus***)** One of several similar species of water crowfoot; an uncommon annual, mainly of the South and West. The stems grow on mud or in water, reaching 2′ (60cm). Floating leaves are 3-lobed.

TWIN-HEADED CLOVER (*Trifolium bocconei***)** A slender, rather hairy 2-4″ (5-20cm) annual. It is one of the Lizard's several rare clovers, growing here in grassland near the sea; it also occurs in Jersey. Heads of flowers are borne, usually in pairs, during June and July.

LARGE LIZARD CLOVER (*Trifolium incarnatum ssp. molinerii***)** One of the Lizard's great botanical attractions is this annual clover; which also occurs on Jersey. Softly hairy, it bears its many-flowered heads in May and June and rarely exceeds 8″ (20cm).

THYME BROOMRAPE (*Orobanche alba***)** Although it parasitizes wild thyme which is not an uncommon plant, this is a rare 3-12″ (8-30cm) perennial of a few scattered chalky rocks and screes, including some around the Lizard. Flowers June-August.

Black and White Warbler

Orphean Warbler

Spectacled Warbler

ORPHEAN WARBLER (*Sylvia hortensis*) A 6″ (15cm) warbler of scrub and open, wooded places in southern Europe and a rare vagrant here. Reminiscent of a blackcap, but stouter, and the cap extends down on to the cheeks. Has a tuneful warbling call.

BLACK AND WHITE WARBLER (*Mniotilta varia*) An attractive 5¼″ (14cm) bird with smart black and white striped plumage. Occasionally blown across the Atlantic on westerly winds. Characteristically, it works its way up and around tree trunks in search of insects.

SPECTACLED WARBLER (*Sylvia conspicillata*) Although lending the bird its name, the pale eye rings of this 5″ (12.5cm) warbler are not conspicuous and it resembles a dark whitethroat. It has a bright, tuneful song and is a rare vagrant from southern Europe and Africa.

American Redstart

Female

Male

Parula Warbler

PARULA WARBLER (*Parula americana*) Distinguished by its bluish and yellow plumage and white wing bars and eye rings, this colourful little 4½" (11cm) warbler is a very occasional visitor to southwest Britain. Like a tit, it often clings to tree trunks.

AMERICAN REDSTART (*Setophaga ruticilla*) This rare vagrant is a very distinctive 5" (12.5cm) bird: males have striking black and orange plumage; females are brown and yellow, with a grey head. It feeds on insects which it catches on the wing.

The Great Black-Backed Gull

Wheeling and crying high above the crashing waves, the ferocious
great black-backed gull is a familiar sight all round our coastline,
yet it is the scarcest of our indigenous gulls.

Weighed down by its long wings, the
great black-backed gull needs a short
run along the ground before it can
become airborne. But once in the air, with wings
outstretched to their full span of five feet
(150cm), the bird moves with ease, its slow,
steady wingbeats lifting its large, goose-sized
body over the waves, where it rides the air currents in long, graceful glides, its hoarse *agh-agh-
agh* calls resounding in the crisp sea air.

KING OF THE GULLS

The great black-backed gull is the largest,
strongest and most maritime of the gulls which
nest in Britain. 30 inches (75cm) from bill tip
to tail, it stands a good head taller than any
other seagulls when in their company. It has a
sooty-black back, pale flesh-coloured legs, a
large and powerfully hooked bill that has a red
spot near the tip of the lower mandible, and
eyes that are pearl grey with a brilliant red ring
around them. It can only be confused with the
lesser black-backed gull, which was once mainly

a summer visitor to our shores, but is now
present in large numbers all year round.
However, this smaller bird has yellow legs and a
lighter coloured back.

Like other gulls, the great black-backed gull
is a scavenger, and flocks round fishing boats
to feed on the waste fish thrown overboard. But
even without the fisherman's larder, this ferocious gull has no difficulty in finding enough to
eat. It is a voracious predator which uses its
heavy hooked bill to rip rabbits, rats, voles, mice
and even sickly lambs apart, turning them inside
out before eating them. It also takes starfish,
molluscs, crustaceans, worms and carrion from
the shoreline, and fish from the sea, flying low
over the water and plunging into the waves to
take the fish from just below the surface. Puffins
are caught in the air by the neck or attacked in
the water as they bob up after a dive. Other
birds, chicks and eggs are also taken – especially
during the breeding season when there are
demanding youngsters to care for. Manx shearwater colonies are particularly vulnerable – the

BIG BULLY
*(above) The largest of our
British gulls, the massive
form of the great black-
backed gull can be seen
around our shores all through
the year. But in the breeding
season pairs of birds are most
likely to be found on rocky
coasts where islets and
offshore stacks offer safe
nesting sites. The male is
slightly larger than the
female, but otherwise the
sexes are alike. Both are
strong and aggressive, with a
powerful hooked bill, which
makes this bird a formidable
predator, and the terror of
many seabird colonies.*

birds are so slow and clumsy as they come out of their nesting burrows to find food for themselves and their young, they are sitting targets for the gulls who literally shake them to death.

During the autumn and winter months the great black-backed gull can be found in a variety of locations all round the British coast – notably on cliffs, but also on sandy shores and salt-marshes, while a few fly inland. But come nesting time their distribution shows an interesting change. At this time of the year they are almost totally absent from the south and east coast, from Berwickshire in the north to Hampshire in the south. This is probably because this part of the coastline is lacking in the rocky cliffs and offshore stacks and islands which are the gulls' favoured nesting sites. These afford them protection from predatory mammals like foxes, which would take a heavy toll on their numbers. Only rarely do birds nest inland, except in Ireland, where they frequently breed on large freshwater lakes.

SHARED PARENTHOOD

Although a gregarious bird in winter, the great black-backed gull is a solitary nester or nests in small groups. There are flourishing scattered colonies on islands such as Mullion, off the Lizard, on the Calf of Eday, Orkney, and on North Rona in the Outer Hebrides. Between May and early June both sexes build a large nest, siting it near a boulder, wall or other vantage point that can be used as a lookout post by the offduty parent which swoops low over any intruder. The nest is up to 16 inches (40cm) across, made from grass, twigs, litter and seaweed piled up in a slight dip in the ground.

The female lays two or three eggs, pale buff or olive-brown in colour and spotted and blotched with dark brown. She and her mate start to incubate with the arrival of the second egg,

before the clutch is complete. The chicks, covered with grey-brown down, hatch out after four weeks. Within a few days they leave the nest to hide in the cover of surrounding plants or rocks. Seven or eight weeks pass before they are fully fledged, but even then they still nag their parents for food.

Eventually the dull, mottled brown immature gulls leave the breeding grounds and fly south. It will be four years before they have full adult plumage and begin to breed. The adults, in the meantime, stay in the British Isles, wintering near their breeding grounds and returning year after year to nest in virtually the same spot.

HIGH FLIER
(below) The heavily built great black-backed gull wheels over the seashore with other gulls. It also flocks to fishing boats far out at sea.

AT THE NEST
(left) Less colonial than other gulls, the great black-backed gull usually nests singly or in small groups, although it is sometimes found in a mixed colony of other gulls. The nest is a large mound of seaweed, heather and grass, made in May or June. The mottled grey and black chicks are cared for by both parents and fledge after seven or eight weeks.

81

The Isles of Scilly

At the mercy of the Atlantic Ocean, some 28 miles south-west of Land's End, lie the peaceful Scilly Isles – a group of over a hundred low-lying islands and rocky islets which are fabled to be all that remains of the Cornish kingdom of Lyonnesse, lost to the sea in King Arthur's time. An area of outstanding natural beauty and dramatic contrasts, the Scilly Isles have been shaped by nature and by man. Today the desolate landscape of the larger islands is tempered by a latticework of evergreen windbreaks and lush sub-tropical plants, supported by the mild climate.

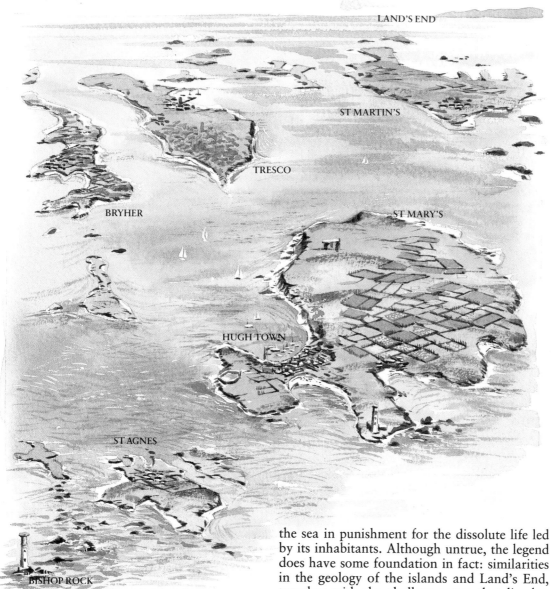

LAND'S END

ST MARTIN'S

TRESCO

BRYHER

ST MARY'S

HUGH TOWN

ST AGNES

BISHOP ROCK

ISLAND COMMUNITY
Of the 200 or so islands, islets and named rocks which make up the Isles of Scilly, only the five main islands are inhabited. St Mary's is the largest – some three miles by two – with the capital, Hugh Town, and all but about 350 of the islands' 2000 population. The four larger 'off-islands' offer a variety of wild and gentle scenery. Tresco is possibly the most spectacular and the site of exotic sub-tropical gardens.

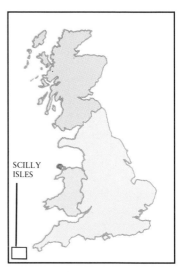

SCILLY
ISLES

the sea in punishment for the dissolute life led by its inhabitants. Although untrue, the legend does have some foundation in fact: similarities in the geology of the islands and Land's End, together with the shallow water that lies between the islands and the mainland suggest that the two may once have been joined, but long before King Arthur's time, perhaps some 300,000 years ago.

ANCIENT REMAINS

When the first Bronze Age settlers arrived, around 2000 BC, Scilly was probably still virtually one island, some ten miles by five, bearing the remains of ancient woodlands with attendant peats and plants. Today, there are few trees on the islands, but the landscape is littered with structures made by neolithic man. Most impressive are the granite burial chambers, up to 30 feet (9m) in diameter, and the clusters of neatly formed graves in early cairn fields. The density of these memorials in this small, remote area – 50 out of 250 in the whole of England and Wales – is a puzzle which has yet to be solved.

Through the centuries man has struggled to eke out a living on the barren, wind-swept islands, growing what he could in shallow sandy soils. Pirates plundered the meagre supplies, and modern prosperity has its roots in the

Almost 30 miles off Land's End, in line with the great granite moors of the South West as they descend in height from Dartmoor to Penwith, is a group of rocky islands, scattered through the sea. These are the Isles of Scilly, low-lying and flat-topped – the fragmented remnants of a single granite mass which was forced up from within the earth some 300 million years ago, when the spectacular granite features of Devon and Cornwall were also formed.

During the last three or four thousand years, a combination of subsidence and a rising sea level of some 9½ inches (24cm) a century have reduced the single landmass to a collection of some 200 islands, islets and reefs arranged in a broken oval around a shallow lagoon. As the land sank, so the sea created vast quantities of sand, now heaped up on beaches and in dunes and deposited on the sea bed, creating shallow clear waters and re-linking some of the islands again.

According to legend, the Scilly Isles were once part of the lost Cornish kingdom of Lyonnesse, an incomparably fertile tract of land ruled by King Arthur before it was engulfed by

PERILOUS SHORES
Weathered granite is much in evidence all round the islands, in stretches of rugged coastline and in reefs and islets offshore. The rocky waters have always been perilous for shipping. As recently as 1967 the giant oil tanker Torrey Canyon *was lost on the Seven Stones reef north-east of Scilly, polluting the sea and beaches for hundreds of miles at vast cost to marine life.*

life-work of Augustus Smith who came to Scilly as landlord in 1834. With great thoroughness he set about creating natural wind-breaks and fixing wind-blown sand with scrub and gorse. Today's landscape – with its small fields surrounded by salt-resistant, evergreen hedges which protect the early narcissus crop, and the colourful sub-tropical gardens of Tresco Abbey – owes much to his far-sighted initiatives.

Because of the sea, and the southerly location, the climate of the islands is milder than anywhere in Britain and temperatures rarely drop to freezing. The low altitudes – the highest point on the islands is only 158 feet (48m) –

means there is less rain than on the mainland, with rainfall averaging about 32 inches (81cm) per year and regular periods between April and September when there is little or no rain.

This maritime climate, with its mild winters and cool summers, is ideal for the winter production of narcissus flowers, and also encourages visitors to the islands. Tourism is now the islands' main industry, but ironically the same visitors and improved farming methods which have brought prosperity to the Isles of Scilly, are also the biggest threat to the islands, imposing considerable pressure on their limited resources.

SUB-TROPICAL PARADISE
Lush vegetation is scarce on the islands as a whole, but on Tresco sub-tropical plants flourish in the gardens created by Augustus Smith. New Zealand ironwoods and Mexican yuccas grow alongside plants found nowhere else in the northern hemisphere. All this is made possible by the mild climate, and by the planting of conifer trees which provide shelter from the violent westerly winds.

Nature Walk

Wherever you go on Scilly, there are monuments to the islands' ancient past and to the sea. Look out for:

BISHOP ROCK LIGHTHOUSE – the tallest in Britain – guarding the south-western approaches.

BURIAL CAIRNS – common in Scilly – dating from neolithic times.

TROY TOWN MAZE on St Agnes, probably made by shipwrecked Scandinavians.

FIGUREHEADS from ships wrecked on the islands' rocks, now in a museum.

Wildlife of the Isles

The tiny but beautiful islands of Scilly contain a wealth of rare and exotic wildlife, from the resident white-toothed shrew to storm-blown birds from America and Asia.

The 145 or so islands which make up the Isles of Scilly bear the direct brunt of the westerly winds and pounding ocean swell from the great Atlantic Ocean, and are dominated by gales, salt spray and dramatic towering waves. Despite this hostile background, the islands teem with life, much of it unusual or even unique.

Many of the islands are merely bare rock or at best overgrown with a sparse covering of dwarf heath carpeting the sharp grey granite. But the five larger islands which are inhabited are softened in places by small green pastures, bulb fields and other intensively cultivated soils, often in tiny fields enclosed by thick, tall evergreen hedges as a defence against the driving winds. A common windbreak plant in these hedges is the exotic cabbage tree or pittosporum, introduced from New Zealand and now naturalized. Plantations have compensated for the lack of natural woodland, and parts of St Mary's and Tresco islands appear quite well wooded. Tresco has a long, quiet pool, impounded by a 35 foot (11m) bank of wind-blown sand; there are smaller pools on St Mary's and St Agnes, as well as several low, wet overgrown 'moors'.

FLOWER FIELDS

Of the overall total of 4000 acres (1600 hectares), 1600 acres (650 hectares) is farmed, almost 40 per cent being devoted to flowers, notably daffodils and other narcissi, irises and tulips. The early flowers thrive in the remarkably mild conditions, with generally warm springs and little rain, but need protection from the salt-laden winds.

By mid-April the flowers have been harvested, and many of the fields become weed-infested and full of wild flowers. Their seeds are a source of food for many visiting birds. The hedges also contain many exotic plants, including tamarisk, pittosporum, escallonia and the commoner spindle, which also provide food and shelter for both migrant and breeding birds, as well as giving much of the Isles of Scilly their lush, almost subtropical character.

Fields are grazed by sheep and cattle and bounded by drystone walls. Surrounding them, the rugged heaths, ablaze in summer with the golden-yellow of gorse, the fresh green of bracken and the purple of heather, run down to the rocky coast. On the tops of the rocks or at the head of the sandy beaches, bright purple, pink and orange hottentot figs run wild, their thick, fleshy leaves covering many feet of soil or sprawling over the low walls. On Tresco, there are planted woods of pines and the famous collection of trees and flowers surrounding Tresco Abbey. Alongside its pools are small reedbeds and patches of willows.

The isolation of the islands, and their extreme exposure to the full force of the Atlantic gales, mean that there are fewer plants than on the nearby mainland, although these include some that are rare there but thrive on the islands – such as white mignonette. Lanceolate spleenwort is an uncommon fern throughout most of Britain too, but grows luxuriantly on Scilly granite walls.

DWARF PANSY
This is one of the rare plants for which the islands are renowned. It is a Mediterranean species that has spread to the west coast of France, the Channel Isles and Scilly, probably reaching the islands as wind-, water- or bird-borne seeds.

WILDLIFE ON THE SCILLY ISLES

Small colonies of shearwaters and storm petrels nest in burrows, returning to land only at night. Fulmars, gulls and razorbills all breed but Lapland buntings occur only on migration and purple sandpipers are winter visitors. Plants such as smaller tree mallow, hottentot fig, orange bird's foot and dwarf pansy occur in few places other than Scilly, and though western gorse, spring quill and three-cornered leek have a wider distribution they are confined to south-western areas. Scilly shrews are closely related to lesser white-toothed shrews on the Channel Islands. Small numbers of grey seals breed. In the clear waters colourful anemones and starfish abound.

KEY TO THE SPECIES

1 Fulmar
2 Razorbill
3 Grey seals
4 Heather
5 Gorse
6 Lapland bunting
7 Great black-backed gulls
8 Manx shearwater
9 Storm petrel
10 Smaller tree mallow
11 Royal fern

12 Western gorse
13 Hottentot fig
14 Spring quill
15 Marram grass
16 Bird's foot trefoil
17 Orange bird's foot
18 Three-cornered leek
19 Common blue
20 Purple sandpiper
21 Yellow horned poppy
22 Thrift

23 Meadow brown
24 Sea holly
25 Dwarf pansy
26 Heart urchin
27 Flat winkles
28 Beadlet anemones
29 Limpets
30 Blunt tellin
31 Scilly shrew
32 Common starfish
33 Small necklace shell
34 Jewel anemones
35 Featherstar

FEATHERSTAR
The crystal-clear, azure-blue waters of the Isles of Scilly contain a wealth of marine life, including brilliant multicoloured jewel anemones, purple heart urchins and tube-dwelling parchment worms, as well as the delicate featherstars shown here. Normally restricted to deep water, this elegant creature can be found in the shallows around Scilly.

CABBAGE TREE
The cabbage tree, or pittosporum, is one of the most noticeable of the many plants introduced from abroad to the Isles of Scilly. A native of New Zealand, it was brought to the islands by one of their leaseholders in the late 19th century to form windbreaks for the protection of the bulbs and other commercially grown flowers.

The islands boast other plants that are rare in Britain. These include the orange bird's-foot and dwarf pansy, found only on Scilly and the Channel Isles. Some of these rarities, such as the elegant, clear yellow Bermuda buttercup, rosy garlic, three-cornered leek and Babington's leek, grow so profusely in the Scilly bulbfields, that they are considered agricultural pests.

Butterflies also provide some pleasant surprises. The coastal heaths, with their stony paths and granite outcrops, would appear at first sight to provide a perfect habitat for graylings, but there are none; nor are there any orange-tips or skippers. But there is a distinct race of the meadow brown and a very restricted race of the common blue found only on the island of Tean.

There is only one species of grasshopper, although the visitor to Scilly in autumn might come across the impressive 5cm-long great green bush cricket.

St Mary's has some frogs, but they do not occur on other islands, and toads, like snakes, are completely absent. There are few mammals, either: no foxes, badgers, otters, stoats, weasels or short-tailed voles. Also, despite their ability to fly across water, no bats have managed to reach the islands.

UNIQUE MAMMAL

The islands do, however, boast one mammal that is found nowhere else in Britain, except for the Channel Isles – the lesser white-toothed shrew. Its peculiar distribution – it is a native of southern and central Europe – indicates that it may have been accidently introduced to the islands in boat cargoes.

Much more conspicuous are the grey seals which haul themselves on to the shores of Scilly each winter to breed. Rookeries of over 100 seals form part of the major breeding population of Cornwall and south-west Wales

and give birth to around 40 pups each year.

But it is in its bird life that the Isles of Scilly have most to offer, particularly in the prime migration month of October, when rare strays blown off course from Asia or America may be expected at any time.

MANX SHEARWATER
Although most renowned for the rare birds they attract, the granite cliffs of the Isles of Scilly also provide nest sites for a variety of seabirds including the Manx shearwater, which nests in burrows in the turf or among crevices in the rocks.

HOTTENTOT FIG
In spring and summer, the islands are a riot of colour as the exotic flowers bloom, including the beautiful pink (or occasionally yellow) hottentot figs. Introduced from South Africa, they also grow on the cliffs of Cornwall and Devon.

the paddyfield and yellow-browed warblers, rustic and little buntings, olive-backed, Richard's and red-throated pipits and rose-coloured starlings, plus a supporting cast of less exotic migrants, such as wrynecks, red-breasted flycatchers and melodious warblers, make a visit to the Isles of Scilly the highlight of the year for many birdwatchers.

The spectacular rarities are not all that the islands have to offer, however. In summer, the colonies of breeding seabirds create a dramatic spectacle, although many are now reduced in number compared with former years. In 1909, Annet Island alone had 100,000 breeding puffins; now there are less than 200 pairs in the whole of Scilly. Annet does, however, have breeding Manx shearwaters and storm petrels, unusual so far south. Razorbills and guillemots also nest there and on the stack of Men-a-var, together with a large colony of kittiwakes. Shags and cormorants are regular breeders and one can see great flocks of shags in the shallow

About 375 species of birds have been recorded in Scilly over the years. This impressive total includes a remarkable score of 'firsts' for Britain. Birds discovered for the first time in the British Isles, sometimes for the first time in Europe, include such varied species as the American purple gallinule, semipalmated plover, greater yellowlegs, common nighthawk, blue-cheeked bee-eater, yellow-bellied sapsucker (an American woodpecker), cliff swallow, green, magnolia and hooded warblers, scarlet tanager and bobolink. Although all but the bee-eater and green warbler come from America, it is the number of vagrants from Europe and Asia, often to be seen on the same day as an American bird, that makes Scilly extra exciting. Birds such as Pallas's warbler,

GREAT GREEN BUSH CRICKET
The most dramatic insect on the islands is the great green bush cricket, which reaches 2 inches long, and thrives in the mild climate.

sounds between the islands throughout most of the year. There are a few pairs of common terns scattered through the islands, and, until recently, at least, half a dozen pairs of the very rare and threatened roseate tern.

There are a few surprising omissions among the breeding landbirds, such as the yellowhammer, reed bunting, jay, magpie, blackcap and garden warbler. Bullfinches, common enough on the mainland, made news by breeding for the first time in 1976, and there are no tree sparrows, ravens, rooks or jackdaws. Even willow warblers are scarce, and although wheatears used to breed, they no longer do so.

Common breeding birds include linnets, wrens, dunnocks and rock pipits; reed and sedge warblers breed in small numbers. With the sad demise of the peregrine around 1928, the only breeding bird of prey is the kestrel.

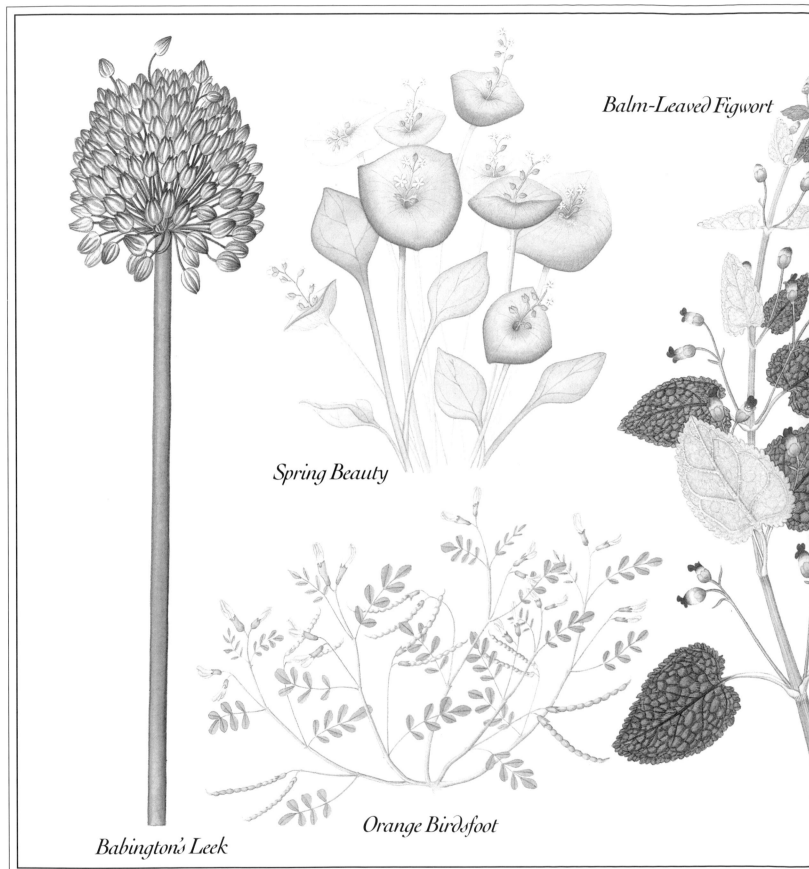

Balm-Leaved Figwort

Spring Beauty

Orange Birdsfoot

Babington's Leek

BABINGTON'S LEEK *(Allium ampeloprasum* ss. *babingtonii)* A perennial with linear leaves and a 24-80″ (60-200cm) stem, the open head of flowers has large buds and smaller heads arising from it. Rare in the South-west, frequent in fields on the Isles of Scilly.

SPRING BEAUTY *(Montia perfoliata)* An upright annual alien 4-12″ (10-30cm), now widespread and often abundant on light, cultivated soils. The flower stems grow up through the middle of its round leaves and flower May-July. Lower leaves are borne on long stalks.

ORANGE BIRDSFOOT *(Ornithopus pinnatus)* This weak sprawling 2-6″ (5-15cm) annual is a rare plant of short turf and sandy paths on the Isles of Scilly and the Channel Islands. Leaves are divided into pairs of leaflets, the flowers and beaded pods are seen April-August.

BALM-LEAVED FIGWORT *(Scrophularia scorodonia)* Confined to the south-west tip of England, where it is profuse in hedges and marshes, this is a downy plant to 39″ (1m) with a square stem. Wrinkled leaves are double toothed, flowers open June-August.

Bermuda Buttercup

Three-Cornered Leek

Smaller Tree Mallow

THREE-CORNERED LEEK
(Allium triquetrum) This is a
garden escape established in the
mildest parts of the extreme South-
west. A perennial, with a triangular
flower stem 8-20″ (20-50cm)
supporting bell-shaped blooms in a
loose head April to June.

BERMUDA BUTTERCUP *(Oxalis
pes-caprae)* Native to South Africa,
now found as a perennial weed of
fields and wasteland in Devon,
Cornwall and Scilly Isles. Heads of
flowers on 4-12″ (10-30cm) stalks
open March-June. Deep-buried
bulbs make eradication difficult.

SMALLER TREE MALLOW
(Lavateria cretica) Growing in
waste places and cultivated land,
west Cornwall, Isles of Scilly and
the Channel Islands, this is a hairy
plant with stems that reach 60″
(150cm). Sprays of flowers arise in
the leaf axils, June-July.

Woodchat Shrike

Juvenile

Adult Winter

Pallas's Warbler

Winter

Red-Throated Pipit

WOODCHAT SHRIKE (*Lanius senator*) Isolated individuals occur rarely in Britain during spring – north of their breeding grounds in south Europe, Asia and north Africa. A 7″ (18cm) shrike with distinctive plumage – females less bright than males – it prefers woods.

RED-THROATED PIPIT (*Anthus cervinus*) Migrating from breeding grounds within the Arctic circle to Africa and south Asia, this 6″ (15cm) bird is a rare vagrant. Similar to a meadow pipit but more heavily streaked, its throat becomes red during the breeding season.

PALLAS'S WARBLER (*Phylloscopus proregulus*) A regular but very rare visitor from Asia, seen in autumn in copses and scrub where it feeds on insects. 3½″ (9cm) long, the conspicuous yellow rump enables it to be distinguished from other small greenish warblers.

Rose-Coloured Starling

Rustic Bunting

Winter

Red-Breasted Flycatcher

ROSE-COLOURED STARLING (*Sturnus roseus*) Numbers of this 8½" (22cm) starling fluctuate widely in south-east Europe and south-west Asia and vagrants arrive in Britain most summers. Females are duller versions of the pink and glossy black male, who has a crest.

RUSTIC BUNTING (*Emberiza rustica*) Breeding across north Asia west into Sweden, rare vagrants may be seen here spring and autumn. 5¾" (15cm), both sexes have brown heads with white eye stripes in winter, but the male has a black and white head in summer.

RED-BREASTED FLYCATCHER (*Ficedula parva*) Nesting in woods, from eastern Europe right across Asia, this 4½" (11cm), insect-eating bird arrives here in small numbers mostly in autumn. Both sexes have white tail patches but only males have the bright rust-red throat.

Rare Birds of Scilly

From the Asian green warbler to the American purple gallinule, the Isles of Scilly have hosted an extraordinary number of rare birds never seen anywhere else in Britain – or indeed in Europe.

As the October rain sweeps across St Agnes, blown almost horizontal by the strong southwesterly wind coming in off the Atlantic, the plaintive *quee-i-lee* of a lone bird is heard out to sea. Soon, a large-eyed, delicate-looking wader flaps sluggishly in over the bay, borne along on the air. Moments later, it crosses the shore and drops, seemingly exhausted, upon the damp green turf.

The bird is a lesser golden plover, a wanderer all the way from Alaska rarely seen in Britain. Migrating south from its North American breeding ground, it was blown off course by the southwesterly winds as it headed for the Caribbean. Swept right over the Atlantic (and separated from its fellows) as it flew south, it has crossed 3000 miles of ocean before finally making landfall on the Scillies.

The lesser golden plover is just one of the many unusual and exotic birds that may be sighted in autumn in the Scillies, for these unique islands, flung far out beyond the southwest tip of England seem to be at a cross-roads for birds migrating from almost everywhere in the northern hemisphere.

DISTANT WANDERERS

Besides the lesser golden plover, many other waders heading south for winter from North America drift off course and make landfall in the Scillies. The distinctive *brrp* of the pectoral sandpiper is often heard over the Scilly Isles in autumn and, every October, a few white-rumped sandpipers and greater yellowlegs are seen settling on mud-flats and lagoons across the islands.

American wigeon, blue-winged teal and other North American waterfowl may be seen over the Scilly Isles, too. Sometimes, the islands may be visited by the American purple gallinule. Dark bluish-purple with a stout red beak, the gallinule looks a little like an overgrown moorhen, and its long dangling yellow legs make it look rather weak in flight, but it is actually an impressively strong flyer, capable of migrating long distances.

More remarkably, North American landbirds may sometimes drop in here in autumn. Their presence is remarkable because, unlike the waders and waterfowl, they cannot settle on the water to rest – so they must have flown thousands of miles over the ocean without stopping, helped along by the strong prevailing westerly winds.

This feat is so surprising that it was once believed they travelled some of the way on

boats, but it is now accepted that these tiny birds fly all the way. Gold and black Baltimore orioles, brilliantly plumaged, rare scarlet and summer tanagers, and at least four species of American thrush and nine American warblers and vireos (including the red-eyed vireo) have all made the crossing to the Scilly Isles. They appear here when depressions move rapidly east across the Atlantic, and the small birds are caught up in strong southwesterly winds to the

GOLDEN ORIOLE
(above) After wintering in tropical Africa, this striking species with its brilliant yellow and black plumage, is a summer visitor to the Scillies. A shy bird, with a fluty, melodious whistle, it is more commonly heard than seen in the open.

south, making their first landfall on the Scillies.

Barely less remarkable is the appearance in the Scilly Isles at about the same time of year of equally small birds from right across the other side of the world – from Asia and China. Two of these rare visitors are the yellow-browed warbler and the rare and tiny Pallas's warbler, both natives of Siberia which normally migrate south to India and China for winter.

LOST MIGRANTS

No-one knows quite why they appear in the Scilly Isles. Some believe that young birds get their line of travel right but fly in the opposite direction, reaching North and West Europe instead of South East Asia, a phenomenon which is known as 'reversed migration'. They then swing south west to reach Britain – at the extreme ending in the Scilly Isles. It may be that they are encouraged by the easterly winds that blow to the south of the belt of high pressure

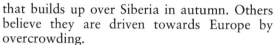

A SPLASH OF COLOUR
(right) The American purple gallinule adds an occasional splash of colour to the Scilly Isles – most typically in November. This unusually-coloured waterbird has much in common with the moorhen, but breeds in the southern USA and Central and South America. It lives in freshwater lakes, rivers and marshes, has a jaunty walk and can run fast over floating water vegetation – such as water-lilies – on its long-toed feet.

A BUOYANT FLIER
(above) The North American ring-billed gull is a regular visitor in south-west Britain for a large part of the year. It is, in fact, conceivable that a few may be nesting – undetected – in European gull colonies. Being strong and buoyant fliers, larger numbers of gulls are able to withstand the trans-Atlantic crossing than many of the smaller vagrants.

that builds up over Siberia in autumn. Others believe they are driven towards Europe by overcrowding.

In spring, the Scillies may receive yet another set of unusual and exotic visitors; wanderers from the south. As the April sun brings an early spring to the Scillies, the heron-like little egret with its dagger beak and long graceful white plumes may wing its way into St Mary's. So too may the rare squacco heron, coming into land with flashing white wings, along with rare shrikes and wheatears. And bringing a splash of Mediterranean colour are the golden oriole and the gaudily coloured bee-eater.

All are birds from the Mediterranean, migrating north for the summer from their African wintering grounds, that have simply overshot their destinations in Southern Europe, perhaps helped along by southerly winds. These birds at least have a chance of correcting their mistake and flying south again for the summer, especially if it turns cold – unlike the autumn wanderers that are unable to return to their homeland and will more than likely perish from cold in the British winter.

SCARLET TANAGER
(right) This bird, with its distinctly tropical appearance, is a member of the finch family. It breeds in the woodlands of eastern North America and is sometimes seen in the Scillies during October. The plumage of the male and female during the breeding season is markedly different – the female being an olive-green and yellow colour, while the male is the vivid scarlet and black shown here.

Breckland

A desolate wilderness of grassy heath, inland sand dunes and enigmatic meres, Breckland occupies some 300 square miles at the heart of East Anglia. The region takes its name from the local word 'brecks', denoting patches of land which were once cultivated and then abandoned as the soil became exhausted. And in fact the Breckland landscape of today is one shaped largely by man; the open areas are the result of thousands of years of forest clearance and intensive grazing, while the vast tracts of conifers are more recent additions, planted to secure the shifting soil.

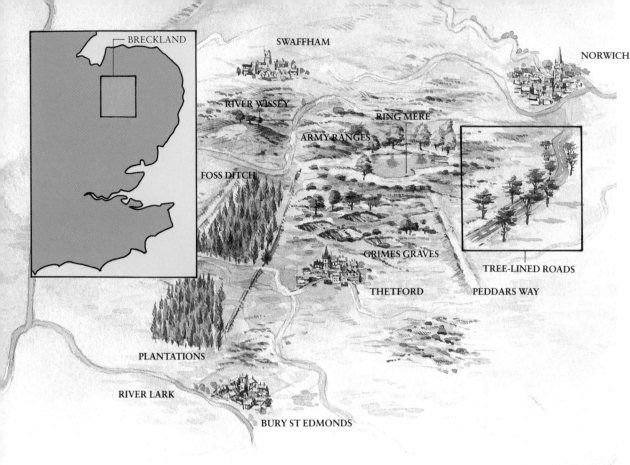

BRECKLAND
SWAFFHAM
NORWICH
RIVER WISSEY
RING MERE
ARMY RANGES
FOSS DITCH
GRIMES GRAVES
TREE-LINED ROADS
THETFORD
PEDDARS WAY
PLANTATIONS
RIVER LARK
BURY ST EDMONDS

A CHANGING LANDSCAPE
Occupying around 300 square miles in the heart of East Anglia, Breckland was quickly settled by early man who mined the rich deposits of flint and exported worked and unworked stone along trade routes such as the Icknield and Peddars Way. These early settlers soon cleared the thinly wooded land and when the light, fast draining soil rapidly deteriorated, they turned the land over to sheep, and later, rabbits. Today, however, Breckland has changed again. Much of it is now used as army ranges or is covered by huge conifer plantations, but a few original 'brecks' still remain.

A wild, low-lying plain straddling Norfolk and Suffolk, Breckland has a long and complex history with its origins in the last Ice Age. Once a wide chalk basin, during the glaciation Breckland was coated with debris: a porous spread of clay, sand and chalk. Subsequently, meltwater and rain attacked this glacial 'drift', washing away the chalk, breaking down the clay and leaving behind a wind-skimmed surface layer of fine sand.

The light, loose, sandy soil of the wasteland which resulted attracted only a sparse covering of trees – a fact appreciated by Neolithic farmers who, in a country blanketed with primeval forest, had to clear land before they could cultivate it. But although the land proved easy to clear, these early agriculturalists soon discovered that the arid, sour sand yielded poor harvests. As a result, crop-growing was kept to a minimum and the early farmers concentrated on raising animals. In doing so they began a tradition of livestock farming which would endure almost 7000 years and which, more than anything else, transformed Breckland into the desolate heathscape we know today. Little by little the forest was cleared, the land cropped for a year or two, then given over to cattle and sheep and thus – through grazing – was never allowed to regenerate. Some tracts of heath, apart from their scattering of gorse and bracken, remain as they were in prehistoric times – uncultivated since the Neolithic farmers first tilled them with flint tools, mined nearby, around 5000 BC.

From these prehistoric beginnings, Breckland developed into an important agricultural area – with the emphasis on livestock. It prospered under the Romans and Saxons and by the

WANGFORD WARREN
Breckland's thin sandy soils are particularly prone to soil erosion – a problem exacerbated in the past by the over-grazing of sheep and the tunnelling of rabbits. The result was often 'blows' and 'floods' of sand which drowned fields, smothered buildings and, in 1668, buried the whole village of Santon Downham.

WEST TOFTS MERE
Ranging from small ponds to 30-acre lakes, Breckland meres can all be strangely enigmatic. Appearing to defy nature, after rain they may be drained dry, while in a drought they can be full to overflowing. The answer lies below – in the water table of the underlying chalk, the level of which depends not on the current weather but that of a month, or even a year, ago.

Middle Ages had established itself as sheep country: the wide heathland then comprised countless grazings, with just enough ploughed strips to provide essential food. It was an ideal environment for sheep: the stubby vegetation – too coarse for cattle – suited them perfectly, while the soil's aridity discouraged foot-rot; and, all around, East Anglia's burgeoning textile industry clamoured for their wool.

But in the wake of the Norman Conquest, the incumbent flocks had a new animal thrust among them: the rabbit. Introduced from France for its fur and meat, the coney quickly became big business in Breckland – and the area was divided into vast territories called warrens which were licensed out to landowners. The names of various warrens still survive today as do the ruins of some warren lodges – stout, fortified buildings in which the warrener kept guard against poachers.

RURAL DEPOPULATION

Towards the end of the medieval era, however, Breckland's prosperity began to wane. The reasons were various and inter-related: rural depopulation – a countrywide phenomenon in the later Middle Ages – emptied much of Breckland to create a landscape of lost villages and abandoned hamlets. The area's marginal soils – stony and shallow – were exhausted and could no longer support cultivation; and, most disastrously, over-grazing by sheep and rampant burrowing by rabbits had totally eroded the fragile topsoil, exposing it to the vagaries of the wayward wind. With increasing frequency, sand 'blows' and 'floods' became a devastating feature of the Breckland scene; great whirling banks of sand drowned fields, smothered buildings and, in 1668, obliterated the village of Santon Downham.

For the next two or three centuries, Breckland was largely left to itself – and the rabbits which were profitably reared until myxomatosis caught up with them. In the 1800s, the Victorians reclaimed and improved peripheral fields for agricultural use; planted shelter belts of Scots pine to stabilize the shifting sand; and populated the heath scrub with pheasants to indulge the current fashion for game – some Breckland shooting parties bagged over 1000 birds in a single day.

In its flint and sheep heyday, Breckland was one of the most densely-populated parts of Britain. Today it ranks as one of the emptiest – due in part to the decline of traditional activities and in part to two major changes in land-use that have happened in the twentieth century. On the one hand, much of Breckland has been appropriated for military purposes – airbases, mock battle fields and NATO training grounds. On the other, some 80 square miles now belong to the Forestry Commission and are covered in conifer plantations. But in between, fragments of heath and occasional meres survive – reminders of the landscape's transformation.

Nature Walk

The desolate and sometimes haunting Breckland landscape holds many intriguing reminders of the distant past. Look for:

PATTERNS of flinty ridges and sandy heather-filled dips, relics of the Ice Age.

PEDDARS WAY – one of several prehistoric tracks which cross East Anglia – improved by the Romans.

GRIMES GRAVES, near Brandon, Britain's most extensive Stone Age flint mines.

PINE-TOPPED BARROWS, burial mounds made by Bronze-Age pastoral tribes. The trees survive because these areas were never farmed or grazed.

Wildlife of the Brecks

The character of Breckland stems from the mix of local climate and
soils, which encourages rare plants, insects and birds, helped –
surprisingly – by the rabbit.

For centuries, sheep and rabbits reigned in
Breckland. Today, most of the sheep are
gone and near one of the few remaining
Breckland rabbit warrens, a quite different
scene unfurls. A rabbit is running at full stretch
over the short, patchy and burrow-pocked turf.
On its tail is a stoat. They disappear down into
the maze of tunnels. All is quiet for a few
moments. Then they burst out again, the rabbit
kicking its weaving course across the grass and

the sleek robust predator gliding after it. Eventually the chase ends in a tumbling, scrapping
death for the rabbit and a meal for the stoat.

On other occasions, however, the rabbit is
too smart in the riddle of underground run-
ways, the stoat pops out of a tunnel alone and
reverts to a busy grooming, indifferent to the
unique habitat which surrounds it.

BRECKLAND'S VARIED HABITATS

Breckland is one of the driest parts of the British
Isles. Hot summers, cold winters and the chalk,
sand and flint of its soils have given it an
unusual and sometimes unique flora and fauna.

The remaining fragments of true Breckland –
a breck was a field left fallow – are hemmed in
by sombre conifer plantations, cereal prairies of
wheat and barley and the thundering air bases
of the Norfolk/Suffolk borderlands. Today, the
few fields left fallow are mainly on reserves.

Here the bright cornfield weeds – poppies, cornflowers, chamomile and others – burst into colour in summer as the long dormant seeds respond to the lack of agricultural discipline.

Whinchats breed among the chaotic and colourful weed jungle, singing from the top of tall thistles and bushes to mark their territories. Their nests are hidden on the ground beneath the poppies and the thorny blue spikes of the viper's bugloss. When the flowers are gone the

SOLDIER ORCHID
(right) This orchid is one of Breckland's surprises. A small colony was found in a chalkpit in a conifer plantation. How these rare orchids found their way there is a mystery, since they are more often seen in woodland borders and chalky grassland.

WILDLIFE ACROSS BRECKLAND'S CHANGING HABITATS
Breckland's sand, flint and chalk soils form pockets of wilderness that attract some unusual species. Conifer plantations hold deer, nesting crossbills and, at their edges, the bee hawk-moth. Sandy heaths harbour adders, the fierce wolf spider and its predatory wasp, the drought-resistant biting stonecrop and butterflies such as the grayling. On stony soils rabbits graze the sparse grass, and lapwings and the scarce stone curlew nests in scrapes. In chalky grassland, flax and thyme grow alongside the unusual moonwort fern. The meres attract nesting ducks.

KEY TO FEATURES AND SPECIES

1 *Old Scots pines*
2 *Male crossbill*
3 *Silver birch*
4 *Mistle thrush*
5 *Skylark*
6 *Lapwings*
7 *Gorse*
8 *Red-backed shrike*
9 *Roe deer buck*
10 *Heather*
11 *Red deer*
12 *Pine plantation*
13 *Stony soil*
14 *Grayling*
15 *Male wheatear*
16 *Teal*
17 *Wigeon*
18 *Wavy hair-grass*
19 *Narrow-bordered bee hawk-moth*
20 *Bracken*
21 *Adder*
22 *Sandy heath*
23 *Stoat*
24 *Sand sedge*
25 *Rabbits*
26 *Stone curlew*
27 *Field wormwood*
28 *Rabbit-proof fence*
29 *Chalky turf*
30 *Quaking grass*
31 *Reed canary-grass*
32 *Essex skipper*
33 *Mere*
34 *Spiked speedwell*
35 *Golden dock*
36 *Spider-hunting wasp*
37 *Biting stonecrop*
38 *Sand catstail*
39 *Maiden pink*
40 *Female common blue*
41 *Flax*
42 *Sheep's fescue*
43 *Moonwort*
44 *Wolf spider* Trochosa terricola
45 *Ground beetle* Carabus nitens
46 *Bird's foot trefoil*
47 *Thyme*

weeds' seedheads feed mixed winter flocks of finches.

But there are rarer wild flowers which grow chiefly, or only, in Breckland. Fingered, early and spring speedwell are modest weeds of a few roadsides and nature reserves. Striated catchfly grows among purple-stemmed cat's-tail and Breckland thyme.

Many of the special flowers grow on the Breckland heaths. They may once have grown from the fallow lands, at a time when heather and grasses came in to make a sward over the stony soil.

The heaths now hold such rare plants as Spanish catchfly, wild grape hyacinth, star-of-

Bethlehem, field wormwood and small medick. These are plants native to the steppes of eastern Europe, but they have flourished in an area of Britain not dissimilar to their vast and wind-swept homeland.

Breckland's unique blend of insects and spiders roams this vegetation. One species of moth, misleadingly known as the viper's bugloss, has never been found outside Breckland. Its caterpillars feed on Spanish catchfly, a flower that is locally common but otherwise rare. The moth was so-christened because the first ever British specimen was found, in July 1868, resting on viper's bugloss.

There are Breckland beetles and bugs, too, like the beetle *Diastictus vulneratus*, found on Foxhole Heath but hardly anywhere else. And there is the uncommon bug *Arenocoris waltlii*, usually a coastal species, but found here on the Breck's inland sand dunes. It occurs at Wangford Warren, where the mobile sandhills have species typical of coastal dunes.

In open stony areas the crab spider *Oxyptila scabicula* goes about its carnivorous business. It can be common here, but is rare outside Breckland. The ·Brecks are the only inland site for several other species of spider, which are more usually found on coastal sands.

A STRONGHOLD FOR RARE BIRDS

The stone curlew, one of Breckland's rarer birds, is active throughout the night but especially at dusk and dawn. Its haunted cries echo through the night air as it hunts insects with the aid of curious, extra-large eyes. It breeds on

MOTH CATERPILLARS *(above)) This mullein moth caterpillar is feeding on a leaf of mullein, a tall, yellow-flowered plant commonly found in the Brecks. The caterpillars feed in groups, decimating the foliage and eating everything but the stem before leaving the plant to pupate at its base. The moth itself, which is modestly drab, flies at night in April and May.*

RED-BACKED SHRIKES *(above left) The red-backed shrike is our only breeding shrike, but there are probably no more than 50 pairs in Britain, most of them in the Brecks and coastal East Anglia. The birds breed in insect-rich areas and require a thorny bush as a nest site. Shrikes sometimes accumulate a larder of insects, birds and small mammals by impaling them on the thorns; hence their old country name of 'butcher bird'.*

CROSSBILLS AND YOUNG *(right) Crossbills expand their range every so often in response to local food shortages (they are particularly fond of spruce seeds). In 1910 a huge influx of crossbills arrived in Britain from the Continent and many have stayed to breed in Breckland conifers.*

some of the heaths and can sometimes be seen in daylight, walking slowly across the grassland, stretching and preening. Locally, the bird is known as the Norfolk plover.

Two other birds whose populations have also declined across Britain – the red-backed shrike and the nightjar – are still to be found breeding regularly in Breckland. The crossbill, however, has expanded its British breeding population in the huge conifer plantations which have replaced many of the heaths. Here, crossbills have established a successful bridgehead since their sudden arrival from the Continent in 1910. Red squirrels and deer can also be seen.

The Scots pine is Breckland's most characteristic tree. It grows happily in the sands, spreading out from the forests and newer plantations to form shelter belts that wander across the landscape. Sentinel-like, it also lines the roads with

ranks of gnarled trunks.

Breckland is not all dry. There are scattered land-locked lakes, known as meres, which fill and empty at the whim of the unpredictable water table. Nesting amid the rich waterside vegetation are various ducks, including the gadwall. It bred for the first time in the British Isles in about 1850, when a pair were released in Breckland.

Breckland's flora and fauna is changing. With the decline in sheep farming and the loss, due to myxomatosis, of a thriving rabbit population, short-cropped swards are few and far between. Taller, ranker grasses have come in and the heather has grown from soft round cushions into tall and leggy bushes. Stone curlews have declined, as have many of the Breckland flowers.

To restore the short sward, grazing has been reintroduced at several sites. Its success is most

marked at Weeting Heath, where the flora and fauna has recovered dramatically due to the fencing in of rabbits. Spiked speedwell flourishes, with rupturewort and breckland thyme. Where there is respite from the grazing, Spanish catch-fly and maiden pink grow. Stone curlews breed here and so do wheatears.

Weeting Heath must be rather similar to the great Breckland warrens of the past, where thousands of rabbits were reared for fur and meat. And, fortunately, enough rabbits have survived the triple dangers of man, myxomatosis and the ever-present stoat to play a vital role in restoring a part of the Brecks to its former glory.

Breckland will probably never again be the barren, flinty wilderness it was until the beginning of this century, but pockets of its special wildlife still survive.

NIGHTJAR AT REST
(above) This nocturnal bird rests on the ground by day, wonderfully camouflaged against its heathland background of stony soil, dry bracken or – as here – a colour-matched, lichen-encrusted boulder. Come dusk, the birds are actively flying in pursuit of insects, which are caught in the wide-open, bristle-edged beak. Nightjars are summer visitors from Africa. Breckland birds nest in small numbers on the heaths and forest rides.

RED SQUIRREL
(centre left) Until about ten years ago, red squirrels could be seen regularly, if fleetingly, in many parts of Norfolk. Now the grey predominates, but reds can still be glimpsed in Breckland, where they hold on in the huge conifer plantations which have replaced many of the original heaths.

SPIKED SPEEDWELL
(left) An attractive but rare flower, spiked speedwell is found in the wild only in Breckland. It is more commonly found as a cultivated plant in gardens. It flowers from July to September, pushing up its spike of bright flowers to a height of 2' (60cm).

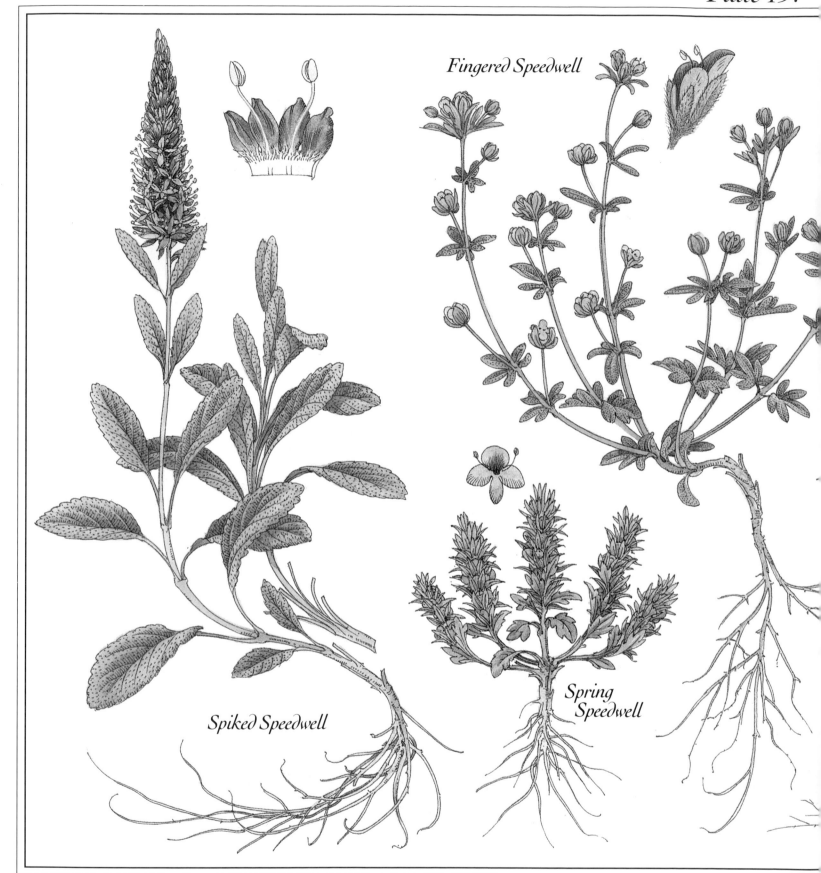

Fingered Speedwell

Spiked Speedwell

Spring Speedwell

SPIKED SPEEDWELL *(Veronica spicata* ssp. *spicata)* On the verge of extinction this rare and protected perennial grows only on the short rabbit-grazed turf of the Brecks. Stems to 24″ (60cm) have spikes of dark blue flowers July to September, the leaves have rounded teeth.

FINGERED SPEEDWELL *(Veronica triphyllos)* Like the other rare Breckland speedwells, this 2-8″ (5-20cm) annual is under threat with changing uses of open, sandy fields. Hairy stems are semi-erect, with 3-7 radiating lobes and deep blue flowers seen from April-June.

SPRING SPEEDWELL *(Veronica verna)* Very rare, this glandular annual has semi-upright, branched stems 1-6″ (3-15cm). Leaves have 3-7 lobes and the clusters of tiny flowers open May-June. Only found in Suffolk, it is seen in dry, bare fields on sandy soil.

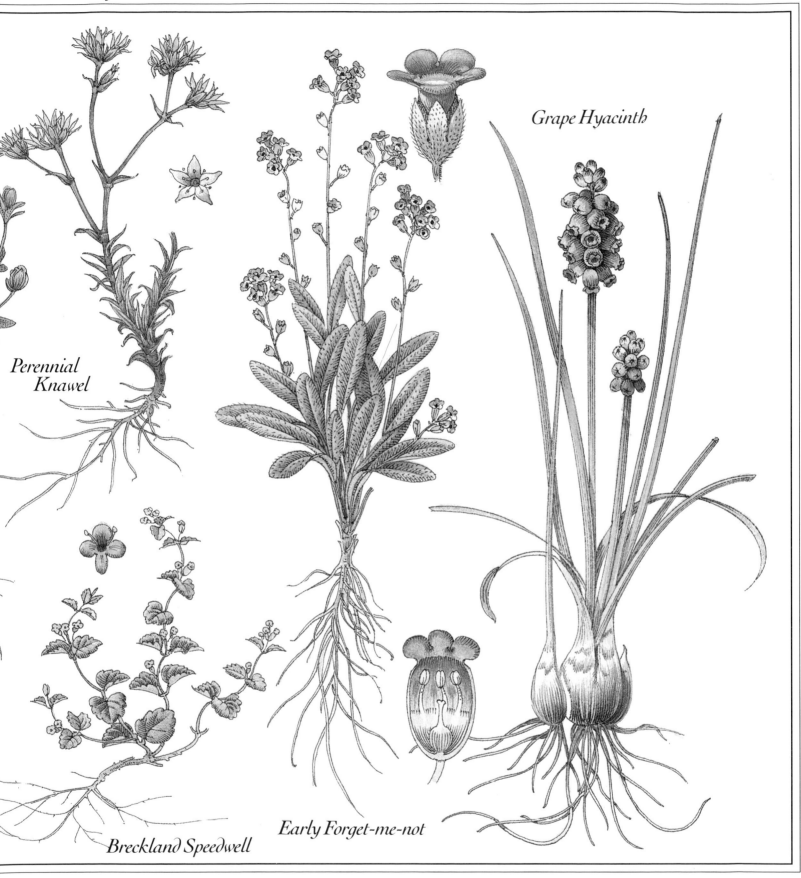

Perennial Knawel

Breckland Speedwell

Early Forget-me-not

Grape Hyacinth

PERENNIAL KNAWEL (*Scleranthus perennis* ssp. *prostratus*) This wiry perennial with semi-erect stems to 10″ (25cm) occurs on bare sandy ground in only a few places in Suffolk, where it is rare and protected. Small, white-edged flowers are seen June-August.

BRECKLAND SPEEDWELL (*Veronica praecox*) Probably an introduction, this 2-8″ (5-20cm) annual, never plentiful, is almost extinct and seen only in a few Breckland fields. Upright stems bear oval, toothed leaves. Flowers appear in March-April, seeds are cup-shaped.

EARLY FORGET-ME-NOT (*Myosotis ramosissima*) A small, hairy annual with slender stems 1-10″ (3-25cm), this is a locally occurring plant of open arable lands and stable dunes throughout Britain, except the North, West and Ireland. Bright blue flowers open April-June.

GRAPE HYACINTH (*Muscari neglectum*) This bulb grows on dry grassy banks and tracks in east England. Readily shaded out by tall plants, it is now very rare. Leaves are narrow and drooping, and an 8″ (20cm) stem bears a spire of deep blue bell-like flowers, April-May.

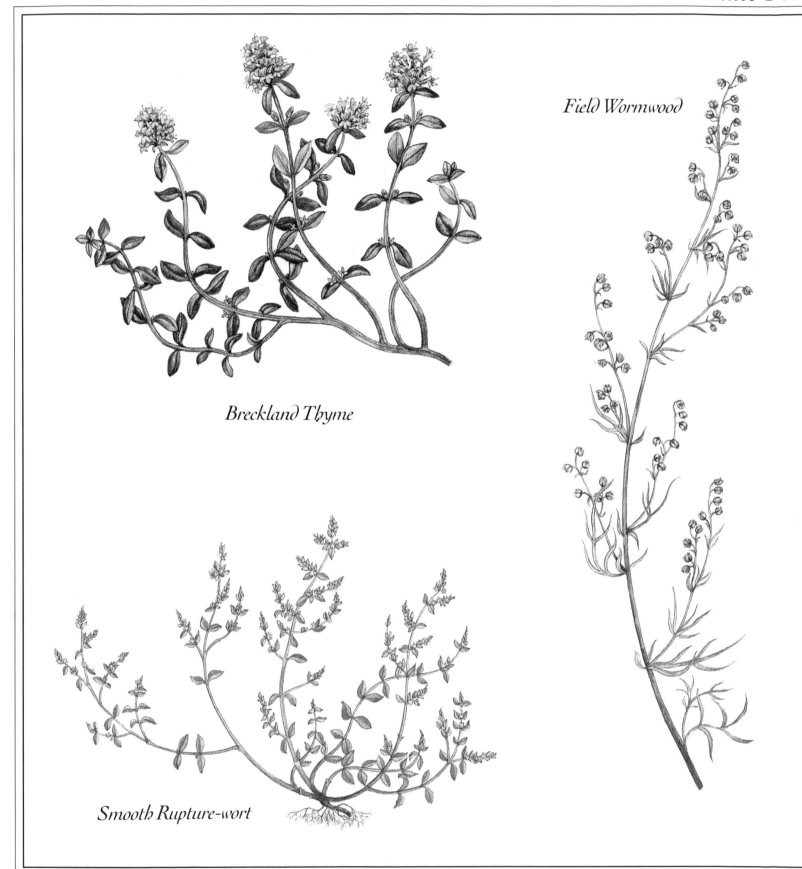

Field Wormwood

Breckland Thyme

Smooth Rupture-wort

BRECKLAND THYME *(Thymus serpyllum)* Prostrate mats of this creeping perennial grow amid short turf and on bare ground – now rare and restricted to a few sites in the Brecks. At most only 3″ (7cm) high, it has tiny, faintly scented leaves and flowers June to August.

SMOOTH RUPTURE-WORT *(Herniaria glabra)* Very rare, this small annual makes a mat of branched stems 2-6″ (5-15cm) long. The tiny leaves are oval, and flowers seen July-September have minute petals. It grows in a few localities in east England on open, coarse sand.

FIELD WORMWOOD *(Artemisia campestris)* An exceedingly rare plant of the Brecks, this scentless perennial grows to 24″ (60cm). Leaves are divided into narrow segments, and the August-September flowers are wind-pollinated. It grows on bare, sandy soil and fields.

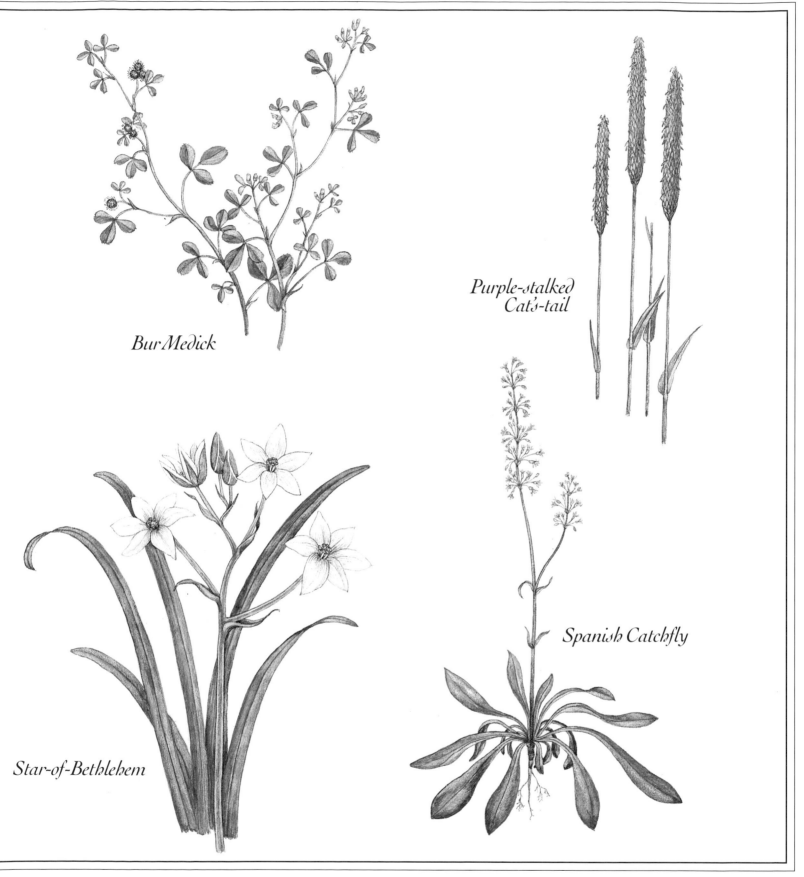

Bur Medick

Purple-stalked Cat's-tail

Star-of-Bethlehem

Spanish Catchfly

BUR MEDICK (*Medicago minima*)
Low-growing, with 2-8″ (5-20cm)
sprawling downy stems, this is a
rare annual found very locally on
dunes, open sandy fields and banks
along the south-east coast and the
Brecks. Flowers appear May-July,
coiled pods have tiny hooked spines.

PURPLE-STALKED CAT'S-TAIL
(*Phleum phleoides*) Local and often
plentiful in dry grassland in the
eastern counties of England, this
perennial makes close tufts 4-28″
(10-70cm). The densely packed
flowerspikes appear June to August,
the leaves are rough-edged.

STAR-OF-BETHLEHEM
(*Ornithogalum umbellatum*) This
attractive bulb has narrow leaves
with a white midrib, and a stem to
12″ (30cm) with 6-15 flowers, April
to June. Grows locally in grassy
places except in the North and West
where it is very rare and coastal.

SPANISH CATCHFLY (*Silene
otites*) This rare perennial is seen in
chalky fields or verges, amongst
short grasses or on bare soil. A few-
leaved flowerstem to 35″ (87cm)
grows from a rosette of leaves, with
open whorls of small, yellow flowers
appearing from June to August.

The Stone Curlew

A rare and shy bird, the stone curlew haunts the open heaths,
downs and farmland of East Anglia and southern England, where its
strange call can be heard at night echoing across the land.

As the light fades from the wide East Anglian sky, the dusky hush is pierced by a series of strange, almost unearthly wails and high-pitched trills. The calls are those of stone curlews becoming active in the deepening darkness. Bird answers bird, as they take wing calling as they fly, impossible to see in the half light.

It is from their most common call – a liquid, haunting *coor-lee* – that the bird gets its name, though it is not a curlew at all. The stone curlew is, in fact, a member of a group called 'thick-knees', which includes several similar, short-billed, large-eyed, long-legged, mottled brown species that favour the dimly-lit, undisturbed worlds of dawn and dusk.

The stone curlew is a somewhat plover-like bird, about the size of a woodpigeon but stands higher off the ground on long, yellow legs. The plumage is pale, streaky brown, paler beneath so that the natural shadow below is cancelled

out – by countershading – providing a perfect camouflage against the rather neutral background of grassy warrens and tussocky heath which it inhabits. The bill has a yellow base, often visible at a great distance and much more obvious than the large, yellow eyes which, surprisingly, are only noticeable at close range. The head stripes are strong, but also become diffuse at a distance. Only the large areas of white on its otherwise mostly black wings provide any strong contrast, making it a much more striking bird in the air.

Stone curlews are found in East Anglia and in southern England from Berkshire to Dorset, where they are thinly spread and very local. The traditional breeding territory was downland turf, but with the decline of sheep farming in the South and the fall in the rabbit population following myxomatosis, much of this habitat has become overgrown and unsuitable. The Breckland heaths also supported stone curlews

HEATHLAND BIRD
(above) Although classified as a wader, the stone curlew is a bird of dry, sandy heaths, stony ground and open farmland. Such territory enables it to keep a watchful eye for signs of danger, and also has plentiful supplies of slugs, snails and insects – its main food. The stone curlew has little in common with the curlew itself, apart from a preference for open spaces and a similar call – a long coor-lee – and the two are not related. At 16 inches (40cm) the stone curlew can best be identified by its long thick yellow legs, white wing bars and huge yellow eyes.

DISPLAY BEHAVIOUR
Stone curlews often indulge in ritual display behaviour, such as during courtship, on preparing to feed, at signs of approaching danger or to guard their territory. This stone curlew (left) is adopting an aggressive pose towards an unseen intruder who he considers to be getting too close to his nest for comfort.

IN FLIGHT the stone curlew has long, broad wings with a double wing bar, striking black and white feathers and mainly white underparts.

on close-cropped sandy places, but such areas are now found only on reserves and one or two other spots, and are often heavily populated by weekend visitors and picnickers. So stone curlews have been forced to show a degree of adaptability by moving into arable farmland.

SUMMER VISITORS

The stone curlew is a summer visitor, arriving in March and early April after wintering in Spain and North Africa. The newly-arrived birds select a site on bare sandy ground for their 'nest'. This is no more than a shallow scrape in the soil and the birds lay their two eggs directly on the ground. These are sandy-coloured, with dark spots and streaks. These markings break up the smooth, regular outline of the eggs, so that the shiny oval shape will not catch the eye of a passing fox or crow.

The eggs are laid in April and May, but a few pairs sometimes lay a replacement or second clutch as late as August. Incubation is shared by both birds and lasts for almost four weeks. The chicks leave the nest scrape within a day of

hatching. They are delightful, downy creatures with thin bands of black along their bright buff backs. They already have yellow legs and soon develop a characteristic stone curlew trick. When disturbed, they crouch flat against the ground, in a 'freezing posture' with head and neck extended and pressed close to the soil. There they stay, relying entirely on their excellent camouflage to avoid detection. As they do not fly for about six weeks, the young need to be alert, wary and quick to crouch down out of sight of predators such as foxes.

In the autumn, before the birds leave for their wintering areas, flocks of a dozen or two will gather in and around Breckland in some favoured field, for stone curlews are basically social birds. Fortunately, farmers who appreciate the sight and sound of these rare, peculiar and beautiful birds are doing their best to protect them. They may yet manage to halt the sad decline of the stone curlew and make its sharp, extraordinary cries in the black of night once again a more familiar sound across the windswept downs and sandy, rabbit-riddled Brecks.

COMMUNAL DISPLAYS are often performed prior to the birds leaving to feed, and involve frantic wing-flapping and leaping.

SHARED NESTING
(right) Both male and female share the task of incubating the eggs which take about four weeks to hatch. Once hatched, the young are initially fed by both parents but are able to feed themselves in two or three days, usually with one adult standing by to supervise. Young stone curlews stay within their parents' territory until they can fly at about six weeks old.

THE EGGS are large, smooth and buff-coloured, with variable brown markings and are blunt-ended; one – but sometimes two – clutches of two are laid in a shallow scrape.

The Norfolk Broads

Made up of meres, channels and rivers, the Broads lace a wedge of the flat, liquid landscape of eastern Norfolk with a spidery 120-mile trail of shallow waterways. They lie within an area that was once a great expanse of wild marshland and were created when the sea level rose hundreds of years ago, flooding the excavations of early medieval people who had long dug for peat there. Since then, the thick pelts of reeds that sprang up at the water's edge and the patches of land that have been steadily reclaimed for farming have shaped the face of the Broadlands as we know them today.

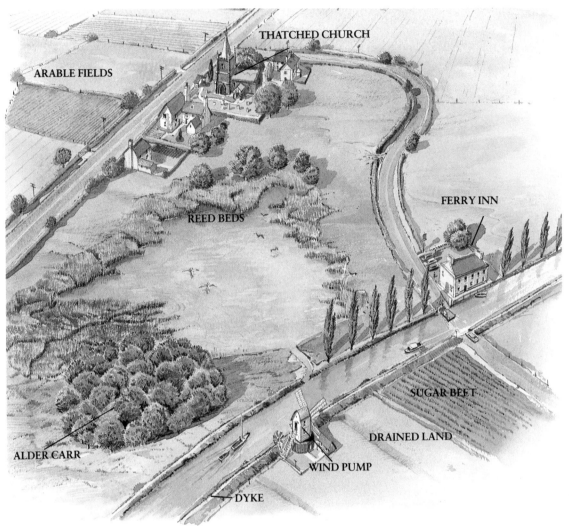

ARABLE FIELDS

THATCHED CHURCH

REED BEDS

FERRY INN

ALDER CARR

WIND PUMP

DYKE

SUGAR BEET

DRAINED LAND

BROAD VIEW
(left) The flat, watery landscape of the Norfolk Broads is made up of 41 shallow lagoons (the flooded sites of ancient peat excavations on ancient natural marsh) some of which are linked to the main rivers of the area – the Yare, the Bure and the Waveney. The horizon may be punctuated by windmill pumps, which are used to drain land lying below river level, and which is protected from water-level rises by barriers or dykes. Characteristically, the margins of the lagoons support thick beds of reeds.

REED HARVESTING
(below) Reeds are harvested in winter, and may be sent as far afield as America for thatch. Reed growth is adversely affected by fertilizers from cultivated fields, and dislodged reed 'rafts' expose the banks.

Carpeted with water lilies, and banked by impenetrable reed-beds which provide shelter for a variety of wildlife, the Broads are a remnant of an ancient wilderness whose magic remains despite their popularity with vast numbers of holiday makers.

The Norfolk Broads lie within a wedge in the north-east corner of Norfolk, roughly between Sea Palling in the north, Norwich in the west and Lowestoft in the east. Three rivers – the Yare, the Bure and the Waveney – meander across the flat landscape, flanked by shallow lakes – the Broads themselves, of which there are 41. Broadland also encompasses open grazing marshes which stretch alongside the lower reaches of the rivers within smell of the sea.

Originally, a trackless swampy waste stretching between the rivers, the Broads in time became quite well settled starting with the Beaker folk of 2000 BC, despite the biting easterly winter winds, and the prevalence of the ague – the native form of malaria. To compensate, the Broads offered plentiful fish and wildfowl, and the hidden bonus of a ready fuel supply in the form of fen peat – the partly rotted remains of reeds and other swamp plants – which burns steadily when dried.

The peat was dug to a depth of two or three metres in open scattered workings alongside the rivers, a process which began in Saxon times and continued throughout the Middle Ages, right up until World War 1. In the 13th century the abandoned workings flooded to create shallow lagoons – the 'broad waters' we see today – whose man-made origins are revealed in places by their obviously unnatural outlines. The flooded diggings were colonized by dense beds of reeds thriving in the calm shallow water, which are still cut for thatching.

Saw sedge was also harvested to be used for capping thatched roofs, and rough hay could be cut or grazed from the marshy ground. Even the tangled scrubby woodland occupying higher ground, and composed mainly of alder and sallow, yielded timber for stakes and other purposes. Fish and waterfowl proliferated, and in time the clear lagoons became water gardens covered with water lilies. With the exploitation of the natural resources, the area prospered, and even supported a great abbey – St Benet's – which is now a ruin.

LAND RECLAMATION

Some of the drier land surrounding the lagoons was drained to improve grazing, a change which was accelerated at the beginning of the 19th century, when systems of dykes were constructed and water was pumped away by wind pumps whose giant sails utilized the relentless winds. These have now been superseded by steam, diesel and electric pumps.

The railways of Victorian times gave the Broads new life, providing transportation for the local fish and wildfowl supplying the London markets, and the reeds for thatching. The Broads also began to attract tourists, lured by the fishing and shooting, and rowing or sailing in this watery paradise.

Today much has changed. The Broads have now become one of the most popular holiday grounds in Britain with over a million visitors staying for a week or more each year. In some places the rivers are now lined by holiday homes, and the villages have expanded.

But the effects of motorized water craft have made one of the greatest changes – for there are at least 2000 motor craft for hire, and another 3000 privately registered. In stark contrast to the sailing craft of Victorian times, these modern

WATER, WATER EVERYWHERE
The reeds bordering broadwater often back on to drier land where twiggy copses of alder and sallow flourish.

boats destroy aquatic plants with their propellers, and the silt stirred up in their wake smothers both plant and animal life. The wash from boats erodes the edges of the waterways and dislodges the reeds, with the result that the 1200 acres of reedbed to be found in Broadland today is only half the area which existed at the end of World War 2.

Added to all this is the hazard of pollution. The sewage from houses and holiday craft once enriched the water of the rivers and lagoons to such an extent that it 'bloomed' turbidly with slimes and algae, which stifled plants and fish. Though this is now under greater control, more intensive arable land use is having a similar effect – where areas of old drainage marsh have been drained and ploughed for sugar beet and other crops, the inevitable wash of chemical fertilizers into the waters has enriched them to the detriment of the wildlife. All is not lost however, for many of the Broads are now completely protected and are being managed to preserve their true character and conserve the wildlife they attract. Even the threat to areas of open grazing land has now eased, as a result of government action. And there is a good chance that Broadland will become a National Park, alongside Dartmoor and the Lake District, as a precious part of our national heritage.

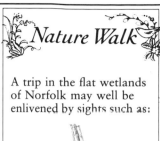

Nature Walk

A trip in the flat wetlands of Norfolk may well be enlivened by sights such as:

WINDMILL PUMPS which were used to drain waterlogged land for pasture or cultivation in conjunction with barriers, or dykes, and sluices.

CHAIN BARRIERS which close off stretches of water to boat traffic, to allow the plants to regenerate.

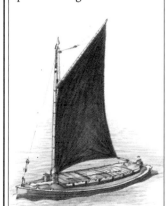

WHERRIES Broad-based trading or passenger vessels with a shallow draught and large high sail specific to the Broads. Very few remain.

Among the Reeds

Fringed by acres of reeds and grasses, and alive with the sight and sound of almost every imaginable water bird, the Norfolk Broads are a unique and delightful refuge for many rare species.

For miles around many of the Broads, the landscape is almost level, and even the lowest vantage point – a boat or a river bank – gives a view clear across the myriad tiny bays and inlets that characterize these vast man-made lakes. At first, little can be seen but acres of still water, miles of reeds rippling in the breeze and the occasional copse of alder. A closer study reveals one of the richest of all Britain's wildlife habitats.

In summer, the Broads teem with birds. If the characteristic 'booming' cry of the bittern is now rarely heard, there are still many other birds to catch the eye and ear. Where sallow and hawthorn bushes grow among the tall reedbeds, summer finds all kinds of warblers thriving in the mixed habitat. Here, reed warblers, red-brown and rather plain, sing their harsh song of even, repeated notes. Here, too, can be heard the more frantic warble of the sedge warbler as it dances through the air on its song-flight. And, very occasionally, the startling staccato song of the rare Cetti's warbler rattles out as it skulks at the base of the sallow bushes.

Once almost as rarely heard as Cetti's warbler, the bell-like call of the bearded tit, or reedling, is now an increasingly common summer sound on the Broads. Occasionally you may glimpse this tiny moustachioed buff and black bird as it whirrs across the reedbeds, carrying food to its young, before diving quickly out of sight.

Easier to see are the birds that live or feed out on the water. Greylag and Canada geese are hard to miss as they flap awkwardly into the air. The beautifully coiffured great crested grebe is less obvious but equally distinctive as it dives neatly for fish in the calm water.

A LAST REFUGE

The Broads have long provided a last refuge for a number of rare species of bird. Summer is the best time to see a marsh harrier, a native Broadlands resident, gliding low over the pools and dykes looking for young water birds, its chocolate and gold plumage glowing in the sun. Sightings are rare, though, for there are less than 30 breeding pairs of this beautiful bird in Britain. The large, white-plumed spoonbill with its distinctive bill is easier to see, but even this summer visitor from Holland is no longer common.

The Broads, too, are the last refuge for one of our rarest and most beautiful insects, the swallowtail butterfly. These lovely butterflies, with their distinctive wing-eyes and long wing-tails, depend entirely on the increasingly rare fenland plant, the milk parsley, and in June they can sometimes be seen sipping the nectar from the feathery white flowers of this small plant.

June also sees many of the Broadland plants at their best. Where water meets land, a rich community of damp-loving plants makes up the fen. The variety is enormous and from a boat you can see a delightful succession of velvety reedmace and other reeds and bulrushes, great hummocks of tussock and saw sedge, and banks of deep-pink agrimony, a favourite haunt of butterflies. Both yellow and purple loosestrife stand tall here, and the bright glow of the exotic Himalayan and orange balsams can often be

BROADLAND SURVIVOR
Protected status has enabled the bearded tit or reedling to survive man's attacks on its natural habitat.

WILDLIFE ON THE BROADS
The peaceful waters of the Broads are a haven for an abundance of birds, small mammals and plants. On a summer's day, the swish of reeds in the breeze mixes with the chattering song of the sedge warbler or a quiet splash as a coypu drops into the water. Out beyond the reeds, all kinds of waterfowl dabble and dive, while on the bank a rare swallowtail butterfly sips on milk parsley. Up above, a watchful marsh harrier scans the reeds for prey and a Canada goose flaps lazily by.

KEY TO THE SPECIES
1 *Marsh harrier*
2 *Great crested grebe*
3 *Water lilies*
4 *Mallard (male)*
5 *Otter*
6 *Canada goose*
7 *Coot*
8 *Coypu*
9 *Heron's nest*
10 *Norfolk aeshna dragonfly*
11 *Bittern*
12 *Water vole*
13 *Sedge warbler*
14 *Sedge warbler's nest*
15 *Meadowsweet*
16 *Heron*
17 *Moorhen*
18 *Swallowtail butterfly*
19 *Milk parsley*
20 *Hemp agrimony*
21 *Purple loosestrife*
22 *Southern marsh orchid*

SWALLOWTAIL
(left) Armed against predators by its ingenious camouflage – which fools birds into aiming for its tail – this lovely butterfly has fared badly against man's attacks on its habitat, and it is now confined entirely to the Broads.

EARLY MARSH
(right) Damp and marshy ground on the fringes of the Broads succour the purple blooms of this rare orchid.

BEWICK'S SWANS
(below) Of all the winter visitors to the Broadlands, few are more beautiful than the Bewick's swans, named after the celebrated 18th century bird illustrator Thomas Bewick. Come autumn, great flocks of these swans, often hundreds strong, wing their way in V-formation over the Broads, some to stay and some to pass on south.

seen. Very occasionally, the wonderful royal fern, with its vast feathery leaves, may be seen here as well. On the landward side, the fen is often backed by 'carr', a light scrubby woodland made up mainly of alders which have invaded the marsh.

Come autumn, the character of the Broads changes subtly. The flowers fade and die, and the reed and sedge warblers leave for Africa. But the departing birds are replaced by an almost continuous stream of migrants flying south from northern Britain, Scandinavia and the Arctic. All kinds of waders, large and small, may stop for a few days or more, before flying on to warmer climes.

Besides waders, all kinds of duck may visit, though less frequently now since pollution has reduced the water plants. Commonest, apart from the ubiquitous mallards, are tufted ducks and pochards bobbing on the water in cleanly patterned flocks, sometimes called 'rafts'. They dive to feed, or doze with their bills tucked under their mantle feathers.

WINTER ON THE BROADS

As winter approaches, local anglers turn their thoughts to pike, for the Broads hold some of Britain's largest. These fierce predators, sometimes weighing up to 40 pounds, lurk among the submerged reeds, ambushing shoals of roach and bream. Otters, too, prey on these fish – they still pass through the Broads and may even breed in very small numbers but they are rarely, if ever, seen. In November, just a couple of dozen bean geese may flap clumsily down into the Yare valley, their traditional wintering ground – one of the few sites in Britain where these large northern birds winter. They are grazing birds, like the white-fronted geese that often accompany them, and the grass marshes of the valley are crucial to their survival.

In mid-winter, the Broads are bleak and cold and little seems to stir in the damp reedbeds. But occasionally a hen harrier may be seen scanning the marshes, or a short-eared owl, hunting for voles. Near dusk they may be joined by a ghost-white barn owl and, as darkness falls, rooks and jackdaws flutter noisily to their roosts, while chevrons of gulls drift in from fields and rubbish tips for a quiet night on the Broads.

As winter loses its grip, lapwings return to the marshes, twisting through the grey skies and tumbling earthwards with hoarse cries, only to swerve up at the last possible moment. Male snipe roller-coaster on the wind, their taut tail-feathers thrumming out a deep bleating note. The snipe is now much less common in the Broads than it was once – since it prefers damp ground for its nest and efficient drainage has reduced the number of possible sites.

In spring, the mudflats on Breydon Water, where the rivers Yare, Bure and Waveney join, come alive. Wheeling in against a backdrop of Great Yarmouth chimneys and rooftops come armies of waders. Most distinctive are the ringed plovers, with their neat black-banded breasts, but 15 or more species of wader may feed here on a busy day, including such rarities as the broad-billed sandpiper.

FLOURISHING DYKES

As spring warms the grazing-marsh dykes, the cleanest of them fill with water-plants once more. Numerous pondweeds (potamogetons) grow beneath the surface, while bright green duckweeds float on top. Most flowers are white, but the water violet adds a splash of colour. Perhaps most interesting is the rare and curious

watersoldier, a fleshy-looking plant which bobs to the surface in late spring after spending the winter well below the water.

These dykes were once the haunt of another strange creature, the coypu. This large rodent was an immigrant from South America, brought to England in 1929 for its fur; it escaped or was released into the wild and was soon considered a pest because of the damage it did to banks and crops. Concerted efforts to eradicate the coypu have been so effective that it is now considered extinct in this region.

As the days lengthen and warm, and summer comes again, the dykes may provide a sighting of one of the Broadlands' most delightful creatures, the lovely Norfolk aeshna (pronounced 'eeshna') dragonfly, as beautiful, fragile and rare as the Broadlands themselves.

NORFOLK AESHNA DRAGONFLY
(above) Unique to the Broads, the Norfolk Aeshna has the scientific name aeshna isosceles *because of the bright green isosceles triangle on its abdomen. In summer, this brilliant dragonfly is often to be seen hawking over the dykes and ponds of the Broads, sometimes well after sunset. Late in the summer, the male supports the female as she lays her eggs in plants or floating wood; when she has finished laying, the male lifts her into the air again.*

Marsh Sow-thistle

Milk Parsley

Cowbane

MARSH SOW-THISTLE *(Sonchus palustris)* Stalkless leaves clasp the thick, angled stem with long pointed lobes. Black glandular hairs clothe the flowers of this 35-120″ (90-300cm) rarity of E. Anglian reedbeds. Pale lemon blooms open July-September.

COWBANE *(Cicuta virosa)* A rare plant of ditches and marshes – but locally common in Norfolk – cowbane is very poisonous. A robust, erect 12-52″ (30-130cm) perennial, the leaflets are almost linear, with sharply toothed edges. White flowers open in July and August.

MILK PARSLEY *(Peucedanum palustre)* A tall, 20-60″ (50-150cm) biennial plant, locally abundant in East Anglian marshes but very rare elsewhere. It is the foodplant of the swallowtail butterfly. Small, greenish-white flowers in July-September are followed by oval, ribbed fruits.

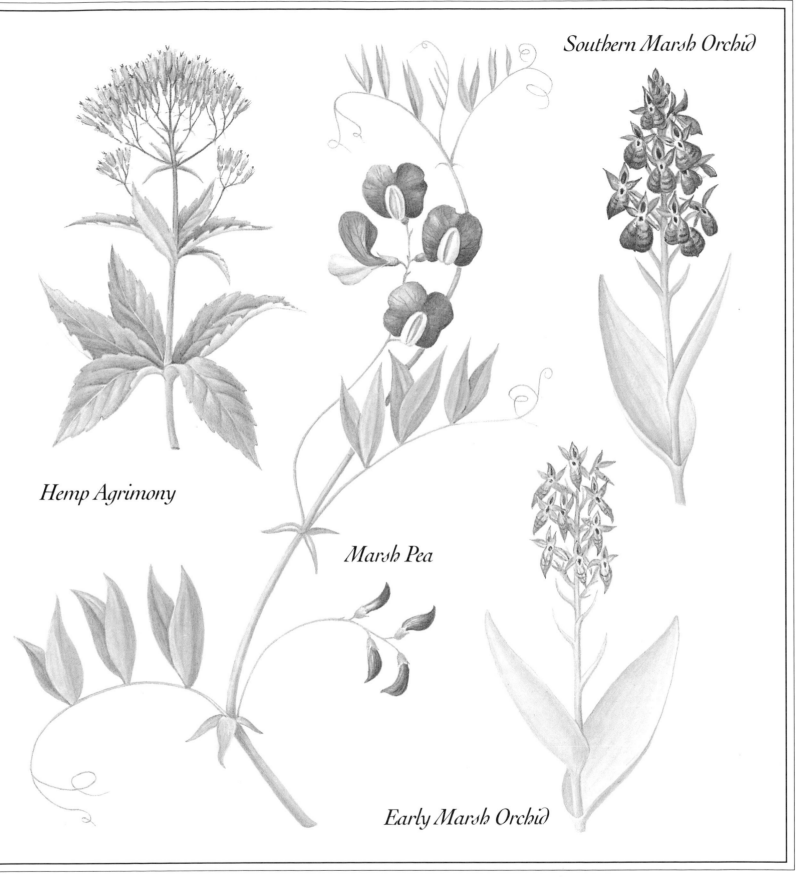

Southern Marsh Orchid

Hemp Agrimony

Marsh Pea

Early Marsh Orchid

HEMP AGRIMONY (*Eupatorium cannabinum*) Belonging to the daisy family, this large 12-48″ (30-120cm) perennial has densely packed heads of dull pinkish flowers from July-September. The reddish stem and the oppositely arranged toothed leaves are covered with short, soft hairs.

MARSH PEA (*Lathyrus palustris*) Rarely seen, this 24-48″ (60-120cm) pea grows in wet meadows and fens, climbing up other plants by means of tendrils. The stems are winged and the 2 or 3 pairs of leaflets narrow. After the bluish-purple flowers in May-July, black pods develop.

SOUTHERN MARSH ORCHID (*Dactylorhiza majalis*) Quite common on areas of wet, alkaline peat in southern and western England and Wales. Flowerspikes of closely arranged rose-purple flowers up to 24″ (60cm) long are seen from June-August. The leaves may be spotted.

EARLY MARSH ORCHID (*Dactylorhiza incarnata*) A very variable orchid – the subspecies *incarnata* is widespread and often abundant in wet, alkaline meadows. The leaves are unspotted and the sturdy 6-16″ (15-40cm) flowerspike bears flesh-pink blooms May to July.

Bittern

Female

Bearded Tit *Male*

BITTERN *(Botaurus stellaris)*
A secretive 30″ (76cm) member of
the heron family living in reedbeds,
concealed by its mottled colouring
and vertical stance. Its deep booming
call is audible up to 3 miles away.
The female builds a nest among the
reeds and lays 5-6 olive brown eggs.

BEARDED TIT *(Panurus biarmicus)*
Now often known as bearded
reedlings, these 6½″ (17cm) social
birds make deep nests of dried
leaves among the reed bases.
5-7 creamy eggs are laid April-July
in each of 2-3 broods. Only males
have black 'moustaches'.

Sedge Warbler

Reed Warbler

Cetti's Warbler

SEDGE WARBLER (*Acrocephalus schoenobaenus*) Distinguished by a pale eyestripe and black-streaked back, this 5″ (13cm) summer visitor nests among dense damp vegetation; 5-6 pale-greenish, finely speckled eggs are laid in May. Harsh and sweet notes make up its song.

CETTI'S WARBLER (*Cetti cetti*) Announcing its presence from deep cover with loud staccato bursts of *chewee*, this shy 5½″ (14cm) bird with a cocked tail resembles a small nightingale in colour. It feeds on insects and lays 4 reddish eggs in an untidy nest in May.

REED WARBLER (*Acrocephalus scirpaceus*) A frequent, loud *chur-chur-chur*, like the grating of two pebbles, gives away this 5″ (13cm) summer visitor. A cup-shaped nest of dried plant material is slung between the reeds and 4 pale green eggs are laid in May.

The Bittern

**The rare bittern – only about half a dozen are left on the Broads –
spends most of its life perfectly camouflaged behind a screen of
reeds, with only its booming call to give it away.**

The marsh is silent. Thin tendrils of mist curl up to mark the hidden ditches and runnels before dissipating above the corn-coloured beds of reed, while splinters of ice on the peaty pools bear witness to the coldness of the night frost. Then from the centre of the marsh echoes a low double note, like a distant foghorn, repeated several times.

Despite the cold early months, the mating season has begun, and a bittern is singing its unique song. Called 'booming' it carries several miles and is the reason for the birds scientific name *Botaurus*, from the latin meaning 'the bellowing of a bull'. Bitterns spend virtually all their lives in the dense cover of the reeds, so a loud locatable song is a necessity both for a male to advertise his territory, and for amorous bitterns to find each other among the reedstems where visibility is often only a few feet.

A large, roundwinged member of the heron family, the bittern is shy and secretive, seldom leaving the cover of the reeds. When it does, it flies with slow, deliberate wingbeats before dropping back into another part of the marsh. Disturbed, the bittern freezes, its bill pointing skywards at the end of a long outstretched neck imitating the vertical lattice of the reedstems, and perfectly camouflaged by its brown, black and gold-flecked plumage. This habit of remaining motionless, and only flying off at the close approach of an enemy, may work with natural predators, but it has proved a disastrous strategy against ill-disposed men with guns.

THE DECLINING POPULATION

Unhappily, the Victorian habit of shooting anything rare or unusual took a heavy toll of the hapless bittern. This, together with the attentions of egg collectors and gamekeepers, and the drainage of fens and marshes meant that bitterns became extinct as a British breeding species in 1886. In 1911, however, booming was once again heard in Norfolk, when a pair bred successfully again. Under the protection of sympathetic land owners, a slow recolonization took place especially in the Norfolk Broads. By 1954, no fewer than 60 boomers were recorded

THE SHY BOOMER
*(left) Sitting in characteristic pose with head
lowered and shoulders hunched up, the female
remains beautifully concealed as she protects
her young. Both sexes are striking brown birds
streaked with black and buff, with black
crowns and moustaches and yellow bills. The
young are similar with paler streaks.*

in the Broads, and bitterns were also breeding in Suffolk and Lincolnshire, and as far away as Lancashire and Somerset.

Unfortunately, numbers began to decline again during the late 1950s for a variety of reasons. Many rivers and streams had been affected by an excess of raw sewage causing massive algal growth and a decline in the aquatic invertebrates and fish on which the bittern feeds. At the same time, an increase in boat traffic on the broads and rivers not only caused direct damage to plants from propeller damage and wash, but also stirred up mud, cutting out light to aquatic plants – the basis of the food chain on which the bittern depends. The bittern population on the Broads may also have suffered from the decline in the cutting of reeds and marsh hay – the cutting had previously kept clear valuable fishing sites which ran right into the very heart of the reedbeds.

Use of pesticides may also have adversely affected the bittern. But while other birds known to be affected by pesticides have increased in number during the last decade as the more harmful chemicals were withdrawn, the bittern population is still going down. In 1985, there were about 35 boomers left in Britain, with just half a dozen on the Norfolk Broads, and over half the national population at only three sites – all nature reserves run by the Royal Society for the Protection of Birds for the Nature

BITTERN REVEALED
(below) Forced out beyond the reedbeds to hunt for food by wintry conditions, a bittern stalks through fronds of mare's tail, its streaky camouflage no longer so effective.

Conservancy Council.

The number of booming males may be less than the number of nests, since bitterns can be polygamous, a male having more than one female. However, after mating, the male takes no further interest in the activities of the female. She builds the nest platform amongst the brittle litter of dead stems from previous years, lays 5 to 6 olive-brown eggs and incubates these until they hatch some 25 days later. After another two weeks, the young begin to leave the nest but the female continues to feed them for some weeks. Like the adults, they quickly become adept at clambering around in the reedbeds, clasping bundles of reeds in each foot and moving slowly through the tall stems like stiltwalkers.

DECLINE AND FALL?

Like many other birds, bitterns suffer considerably in cold winters, when their food is locked up by the ice and the reedheads hang heavy with hoar frost. They eat fish, eels, water insects, frogs, toads, earthworms, small mammals and birds – most of their food comes from the water. During hard weather, bitterns have often been picked up, emaciated and suffering from starvation, although quite a number of these are probably continental birds which have come to Britain to escape the worst of the Northern European winter.

For British bitterns the future is uncertain, and it remains to be seen whether numbers will continue to decline. It would be sad if a bird which has come back from extinction as a native breeding species within living memory, were to disappear again.

IN FLIGHT the heavily barred wings, appear broad and rounded. Wingbeats are slow with the head hunched into the shoulders.

THE FEET are long and strong for clambering about among the reeds and climbing up the stems.

THE EGGS 5-6 are laid on a flat pile of reedstems amongst the dense vegetation in April-May.

The Peak District

The Peak District – Britain's first national park – occupies a 540-square-mile oval of magnificent scenery set like a haven in the heart of the country. Here, the Pennine Hills snake through the region, forming the tail-piece to England's geological backbone and presenting a natural barrier to the encroachment of the giant industrial cities which flank the Peak District on all sides. In the north, high bleak moorlands and peaks over 2000 feet high melt gradually southwards over sweeping panoramas to soft green dales which echo year-round to the melodic burble of swift rivers.

THE DARK PEAK

HIGH MOOR

DRY-STONE WALLING

SHALE OUTCROP

CLOUGH

RESERVOIR

ASHWOODS

LIMESTONE CLIFFS

THE WHITE PEAK

QUARRY

DALE

OLD MINE WORKINGS

LAND OF CONTRASTS
*(above) The Peak District has
two distinct sections, which,
effectively, mark the dividing
line between upland and
lowland England. The hard
gritstone of the Dark Peak
tends to bleak moorland,
with livid gashes of exposed
rock. By contrast, the light
limestone of the White Peak
is richly clothed in green.*

THE PEAK
DISTRICT

The Peak District as a whole comprises
two main areas of different character,
known as the White Peak and the Dark
Peak. The White Peak is the southern plateau of
limestone, bounded by Ashbourne in the south
and a northern arc of towns comprising Buxton,
Castleton, Bakewell and Matlock. This is a
pastoral area with large fields edged by limestone
walls and a river system that has carved deep
into the bright soft rock to produce the gorges,
cliffs and valleys of the Dales. Here the Wye,
Derwent, Manifold and Dove rivers flow swiftly
along their narrow valleys, following the courses
set in the great Ice Age; the vertical gorge cut
by the Dove reveals a slice of multi-layered
young rock, showing different striations down
to the snaking river-trench in the ancient limestone base. In places monolithic spurs, such as
Tissington Spires and Ilam Rock, have become
separated from the rock wall by the action of
water and ice.

Travelling northwards from Ashbourne – the
gateway to the Peak – the air begins to get
noticeably colder. In winter, the landscape may
suddenly fill with driven snow, under which the
great fields lose their chequering of low walls,

and wind-sculpted drifts block the roads and
bar entrance to the Peak.

The Dark Peak sits on the White Peak like a
helmet, its brooding presence a barrier on all
sides except the south. A harsher country, the
darkness stems from the gritstone and shale, the
mantle of peat bogs, the brown heather, and
the burnished acidic water. Coming eastwards
from the flat Cheshire plain, the dim blunt-
sided plateau of Kinder Scout – at 2088ft the
highest of eight peaks over 2000ft in the area –
never seems to get any closer until suddenly, at
the little 19th century textile towns of Glossop
and Hayfield, the mountain moor looms directly
overhead, its steep sides scarred by generations
of hiking boots. In the dead of winter the torrent
of Kinder Downfall freezes solid over its headlong fissure at the brink of this plateau. The top
of Kinder Scout is a maze of deep peatbogs and
confusing horizons, upon which impenetrable
mists can drop in seconds: it is a dangerous
place and has claimed many lives.

LIMESTONE AND GRIT

The smooth pastoral undulations of the White
Peak and the primeval scars and livid outcrops
of the Dark Peak owe their differing natures to
startling geographical transformations which
can be traced back three hundred million years.

At that time the limestone heart of the Peak District began to build up at the bottom of a shallow sea. Over the following millenia shell-sand, corals and huge, dead sea lilies accreted layer by layer, enclosed by reefs which can still be identified in the fossil-rich hills and ridges of Castleton and the upper valley of the Dove, now around 1000 feet above sea level. River mud from the north slid gradually into the deeper water around a shallow central lagoon and in time became shale. The rivers also brought down hard gravelly sediments which petrified into millstone grit – hard, durable rock which was used to make millstones. In the north, this dark rock forms the landscape's massive skeleton, from which all else has been scoured away by the action of wind, frost and water.

Millstone grit rears up dramatically from north to south along the Derbyshire Dome. This was the largest of a great series of folds in the area caused by enormous pressure from within the earth's crust. Upthrusting revealed the layers of grit, shale and coal, laid down earlier. As the land alternately rose above the water of the lagoon and sank beneath it during folding, forests grew, which turned to peat and, finally, after resubmersion, coal. When the Dome was again thrust up from warm seas, after the 120 million years of the Mesozoic era,

it became riddled with complex drainage channels scoured out by the sea sluicing away from the long humps of earlier folds. These were the antecedents of the valleys which, scraped bare by the glaciers of the Ice Age and further eroded by the water of countless winters, still fissure the high bleak plateaux. Weathering later stripped out the shale and coal, leaving only the grit-stone, except for a patch in the south where that too has been worn away down to the limestone core.

THE PEAK'S EARLY SETTLERS

Despite winter's biting cold, there are signs that humans settled in the Peak District from the Ice Age onwards. Neolithic farmers were the first to settle, around 3000 BC, and their tombs remain in the form of eight chambered barrows in the White Peak, among which is Five Wells on Taddington Moor, the highest megalithic tomb in Britain at 1400ft above sea level. About 1000 years later, men of the late Neolithic Age erected the 40 stones of Arbor Low circle: weighing 8 tons each, and fashioned with tools of stone, bone and antler, these lie on an earth platform surrounded by a ditch and a 50ft mound. Dominating the skyline from the frowning hill of Mam Tor is the largest of a dozen Iron Age forts, dating from about 500 BC. Castleton village, in its shadow, housed later settlers who mined the fringe of the exposed limestone for lead or Blue John – an attractive fluorspar veined with colour from pink to dark purple. And the lofty isolation of Flash – at 1518ft the highest village in England – made it a safe refuge for coiners, whose activities immortalized the village name as the underworld term for counterfeit money.

A region of startling contrasts, with open sunny pastures, wooded rivulets and naked frost shattered pinnacles, the Peak District is home to a wealth of beautiful and unexpected flora and fauna.

GRITSTONE RIDGE *(above) Standing to the east of the Dark Peak, Stanage Edge is much favoured by climbers – its dark gritstone and heather moorland presenting sombre and dramatic views. Unfinished millstones are still to be found strewn at the bottom of the Edge.*

GREEN DALE *(left) The valley of the Dove typifies the green and gentle southern area of the Peak District. Here, the limestone landscape is softened by abundant ashwoods. The valley cuts through a gently undulating plateau 1000ft above sea level.*

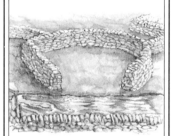

127

Peakland Wildlife

The variety of habitats in the Peaks benefits a wide range of wildlife: red grouse, a dwarf butterfly, mountain pansies, wood tiger moths and curlews are just some of the species to be seen.

The Peak District, with the Dark Peak to the north and White Peak to the south, straddles the divide between the low ground of southern England and the uplands of the North. Here, northern species such as cloudberry and bearberry have their southernmost limits; while southern species, such as white bryony, a hedgerow scrambler, are absent or very much scarcer farther north.

The Dark Peak is itself subdivided, comprising the High Peak north of the Sheffield–Whaley Bridge road and the West Moors south of it. Kinder Scout is the central spine of the High Peak, clothed in heather moor and bursting out into dark outcrops of hard rock along the ridges. The valleys below have clear, rapid streams and large, deep reservoirs; many of the side slopes are clothed in forestry plantations of exotic conifers, where sparrowhawks are frequent and red squirrels may still be found. The moors themselves have red grouse in the tall heather and golden plovers in the eroded peat hags and cotton grass moors. The grazing areas on the moors are divided by dry-stone walls of the same dark stone as the rock outcrops where ring ouzels and wheatears sing in spring. It is a rich, dark landscape which blends gently into the dark industrial towns on its fringe.

FROM DARK TO WHITE

The White Peak is quite different. Here, the high ground is clothed with bright green grass, cropped short by hundreds of sheep, and crossed by dry-stone walls which shine white in the sun and draw a pattern of thin white lines on the land. Big new quarries scar the lower slopes; old ones have blended in with the softening effects of years of erosion. The limestone itself is riddled with caves. Rivers and streams disappear underground and flow through deep potholes before emerging once more into the light, to flow quickly through narrow valleys, beloved

FOREIGN TROUT
(left) The rainbow trout was brought to this country from North America in the 19th century, and now threatens to oust our native brown trout from the few well-oxygenated streams where they both thrive. Living a maximum of nine years, it has established successful natural breeding populations in a few areas.

by dippers and grey wagtails.

The sides of the valleys are draped in ash-woods. Pollen analysis from nearby peat bogs reveals that there was little or no ash present in the woods after the last Ice Age relented. Perhaps wych elm was dominant then; but oakwoods would not have been common on the limestone. Oaks grow freely on lime only where it is very wet, such as in western Ireland. With oak unable to take a strong hold, the way was clear for the ash, which thrives on lime, to become dominant when woods flourished once again.

Some fine ash woodlands can be found at Dovedale, one of the most famous and picturesque dales of the Peak. Other ash woodlands are in the Wye Valley, and more can be explored in Lathkill, Monsal and Miller's Dale.

WHITE PEAK WILDLIFE
Woodland on the edge of the dales is of ash, yew and whitebeam. Here shelter escaped fallow deer and occasional badgers. Merlin and ring ouzel can be spotted in the Dark Peak. The introduced little owl eyes up a sunbathing lizard – a potential meal. A glow-worm – the female beetle emits the most light – shelters by day on a plant of the hillside, the beautiful, bright-yellow globe flower.

KEY TO FEATURES AND SPECIES
1 Dark Peak
2 Wooded clough
3 Ash
4 Wych elm
5 Limestone cave
6 Dale
7 Whitebeam
8 Little owl
9 Yew
10 Wood tiger moth
11 Female merlin
12 Dark green fritillary
13 Fallow deer
14 Orange tip
15 Badgers
16 White bryony
17 Globe flower
18 Dipper
19 Meadow cranesbill
20 Butterbur
21 Greater burnet saxifrage
22 Ring ouzel
23 Hart's tongue fern
24 Bird's foot trefoil
25 Thyme
26 Glow-worm
27 Monkey flower
28 Common lizard
29 Lily of the valley

129

These ashwoods have an extremely rich flora and luxuriant undergrowth. The soil is relatively rich, and the tree canopy thin and broken, allowing in plenty of light to the benefit of shrubs and ground cover. Hazel, dogwood, spindle, buckthorn, privet and elder are all common; mountain currant is plentiful in the Dovedale woods.

Limestone cliffs and grassland also have fascinating plants. Bird cherry and globe flower sprout from crevices out of reach of grazing animals; bloody cranesbill, mountain pansy and Nottingham catchfly are among the local plants to be found here. Birdsfoot sedge is found only here and on the Cumbrian coast where it grows less plentifully. There are some fine butterflies, too. Dark green fritillaries – large, chequered orange insects – are sometimes seen over the hills, whereas a dwarf form of the orange tip can be found in the dales, where wood tiger moths also fly by day.

Here and there are lead mines, old and disused now, with spoil heaps colonized by some special flora – alpine pennycress and spring sandwort, pansies and thyme. Where old mines and quarries have spilled out rock and scree, wheatears take advantage of the rough ground and nest in cavities under loose stones. Little owls may hide away in deep holes or on flat ledges in the old quarry face.

The White Peak has some special birds of its own. Black grouse still hang on, though numbers

UPLAND PLOVER
(above) A golden plover incubating its eggs achieves a successful disappearing act, melting into the grassy moorlands on which it breeds. The off-duty bird often stands guard on a nearby hummock. About 400 pairs breed in the Peak District National Park.

DOVEDALE MONKEY FLOWER
(above right) The monkey flower is a garden escape, and came originally from an island near Alaska. It has become naturalized in the wet places of Britain by following the waterways of 19th century canals. It spreads by means of creeping roots.

GRASS IN SEED
(right) Common cotton grass is a native perennial, whose fluffy cotton-wool seed heads dance 24in. (60cm) above spreading roots. The seed tufts make excellent stuffing for cushions and pillows.

INTRODUCED HARE
(left) The mountain, or blue, hare inhabits open moorland, feeding on heather, cotton grass, bilberry shoots and rushes. Indigenous to Scotland, the mountain hare of the Peak is at the southern limit of its British range.

have declined lately – partly due to disturbance of their habitat and partly, it is thought, due to shooting. The remnant population is isolated by many miles from the other British groups which are found in Wales, the North and Scotland. Short-eared owls hunt the moors, while whin-chats occupy the grassy fringes; and common sandpipers haunt the shallow streams. A few pairs of twites, upland finches akin to the linnet, also breed here.

way up above the mosses. Overhead, snipe may be heard 'drumming' – the bleating noise they make as they dive steeply down – caused by the stiff outer tail feathers throbbing through the rushing air.

Visiting birds have nested in the Peak in recent years. The fieldfare, normally a winter visitor to Britain which comes here to escape the worst of the harsh continental winter weather, has settled to breed on Staffordshire and Derbyshire moors. But why it has chosen the Peak, when breeding is almost unknown in Britain as a whole, is a mystery.

There are also two unusual mammals in the Peaks District. Neither is commonly seen as their populations are small. In the Dark Peak, mountain hares, introduced from Scotland, hold on in small numbers. Further north, these hares turn white in winter but in the milder climate of the Peak they remain brown. The most extraordinary animals on the moors are the escaped red-necked wallabies, sometimes seen bounding over the tops, to the surprise of many walkers.

WOOD TIGER MOTH
The dramatically coloured males of this species can often be seen darting low over the heather and grassland, from late May to July, in search of the female, which stays under cover until evening. The caterpillars of the single brood feed on plantains and other low growing plants before hibernating.
They emerge in spring to feed again, then pupate.

HIGH SUMMER

A walk on a fine summer's day in the Peak District is a real joy – the sights and sounds a delight to eye and ear. The dales offer peace and seclusion, with still, deep pools beside dilapidated mills, and fast, clear streams running from them. Here, brown and rainbow trout rise as little grebes dive. In the surrounding woods, great spotted woodpeckers tap the tree trunks and pied and spotted flycatchers sally out from a perch to take a flying insect with acrobatic precision. In the tall ashes, but more especially where there are oaks too, the plaintive piping song of the wood warbler alternates with its other, more frequent, song – a long, shivering trill. The dipper's loud *zit zit* may be heard over water, as it flies upstream.

Away from the sheltered dales, cliff- and quarry-nesting kestrels hunt over the open fields and moors. Wheatears fly along the stone walls and stop to flick their tails and make harsh, irritated calls. Coming to the higher moors, red grouse may be heard defending their territories sometimes fighting, challenging one another with their *go-back, go-back* calls. Meadow pipits seem to be everywhere, rising in a slow, weak-looking flight to turn and sweep down, turning and banking from side to side as they come, uttering their thin little songs. Watching them, perhaps, may be cuckoos, intent on finding a pipit's nest in which to lay the unwelcome egg.

In spring and summer the air rings to the sound of singing curlews, and here and there the keen observer might trace unfamiliar calls to a displaying golden plover, in its song flight

GLOBE FLOWER
(left) The globe flower opens its shiny round flowers between May and August. This native perennial can reach 24in. (60cm) in height, and is common in parts of Scotland and the north of England, where it favours damp meadows, woods and scrub. A member of the buttercup family, it can be found in the Peak in moist, grassy areas.

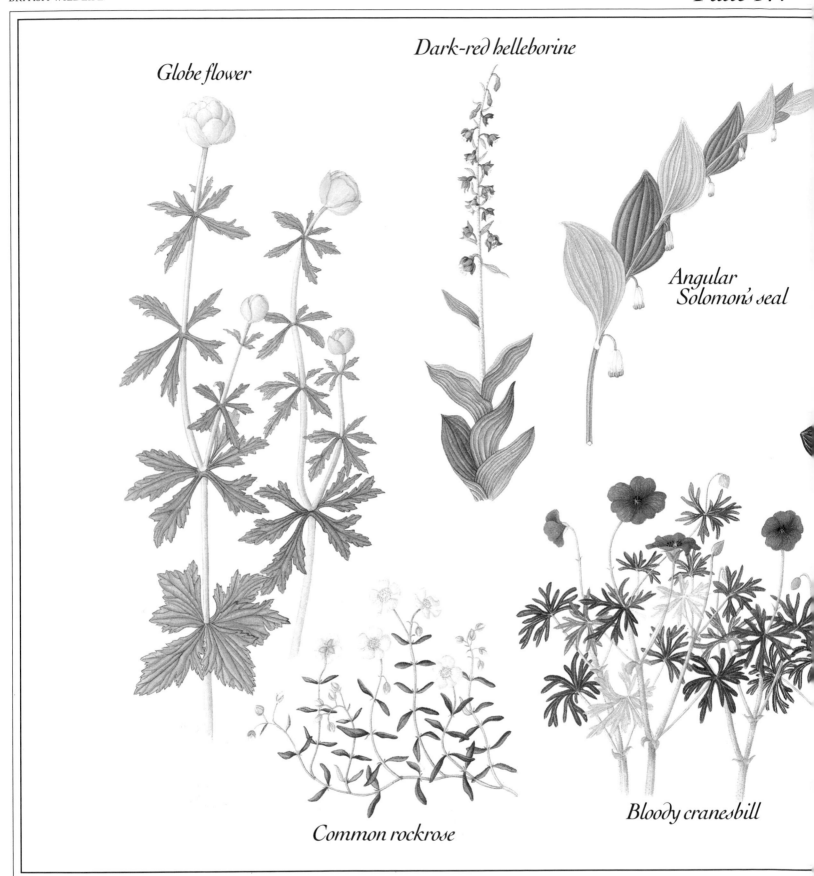

Globe flower

Dark-red helleborine

Angular Solomon's seal

Common rockrose

Bloody cranesbill

GLOBE FLOWER *(Trollius europaeus)* Forming clumps 8-24″ (20-60cm) high, this perennial grows in wet meadows and glades in upland areas north from south Wales and Derby. Leaves are deeply lobed, lower ones stalked. Pale globular flowers appear June – July.

COMMON ROCKROSE *(Helianthemum nummularium)* Common in chalky scrub and grass except in the far North, the sprawling 2-12″ (5-30cm) stems root where they touch the ground. The stalkless leaves are white below. Fragile flowers are seen June – September.

DARK-RED HELLEBORINE *(Epipactis atrorubens)* A local rare orchid of limestone rocks and woods in the North and West, single erect 8-24″ (20-60cm) stems are downy, with stalkless, folded leaves. A spike of slightly scented flowers is seen in June and July.

ANGULAR SOLOMON'S SEAL *(Polygonatum odoratum)* A rare plant of shade, in limestone woods of the North and West, stalkless, oval leaves are arranged on curved stems 6-8″ (15-20cm) long. Tubular, scented flowers hang on thin stalks June-July; round fruits are blue-black.

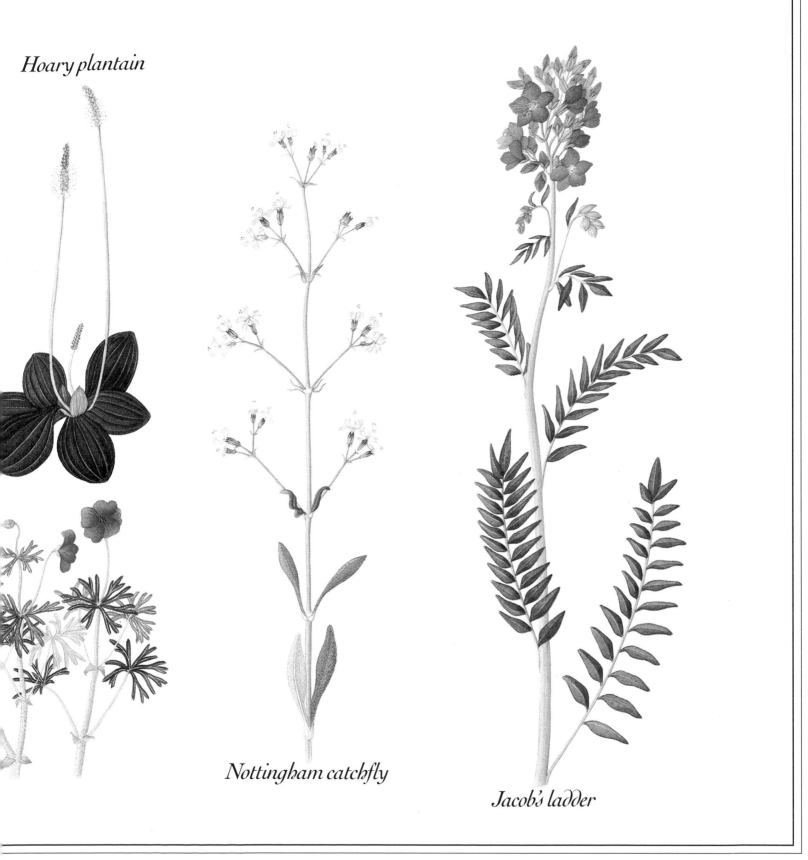

Hoary plantain

Nottingham catchfly

Jacob's ladder

BLOODY CRANESBILL *(Geranium sanquineum)* Large, solitary flowers are borne on 4-24" (10-60cm) stems July-August. It is a creeping, hairy, branched perennial, with round leaves cut deeply into narrow lobes. Found on limy grassland and rocks: widespread except in South-east.

HOARY PLANTAIN *(Plantago media)* Unlike other plantains, the dense heads of scented flowers are insect-pollinated. The flower stems, seen May-August, reach 12" (30cm). Oval leaves are hairy, with prominent veins. Common and widespread except on acid soils and in the North.

NOTTINGHAM CATCHFLY *(Silene nutans)* A scattered, local plant of dry chalky slopes and rocks. 10-31" (25-80cm) stems are sticky above to trap tiny flies. The leaves are softly hairy and nodding. Scented flowers with two-lobed petals open at dusk May-July, attracting moths.

JACOB'S LADDER *(Polemonium caeruleum)* A lovely but very local plant of slopes and remote valleys of northern, limestone mountains. 12-35" (30-90cm) unbranched stems bear leaves divided into 6-12 pairs of narrow leaflets and a loose head of vivid flowers, June and July.

Chinese character

Shoulder stripe

Pale tussock

CHINESE CHARACTER *(Cilix glaucata)* Common and widespread in England and Wales, this moth tricks predators when at rest by looking like a bird dropping. Two generations each year, adults fly at night in spring and again in summer. Larvae feed on thorn bushes.

PALE TUSSOCK *(Dasychira pudibunda)* Flying at night in May, large paler females have a wingspan of 2¾″ (7cm); males are smaller with highly sensitive antennae. Larvae have loose tufts of hairs – they feed on hops and deciduous trees, pupating over winter.

SHOULDER STRIPE *(Earophila badiata)* This moth flies March to April, and is abundant in hedges and copses where wild roses grow – the larvae feeding on the foliage at night, May-July. They pupate underground all winter. Widespread, but absent from the far north of Scotland.

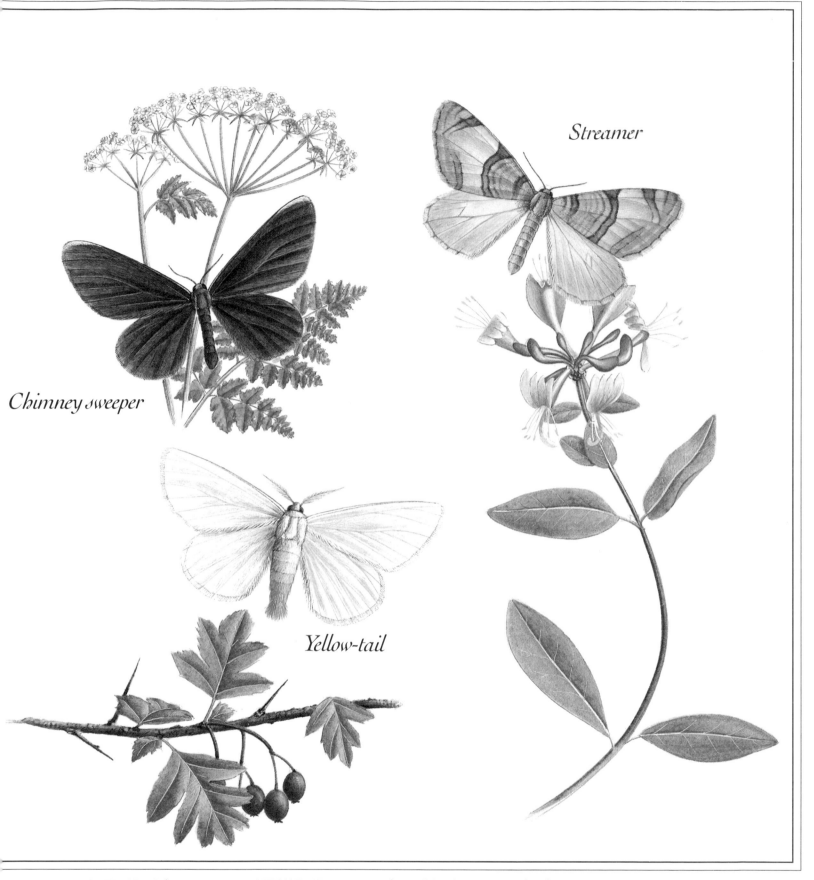

Chimney sweeper

Yellow-tail

Streamer

CHIMNEY SWEEPER *(Odezia atrata)* A distinctive, sooty moth that flies by day June-July, visiting flowers. Locally frequent in Wales, mid to north England and south Scotland in wet fields and woods. The larvae feed on pignut leaves and pupate underground over winter.

YELLOW-TAIL *(Euproctis similis)* Widespread, these hairy moths fly July-August. Males have dark dots on the forewings; females hide their eggs with hairs from the 'tail'. Black, patterned larvae overwinter, feed on tree leaves and pupate in May.

STREAMER *(Anticlea derivata)* A widespread moth occurring almost everywhere close to the foodplant, wild rose. The adults can be found at dusk in April and May, flying by hedges and copses. Long, twig-like larvae pupate June-July, emerging in spring.

The Curlew

The beautiful bubbling song of the curlew brings life to
the lonely moorlands each spring as this long-billed
wader flies in from the coast to nest and breed.

The haunting, melancholic call of the
curlew is one of the most memorable
summer sounds of the north and west
uplands. Returning each spring to their lonely
moorland breeding grounds, the curlews' liquid
cries echo across the valleys, advertising their
arrival long before the birds themselves come
into view.

Flying leisurely on long pointed wings, the
birds wheel in to land, flashing the white V on
their backs as they alight on the springy surface
of the boggy moor. Once settled, the curlew
melts into its surroundings, its speckled ash-
brown plumage providing a perfect camouflage
against the broken moorland. But though the
curlew can be difficult to spot, once seen, it is
certainly not hard to identify.

Almost the size of a herring gull, the curlew is
Britain's largest wader, but its most distinctive
feature is its remarkably long, decurved bill,
up to three times the length of its head. This
long slender bill – rivalled only by that of
the similar whimbrel – possesses a flexible
tip which is sensitive to movement, allowing
the curlew to detect and catch prey up to six
inches below the surface. So both at the water's
edge in winter and on the hillside in summer
the curlew can exploit food sources out of
the reach of other birds.

RETURN TO THE MOORS

Most curlews are paired before they arrive at
the breeding grounds, and probably remain
faithful to the same territories year after year.
The males lay claim to their territories by
circling above them and letting their rivals
know they are back.

As the curlew soars, so it sings, a breathtakingly beautiful song that begins slowly with
long, drawn-out, fluid notes during the glide.
These become faster and higher, until they
erupt into an exultant bubbling trill.

INLAND NESTER

*During the spring and
summer the curlew abandons
its coastal home for the damp
upland meadows and lonely
inland moors that offer
undisturbed nest sites and an
abundance of insect food.
Curlews may also be found
exploiting other inland
niches, nesting on lowland
pastures, arable land, heaths
and even sand dunes. This
adaptability has led to a
steady rise in their numbers
and there are now between
50-60,000 pairs breeding
in Britain.*

PRECOCIOUS CHICKS
Only 24 hours after hatching the curlew chicks are running in the grass around their nest hollow. Even though well camouflaged by their black and tan down, for the next 5-6 weeks, until they can fly, they stay very close to their protective parents. Come autumn, when the inland food supply wanes, they return to the coast to feed on invertebrates.

After his song flight, the male flies down and, prior to mating, runs after his mate with lowered breast and raised rump, his head drawn back and bill pointing down. Sometimes the pair may even play leapfrog. Males may also indulge in ritualized fighting among themselves, occasionally beating at each other with their wings and legs.

Having established their territory and re-affirmed their bond, the pair mould several hollows in the vegetation with their breasts. Then, choosing one, they line it with grass to form a soft bed for the 4 eggs, which are laid later at intervals of about 2 days.

DUTIFUL PARENTS

Both parents take it in turns to incubate the clutch, changing places twice-daily. Marauding crows with an eye to egg robbery are usually driven off by the off-duty bird, whose harsh alarm calls shatter the peace of the moor.

The chicks hatch after about 4 weeks. Well-camouflaged by their black and tan markings they leave the nest within 24 hours. If the chicks are threatened by a predator, the parents will feign injury, dragging one wing across the ground, to lure attention away from them.

A VARIED DIET

On moving inland to breed, the curlew exploits a wide variety of food, in particular, earth-worms, leatherjackets and other grubs which they prise out of the soft soil with their long bills. Curlews supplement this diet with snails and even small frogs, and they also eat seeds of grasses and the berries of other moorland plants. The young are soon able to forage for themselves, but a parent bird will often lead them to choice feeding places. Initially, the young curlews' bills are straight, but they soon start to lengthen and curve, reaching full length after about four months. Their plumage, too, is warmer brown than their parents' at first, though this gradually lightens to the adult colour.

When autumn comes to the moor and the heather flowers make great splashes of purple, the curlews, young and old, start to migrate, mostly southwards and westwards, to the lowland bordering the coast. Some spend the winter as far west as Ireland while others migrate as far south as France and Spain. But the travel is two-way, as immigrants from the Continent contribute to the 150,000 curlews which remain in Britain each winter.

CURLEW DISPLAY
As a climax to his breeding display – a trilling song flight followed by a running ground display – the male curlew may lift his wings, tips pointing backwards, quivering them to reveal their finely barred, silky white undersides. He then mates with his partner who then lays a single clutch of 4 eggs.

IN FLIGHT wingbeats are slow, steady and purposeful. There is a conspicuous white V on the back and the whitish underwing is heavily barred.

THE BILL can be up to 6″ (15cm) long in the female curlew but is shorter in the male.

THE EGGS are pointed, glossy and greenish-buff, spotted with brown. 4 are laid April-May in a hollow.

The Red-Necked Wallaby

**An astonishing sight on a grey winter's day in the Peak District,
the red-necked wallaby is a small Tasmanian marsupial now
regarded as a wild animal of Britain.**

Visitors to the Peak District rub their eyes in disbelief as they startle a small, hare-sized creature which bounds away at lightning speed across the moor and into cover, leaving the bewildered observers wondering if they have been seeing things.

EXOTIC IMMIGRANTS

The animal they have seen, unlikely though it seems, is the red-necked or Bennett's wallaby, a marsupial (pouched mammal) native to south-eastern Australia and Tasmania. From a handful of escapees from a private zoo near Leek during World War 2, a small population of these attractive aliens has managed to survive on heather moorland and thick scrub north-west of Leek and in woodlands near Hoo Moor in neighbouring Derbyshire. As well as the Peak District population, there is a small colony of feral red-necked wallabies in Ashdown Forest in Sussex, also the result of an escape from a private collection.

The Peak District population has fluctuated considerably over the years; the exceptionally hard winters of 1947-8 and 1962-3 took a heavy toll and several wallabies were found dead on the frozen moorland, cut off from their food by the thick blanket of snow. By 1970 there were less than a dozen animals. Numbers soon increased, however, and by 1977 there were about 20. But the wallabies were soon faced with a new threat – the land on which they lived was sold for sheep farming. The wallabies could not compete with the newcomers for grazing and shelter, and the bitter winter of 1978-9 brought them to the brink of extinction. Fortunately, the Peak Planning Board came to their rescue and purchased a large area of their habitat, from which the sheep were excluded, and 20-30 animals thrive in the Peak today.

LITTLE BOUNDER

In summer the wallabies hide in vegetation, but in winter they are easier to see and track over snow. At 24 inches tall, the wallaby is two inches taller than a hare, with a tail slightly longer than its body. It has short ears, and the typical kangaroo habit of bounding along on its hind legs with its front legs held close to its chest. Although active by day, wallabies are shy creatures, spending

AN INCREDIBLE JOURNEY
Only a fraction of an inch long at birth, the baby wallaby uses its minute front legs to haul itself up into its mother's pouch, finding its way by scent.

PASSENGER FARE
(left) Female wallabies produce two different kinds of milk at the same time – one to suit the newly born young, and another for the older sibling nearing independence. After a few months, the young wallaby will snatch plants from the safety of its mother's pouch, as she bends forward to feed. Like sheep or cattle, adult wallabies 'ruminate' to make the best use of poor quality vegetation – the finely shredded food passes into a special part of the stomach, where bacteria break down the tough cellulose walls of the plants. The resulting 'cud' is passed back to the mouth to be chewed a second time.

much time in cover from which they usually emerge only to feed.

If encountered in the open, a wallaby usually leaps away, alerted to danger by its acute hearing. When travelling at top speed it can reach over 40 miles an hour, and is airborne for as much as 70 per cent of the time. The long hind legs maintain a powerful spring-like action, and the heavy tail acts as a counterbalance.

PROTECTIVE POUCH

The wallaby lives on a diet composed mainly of heather, but also eats grasses, bilberry and cowberry leaves, bracken, birch leaves and pine needles. They grip the plants with their elongated lower incisor teeth, and chew them with a shearing action of their molar cheek teeth.

Female wallabies have pouches in which the young, which are born in a very immature state after a gestation period of only one month, are

BOXING RIVALS
(right) Before mating, rival male wallabies may fight for the females, boxing with their forepaws and kicking out with their powerful hind legs. Pregnancy does not necessarily immediately follow mating as the female can hold a foetus 'in store' – called embryonic diapause – enabling her to give birth to another baby as soon as the previous one has matured.

MOTHER AND JUVENILE
(below) Adult wallabies are usually solitary, though a juvenile may stay close to its mother for some months.

reared. At birth, the tiny wallaby clambers unaided over the mother's fur to reach the pouch. Once inside, it grasps one of the four teats, which acts as an anchor as well as a source of food. The baby grows fast, doubling its weight every 4½ weeks. It stays clamped to the teat for about 19 weeks, its eyes open five weeks later, and at 26 weeks it is fully covered with fur. By about 30 weeks, the young wallaby – known as a joey – takes its first look at the world, poking its head and forelimbs out of the pouch. It soon tries eating grass for itself when its mother stoops to feed. Later, it leaves the pouch for short exploratory journeys. As it gains confidence it stays out longer and longer, until at about 10 or 12 months, its mother refuses to let it return to its snug home. The joey stays close to her for a further few months, by which time her pouch may well be occupied by another tiny wallaby.

The Yorkshire Dales

In places awe-inspiring and in others intimate, the landscape of the Yorkshire Dales – an area of some 680 square miles – is one of dramatic variety. Bleak, open moorland is softened by the green, part-wooded valleys of Swaledale and Wensleydale to the east and Wharfedale and Ribblesdale to the south – rich, peaceful pasturelands criss-crossed by drystone walls. In the south limestone predominates, emerging triumphantly as towering cliffs and craggy outcrops, cut by swift-flowing streams which nourish the surrounding countryside.

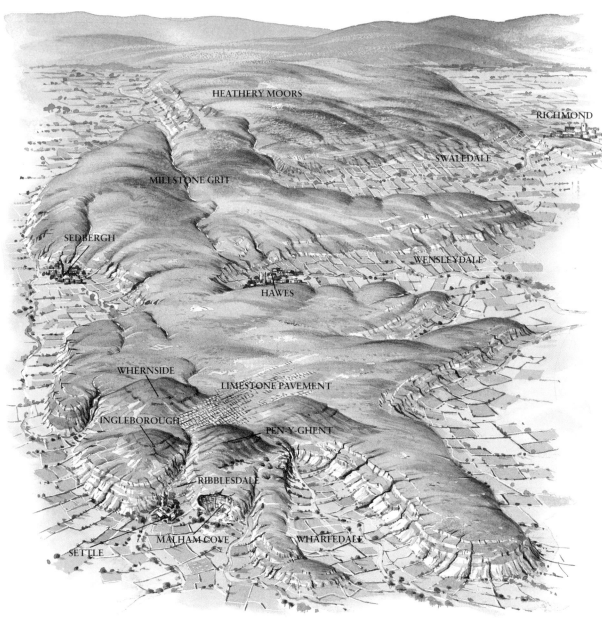

HEATHERY MOORS

RICHMOND

SWALEDALE

MILLSTONE GRIT

SEDBERGH

WENSLEYDALE

HAWES

WHERNSIDE

LIMESTONE PAVEMENT

INGLEBOROUGH

PEN-Y-GHENT

RIBBLESDALE

MALHAM COVE

WHARFEDALE

SETTLE

A RICH TAPESTRY
Situated in the central Pennines, the Yorkshire Dales is one of the most beautiful and varied landscapes in Britain. The tilting plateau of wild moorland is incised by a series of valleys which display an impressive range of limestone features.

THE YORKSHIRE DALES

Anyone who visits the Yorkshire Dales cannot help but be overwhelmed by the majesty and gentle beauty of this most distinctive landscape. Sitting astride the central Pennines, much of the Dales country comprises high heather moorland rising to over 2000 feet (600m). But the bleakness so characteristic of the Pennines to the north and south is tempered here by vast areas of limestone pasture and bright white rock and numerous long, green valleys – the Dales – which slash into the very heartland of the high moor country.

LIMESTONE LANDSCAPE

It is the limestone which dominates the scene, particularly in the southern part of the area where it forms fells over 1300 feet (400m) high. Not only is this rock visually dominant where it has been weathered white in the crags, scars, walls and buildings of the Dales, but it also forms a most intriguing assemblage of landforms resulting from the solution of the rock in slightly acid rainwater. Such a landscape is known as 'karst' (named after a region in Yugoslavia) and when combined with the effects of

glaciation as it is in the Dales, it is more correctly called 'glacio-karst'. Dry valleys and gorges and large areas of limestone pavement, disappearing and reappearing streams and extensive cave systems distinguish the Dales as one of the finest glacio-karst areas in Western Europe.

The karst is most spectacularly developed on the Great Scar Limestone, a 650 feet (200m) thick slab of limestone deposited some 330 million years ago in Lower Carboniferous times. The Great Scar and the Yoredale Series of rocks – a repeating sequence of shales, sandstones and limestones which overlies the Great Scar Limestone – form the basis of the Dales' geology. Because these beds rest upon a rigid, tilted block of the earth's crust they remain unfolded, but dip gently to the north and east. Elevated in the south-west, the Great Scar Limestone forms dramatic landscapes in the Three Peaks and Malham areas, but is overlain by a thick layer of Yoredale rocks in the north.

Glaciers and their meltwaters moulded the overall relief of the Dales country. Most main valleys have been deepened by the glacier ice and the evidence of glaciation is plain to see

142

When walking in the Dales, look out for the natural and man-made features which make this landscape so spectacular. Examples are:

DRY VALLEYS like Gordale Scar and Trow Gill, made by glacial meltwaters cutting through the frozen ground.

LIMESTONE SHELVES formed by natural weathering of the rock.

RUINED ABBEYS whose monks once reared sheep and mined for lead and iron ore.

CAVERNS formed by underground rivers. Gaping Gill is the largest limestone cave in Britain

---

lakes and wetlands all enveloped by vast tracts of forest. The first groups of wandering hunters and gatherers made little impression on the landscape, but as man became more sedentary so he began to change the face of the Dales.

Perhaps the biggest impact was made by forest clearance. Felling and grazing from Neolithic times have created in parts of the Dales an almost treeless landscape, and ancient woodland now survives only on steep and rocky slopes too inhospitable to farm. In contrast, man's historic structures have added greatly to the landscape. Early man left walled enclosures, henges and earthworks; Romans left roads; Norsemen left homesteads; Angles created the early nucleated villages, and medieval farmers left cultivation strips – lynchets – terracing many of the fells. Man's most spectacular contribution has been the enclosure of the land with thousands of miles of stone walls and the building of the Dales' wonderful stone villages.

Today, this pastoral landscape is increasingly threatened by modern mineral extraction, farming and afforestation, together with the pressures for greater tourism and recreational opportunities. Change should continue to take place, but there needs to be continuing harmony between man and nature to secure the future of the beautiful Dales landscape.

---

throughout the Dales. Many features are landmarks – Kilnsey Crag in Wharfedale is an ice-eroded spur; Cautley Crags in the Howgills are part of a glacial corrie; Raven Ray in Kingsdale is a glacial end moraine (sand and rock deposits at the snout of a glacier), and Ribblehead and Wensleydale contain major drumlin fields (hillocks of glacial deposits shaped beneath the moving ice).

Ice last retreated from the Dales about 13,000 years ago, leaving a harsh, barren wasteland in its wake. Gradually, however, as the climate warmed, plants and animals recolonized the area, and when early stone-age man returned to the Dales about 9000 years ago he entered a land of rich natural habitats, with streams,

THE UPLAND STREAM (above left) *Fast-flowing streams are a feature of the landscape, and cut through the limestone, tumbling over boulders, to form narrow, sometimes wooded, gorges. In places they emerge from the rock as a plunging waterfall, known locally as a 'force', before flowing on, becoming ever wider as they meander along the valley floor.*

LIMESTONE HILLS (left) *On the southern edge of the Dales the underlying limestone breaks through the surface, emerging from the emerald turf as craggy outcrops. Elsewhere it towers from the surrounding lowlands in sheer cliffs, and stretches along the hilltop as a broken limestone pavement.*

From Moor to Dale

From the high, heather-clad grouse moors, down to the
meadow-flanked trout streams which wind in the valley bottom,
the Dales' varied habitats shelter a wealth of wildlife.

Day breaks mistily over the dewy heather
and against the pale light of morning the
shape of the moorland is revealed. Cock
red grouse flutter in territorial flights; their
quacking songs seem almost to be telling the
traveller to *go back – go back – go back!* A
curlew bubbles its melancholy tribute to the
breaking of the dawn as it climbs steeply through
the chill air, then glides down over the wind-
swept moor on quivering wings.

Amid the ling a large black and green banded
emperor moth caterpillar lies still, awaiting the
warming rays of the sun. Shaggy-coated, horned
sheep forage among the poor vegetation while
healthy lambs slumber in cosy, bilberry-clad
hollows.

Small brown meadow pipits dash for cover as
a sleek little merlin breaks the skyline over a
ridge. Its flight is unusually laboured, however,
for the merlin has already struck and is holding
the limp-feathered form of a pipit in its talons.
The merlin's brood of four downy young sit in
an austere nest at the base of a tall clump of
heather, eagerly awaiting the return of their
parent with breakfast.

FROM THE TOP DOWN

A journey down through a Yorkshire Dale fittingly begins at the head, high up on the moors
of the Pennines. As the mist clears, the lower
lying areas of the moor are covered white,
almost snow-like, with masses of flowering
cotton grass – a useful guide for the fell walker
as it indicates the damper areas. With the sun
now climbing above the ridge, the first of the
black flies begin to plague the sheep, causing
them to stamp and twitch.

Where the ground falls away, dry-stone walls
enclose rough fields. Here, at the interface between agriculture and grouse moor, bracken
has encroached. Bracken flourishes because it
contains a compound of cyanide which acts as a
very effective defence mechanism against grazing; neither sheep or rabbits will eat bracken.
The grasses – sheeps fescue, moor mat grass
and brown bents – have, however, been eaten
hard back. Whinchats and wheatears – both
summer visitors – nest in this rough area. At the

edge of the heather, wild strawberries and soft
yellow rock-roses grow. A female brown argus
butterfly, whose caterpillars feed on rock-rose,
examines the foliage of this straggling plant in
search of a place to lay her eggs.

A lively stream bubbles out of the moorland
peat and has carved a steep sided valley. Large
naked boulders protrude. Gnarled by the harsh
environment, rowan trees struggle to maintain
a foothold. A white breasted cock ring ouzel
chatters anxiously as he keeps watch close by
his freshly hatched brood.

The underlying rock here is limestone and
where the hills roll over into the dale, white
stone outcrops. These calcareous hillsides have
a specialist flora of lime-loving plants. It is just
the sort of habitat in which the dark red helleborine – a very rare orchid – might be found.

Some of the stones are covered by a velvety
carpet of sheep-grazed turf, forming a tussocky
terrain. From here a pair of lapwings take to the
air to meet an intruding carrion crow. The lapwings' chicks are freshly hatched and at a very

COMMON COTTON GRASS
*(left) A lover of damp, peaty
soils, cotton grass is growing
here near the head of the
dale. Higher up, it will carpet
waterlogged areas of
moorland. Until the
cottony fruiting heads
appear in June the plant –
related to the sedges rather
than the grasses – is
inconspicuous.*

WILDLIFE IN THE YORKSHIRE DALES

Gritstone boulders break through the thin soil of the high moor but, lower down, the scars (cliffs) are of limestone. On these scars and on the broken limestone pavements grow lime-loving plants, finding shelter in the cracks. In addition to those seen here, wild thyme, purple saxifrage and dark red helleborine can be found, as well as polypody, spleenworts and other ferns. The brown argus butterfly is at the northern edge of its range in the Dales and may be replaced by the northern brown argus: both lay their eggs on rock-rose. Ravens and ring ouzels are birds of the hills. The raven will nest in a tree or on a rock ledge; the ring ouzel, too, nests on rock ledges or in a dry-stone wall or on a heathery slope in a gully. Herons and grey wagtails both rely on the stream for food, while the lapwing unearths insects from the fields. The widespread weasel hunts voles, mice and nesting birds.

KEY TO FEATURES AND SPECIES

1 *Ash*	12 *Walled fields*
2 *Limestone scar*	13 *Whinchat*
3 *Wych elm*	14 *Weasel*
4 *Shrub layer*	15 *Mountain everlasting*
5 *Grey heron*	16 *Limestone pavement*
6 *Grey wagtail*	17 *Thistle*
7 *Lapwing*	18 *Common rock-rose*
8 *Sycamore shelter belt*	19 *Mountain pansy*
9 *Heather*	20 *Lichens*
10 *Raven*	21 *Brown argus*
11 *Gritstone*	22 *Cock ring ouzel*

dangerous stage in life. Climbing and diving repeatedly, the irate parents force the black intruder to alter its tack.

Such is the intensity and vigour of the attack that the crow's mate has been allowed to slip in undetected. Perching on a rock, it cocks an inquisitive eye. A cryptically marked, downy plover chick sits tight, but its movement has already been detected by the crow. As its mate continues to distract the angered plovers, the robber pounces, quickly killing the chick with its strong black beak and then airlifting it away to feed a fast growing brood of young crows.

The unimproved pasture here is rich in flowering plants that provide a source of nectar for the diminutive small copper butterfly which pollinates the flowers as it feeds. Yellow birdsfoot trefoil, buttercups and tormentil, purpley-blue bugle, thymes and speedwells, and white daisies, chickweed and dropwort all grow flat on the ground, thus avoiding the grazing jaws of sheep and forming a marvellous miniature world of colour and delicate form.

FLANKING THE RIVER

By midday the sun is high above the dale and the horse-flies, known as clegs, are biting. Viewed from the shade of a dry-stone wall, the panorama of the flat-bottomed dale stretches below. Old hay meadows, mellowed by the flowering heads of buttercups, daisies, meadowsweet and great burnet, flank the river, whose course is traced by mature deciduous trees on either bank as it winds its way down the dale.

In the clear waters of the river, swim silver grayling, trout, salmon parr and myriad minnows, feeding on the darting mayfly and stonefly nymphs, and the larvae of caddis flies. In places the river disappears underground, only to reappear hundreds of yards downstream. In the winter months, when the water table is higher, the waters flow in full spate over the bleached stones of the now dry river bed.

A bushy tailed vixen, out in broad daylight in search of a meal for her cubs, pops over a stone wall. A pair of black and white oystercatchers pipe nervously. They run along the dry, stony river bed to lure the fox away from their young. The old vixen pays little attention to their antics for the prospect of dining on oystercatcher chick does not excite her. At this time of plenty a fox can afford to be a little more choosey.

An old ash woodland rises up the valley side from the river edge. Ash woodland is the climax vegetation in these northerly parts and probably forms the richest wildlife habitat. Sadly, all too little exists now. The ground flora and understorey are quite special, although the pungent smell of wild garlic is a not uncommon woodland aroma. Bird cherry, however, is an unusual sight, as this white flowering tree is rarely met with outside the northern ash woodlands. Its dark, bitter berries are loved by birds.

Although the ash is one of the last trees into leaf, the canopy closes over by midsummer and the woodland floor is well shaded. In this dim,

COCK WHEATEAR
(left) Perched at the entrance to the nest, this male wheatear has arrived with a beakful of caterpillars and other invertebrates for his brood. Dry-stone walls make excellent nest sites but the birds take equally well to natural rock crevices or subterranean holes such as rabbit burrows. Wheatears winter in Africa, south of the Sahara, arriving back in Britain as early as March. They are very much birds of the uplands these days, though small numbers still nest in the South in areas where both nest sites and short grazed turf can be found.

COCK RED GROUSE
(above) These handsome gamebirds can occur in large numbers on the moors but may seem to be absent – particularly on and after the Glorious Twelfth! They frequently skulk low among the covering heather, and only a warily raised red-browed head reveals their presence.

FLOWER MEADOW
(right) The rich purple of meadow cranesbill, and myriad bright yellow buttercups, enliven the hay meadows of the Dales. Cranesbill is named after the beak-like projection which covers the seed cluster.

ROVING BADGER
*Although badgers are
generally nocturnal, they
may venture abroad during
daylight hours in areas
where they are free from
human disturbance. This is
especially true in autumn
when they are fattening up
for the winter ahead. In the
Dales their setts are usually
in the ash woods but may be
up on the moors.*

COMMON POLYPODY
*(below) Dry-stone walls
provide a convenient niche
for this fern which is
common throughout Britain
and Ireland. Lichens and
mosses also coat the
weathered stones.*

damp environment delicate water avens, poisonous flowered herb Paris, angular Solomon's seal,
and baneberry or herb Christopher all flourish.
Amid the undergrowth a roe fawn lies
motionless.

From the shrub layer, blackcaps sing out
above the noise of fast flowing water. Common
sandpipers bob incessantly by the water's edge,
clambering about the stones in search of invertebrate quarry. An elegant grey wagtail joins in the
search for food. Sallying out from a low bough,
a pied flycatcher grabs a mayfly and returns to
its perch. All around, wood warblers reel out
their song.

BETWEEN THE WALLS

Beyond the woodland's edge the sunlit road
verge is strewn with mauve flowers of meadow
cranesbill. Dry-stone walls encrusted with orange
lichens edge the narrow roads and form a place
for herb Robert to drape. Dashing from cover, a
stoat runs with its head held high, carrying a

rabbit kitten back to its nest of young, secure in
the foot of a wall.

A small, unkempt field sports the tall, single
purple heads of the melancholy thistle and a
mass of yellow ragwort, a tenacious weed.

A cry from the sky, high above a limestone
crag, draws attention to the powerful, stream-
lined form of a peregrine falcon. It closes its
wings and stoops dramatically across the rock
face, screeching as it does so. Climbing once
more on winnowing wings, it repeats the performance. Quite suddenly the peregrine is joined
by another. The tiercel (male) has coaxed his
mate from the nest and they join together in a
wild, wheeling flight above the crags. In this act
of mutual understanding the bond between the
pair is strengthened and prepares them for the
co-operation they will need when working together to rear their youngsters. Flying freely
above the moor, these exciting birds of prey
encapsulate the spirit of wild beauty that is the
Yorkshire Dales.

BITING CLEG
*(above) Several species of
horse-fly are known as clegs.
The females are blood-
suckers, attacking horses,
cattle and humans and
inflicting a painful bite. Some
species approach silently,
while others home in with an
ominous hum. The males,
meantime, go peaceably
about their business, sucking
nectar from flowers.*

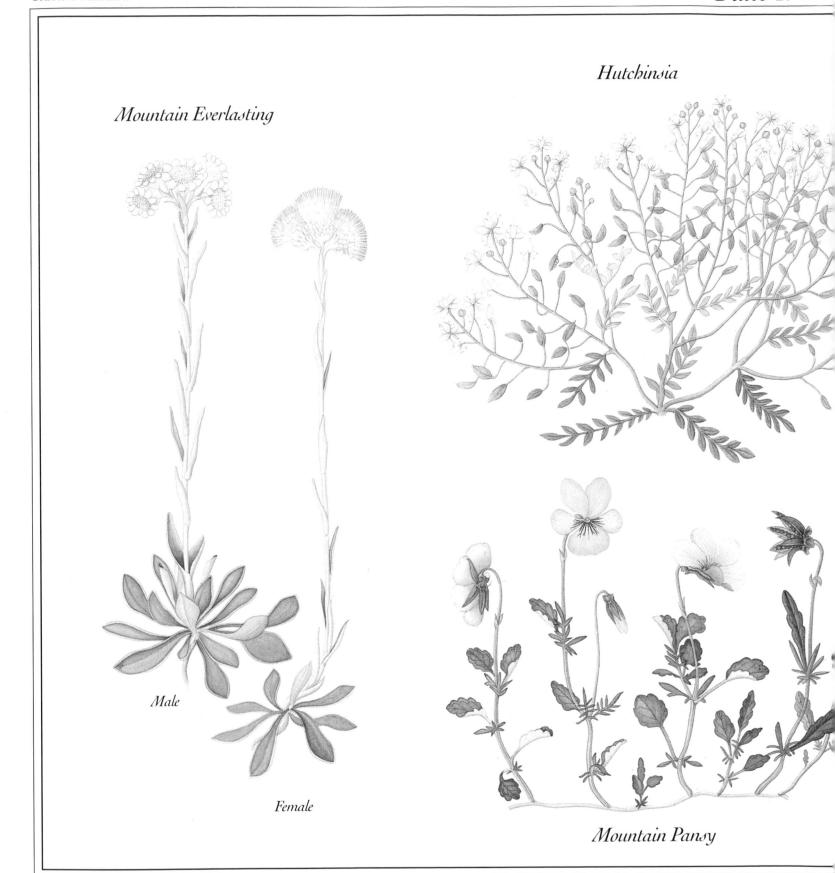

Mountain Everlasting

Hutchinsia

Male

Female

Mountain Pansy

MOUNTAIN EVERLASTING
(Antennaria dioica) This perennial
grows in small clumps on the dry,
limy uplands of north Britain. An 8″
(20cm) woolly stem, with close-
pressed leaves grows from a rosette
of leaves. Heads of tight-packed
flowers open June-July.

HUTCHINSIA *(Hornungia
petraea)* A rare 2-6″ (5-15cm)
annual of dry, limy rocks and dunes
of Somerset, Derbyshire, Yorkshire
and Wales. Branched stems have
small leaflets and tiny flowers on
short stalks from March-May,
which lengthen into fruit.

MOUNTAIN PANSY *(Viola lutea)*
Locally common, mostly on
limestone hills in north Britain and
Ireland, the single 3-8″ (7-20cm)
stems bear oval leaves and lobed
stipules. Yellow, purple or bi-
coloured flowers with thin spurs
appear June-August.

Birdseye Primrose

Dwarf Milkwort

Alpine Bistort

DWARF MILKWORT *(Polygala amarella)* A very rare perennial of a few localities on damp, northern limestone and chalky downland in Kent. The short branched stems to 4″ (10cm) have oval, stalkless leaves. Pale flowers seen June-August may be bluish or pink.

BIRDSEYE PRIMROSE *(Primula farinosa)* Though restricted to wet, limy grassland and mires of north England and south Scotland, it is often locally common. Clusters of flowers, May-July, are borne on a 6″ (15cm) leafless stem. Basal, scalloped leaves are mealy beneath.

ALPINE BISTORT *(Polygonum viviparum)* A perennial of upland pastures and wet rocks in the North, thin, upright stems 2-12″ (5-30cm) arise from a creeping rootstock. A terminal spike of flowers, June to August, also bears tiny buds.

Black Grouse

Red Grouse

BLACK GROUSE *(Tetrao tetrix)*
Common on open woods and
moors in the North and West, but
absent from Ireland. In summer the
21″ (53cm) polygamous males sport
their black breeding plumage,
leaving the mottled 16″ (41cm)
females to care for eggs and young.

RED GROUSE *(Lagopus lagopus)*
Common on heather moors of
upland Britain and Ireland, stocks
of this dumpy, 13-15″ (33-38cm)
bird are maintained for sporting
interests. 6-11 brown-blotched eggs
are laid in a shallow hollow which
the darker red male helps to guard.

Yellow Wagtail

Ring Ouzel

Goshawk

GOSHAWK (*Accipiter gentilis*) A powerful 19-24″ (48-61cm) hawk, the female is larger than the male. Very rare, with a small breeding population, it nests in conifer woods – laying 2-3 whitish eggs in May – and hunts along the open tracks.

YELLOW WAGTAIL (*Motacilla flava*) This slim, long-legged 6½″ (17cm) summer visitor breeds in England, Wales and south Scotland. Two clutches of 2-5 speckled eggs are laid in a hair-lined nest built on lowland meadows or open moors, near water.

RING OUZEL (*Turdus torquatus*) Widespread but infrequent in upland valleys – above 1000′ (300m) – this 9½″ (24cm) summer visitor announces its presence with a clear call. Females are a browner version of the male. 4-5 blotched, blue eggs laid in a grassy nest.

The Ring Ouzel

A summer visitor to Britain, the ring ouzel makes its home in our
wild uplands, wheeling over the craggy peaks and sheltering among
the scant vegetation and rocks which make up the landscape.

The loud, clear piping song of the ring ouzel – *pee-u* – carries across the desolate rocky wastes of moorlands and mountainsides throughout upland Britain – a distinct, familiar sound in an otherwise quiet landscape. The disjointed song proclaims the bird's presence long before you see it, far in the distance, perched high on a crag or rocky outcrop. Known as the 'upland blackbird', the ring ouzel is a denizen of high, open spaces – a shy, nervous bird which shuns the inhabited areas favoured by its near-relative.

At 10 inches (25cm) long, the ring ouzel is the same size as the blackbird, but its colouring and the wide white band or 'gorget' which crosses its lower throat distinguish it from the more familiar lowland bird. The male is sooty-black in colour, with silvery feather margins on the wings and underparts. The adult female is browner than the male, and while the pale wing patches and crescent feather edging are more pronounced, the gorget is narrower and less well defined. Both birds have yellowish bills with a dark tip, but these are not as prominent as the blackbird's bright yellow beak.

The ring ouzel is not a resident bird in Britain. It winters in southern Europe and North Africa and flies northwards in early spring to breed, arriving in the south-west of England and southern Ireland in early March, and reaching North Yorkshire and the Lake District by April and the Scottish Highlands by May.

A HEAD FOR HEIGHTS

It has few breeding grounds below 800 feet (250m), and some have been found as high as 3300 feet (1000m) and more. A pair's nesting territory usually includes a crag or gully and sometimes a few stunted bushes or trees. The choice of nest site varies, but is typically in a clump of vegetation. This may be of bilberry, grass, heather, woodrush or other plants typical of the upland habitat. Such plants often overhang steep rock faces, and nests are frequently found at the top of a cliff or on a rock ledge. Nests also occur on flat ground among heather or bracken; only occasionally are they made in bushes or trees.

The nest itself is made of coarse grasses built upon a foundation of thicker heather twigs or earth. Inside, a lining of finer grasses cushions the one or two clutches of eggs laid in April and May. The pale blue eggs are rather like those of the blackbird but are more heavily blotched with dark red-brown. Clutches usually comprise four eggs, but five are not uncommon, and six

are sometimes found. Incubation is shared by both sexes and the eggs hatch after 14 days. The buff-coloured nestlings grow quickly, fed by both parents, and leave the nest after two weeks.

NOISY CHATTER

It is during nesting time that the ring ouzel displays its aggressive nature, screaming a hard, loud *tac-tac-tac* which is run into a rattling chatter, often without much provocation. It will chase off crows, buzzards and other larger birds when defending its nest and territory. Disturbed from its nest, it will sit on a high rocky

THE UPLAND BLACKBIRD
A distinctive bird with sooty black plumage and a broad white crescent at the throat, the ring ouzel inhabits the high moors and mountainsides of the British Isles, where it is the upland equivalent of its near relative, the blackbird. Usually seen only from afar, it announces its presence with a penetrating whistle.

A PRECARIOUS PERCH (left) The ring ouzel's nest site varies, but is usually a sheltered spot – a gully or a ledge on a rocky mountainside, a heather-covered hollow on open moorland, or the grassy bank of a fast-flowing stream. While most sites are natural, many are unnatural rock habitats such as walls, derelict buildings, quarries and mine shafts, where nests have been found up to 15ft (5m) below ground level.

IN FLIGHT the pale edges of the flight feathers and the adult male's white crescent are clearly visible.

perch and scold and shout at the intruder.

The ring ouzel remains in the north of Britain until July, when it begins its southerly migration. Late summer often sees families of birds banding together in loose flocks, complementing their usual diet of molluscs and other invertebrates with moorland berries and even cultivated fruit, plucked from a garden in the quiet of the morning on the journey south. By the beginning of October the last of these summer visitors have left Britain.

There is some evidence to suggest that the range of the ring ouzel is contracting and that it is no longer breeding in some of its former haunts. Over the last hundred years a definite decline in numbers has been recorded in Ireland and breeding may have ceased completely in Cornwall and the Isle of Man. This decline may be related to the increased numbers of the blackbird, which seems to have extended its range to exclude the ring ouzel from some areas. Climatic changes may have played some part in this, with milder weather discouraging ring ouzels from breeding in marginal habitats, and encouraging lowland blackbirds to inhabit higher altitudes. This may be especially true of Ireland, where there is less high ground for the ring ouzel to dominate.

THE THROAT MARKING is less distinct on the paler female, and completely absent from the juvenile, which is heavily speckled.

A TYPICAL FAMILY (right) Well-hidden among moorland bracken, this brood of five nestlings is visited by the male bird. Both sexes feed their young on a diet of flies, worms, caterpillars and other invertebrates. The young quickly gain strength and leave the nest two weeks after hatching, venturing out with their parents in a noisy group.

THE EGGS are normally produced in two clutches of four. Laying begins in April or early in May.

153

Hill Sheep

These hardy native sheep with their thick shaggy coats, are a
characteristic feature of the rugged Pennine falls, withstanding
biting winds, rain, snow and the coldest temperatures

Early September in the northern Pennines and already the first mists of autumn are veiling the dark flanks of the fells, soaking the heather and the coarse upland grasses. In the grey, watery light the landscape is bleak and apparently deserted, but half-way down the road which winds between stone-walled pastures to the head of the dale, the way is blocked by a huge flock of sheep, being driven down to the farmstead by the shepherd and his pair of watchful dogs.

The sheep are Swaledales, stocky purposeful animals with long coarse wool hanging to their knees in matted ringlets. Bright-eyed and alert, they are more intelligent than the woolly simpletons of the lowlands. For much of their lives they have to weather the harshest climate in England, feeding themselves and their lambs off the thin pickings of the high tops.

The main purpose of the autumn 'gather' is to put the flock through the sheep dip – a compulsory bath of insecticide which destroys skin parasites – but it also gives the shepherd a chance to sort out his sheep for the new breeding season. Only the hardy young ewes will be returned to the fells, the older – usually three-year-old – ewes will be kept on the richer enclosed pasture near the farm. Here, the better conditions enable them to carry on producing lambs when they are no longer fit for the rigours of the open moor.

These older ewes are mated with rams of low-land breeds such as the Bluefaced Leicester, which is meaty, fast-growing and productive. The ram lambs are mostly sold for meat, only the lucky few being selected for breeding. The female lambs resulting from this cross are,

A TOUGH LIFE
*(above) Hill sheep such as
the Swaledale, Dalesbred
and Rough Fell breeds,
are extremely hardy
animals, capable of
surviving harsh weather
on a diet of poor quality
grasses and scraggy, fibrous
vegetation. They are only
brought down to the lower
pastures for breeding in
the autumn or to shelter
from the coldest extremes
of the Dales' winters,
such as when sudden
blizzards smother the
fells with snow.*

however, worth a lot of money to the lowland farmer as they are cheap to keep, yet able to produce a lot of high-quality lambs.

The older ewes are usually mated in early November, so that when the lambs are born, 21 weeks later, the new spring grass will be coming through. Before mating, the mothers are fed up well for about three weeks to get them into ideal condition. Then the rams are let in, one to every 40 or so ewes, each equipped with a coloured marking crayon strapped to his chest. Only when every ewe is adorned with a bright patch of colour on her rump are the rams called off for a well-earned rest.

The young ewes which return to the high land are mated to pedigree hill rams about a month later than their elders, as the grass comes through rather later on the fells. Once mated they go back to the hills, because there is never enough valley grazing to feed the whole flock.

Winter is the start of an anxious time for the shepherd, for winter weather on the fells can be severe and while all may be well in the dale, up on the fell a full-scale blizzard may be piling up great drifts of snow, burying flocks where they shelter in hollows.

SPRING LAMBS

By the start of the lambing season, the worst of the weather is over, but even so all the sheep are gathered off the fell and brought down to sheltered pastures in the dale. Although hill sheep are self-reliant creatures, there are always exceptions. Twin lambs and their mothers need particular vigilance and are often housed under cover, in temporary pens built of straw bales.

A lamb relies on its mother's milk for two or three weeks, before beginning to nibble at the grass. The shepherd will always try to return them to the fells as soon as possible, so that the grass they eat is clean and fresh. In the dale, constant grazing by other sheep infects the grass with parasites and any lambs which stay down-hill for observation have to be repeatedly dosed against a host of unwelcome guests.

It is four months before the lambs are properly weaned. Most of that time is spent on the high land, with a downhill excursion when their mothers are gathered off the fell for shearing. The wool of hill sheep is long and coarse, but nevertheless fetches a high market price.

In August, the lambs are weaned and are separated from their mothers on the fell and brought down to the farm. Before long, most of them are packed off to market. However, the ram and ewe lambs retained for breeding will spend a comfortable winter in the dale before joining the other sheep on the moorland pastures, by which time the next season's lambs will be sampling their first taste of spring grass.

SWALEDALE SHEEP
(above) The Swaledale is the most numerous of the Dales' breeds and is distinguished by its black face, grey muzzle and large rounded horns. The Swaledale's long, shaggy coat contains a dense undercoat to protect it from the cold and their coarse wool is used for making carpets and tweed.

SHELTER OF THE PEN
(left) Lambs are born in the sheltered low pastures of the Dales – often inside a pen built of straw bales – usually in March or April. Ewes generally give birth to one lamb, although twins are not uncommon. During the birth, the ewes are closely watched by the shepherd but help is only given if problems occur, such as the lamb being in the wrong position for a safe delivery.

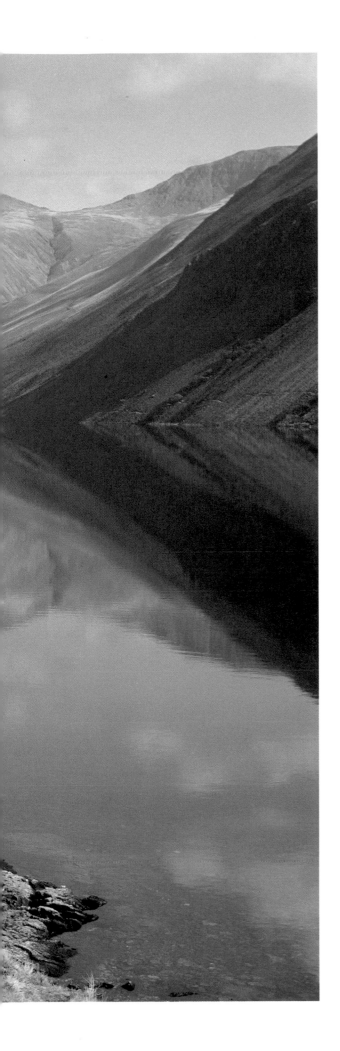

The Lake District

A region of breathtaking beauty, the Lake District enshrines the scenes of a 500 million-year-old geological drama that has produced a landscape full of contrasts. Rent by wild and jagged volcanic pinnacles at its centre, pierced by the cones of slate-hearted Skiddaw in the north and falling to the gentle wooded undulations of Coniston in the south, Lakeland softens at its edges to swathes of rolling farmland. Man, too, has left a mark on this land – in prehistoric stone circles, in the many mines where minerals have been sought, and in some of the lakes themselves.

STONE CIRCLE

CONIFERS

OAKWOOD

REEDS

WATERFALL

QUARRY

DISUSED MINE

SHEEP FOLD

LONG HOUSE

SHIPPON

COUNTRY OF CONTRASTS
(left) The Lake District has within its small confines, the highest point in England, Scafell Pike, the largest lake, Windermere, and the deepest mere, Wastwater, which plunges down 258 ft. There are also fertile valleys beneath barren crags, marvels of modern engineering damming lakes and, on the hillsides, Viking field patterns defined by ancient walls.

THE LAKE DISTRICT

The Lake District nestles in the northwest corner of England between the Pennines and the Irish Sea, stretching northwards from the sands of Morecambe Bay towards the Solway Firth.

Within this small area, nowhere more than 25 miles across, there are mountains reaching 3000 feet, and a great variety of rock formations – the wrinkled and scarred relics of violent prehistoric birth-pangs.

The high ground lies in three main ranges. First, and most ancient, are the livid slates and granite making up the smooth slopes of Skid-daw and Saddleback – the time worn remains of a huge mountain range. Below these are the rugged Borrowdale volcanic mountains, among which rises the sheer dark precipice of Scafell Pike, at 3,210 feet the highest peak in England, from the summit of which the mountains of Mourne are sometimes visible across the Irish Sea. Third, to the south, the gentler wooded slopes of Windermere and Coniston are found.

ANCIENT UPHEAVALS

Among the mountains are traces of other ages and upheavals – limestone and coal strata come from a time when the area sank beneath the sea; sandstone and gypsum are remnants of an arid desert formed when Britain lay on the equator.

The final eruption occurred at the same time as the Alps formed, and was followed by per-

iods when massive ice-crusts scooped and scoured the land, leaving sharp crags, corries, fertile flat valleys, and deep gorges. These fan out from the heart of the Lake District and contain deep lakes, the larger of which are known as 'waters' or 'meres'.

The lakes, together with smaller tarns and pools are fed by clear streams and rivers, and by tumbling becks which cascade down the hillsides after rain. Downpours are frequent, for the Lakeland hills are the first to be met by rain-laden Atlantic airstreams, and the head of Borrowdale is the wettest place in Britain, with 130 inches of rain annually. Rain and frost continue the work of the glaciers; cracking off layers of rock, and washing the soil inexorably down the hillsides to fill the lakes with sediment.

Despite the heavy rain and lofty isolation, the area has been settled from prehistoric times, and the legacies of the many invading cultures may still be seen, from 'Druidical' stone circles to Roman roads. The pace of change is slow in Lakeland, and many of today's farms and hamlets were established by the descendants of 8th century Viking raiders, whose memory is preserved in place names ending in 'force' (meaning waterfall), 'gill' or 'ghyll' (ravine), 'by' (village) and 'thwaite' (meadow). Their shepherding tradition survives also, with animals wintered in sheltered valleys, and grazed high on the hills in summer.

VICTORIAN RESORT
Ambleside, which nestles snugly in its sheltered valley, is an indirect tribute to the 19th century poets who eulogized the beauties of nature so successfully that entire towns had to be built to accommodate their disciples. Built near the site of one of the forts of the Roman Emperor Trajan, Ambleside is a perfect holiday centre, with easy access to waterfalls, crags, lakes and woods.

In the 10th century Dunmail, the last king of Cumbria was defeated, and his kingdom handed over to the Scottish king, Malcolm. For the next seven centuries until the union of England and Scotland in 1603, the Lake District was snatched back and forth, and its inhabitants subjected to constant harrassment. In self-defence they erected 'pele' towers – small square towers, whose massive walls protected the owner and his family upstairs, and his livestock below. Many of these remain, along with ruined castles, as grim reminders of dangerous days.

From the 16th century, the countryside was plundered yet again, but this time for its rocks and minerals – the fells are still dotted with abandoned mine workings and old quarries – and great swathes of original forest were ravaged to make charcoal for smelting.

But the Lake District has also enjoyed benign human influence: in the mild valleys where picturesque stone or whitewashed farms nestle among trees and fields; in some of the lakes themselves which owe their tranquil beauty to Manchester Corporation which created them (Tarn Hows, Hawes Water and Thirlmere are all artificial); and in the care exerted by the National Trust, which protects around one fifth of the area. In 1951, 866 square miles of the Lake District were designated National Park and put under benevolent government patronage to preserve its rich diversity.

WINTER WESTMORLAND
(left) The slopes of Wetherlam above Tarn Hows just north of Coniston retain their winter snow cover well into the year, as do many of the Lake District mountains, particularly on their northern sides. The flat glacial valley provides rich pasture for grazing animals contained in stone-walled enclosures. As the summer progresses they move up the gentle slopes to fresh grounds, a pattern established by the Vikings.

Nature Walk

When rambling among the lakes and fells look out for these enigmatic features of the landscape:

PACKHORSE BRIDGES Narrow stone bridges spanning the valley once used by packhorse trains.

SHEEP PENS Circular dry-stone walled enclosures built to pen the hill sheep.

HANGING VALLEYS Left high, but not dry, as glaciers cut the main valley. Side valleys often end in waterfalls.

PELE TOWERS Defensive structures built in the late Middle Ages as protection against marauding Scots.

Around Lakes and Fells

**An area of great natural beauty, enjoyed by many, Lakeland holds
some rare and exciting wildlife, ranging from nesting eagles and peregrines
to deer on the fells and red squirrels in the woods.**

Sweeping mists of rain fill the valley head as they have all morning. But then they part, to show a handful of wild red deer hinds, here unexpectedly grazing among the sheep. The silence, broken only by the steady tumbling of a beck down the hillside, is further enlivened by the catlike mewing call of a soaring buzzard. High above the crags, in a patch of blue sky, a solitary golden eagle spirals away, surveying the ground for prey.

Red deer and golden eagles are only to be seen in the more remote and rugged parts of Lakeland but are all the more remarkable in what is now a popular holiday area. Despite the human pressure the Lake District is full of wildlife.

The Lakeland crags are a regular haunt of ravens. These intelligent birds, the largest of the crow tribe, can be recognized by their heavy bill, their coarse croaking, and their agile aerobatics. They were once common everywhere but nowadays the windswept hills are their stronghold.

Here, too, the buzzard soars, riding the air currents on broad wings. They prefer open hillsides for hunting, but with woods to hand for nesting, and many of the more secluded Lakeland valleys suit them well. Buzzard numbers dropped in the 1950s when rabbits – their principal prey – were almost exterminated by the disease, myxomatosis. And when buzzards then turned to mutton carrion their breeding success was badly affected by the chemicals used in sheep dips. These organo-chlorines have since been banned and the buzzard population has recovered well.

ON THE FELLS

From behind one of the last stone walls, a fox appears, quite happy to hunt in daylight in this undisturbed valley where no danger signals alert it. It is after voles most likely. It stops to bask awhile, yawning in the sunshine which has by now all but dispelled the last of the mist. (And with that cover now gone, the red deer have also secretly slipped away, around the corner of the crag.)

There are many foxes in the Lake District, both on the open fells and in the woods. In the days of John Peel, they hunted the hill fox hereabouts: a larger and rather greyer animal than the lowland woodland fox. The old hill foxes may now have died out, however, for there have been no reliable sightings for some years. Their place on the open fells has been taken by woodland foxes which have extended their territory. Failing an old rabbit hole, they make shift with an earth in a tight crevice at the foot of the crag. In the clear, rain-washed air, the rank smell of the den can be picked up some way away.

Past the stone walls, the open fells stretch up and away. It is an open landscape patterned with the shadows of clouds, and scattered with

MOUNTAIN RINGLET
(left) Found on high, boggy ground up to the tops of the fells, the mountain ringlet is confined, in Britain, to the Lake District and the Highlands of Scotland. It appears to have died out in Ireland. Caterpillars feed on mat grass, hibernating over winter and completing their growth the next spring. Adults emerge from pupae in early summer and can be seen flying on sunny days from June to August.

WILDLIFE BY A LAKELAND MERE

All the birds here breed in the Lake District and all, except the summer-visiting pied flycatcher, are residents. Mergansers, however, generally move to the coast in winter and may well be joined by the redshanks and the peregrine. The numbers of nesting peregrines have increased in recent years following the decline caused by pesticides in the late 1950s and early 1960s, but human disturbance is a growing threat. The aerobatic raven – here mobbing a buzzard – will harry any bird of prey in its territory, especially near the nest. Pine martens and red squirrels favour stands of old pine but have taken readily to the newer conifer plantations that clothe many hills. Encouraged by the damp, clean air, lichens bedeck walls and trees, while touch-me-not balsam and yellow loosestrife grow alongside reeds and rushes at the water's edge. On the fells, red deer and hardy hill sheep – particularly Herdwick – graze the rough grass.

KEY TO FEATURES AND SPECIES

1 Oak	16 Hill fox
2 Raven	17 Red squirrel
3 Buzzard	18 Common reed
4 Juniper	19 Mallard
5 Larch	20 Common club-rush
6 Alders	21 Holly
7 Black-headed gulls	22 Pied flycatcher
8 Redshank	23 Wild daffodil
9 Peregrine	24 Touch-me-not balsam
10 Red deer	25 Yellow loosestrife
11 Sheep	26 Eel
12 Conifer plantation	27 Pine marten
13 Red-breasted mergansers	28 Mountain ringlet
14 Goosanders	29 Lichen Usnea species
15 Teal	30 Hawkweed

GREY FOX

Some foxes of the Lake District are larger and greyer than their lowland cousins. They may be descendants of the (possibly) now extinct hill foxes of the region, and live a more spartan existence than lowland and urban foxes, subsisting largely on voles, hares, insects, fruit and whatever carrion is available. They have a hard time at the hands of farmers and gamekeepers, due to their habit of taking young lambs and grouse, and are much persecuted in certain areas.

ROYAL FERN

(left) This is one of the tallest European ferns, its leaves sometimes growing to 9 feet in length. It is found in damp places, often by lakes and streams. In summer, when the central leaves are topped by reddish-brown spore cases, the fern looks like a flowering plant.

VERSATILE EEL

(below) Eels may sometimes be encountered on land, wriggling through damp grass. This overland migration usually takes place at night and enables these fish to reach land-locked lakes. They occur throughout the becks and meres of the Lake District.

colourful as in a rock garden.

What sheep do not touch, however, is bracken. Dense blankets of this fern have covered many hillsides in recent decades. Though relishing the wet, bracken likes good drainage and often ends in a line at the foot of a slope where the ground becomes waterlogged.

The sheep which graze the fells occasionally disturb a dunlin or curlew nesting among the grass tussocks. The meadow pipit is common, too, at these heights. It is host to the cuckoo, whose echoing call resounds among the valleys on spring mornings. A brown butterfly seen fluttering at this height is the mountain ringlet. It is found only above 1800ft in the Lakes, and in some parts of the Grampians, but nowhere else this side of the Alps.

Leaving the fells behind, another world is found within the woods clothing parts of the valleyside. Some of these woods are of larch or other conifers planted in Victorian times. These older plantations may encourage the pine marten which, though rare, is present in the area.

rocks. There are patches of boggy ground, and the grass and rushes grow in low tussocks. But there are no heathery hummocks and no trees or bushes to be seen, bar a few low junipers.

This is the result of sheep grazing. In some ways the Herdwicks, the local breed of sheep which graze these fells, can be counted part of the wildlife interest. They are hardy enough to be left out in winter, and their ceaseless hungry nibbling keeps the ground clear of trees, which can grow only from rock crevices or along streamside gullies. Though a magnificently bare terrain is created, few wild flowers are seen. They, too, flower only out of reach on crags and along streamsides, but here they can be as

RED SQUIRREL
(above) Our native squirrel still occurs in the Lake District where, coincidentally, the grey squirrel is hardly found. The red squirrel is well adapted to old pine woods, where the cones provide a plentiful diet of seeds, but it can also be found foraging in stands of hardwood trees.

TOUCH-ME-NOT BALSAM
(above right) A very attractive flower, our only native balsam is, sadly, quite rare. Growing by streams and in damp, shady places, it is naturally confined to the Lake District and North Wales but has been introduced in other areas.

NEWCOMERS TO THE LAKE DISTRICT
(right) Red-breasted mergansers have long nested in Ireland and Scotland but it was not until 1950 that they first bred in the Lake District. Since then they have colonized the area and spread to the Peak District and North Wales. The nest is usually well hidden in dense bankside vegetation, often among brambles or gorse. The female lays and incubates up to 20 eggs and when they hatch, a single female may look after other broods, shepherding as many as 50 chicks around a lake.

Many valleyside woods are of native sessile oak. Ash, holly, birch, rowan and alder can accompany the oak and also grow elsewhere; massive old holly and ash trees often adorn the older stone walls. Today these woods are often used as sheltered grazing for sheep and there is not much to be seen on the ground except grass and moss, with ferns in profusion in the rocky gullies.

From an exposed bough, the pied flycatcher makes a swift sortie before returning to its perch. Here, too, melodiously sing the redstart and the wood warbler. This trio of birds is characteristic of these rather open hillside woods.

A brilliant flash of colour reveals a red squirrel, actively searching the branches. The Lake District is one of its remaining strongholds.

Towards the lake shore, the wood changes, with alder becoming more common. And where it opens out into wet grazing, the dainty wild daffodil grows.

As for the lakes themselves, in their sheer size and depth they resemble reservoirs but, though one or two are dammed for water supply, their shores are by and large natural. The shallows attract many waterfowl, teal and mallard among them. The red-breasted merganser now also nests in some places. Black- and red-throated divers visit, but the most dramatic visitors are surely the whooper swans which come in winter.

Below the surface lurk pike, eels and trout. Here, too, are char and whitefish, such as vendace and schelly. Many of the major lakes have their own populations, trapped by falling water levels after the last Ice Age. The vendace, for example, is found in Derwentwater and Bassenthwaite, but not in Ullswater or Red Tarn, where it is replaced by the schelly. Each of these long separated populations has features which differentiate it from the same species in other lakes.

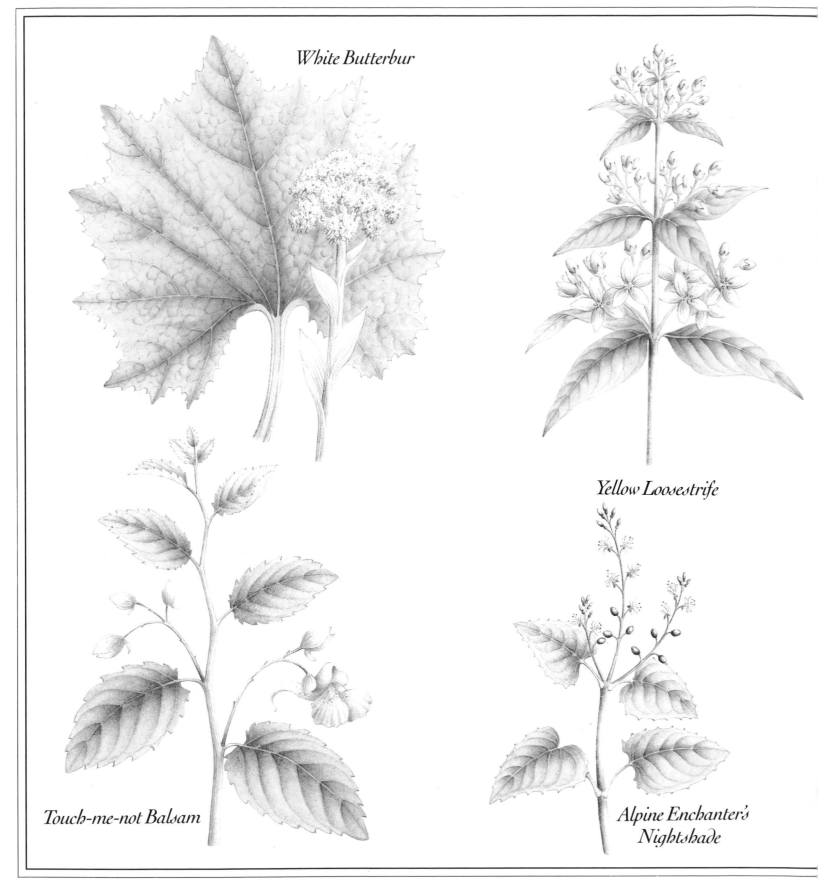

White Butterbur

Yellow Loosestrife

Touch-me-not Balsam

Alpine Enchanter's Nightshade

WHITE BUTTERBUR *(Petasites albus)* A garden escape established in woods and waysides in the North, this spreading plant has branched rhizomes. The scaly 4-12″ (10-30cm) flower stem has scented blooms from March-May. The leaves, appear after the flowers.

TOUCH-ME-NOT-BALSAM *(Impatiens noli-tangere)* Native and local in Lake District and N.Wales, this balsam has succulent 8-24″ (20-60cm) stems and alternate, toothed leaves. Spurred flowers appear July to September, followed by explosive seed capsules.

YELLOW LOOSESTRIFE *(Lysimaca vulgaris)* Clumps of 24-60″ (60-150cm) erect, downy stems grow from thick rhizomes. Dotted with tiny orange or black glands, nearly stalkless spear-shaped leaves are in whorls or pairs. It flowers July-August.

ALPINE ENCHANTER'S NIGHTSHADE *(Circeae alpina)* A rare plant of upland rocky woods in the North-west. Reaching 12″ (30cm), the fairly erect stems bear clusters of flowers July-August – the fruits beome spaced out as the stem elongates.

Lakeland Flowers

Lesser Meadow Rue

Alpine Saw-wort

Grass of Parnassus

Alpine Lady's Mantle

LESSER MEADOW RUE
(Thalictrum minus ssp. *minus)* Local on limestone mountain ledges and screes, a 10-20″ (25-50cm) plant with leaves divided 3 times, giving leaflets that have stalked glands below. Spreading sprays of flowers have many long stamens, June-July.

ALPINE LADY'S MANTLE
(Alchemilla alpina) Perennial, the 5-7 lobed leaves grow from a short rootstock. Leaflets are silky-white below, toothed at the tips. Flower stems reach 8″ (20cm), topped by heads of blooms, June-August. Abundant on open mountainsides.

ALPINE SAW-WORT *(Saussurea alpina)* Resembling a thistle, but spineless, this 3-16″ (8-40cm) erect perennial has scented flowerheads August to September. The stem and undersides of the toothed leaves are woolly. A rare plant of wet mountain ledges in the North-west.

GRASS OF PARNASSUS
(Parnassia palustris) Small tufts of this delicate 4-12″ (10-30cm) perennial grow on wet moors. Basal leaves are long-stalked – the flower stem bears a single stalkless leaf and green-veined flower, July-September. Common in the North

Scottish Blackface

Herdwick

Lonk

SCOTTISH BLACKFACE The most popular mountain breed, with a high Roman nose. Hardy and energetic, both sexes have horns. Mature ewes may weigh 130lb (59kg) and are mated with Border Leicester rams to give greyface crossbreds.

LONK Originally from Derbyshire, this breed has a shorter fleece than many other hill sheep, has legs free of wool and is not quite as hardy. It is agile and kept on Yorkshire moors, and in the Pennines and Lake District. All these old breeds of sheep are carefully maintained.

HERDWICK Originating from black-faced Pennine and tan-faced Viking sheep, this breed is known for its unrivalled hardiness, thriving on poor, upland pastures. Born black, the long coarse adult fleece turns light brown to pale grey. Only the rams have horns.

Dalesbred

Swaledale

Rough Fell

SWALEDALE Both sexes of this hardy sheep have horns. Spreading from the Pennines, it has won favour for the prolific 120lb (55kg) ewes and good fleece for carpets and tweeds. It is mated to Bluefaced Leicester and Teeswater rams to give crossbred Mule/Masham ewes.

DALESBRED Another sheep bred to survive harsh mountain climate. Coming from Upper Wharfedale, they are related to Swaledales but have an outer layer of crinkly wool. Both sexes have curling horns. They are mated with Teesdale rams to give the Masham crossbred.

ROUGH FELL Less popular than Swaledales but also originating in the Pennines, this sheep is kept on the High Shap Fell area. Despite very long coarse wool, nearly to the ground, it has great agility. Ewes 'drafted' to lower pastures are used to breed Masham crossbred ewes.

The Raven

Long persecuted and much maligned by man, the raven is a handsome
bird of legendary intelligence, whose cautious dignity on foot
belies an ability for exhilarating aerobatics on the wing.

BIG CROW

*As big as a buzzard, with a
formidable bristled bill, the
raven is beyond the scope of
any predator bar man.
Breeding ravens mob herons
and peregrines, taunting
them with grating abuse and
defiantly gaping their beaks.
They have a wide repertoire
of threat and defence
postures, involving different
beak positions, and ruffling
specific areas of their
iridescent glossy plumage.*

Big, bold and black – the raven is a fitting
inhabitant of the wild places of the earth.
With a range extending from the shim-
mering sands of the Sahara to the icy shores of
Greenland, this large intelligent crow has
adapted to life in the forgotten corners of the
world.

But it was not always condemned to live in
the wilderness – ravens were once a familiar
sight in London, roaming the streets in search
of edible refuse. But in the 17th century a price
was put on the raven's head, and country
farmer and city rat-catcher alike cashed in on
this lucrative genocide, so that by the beginning
of World War 1, the raven was becoming quite
rare. Since then legal protection and a more
benevolent attitude on the part of farmers and
gamekeepers has allowed it to return to long-

forsaken roosts; but it is still largely confined to
the mountain fastnesses and remote moors of
the North and West. Illegal killing continues,
particularly in pheasant-shooting and sheep-
rearing country, despite the fact that the raven
takes few game birds or eggs and its predilec-
tion for carrion may actually help to protect
sheep from harmful blow fly maggots.

COMICAL CORVID

Understandably, in the face of widespread persecution, the raven's high intelligence usually
manifests itself in extreme caution, and even
when approaching carrion it will keep its wings
spread, ready for an emergency take-off. This
innate wariness contrasts strangely with a dis-
arming and unexpected sense of fun. Comed-
ians of the bird-world, ravens like to mimic

FAMILY GATHERING
Young ravens bask in the security of parental protection for up to five months.

BAD OMENS
Black-clad harbinger of disaster, the raven has long been associated with battle-ground and gibbet. Superstition has it, that if the ravens leave the Tower of London it will collapse.

strange noises as part of their large and varied repertoire of calls; they have been known to play hide and seek with cats and dogs; to play group games passing sticks or stones from beak to beak; and to indulge in aerial clowning — tumbling, somersaulting and nose-diving with great relish.

Similarly, courting involves a sophisticated variety of postures and calls, with bubbling and popping noises added to the usual range of croaks, metallic notes, rattles and knocking sounds. The female, having been preened and 'kissed' repeatedly by her suitor, will jump up and down to signal acquiescence. The breeding pair fly together and perform aerial stunts. A common sight in raven country is a male suddenly tipping over sideways in level flight, turning right onto its back, then rolling upright

EASY PICKINGS
Omnivorous feeders, ravens are partial to carrion, and strip carcases meticulously clean.

again. After such a performance a pair may perch together, and preen each other to increase mutual trust and reduce aggression.

Once the pair is established — ravens do not pair or breed until their third year — the nest site is chosen and building or repair get underway. Ravens nest unusually early in the year often beginning in early February, and hard weather does little to delay progress. Some sites have probably been used by breeding ravens for centuries with some nests built up until they become towering six foot stacks. Both birds build the nest out of large sticks with a layer of thinner twigs inside, lined with earth and roots, and finally wool and fine grass.

UNKIND RAVENS?

Between three and seven eggs are laid in March. They are incubated by the female alone and hatch after 18 or 19 days. The collective term 'an unkindness of ravens' is grossly unjust; the male of the pair feeds his mate solicitously while she is brooding, and they continue to look after their rapidly growing young for such an unusually long time — 6 weeks or more — that the adults are obliged to roost away from the nest for lack of space.

Until they are old enough to breed, young ravens roam the moors and cliffs in flocks which have been known to number 1200. Groups often gather where there is food, and their early start means that they are able to take advantage of the inevitable springtime mortalities of newborn birds and mammals — especially lambs. A nutritious and reliable start to an astonishing potential life-span of 50 years and more.

The Welsh Hills

Shaped by volcanic fire and glacial ice, the Welsh Hills offer some of Britain's more spectacular and attractive scenery. Sweeping north to south in rocky grandeur is the backbone of the region – the Cambrian Mountains, which connect the Brecon Beacons and Black Mountains with Snowdonia. Here, on the empty hills – amongst the highest in the land – the howling wind cuts across the landscape like a knife, while countless streams gush urgently over the hard rock, plunging down gorges and cascading waterfalls, to the hushed calm of the forested valleys below.

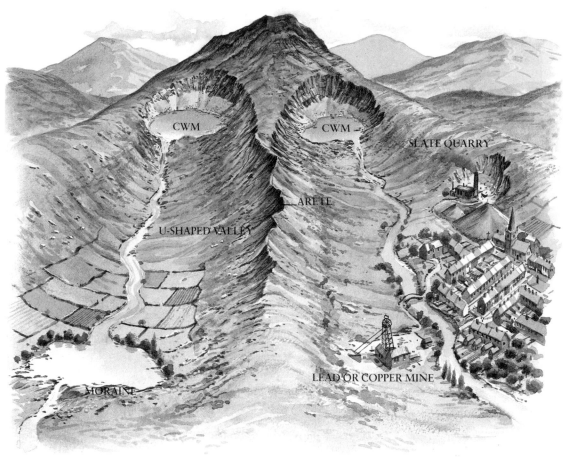

Labels on illustration: CWM · CWM · SLATE QUARRY · ARETE · U-SHAPED VALLEY · LEAD OR COPPER MINE · MORAINE

GLACIATED LANDSCAPE
(left) Many natural features of the Welsh hills chart the paths of Ice Age glaciers. When the glaciers began to move they scooped out steep-backed basins – in Wales called cwms – in which lakes later formed. From there the glaciers moved inexorably forward, carving out U-shaped valleys with high, knife-edged divisions – arêtes – between each glacial valley. When at last the ice retreated, piles of rocky debris – moraines – were deposited which led to the improved fertility of the valley floor.

THE GREEN VALLEY
(right) In sharp contrast to the stark beauty of the naked mountain tops, the lush green valleys, fertile and rich in natural resources, have long supported the agrarian and industrial activities of the population.

Snowdon, the cloud-breeder, stands sentinel at the head of a range of high ground which follows the spine of the Cambrian Mountains to the Brecon Beacons and the Prescelli and the Black Mountains in the South. To outsiders they are grouped together as remote and enigmatic fastnesses, and the names are redolent with legend – The Devil's Kitchen, Slippery Witch's Head, The Castle of the Winds and The Well of the Moon.

This is a land of many moods – a gentle climb started in bright sunshine can quickly turn into a slog past towering crags and precipices bathed in icy mist. But this mist can just as quickly dissolve to reveal spectacular panoramas.

ICE AND FIRE

The Snowdon range dominates north Wales. Though Snowdon itself is a high mountain, it was once at the bottom of a downfold, and immense volumes of what was the higher ground have been eroded away on each side. Volcanic ash and lava flows can be found around Snowdonia, signs of the great contortions that took place, but the face of the Welsh landscape has largely been fashioned by the glaciers of the last Ice Age. In its cold grip the snow that fell became compressed into vast rivers of ice which forced its way down from high ground. At the head of the glacier, the edges froze on to the walls of the valley, and dragged large chunks of rock with them, with which they carved great scrapes along the mountain-side. In time the glacier scooped out giant basins, known in Wales as cwms – a feature of Snowdon and Cader Idris – which have since collected water and become highland lakes.

Moving forward inch by inch, the ice of the glacier armed with rock debris acted as a giant file, grinding away the valley bottom and sides leaving a U-shaped cross-section.

As the glaciers melted after the Ice Age, they unloaded their burden of rocks at the point of furthest advance, forming small hillocks at intervals along the valley floors. Sometimes these 'moraines' acted as dams across streams which later flowed down the valleys, creating lakes. Some of these lakes have since dried out, leaving a patch of fertile soil which shows itself as an unexpected huddle of fields which man has long cultivated. Another sign of glacial action is the presence of isolated giant boulders on the landscape. These were carried within the

SLATE QUARRY *(left)*
For over two centuries, reaching a peak in the slate rush of the late 19th century, slate was a highly popular roofing material. The prosperity of the quarrying areas of north-west Wales encouraged the growth of villages near the quarries. But with the introduction of clay tiles for roofing at the turn of the century, both quarries and villages declined.

Nature Walk

Walks in the Welsh Hills will reveal relics of their glacial past, as well as man's mark on the landscape.

ROCK SHAPES In lakes you may see rock outcrops smoothed into shape by a glacier as it passed.

GOLD MINES Many mines now lie as ruins although Welsh gold is still used to make Royal wedding rings.

NARROW GAUGE During the 19th-century slate boom, networks of railways grew, to take dressed slate to the ports.

SLATE MILL Although still quarried, slate is no longer in such great demand as it was when it roofed much of Victorian Britain, and many formerly booming quarries are deserted ruins.

ice and later dumped as the glaciers retreated.

In more recent times Wales was the final refuge of the free Britons, peoples of Celtic stock fleeing from the armies of Rome. It was never subdued, and the Welsh have jealously guarded their identity ever since, resisting the harsh rule of the Plantagenet kings of England, who built magnificent brooding castles, such as Harlech, particularly around the coast.

Burial cairns of the ancient tribes remain, but much of today's folklore, from black Merlin to white-robed Druids, is no more than myth – the Welsh link with the Druids was a Victorian invention. Geologists have immortalized the names of the defiant tribes, however, in the old rocks for which Wales is renowned: ancient rock formations are named after the Ordovices who lived in the North, and the Silures of the South.

The Welsh valleys are often scarred by mines, for the ancient rocks yield many minerals – gold in some places, which is traditionally used for royal wedding rings. Around Blaenau Ffestiniog,

to the south of Snowdon, gigantic quarries have transformed the landscape completely – they were dug for slate which roofed much of Victorian Britain. Not surprisingly, in a corner of the world which has between 100 and 200 inches of rain annually, these have sometimes filled with water, and become small lakes.

Today, like many of the wilderness areas of these islands, much of the high ground has been given over to dark avenues of coniferous forest, which supports little life, and may add to the acidity of the streams. To create these plantations, tracts of peat bog and moorland – dwindling and fecund habitats for a rich variety of living things – have been reclaimed. Elsewhere sheep graze the indigenous plant-life to extinction, preparing the ground for an invasion of coarse grass.

The Welsh hills have long been prized as a wildlife treasury – some of the earliest naturalists visited the glacier-formed scenery, finding species found nowhere else in Britain. With a little care, they will remain for future generations.

In Hills and Valleys

The late return of spring unlocks the snow-bound Welsh
hills to reveal rare flowers and ferns, unexpected butterflies, dashing
birds of prey and elusive mammals, such as the polecat.

Amid the Welsh hills winters are long and bleak. Snow and frost take an early grip and last well into the spring. Peaks are white, and upland lakes are locked beneath thick, glassy ice. The scenery is spectacular, but the conditions are harsh for wildlife and few wild creatures spend the winter on the hills. Domestic stock, too, find the going tough and many sheep succumb to the extremes of winter. All too often at lambing time, a late fall of snow or long spell of stormy weather will take its toll of both lambs and ewes.

Few living things benefit from this severity, but the raven appears more successful than most. This great black crow of the hills nests early, no matter how harsh the weather. Pairs show interest in breeding from January and will

have laid by late March. By the time the young hatch there will be an abundance of food in the form of dead sheep and other carrion.

Spring sees the drab brown of the upper slopes grudgingly turn to green. Lower down, the orange-brown of dead bracken takes a long time to change as the new, vivid green fronds slowly uncurl. In some areas, now declining and increasingly precious, the moors remain dark brown with a thick carpet of heather which only blooms in late summer, tinging the slopes with pink.

With the warmer weather, meadow pipits return to the moors, pursued by merlins – rare and dashing falcons which feed on small birds. On the rushing streams in the small side valleys, the first spring migrants are the grey wagtails and dippers, moving up from the larger lowland rivers where they have spent the winter. Common sandpipers are later arrivals. Having flown back from Africa, they are the first of the true summer migrants from overseas.

Down in the little valleys, cowslips, primroses and celandines greet the increased warmth, while brimstone butterflies flicker along the lanes and woodland edges. Later, orange tip butterflies look for lady's smock on damp verges and in the wet meadows where early purple orchids flower.

SCREE LIFE

At the foot of the slope there may be a patch of larch or spruce, or one of the fragments of oakwood still left on the Welsh hills. Such woodland often merges into bracken slopes and areas of very rough ground, where big, loose boulders form block scree, matted with luxuriant green mosses and lichens. In sheltered cracks, where sheep cannot reach, grow ferns, including, in isolated places, the parsley fern and holly fern. On a few screes in Snowdonia, juniper – once abundant – spreads in mats across the blocks. Where the screes are composed of smaller stones there will be flowers, including rarities such as mossy and starry saxifrage, alpine meadow-rue and alpine enchanter's nightshade.

Where the slopes level out there may be tracts

MALE WHINCHAT
(left) Flying in from its winter quarters south of the Sahara, the whinchat arrives in the Welsh hills in late April. It is common on bracken-covered hillsides and in young forestry plantations where it can find its two nesting requirements – tussocky grass and a prominent song post. Once frequent in southern and eastern England, it is now mainly found in the hills below the high moorland.

THE HARDY LIFE OF THE HILLS

Feeding chiefly on carrion in winter, the raven haunts the hills throughout the year, breeding early to take advantage of the mortality at lambing time. The red kite, too, is resident in the hills, nesting in the valley-side oakwoods and feeding on prey ranging from sheep carrion to small mammals, birds and frogs. Both the merlin and its principal prey, the meadow pipit, return from lower ground in spring to breed in the hills, while the insect-eating ring ouzel and wheatear are migrants from Africa, arriving to nest in April. On the lower slopes the polecat hunts mice, voles and frogs. The frogs themselves may lay their spawn in the boggy streamside. Caterpillars of the antler moth feed on grasses and rushes and may devastate large areas of upland grazing. The trees and flowers of the hills often grow in rocky crevices out of reach of grazing sheep and feral goats.

KEY TO THE SPECIES

 1 *Red kite*
 2 *Aspen*
 3 *Raven*
 4 *Rowan*
 5 *Merlin*
 6 *Sheep*
 7 *Juniper*
 8 *Meadow pipit*
 9 *Ring ouzel*
10 *Feral goat*
11 *Wheatear*
12 *Lichen*
13 *Golden saxifrage*
14 *Moss campion*
15 *Parsley fern*
16 *Mesh-web spider*
17 *Polecat*
18 *Antler moth*
19 *Short-tailed vole*
20 *Bilberry*
21 *Common frog*

of purple heather moorland, but where it has been burnt too often and then overgrazed, carpets of bilberry and sorrels will colour large areas brilliant crimson.

BIRDS OF THE SLOPES

Rock is usually not far from the surface and frequently bursts through the thin, poor soil. Such outcrops are popular perches for wheatears – busy, bright little birds which flit from rock to rock flashing the pure white of their rump and tail and calling sharply. On bigger rocks and crags, or in deep, rocky gullies with thick heather below and the odd rowan or hawthorn growing out from the side, there may be ring ouzels too.

Slopes which are covered with heather and bracken and scattered with scrubby hawthorn and tall larches are the favourite haunt of nesting whinchats. Tree pipits are also commonly seen as they parachute down to the bush tops during their early summer song flights. The familiar call of the cuckoo also resounds among the hills.

There may be more exciting finds on these slopes. A black grouse might be flushed from the bracken, making off in low, fast flight across the valley, beautiful in blue-black and white. Old stick nests of carrion crows, which are also common in the hills, are appropriated by pairs of merlins, or even long-eared owls where the scrub is dense.

From the edge of an old, remote wood a foraging polecat may venture out in search of

PEREGRINE AT NEST
Though still at risk from egg collectors and rogue falconers, the peregrine is returning to breed on ancestral crags in the Welsh hills.

PARSLEY FERN
(below) This attractive plant of the mountains grows both on stone walls and on the loose rock screes where drainage is good.

short-tailed voles on the more open slopes. Less likely to be encountered, and very much rarer, is the pine marten whose dwindling population is still holding on in the face of increased disturbance.

Huge areas of the lower slopes, and increasingly the higher ground too, are devoted to growing conifers. The new plantations provide a home for whinchats, grasshopper warblers and meadow pipits, but are rarely occupied by short-eared owls or hen harriers, species which take readily to similar plantations in Scotland. The harriers like the heather moors, which survive

only where they are managed for grouse; merlins too, prefer the tall heather but will hunt in the plantations so long as some open ground remains.

Where the land is flatter and the bobbing white heads of bog cotton mark out the swampy, marshy ground, there may be a special butterfly of the hills – the large heath.

In Snowdonia and one or two places elsewhere, the undulating, extensive plateau of sheepwalk or heather moorland, so characteristic of mid Wales, is replaced by higher, bolder countryside. Among the rocks, rowans and aspens may grow from crannies where they are inaccessible to sheep – the rowan seeds perhaps deposited in the droppings of a ring ouzel. High on these mountains there are feral goats – not true wild animals but domestic goats gone wild, they can be found from Cader Idris in the west to Snowdon in the north but they are becoming an increasingly rare sight as their numbers are declining.

Apart from ravens searching for carrion, buzzards may be seen high above the hills, wheeling for minutes on end, searching the ground below for prey such as voles, small rabbits and even

BRIGHT WELSH POPPIES
*Found in damp, rocky places, this plant grows
in Wales, Ireland and south west England.*

worms. Many hunt by sitting quietly on a stump or post, watching carefully for a careless mole to break the surface or a mouse venturing unwisely into the open.

In mid Wales, the uplands are hunted by the splendid red kite – once nearly wiped out and still, at barely 40 pairs, one of our rarest birds of prey. Yet the merlin, in Wales, is now rarer still. In a much healthier state in the Welsh hills is the peregrine, which may be seen soaring high over the peaks or flashing out of sight across a moor.

On the very high tops, it is bleak, wild and, above all, wet. If the summit is rounded and smooth, there could be golden plovers breeding. In spring, a party of dotterels may stop a day or two on their way north, although occasionally a few have stayed to breed. Meadow pipits and skylarks reach nearly to the top, but nowhere in Wales is quite high enough to have the special birds of the Scottish peaks – ptarmigans, golden eagles or breeding snow buntings. But there are other, more familiar birds – swifts everywhere in summer, sweeping the skies for insect prey; and, right to the very top of Snowdon, gulls will scavenge for the scraps left by tourists.

Much less evident are the rare plants of the high tops – alpine woodsia, mountain avens, Snowdon lily, hoary whitlow-grass, alpine cinquefoil and others – all remarkable little gems well worth the climb and the close searching.

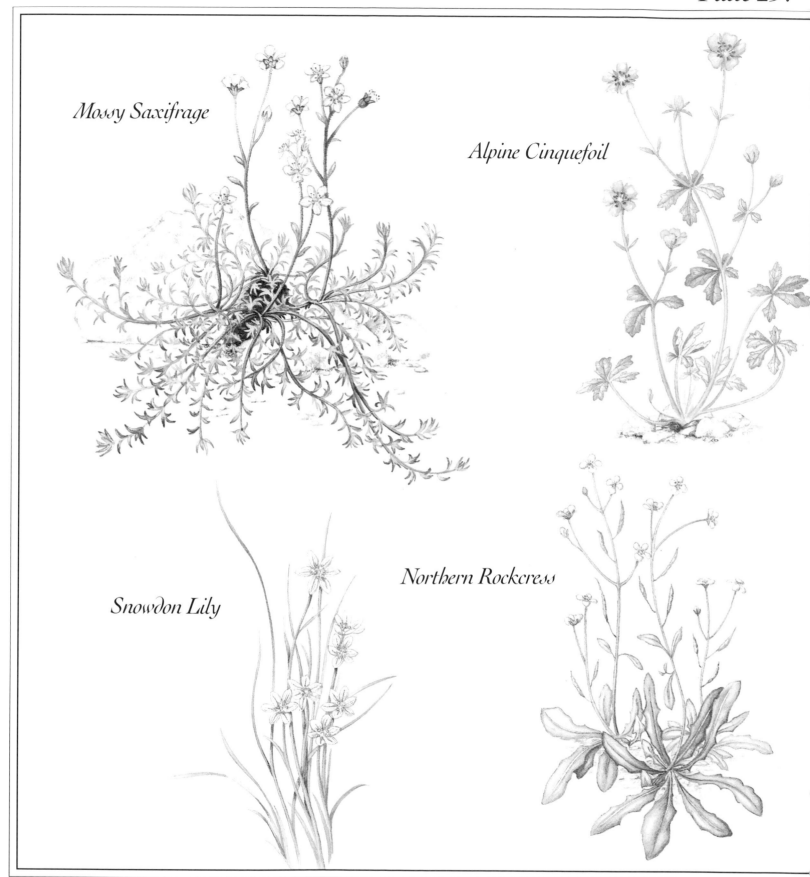

Mossy Saxifrage

Alpine Cinquefoil

Snowdon Lily

Northern Rockcress

MOSSY SAXIFRAGE *(Saxifraga hypnoides)* Forming moss-like clumps, or mats of prostrate stems, this rare perennial grows on ledges and stony slopes of limestone mountains. The erect 2-8″ (5-20cm) flowering stems bear 1-5 white, five-petalled blooms from May to July.

SNOWDON LILY *(Lloydia serotina)* A slender perennial up to 6″ (15cm) tall, this rare lily is a protected species growing on precarious rock ledges throughout Snowdonia. Each plant has 2-4 fine leaves and produces 1 or 2 white, purple-veined flowers in June.

ALPINE CINQUEFOIL *(Potentilla crantzii)* Growing on ledges and in crevices in rocks where it is safe from grazing animals, this is a fairly erect plant 2-10″ (5-25cm) high, flowering June to July. It is found only locally on limestone mountains from N. Wales to Scotland.

NORTHERN ROCKCRESS *(Cardaminopsis petraea)* An early colonist of the bare, rocky slopes of high, limestone mountains, its flowering stems 4-10″ (10-25cm) arise from a basal whorl of leaves – the flowers open from June to August.

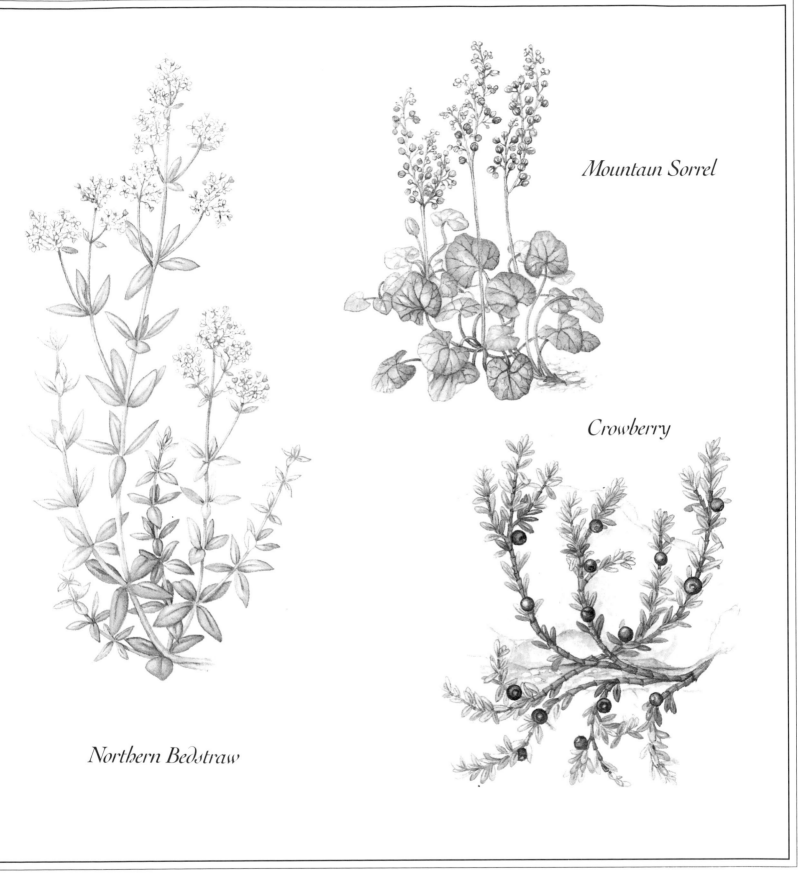

Mountain Sorrel

Crowberry

Northern Bedstraw

NORTHERN BEDSTRAW
(Galium boreale) Distinguished
from other bedstraws by three veins
on the rough-edged leaves, this
8-18″ (20-45cm) plant can be quite
common on rocky mountain slopes.
After flowering in July and August,
fruits with hooked bristles appear.

MOUNTAIN SORREL *(Oxyria*
digyna) A characteristic plant of
damp mountain flushes, this rare
2-12″ (5-30cm) perennial has fleshy,
kidney-shaped leaves and bears
red-edged, greenish flowers in
July and August. It requires a
light, open aspect.

CROWBERRY *(Empetrum*
nigrum) This is a low, 6-18″
(15-45cm) spreading, heather-like
shrub which grows on acid, peaty
soil often in very harsh conditions.
It produces small, pink flowers with
six petals in May and June and
round, black berries July-September.

Female

Merlin

Male

Raven

MERLIN *(Falco columbarius)*
These rare, small 10½-13″
(26-33cm) falcons fly low over open country after small birds, chattering a shrill 'quik-ik-ik'. 3-5 buff, heavily red-brown blotched eggs are laid among the heather in May.

RAVEN *(Corvus corax)* The largest member of the crow family, the 25″ (64cm) raven has a very impressive 4′ (1.2m) wingspan. It lives in bleak mountains, where its harsh, deep 'kronk' can be heard as it soars high in the sky. Its diet consists of carrion, plant material and live prey – insects, young birds and small animals. Breeding often as early as February, ravens choose remote sites and make a deep twiggy nest thickly lined with wool and moss. 4-6 pale green or blue eggs with dark markings are laid from March.

Juvenile

Red Kite

Male

Chough

CHOUGH (*Pyrrhocorax pyrrhocorax*) A member of the crow family, the 15″ (38cm) chough is a social bird with a strong, soaring acrobatic flight. Juveniles are not as glossy as the adults and have orange-yellow bills. The chough feeds on flat, short-tufted pastures digging up insects with its long, curved beak. Its call is a range of shrill and tuneless notes. Territorial when breeding, nests are well hidden in caves or old mine shafts in hills and cliffs near the sea. 3-6 white eggs tinted with green and blotched with brown are laid April-May.

RED KITE (*Milvus milvus*) Giving its name to the kite we fly, this rare and protected 24″ (61cm) bird of prey is easily identified in its effortless flight by a deeply-forked tail, narrow wings sharply bent back and white patches on the underwings. The red kite feeds on rabbits, birds, insects and some carrion and calls a shrill, mewing 'weeoo-weeoo-weeoo'. It builds a nest of sticks and earth, often on an abandoned bird's nest, high in the trees in the wooded valleys of central Wales, and lays 2-3 white eggs with red-brown speckles in April or May.

The Salmon

At the sounding of a mysterious signal, mature salmon are drawn
from their deep-sea feeding grounds to make a demanding
journey home – a journey from which they may never return.

Lured from rich ocean feeding grounds by an overwhelming urge to mate, male and female salmon start on a journey which demands endurance, strength, amazing powers of orientation, and above all, the persistent driving force to spawn to carry them through the hard months ahead. One of the mysteries connected with this fish is how it finds its way back from the open sea where it spends its first few years after leaving the river of its birth. It is believed that the salmon retraces its outward route by following a 'scent path' of the original journey, which may have been over 1000 miles, which it retains as a 'chemical memory'.

As they pause in the estuary, prior to their extraordinary pilgrimage upriver, salmon are at their best. After feeding voraciously at sea on a diet of shrimps – from which salmon flesh gets its colouring – and small fish, adult salmon are usually eight to forty pounds of solid silver-clad muscle. These prime salmon wait in shoals at the river-mouth, adjusting from salt water to fresh, and waiting for a spate of flood water to aid their journey upstream. They have had their last meal – they will not feed again until they have completed their mission, which may take as long as a year. The journey starts at any time of year, but mating itself only takes place in

FISH A LEAPING
(above) Driven by the urge to reproduce, salmon make a seemingly impossible journey from the sea, upriver to the spawning grounds where they were born. In the higher reaches of the river they encounter the rushing steep waters of waterfalls, which the salmon can clear with often quite prodigious leaps. Leaps of falls over 12ft (3½m) have been recorded.

winter, so that whenever they set off, salmon usually arrive in their upland streams from November until mid-January to spawn.

As they begin their leisurely journey, moving faster when the water is warm, and resting when it is cold, they gradually lose their stream-lined and silvery good looks. The females turn almost black and bulge with their heavy load of eggs, while the males turn rust red and develop a hook, or kype, on their lower jaw which they use as a weapon in courtship skirmishes.

THE LEAPER

As the mating urge intensifies, the salmon are compelled to perform high-jumping feats to pass over waterfalls. From a relaxed standing start in a pool, they can, with a flick of muscular tail, clear a 12 foot obstacle, hence the Latin name *Salmo* 'the leaper'.

Once the perilous journey is complete, the male will find a female, and pay court, nudging her with his snout, and feigning to assist her in her task of nest making. The female scoops a hollow in the gravel of the stream-floor and into this scoop, or redd, she deposits her eggs, which the male covers simultaneously with a cloud of 'milt' – sperm. The female then moves on and digs another scoop, the gravel from which covers and protects the first batch of fertilized eggs. She will produce 8-900 eggs per pound of body weight, and will lose between one third and one quarter of her weight in spawning.

Mating over, the male and female salmon may not have strength enough to return to the sea. Many kelts, as the exhausted salmon are called, die on the way back to the sea. Still

fasting, they drop downstream, tails first, gaunt and sometimes fungus-infested shadows of their previous glittering selves.

Meanwhile, back upstream three or four months later, there will be signs of life in the gravel on the stream bed. Tiny translucent fish – alevins – are hatching. Two to five years elapse before the slender six inch fish develops salt-excreting cells in its gills, dons its silver scales, and negotiates a dangerous journey to the sea as a smolt. The sea is full of enemies, but it is also the storehouse which provides enough food to allow a thirty-fold weight gain in a year.

So the cycle repeats itself, with a tiny fish setting out for the cold waters of the north, with the route of this incredible migration imprinted on its memory.

SEX CHANGES
(left) Male salmon in breeding condition lose their silvery good looks and take on a rusty red hue. They also develop large hooks on their lower jaws, known as kypes, which are used as offensive weapons by competing male suitors. The real competition however comes not from adult males, but from parr which have not yet made it to the sea, and which hide near the mating pair. With split-second timing the parr can insinuate itself between them, and fertilize the eggs.

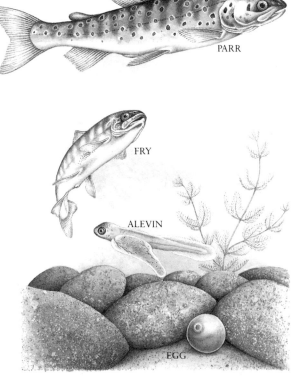

SIGNS OF LIFE
(left) Several months after spawning, tiny translucent fish, called alevins, hatch.

THE IMMATURE SALMON
(right) There are several stages in the river life of the immature salmon. First eggs hatch into alevins, which use their built-in life-support systems, yolk sacs, to nourish them. After a month they become fry, feeding on a variety of aquatic insects. They develop dark smudges along their bodies for camouflage. When they are about 6in. (15cm) long they are parr. Parr remain in the river from two to five years, before heading for the feeding grounds in the seas off Greenland. They make this journey as smolts, and if they return after only one sea winter it is as grilse. If they remain at sea longer they return as mature salmon.

PARR

FRY

ALEVIN

EGG

Anglesey

Flung off the north-west tip of Wales there lies the ancient Celtic outpost of Anglesey, whose bleak galeswept landscape bears the traces of prehistoric civilisations and man's quest for minerals. Many a ship has foundered on the treacherous north coast where the jagged and contorted rocks are among the oldest in Wales. To the south, from rolling sand dunes, distant Snowdonia can be seen across the Menai Strait. Inland, small farms nestle among the cornfields which once sustained Gwynedd's princes – who called this place the Mother of Wales.

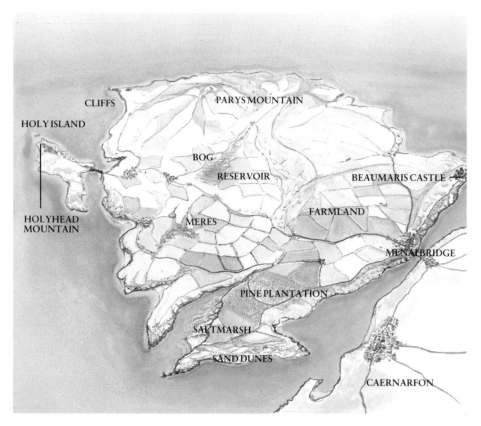

century. A major fracture in Anglesey's rocks runs across the island in this area, and movement along this line has preserved a sliver of coal-bearing beds. This is just one of a number of places on the island where man has exploited the geology. Edward I used local limestone from Penmon when building the castles of Beaumaris and Caernarfon; Telford chose the same material for his bridge; and hard quartzite from Holyhead Mountain was used in the construction of the port's 7860 foot long breakwater.

But the most spectacular site of man's exploitation of the island's rocks is Parys Mountain. The stark landscape of these naked russet slopes is testimony to the intense activity which once took place here at what was the richest copper mine in Europe during the 18th and 19th centuries. The Romans and possibly the Celts mined here, but their inroads were nothing compared to the waste-covered hillside riddled with mineshafts and tunnels left by their 19th century counterparts.

PLUNDERED LANDSCAPE
(below) Parys Mountain is brutally scarred by 18th and 19th century copper mines. A gaping hole at the top of the mountain remains – the Great Opencast Pit.

ISLAND OF CONTRASTS
(above) Within its small area (276 sq. miles), Anglesey has a variety of different landscapes – from the jutting cliffs of contorted ancient rock in the north, to the recently formed sand-dunes in the south. Inland there is rolling fertile farmland, contrasting with the desolation left by man in his quest for copper and coal. The moorland of Holy Island suffers heavy rain which sweeps across the island to the green and wooded south east shore by Menai Bridge.

ANGLESEY

Traces of human settlement and conquest can be found all over Anglesey, from the prehistoric burial chamber of Bryn Celli Ddu – 'the Mound in the Dark Grove' – to Beaumaris Castle. Anglesey's position on the west coast offers easy access to other parts of the Celtic fringe, and with its rolling fertile countryside, it has always been a magnet for man.

Cairns and cromlechs (stone circles) abound. Relics of Celtic settlements remain at Holyhead Mountain and Lligwy. Here a hoard of weapons and chariot fittings has been discovered – perhaps intended as an offering to a lake god by the Celtic priests, the Druids. The Romans left their mark also, establishing a fort at Holyhead and working the copper ores of Parys Mountain.

In later times the island was described as the Mother of Wales, because her cornfields fed the medieval princes of Gwynedd in their Snowdonian fastnesses. The campaign of King Edward I in the 13th century to quell the rebellious Welsh brought the English across the Menai Strait to annex this rich supply of food. At Llanfaes they banished the locals to the opposite end of the island, and marked their victory with the building of Beaumaris Castle.

The arrival of Thomas Telford and his road-makers in the early 19th century caused another population shift. With the development of Irish Sea ferries, road links with the mainland were improved. Telford built a spectacular suspension bridge across the Menai Strait and a new road straight to Holyhead.

A few miles further on, Telford's road crosses a narrow strip of marsh, now bearing few traces of the coal mine which operated here in the last

volcanoes here and great submarine landslips. The grey limestone between Lligwy and Benllech, and at Penmon, was formed from the shells of animals in a warm tropical sea about 300 million years ago. The climate encouraged swamp forests, whose remains form the coal that was once mined at Pentre Berw.

It is Anglesey's magnificent coastal scenery which allows geologists access to its rocks. Inland, the island's complex structure is masked by thick layers of sand, mud and boulders deposited 18,000 years ago during the last Ice Age. As the glaciers melted, the material with which they were laden was dumped: boulders picked up in Scotland and the Lake District were carried to Anglesey and left as massive memorials to the power of frozen water. The sea level slowly rose after the Ice Age, forming the Menai Strait as two river valleys were submerged, and Anglesey became an island.

In recent times the forces of nature have again asserted their power. Medieval farmland and the harbour at Abermenai were smothered by sand blown inland by storms, forming to-day's dunes at Newborough Warren. The farmer's loss however, has been the naturalist's gain – the unique geography of Anglesey has given shelter to a wealth of plant and bird life.

DRIFTING DUNES
In medieval times, Newborough Warren was part of Anglesey's rich farmland, now buried by sand.

Yet man's contribution to the landscape of Anglesey is minute in comparison to the changes recognized by geologists in the record of the rocks. Much of Anglesey is made up of ancient rocks which have been heated, squeezed and contorted. The spectacular crumpled formations of the South Stack cliffs are evidence of the enormous pressures which have affected what were once, over 500 million years ago, soft sands and muds on a sea floor. Other rocks of the same age suggest that there were underwater

Nature Walk

This remote corner of Wales has always attracted people to live and work, signs of which remain, such as:

BEAUMARIS CASTLE, begun by Edward I in 1282 to protect him from his unwilling subjects. It is built from local limestone.

BURIAL MOUNDS, up to 4,000 years old, containing carved stones and flint tools. This is Bryn Celli Ddu, which faces Snowdon.

MINING REMAINS, the legacy of exploitation of the island's rich mineral resources. Anglesey was once Europe's major source of copper.

SETTLEMENT RUINS – these are the 'Irishmen's Huts', 20 of which were occupied in the third century AD under Roman rule.

Around Anglesey

Anglesey's heaths and lakes, ringed by cliffs, beaches and dunes, host over 90 species of breeding birds, countless insects and many specialized flowers in a bewildering variety of habitats.

The interior of Anglesey, its small fields divided by dry-stone walls, is bright with yellow gorse, purple heather and the green of fresh bracken. Pheasants stalk the fields and introduced golden pheasants have bred in the wild here. Sparrowhawks abound and the occasional pair of small merlins nests in the heather. They fly down the abundant meadow pipits and linnets.

Cefni Reservoir and the lakes of the interior hold good numbers of wildfowl. In addition to commoner species, dabchicks, great crested grebes, Canada geese and, on some waters, shoveler can be found breeding. In winter, many birds fly in. From the Arctic tundra come whooper and Bewick's swans, to be joined by white-fronted geese from Greenland. Up to 7,000 wigeon have been counted on Llyn Coron and pintail, teal and goldeneye also fly in.

Insects are plentiful on the lakes. More than half a dozen damselfly species may be seen, and just as many dragonflies. A local speciality, here found at its most westerly point in Britain, is the hairy dragonfly. The female, especially, lives up to the species' name. From May to early July the male is most likely to be spotted along the streams that feed the lakes. In addition to hunting down insects, he searches for the females which only approach water to mate and lay their eggs.

The margins of several lakes are rich in plants. Here grow fen sedge, saw sedge, bog-rush and pale dog violet. Some areas hold masses of orchids. Nine species occur at one location, including fly orchid and frog orchid, as well as marsh fern.

AROUND THE COAST

Anglesey's chief glory is its varied coastline which attracts birds throughout the year and harbours a wide range of plants and insects.

The nesting seabirds at South Stack are active from May to July. On the rock ledges nest guillemots, razorbills, fulmars, kittiwakes and herring gulls. Puffins, too, can be seen busily flying out to sea on fishing trips.

Peregrine falcons may be glimpsed, perhaps nesting nearby in the abandoned nest of an early breeding raven. Stock doves and rock pipits nest in rock crevices, but one of the most exciting birds is the chough. A member of the crow family, this red-billed bird indulges in dramatic aerial chases and, early in the day, may be seen probing the short cliff-top turf for ants.

TERNS IN FLIGHT
These Sandwich terns, named after the Kentish place where they once bred, are the largest of our five breeding terns. Like other terns they fish by diving into the sea, emerging with sand-eels or sprats. They nest in colonies on sand or shingle bars in association with aggressive gulls – this seems to offer protection from predators.

WILDLIFE ON ANGLESEY

Fulmars, kittiwakes and choughs are among the cliff-nesting birds of Anglesey. Lapwings, oystercatchers and other ground-nesting waders breed among sparse vegetation. Newborough Warren's rabbits still crop its many grasses and flowers. Also attracted to the flowers is the marsh fritillary, whose caterpillars feed on scabious. Reptiles, such as the adder and lizard, feed on the plentiful insects. Prickly, but attractive, sea holly grows by the shore, and on the nearby dunes, stabilized by marram grass, marine ducks nest in old rabbit burrows.

KEY TO FEATURES AND SPECIES

 1 Fulmar
 2 Kittiwakes
 3 Juvenile kittiwake
 4 Corsican pine plantation
 5 Sea cliff
 6 Chough
 7 Estuary
 8 Oystercatchers
 9 Sea rush
10 Lapwings
11 Lagoon
12 Dune

13 Dune slack
14 Marsh helleborine
15 Marsh fritillary
16 Rabbits
17 Dark green fritillary
18 Silver-studded blue
19 Marram grass
20 Shelduck at nest
21 Dune helleborine
22 Sheep's-bit scabious
23 Wild pansy
24 Five-spot burnet

25 Beach
26 Female red-breasted
   merganser at nest
27 Leaf beetle
28 Female adder
29 Grayling butterfly
30 Male common lizard
31 Banded snail
32 Sea holly
33 Creeping willow
34 Wolf spider
35 Wild thyme

ANNUAL ROCK-ROSE
(top) Rare in the British Isles, its main sites are in the Channel Islands, North Wales and Western Ireland. It grows among the dry turf on the South Stack headland, flowering from June to September.

The nodding pink flowers of thrift are everywhere on ledges and the cliff top. The bright yellow blooms of annual or spotted rock-rose also enliven the scene. Other plants tolerant of salt spray to be found here include kidney vetch, wild carrot, wild thyme, English stonecrop and common scurvy-grass. Blackthorn bushes, stunted by the wind, provide cover for linnets and whitethroats. The flowers attract not only bees in search of nectar but numerous butterflies, including the marsh fritillary.

The brackish lagoon at Cemlyn Bay is a breeding site for many birds. All five species of British terns have bred recently on Anglesey. At Cemlyn screaming hordes of common and Arctic terns are certain to be seen, diving for fish in the lagoon or the bay. Here, too, may be smaller numbers of little terns and perhaps the

wary Sandwich tern. Sandwich terns are easily disturbed and will desert a colony, even after laying, to re-establish themselves elsewhere.

Two marine ducks also nest in the Cemlyn dunes. Shelducks often lay their eggs in the old rabbit burrows. So, too, may red-breasted mergansers. The merganser's nest may also be hidden under a bush. The bulk of the population nests further north in England and Scotland but mergansers colonized Wales in 1953, nesting on Anglesey that year.

On the shore grow plants able to cope with

PEREGRINE AT NEST
Anglesey's cliffs are a traditional nesting haunt for these magnificent falcons. A dramatic slump in their nationwide breeding success in the 1950s first alerted scientists to the dangers of DDT pesticides, leading to a ban on these chemicals. Peregrines have recovered and returned to their old eyries.

COMMON LIZARD
(right) The heathland of much of central Anglesey is favoured by this sun-loving reptile which may be seen basking on walls, south-facing slopes or sand dunes.

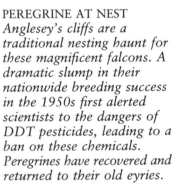

the vagaries of storm and spray. Sea beet, the wild ancestor of beetroot, sugar beet and spinach, grows sturdily, as do clumps of white-flowered sea kale, whose leaves are just about edible. More attractive than the latter plants is the tall yellow horned poppy which flowers through the summer.

Further east, in Lligwy Bay, porpoises can be seen swimming in summer. And just off-shore, on the small island of Ynys Moelfre, grey seals haul themselves out of the water. These seals breed in caves at the foot of the cliffs in Gigorth Bay, on Anglesey's Holy Island.

Puffin Island, not surprisingly, is home to breeding puffins. These hole-nesting birds fall prey not only to the large great black-backed gulls but also to introduced brown rats.

At the southern end of Anglesey the dune system of Newborough Warren is the finest in

COMICAL PUFFINS
(above) These remarkable, almost human looking birds nest both at South Stack and on Puffin Island off the Anglesey coast. The birds were once collected and eaten as pickled delicacies. Today, great black-backed gulls are their worst enemies, preying especially on the plump chicks.

CONEHEAD
(right) The short-winged conehead is a bush-cricket which is near the northern edge of its range in Wales. The female, shown here, has a prominent ovipositor for laying eggs in the stems of rushes and sedges.

DARK GREEN FRITILLARY
(above left) Perched here on knapweed, this fritillary is a fast flyer, seen during July and August. Sea cliffs are a favourite haunt.

SEA BINDWEED
(left) Related to the familiar white bindweed or convolvulus, this species grows on sand dunes and sea shores. Its trailing stems are shorter than those of its cousin, growing to a length of 20" (50 cm). The pink and white flowers, visible from June to August, close up at night. It occurs, among other places, on Llanddwyn Island, near Newborough Warren.

Wales. The National Nature Reserve here covers over 1,500 acres. In the Corsican pines of the forestry plantation, red squirrels strip the cones.

Red beetles, rather like ladybirds without spots, crawl over the carpet of creeping willow in the dune slacks. Spikes of marsh helleborine project skywards. Ruby tailed wasps buzz past and, flying more gently, silver studded blue butterflies. Here, the blues breed at their most northerly British location. Grayling butterflies also occur and, on the dunes themselves, dark green fritillaries home in on wild pansies.

The dunes are rich in lime from crushed shells, encouraging a varied flora among which browse white striped snails and yellow banded snails. Lurking here, too, is *Zelotes electus*, a nocturnal hunting spider.

On the saltmarsh along the river Cefni grow Britain's largest stands of sea rush. Waders, including greenshank, spotted redshank, stints and whimbrel, come here in autumn and may be joined by both brent and greylag geese.

And so back to South Stack, where the breeding birds have dispersed to be replaced by an autumn and winter passage of skuas, Manx shearwaters and gannets from the Pembroke-shire island of Grassholm further south.

Viper's Bugloss

Maiden Pink

Welsh Marsh Orchid

VIPER'S BUGLOSS *(Echium vulgare)* A stiff upright plant with bristly hairs. Stems up to 36″ (90cm) bear short sprays of pink buds which turn blue when fully opened, June-August. Leaves are rough and narrow. Locally common on light, dry soils in England and Wales.

MAIDEN PINK *(Dianthus deltoides)* This perennial grows in open tufts 6-18″ (15-45cm) in dry, grassy fields and slopes throughout Britain except north Scotland. Clove-scented flowers with toothed petals are seen June-September. The leaves are bluish and narrow.

WELSH MARSH ORCHID *(Dactylorhiza majalis cambrensis)* Sometimes reaching 24″ (60cm) tall, the almost solid stem carries a spike of light magenta flowers marked with darker lines, June-August. Found only in marshes of NW Wales and Scotland.

PLOUGHMAN'S SPIKENARD *(Inula conyza)* Thriving on chalky, dry grassland, this upright plant has wiry, red-tinged stems up to 39″ (100cm). Many narrow flower heads are borne singly on branchlets July-September. Lower leaves are toothed and hairy, stem leaves are stalkless.

Ploughman's Spikenard

Yellow Bird's Nest

Seaside Pansy

Dune Helleborine

Shore Dock

YELLOW BIRD'S NEST (*Monotropa hypopitys*) Hooked waxy stems 3-12″ (8-30cm) have clasping leaves and clusters of bell-like flowers June-August. Lacking chlorophyll, it feeds on the rotting vegetation of dune pinewoods. Found throughout Britain, though scattered and rare.

SEASIDE PANSY (*Viola tricolor ssp. curtisii*) Tufts of this 1-6″ (3-15cm) high perennial are locally common on most grassy coastal dunes though absent from NE Scotland. At the base of oval leaves there are lobed stipules. Pods splitting into 3 follow flowers April-September.

DUNE HELLEBORINE (*Epipactis dunensis*) The spikes of bell-like flowers open June-July on slim 8-24″ (20-60cm) stems. Stiff, folded leaves are yellow-green and wavy edged. This orchid occurs only very locally in peaty hollows of dunes in Anglesey, Lancashire and Northumberland.

SHORE DOCK (*Rumex rupestris*) Growing very locally on rocky or sandy shores and damp hollows in dunes of SW England and Wales, this perennial dock has erect, branched stems up to 28″ (70cm), with broad, blue-green leaves. Whorls of flowers open June to August.

193

Tree Mallow

Scurvy-grass

Spotted Rockrose

TREE MALLOW (*Lavatera arborea*) Seen on cliffs and waste places near the south-west and west coasts, this is a branched woody biennial reaching 10′ (3m). Broadly-lobed leaves and upper parts of the stem are softly hairy. Purple-veined flowers open July-September.

SPOTTED ROCKROSE (*Tuberaria guttata*) Found on open rocky places in N Wales and Ireland, this rare annual only reaches 4″ (10cm). The branched stems grow from a leafy rosette, stem leaves are in opposite pairs. Short sprays of red-spotted flowers open June-September.

SCURVY-GRASS (*Cochlearia officinalis*) A fleshy-leaved 2-20″ (5-50cm) plant of sea cliffs and dry banks on saltmarshes all round Britain. The lower leaves are almost circular. 4-petalled flowers are seen April-August, followed by globular seed pods.

Ducks

Goldeneye Duck

Female

Male

Shelduck

Female

Male

GOLDENEYE DUCK *(Bucephala clangula)*An 18″ (46cm) sea and freshwater duck, the distinctively shaped head is brown in females, and black in males with a white spot. White wing patches and the whistling sound made by the wings identify them in flight. Although some now breed in Scotland, it is mostly a winter visitor to sheltered bays all round Britain, diving for molluscs and crustaceans in shallow water. After a noisy courtship, one clutch of 6-11 pale greeny eggs is laid in a tree hole. The young leave the nest after 24 hours.

SHELDUCK *(Tadorna tadorna)* Both sexes of this sturdily built 24″ (61cm) duck have the same bold colouring, though only males have a red knob at the base of the bill. Seen all round the coast on flat, muddy or sandy shores and estuaries, they eat invertebrates and seaweed. A single clutch of 8-15 off-white eggs is laid in May. The nest, made of plant material lined with down, can be built as far as 10′ (3m) down a rabbit burrow. Males stand guard as the female broods; both parents escort the black and white ducklings to the sea.

The Chough

Long revered as the embodiment of King Arthur's spirit, choughs are intrepid monarchs of the air, whose fearless displays on the wing combine natural exuberance with a desire to impress their mate.

Supreme masters of the air, choughs can be seen wheeling, soaring and diving along the wild rugged coasts of their strongholds in western Britain. Along the south and west coasts of Ireland, the Isle of Man, and the west of Scotland and Wales, the harsh ringing cries of these elegant red-billed crows can be heard clearly above the crashing of the waves.

Part of the object of the display is to impress a mate. Choughs pair for life, cementing their pair-bond with breathtaking aerial chases – the birds revelling in their superb powers of flight – interspersed with affectionate mutual preening. Choughs are among the world's highest flyers – reaching 29,000ft (8840m). One minute they are floating high in the blue sky like tiny scraps of charred paper blown about in the wind; the next, they are plummeting down like black arrow-heads, almost dashing themselves against the rocks far below before pulling out of the dive to sail effortlessly up and alight on the cliff top. Here they display to each other, bounding about with comical exaggerated hops, and flicking their wings and tails as they bow to one another, their brilliant red bills contrasting dramatically with their iridescent black plumage.

CLIFF-FACE NURSERY

In April, the female finds a safe place in which to rear her family. Favourite nest-sites are on cliff ledges, often in the shelter of an overhang, and in caves or rock crevices. Here the pair build a stout nest of sticks, grass and the stems of heather and other plants, lined with sheep's wool. The blotched glossy eggs, are laid in April or May. The female alone incubates them for 17 or 18 days, during which time the male works hard at keeping her supplied with food, and regularly calls her off the nest for a short spin to exercise her wings.

The chicks are fed on regurgitated insects by both parents, and take a month to fledge. The young look rather like overgrown starlings, with straw-coloured bills and dull orange-red legs. Soon family groups join together to form loose flocks which feed together on the cliff tops.

Choughs have a unique range of feeding techniques, which gives them an advantage over jackdaws and crows, as long as they can find areas of turf kept short by grazing sheep or rabbits. They can use their brilliant red scythe-shaped beaks as probes, thrusting them into the soft turf or heather of the clifftop. They also

use their bills like crowbars – levering stones aside to search for woodlice, worms, beetles and other small prey. In addition, they can use their bills like pick-axes to hack away at the turf, stripping it away to reveal insect grubs and other food. They are very fond of ants and use the delicate fine pointed tips of their beaks like tweezers to snap them up, having reached them by probing or hacking.

YOUNG CHOUGH
(above) Choughs rarely stray more than a mile inland. They are resident all the year round, battling with the full fury of Atlantic storms in winter. Sociable birds, they are known collectively as a 'clattering of choughs'.

ON THE WING
A couple of inches larger than its close relative the jackdaw, the chough has much glossier, blue-black plumage and longer, broader wings whose tips are splayed out like the outstretched fingers of a human hand. Choughs fly with superb virtuosity, and perform aerial stunts out of pure exuberance.

They eat large quantities of ants, particularly during the breeding season. Like other crows, they have a wide diet, including small crustaceans from among the seaweed, carrion, and grain.

Unfortunately, the 700-800 pairs of breeding choughs are a fraction of the number there used to be in the British Isles. The scarcity of rabbits in some places, due to myxomatosis, and the abandonment of sheep rearing on some of the poorer coastal pastures, have deprived choughs

PREENING PAIR
(below) Choughs mate for life, and constantly reinforce their relationship by mutual preening and aerobatic displays.

HERALDIC CROW
Choughs feature on the coat of arms of many Cornish families, to whom they symbolized the earthly presence of King Arthur's spirit. They vanished from Cornwall in 1968, and Canterbury, whose coat of arms is shown below, lost its resident population early in the 19th century.

of feeding sites with short turf. They may also have suffered from unusually severe winters, when the turf has lain frozen for some time, making it impossible to feed. Their retreat over the years to the milder west coast supports this suggestion.

Choughs have few natural predators – an occasional bird may fall prey to a peregrine falcon or raven. But man has always presented a threat and choughs are still sometimes shot: egg collectors also rob their nests, and the chicks are occasionally stolen to be kept as pets.

However, the chough is unusual among British crows in that the adults, their eggs and chicks are legally protected throughout the year. This is fortunate, for these birds are handsome additions to our coastal wildlife.

The Scottish Highlands

Rising in brutal splendour in north-west and north-central Scotland, the mountains and hills of the Highlands form Britain's most majestic and exciting scenery. Sculpted from some of the earth's most ancient rocks, countless jagged peaks and lofty crags plunge to dark, mysterious lochs of awesome depths, or fall to lush green glens bronzed with peaty torrents. In the past the hills were home to many more people than now live there, yet through depopulation and excused of man's worst excesses the Highlands have been preserved as one of Europe's last great areas of wild, unspoiled beauty.

The following labels appear on the illustration: ISLAND, DEER FOREST, HIGH PEAK, GLEN, CORRIE, RESERVOIR, GROUSE MOOR, SCREE, CONIFER PLANTATION, RUINED CROFT, RELIC PINE FOREST, LOCH

The Highland frontier lies along a fault, a massive rock fracture running up from the Firth of Clyde to just south of Aberdeen. North of this lie mountains ranged in a general SSW to NNE direction. By no means is all of this high ground, however: there are 'lowlands' towards the north east, and the hills themselves are separated by vast, steep-sided, ice-cut valleys, the Great Glen among them, often containing long lakes or lochs.

Although they nowhere match the Alps, the hills are the highest in Britain. Some are huge pyramids set on flat tableland, whose frowning precipices merit the name mountain (the Scots themselves always refer to them as hills). Their form is very varied, however, partly as a result of their rock type. The smooth slopes of Ben Nevis and the Cairngorms are of granite (the latter range is, in effect, a plateau cut by valleys); some of the hills are limestone while the rock called gabbro produces the finest crags.

Over the years, generations of Highland Scots have, either from choice or desperation, left this lovely land and emigrated to North America and Australia and elsewhere, carrying with them the memory of the purple hills of their ancestral home. Their departure resulted in and from great changes in the way the land was used. Nowhere else in Britain is the face of the landscape we know today so closely linked with actual historical events.

THE HIGHEST LAND IN BRITAIN
From the glassy-smooth sea lochs to the snow-capped peaks, some 4000 feet high, the character of the Highland landscape has been formed by climate and land use as well as geological forces.

SNOWCAPPED PEAKS
Depopulated over the centuries, the Highlands have an eerie, lonely quality that has made them such a popular refuge that tourism has become a vital part of the Highland economy.

HIGHLAND HISTORY

The Highlands were settled in early times, and eventually a people called Picts held much of the territory – they faced, but were never tamed by, the Romans. After the Roman withdrawal from Britain, Scots from Northern Ireland settled in Argyll and in time they gained mastery over the Picts, who suffered the worst of the Viking attacks on the North. Later, about 1000AD, great inroads had already been made on the native pine forest which since the Ice Age had covered much of the ground up to the natural tree line. Much more was cleared during medieval times, as by then the clan system was well established, and crops and woods were regularly fired in raids and reprisals. Sometimes the forest was burnt to smoke out refugees, but much was deliberately cleared as protection against the wolves which inhabited it.

The last wolf was killed in about 1750, and by then the traditional husbandry based on cattle was doomed. The last serious rebellions against rule from London collapsed at this time, which led not only to severe and brutal punishments and transportations, but the enforced introduction of sheep and new crops, such as turnips, which were planted on a large scale as winter feed for sheep. Sheep are voracious grazers, and with their introduction, any hope of the forest regenerating itself on the open hillsides disappeared.

Thus the way the Highlands were used changed. Much forest was also cleared when attempts were made to start iron smelting and other industry in some areas. Two hundred years ago, however, sporting interests were also having an effect and landlords set aside vast areas above the sheepwalks where heather was encouraged for grouse and ptarmigan. Heathery grouse moors still cover much ground, the heather being regularly burnt in patches to give the varied cover the grouse require. The rapid-firing, breech-loading gun introduced in the 1860s led not only to butt shooting, but to the near extinction of many wild species, for the keepers could more easily kill eagles, buzzards, and wild cats, which they considered 'vermin'.

In recent years, the Highlands have seen the growth of tourism, hydroelectric schemes and other development, but, fortunately, many parts have become wildlife parks.

HIGH ABOVE THE TREE LINE
Far above the tree line, high plateaux are covered by treacherous, uncharted bogs produced by the teeming rain. Up to 100 inches per year falls on the hard highland rocks.

Nature Walk

Man and nature have both left their mark on the craggy face of the Highlands. Look for:

PEAT TRENCHES For centuries highlanders have fuelled their fires with peat cut from ancient bogs.

BLACK FACED SHEEP Since the late 18th century the hills have been populated by more sheep than people.

TARN These high mountain lakes were scooped out by glaciers during last Ice Age and filled by meltwater.

BROCH Dry-stone, circular hill forts were built by Iron Age Scots to defend their north-western coastal frontier from sea-borne marauders. Some brochs contain galleries in the walls.

Wildlife of Hills and Glens

Although grandly picturesque, the High-lands, at first sight, may seem rather empty of wildlife. Closer inspection, however, reveals a fascinating diversity of both plant and animal life. Climate is one key to this diversity, as weather conditions fluctuate widely across the large area which the Highlands occupy.

The basically cold climate, which affects the vegetation so strongly high up in the hills, is markedly milder in coastal areas, even in the far north. Inland the weather is more 'continental', and the hills tend to have less rain but are subject to greater extremes of temperature, and often are very cold. Rainfall can vary dramatic-ally from one side of a mountain mass to the other, and the wetter sides of the mountains are not only more waterlogged but are often sunless and gloomy, as clouds hang over them. The wind is also an important factor in mountainous country. On Ben Nevis, for instance, a wind blowing at 50 miles an hour or more whips across the slopes for more than 200 days in the year. In the lowlands, sea-borne gales lash the coast with even greater ferocity.

Such conditions affect the natural tree line – the height to which trees will grow up the hillside. Because of the gales, trees near the coast may not grow above 200ft (60m) above sea level but, inland, where the wind has lost some of its sting, the same species can be found growing at heights up to 1800ft (550m) on some mountainsides.

In addition to the effects of climate, the vary-ing bedrock (of which there are many kinds) and man's historical and current uses of the land affect the vegetation of both the glens and the slopes above them. These three factors – climate, bedrock and man's usage – have long determined the pattern of natural life in the Highlands.

On the grouse moors, which usually lie above

OUT OF REACH
Large herds of red deer roam the high ground to escape the incessant biting of midges.

SUN WORSHIPPER
The mountain ringlet (above) only flies when the sun shines.

HIGHLAND WILDLIFE
The exciting wilderness of the Highlands is a stronghold for species rarely seen elsewhere in the British Isles, such as the golden eagle, mountain ringlet, alpine lady's mantle and the ptarmigan.

KEY TO FEATURES AND SPECIES
1 *Immature golden eagle*
2 *Snow buntings*
3 *Summit heath*
4 *Late snow*
5 *Grouse moor*
6 *Ptarmigan*
7 *Red deer*
8 *Sheep*
9 *Boggy 'flow'*
10 *Tumbling stream*
11 *Grassland*
12 *Mountain ringlet*
13 *Dipper*
14 *Sandpiper*
15 *Cowberry*
16 *Thrift*
17 *Starry saxifrage*
18 *Alpine lady's mantle*

WHITE-TAILED EAGLE

BUZZARD

GOLDEN EAGLE

OSPREY

LARGE HIGHLAND BIRDS OF PREY
White-tailed sea eagles are characterized by their broad wings – only the adults have white tails. Buzzards have brown and white underparts and short, broad heads. Adult golden eagles are huge, dark and have fingered wing tips. Ospreys have pale heads and black and white underparts.

the sheepwalks, there may be extensive bogs, called 'flows', in addition to the dominant mosaic of old and new heather. Apart from the red grouse, meadow pipits abound here, as do the highly vocal greenshanks which make their virtually untraceable nests both in the young heather and on the flows. Among the moorland heather, berries – such as cowberry and bilberry – are common and provide additional food for the grouse, while wet-loving shrubs such as cranberry lurk in the flows.

ABOVE THE TREES

The deer forests, despite their name, are usually located above the tree line far beyond the sheepwalks and grouse moors, at heights over 2000ft (600m). Here trees are scant, except for a few birch. Heather may be absent, too, and grasses and sedges often cover much of the ground. The red deer would naturally retire to such places to avoid man, but they are also driven this high in summer by the midges which infest much of the Highlands. On well-managed estates, regular culls take place to keep the herd healthy and in balance with the foraging.

Up here you may see a blue hare and sometimes a pine marten, perhaps occupying a lair in open ground. Wild cats, however, tend to remain on the lower wooded slopes. Equally unexpected may be the sight of feral goats, domestic stock which has taken to the wild, though they are more often seen lower down. Small mountain reindeer roam parts of the Cairngorms where their special diet can be found. They were hunted to extinction in the Middle Ages and today's herds were introduced from Lapland some thirty years ago.

Few butterflies take wing in the thin cold

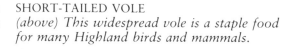

SHORT-TAILED VOLE
(above) This widespread vole is a staple food for many Highland birds and mammals.

mountain air, but on sunny days the mountain ringlet may be seen fluttering around a patch of boggy grass high above the grouse moors. In Britain, it is found only in the Highlands and the Lake District, and its nearest cousins are in the Alps. Another mountain grass butterfly, the Scotch argus, is less restricted and may be seen on somewhat lower ground.

In areas of extensive soft boggy land, waders come to breed in summer as they do on other moors, while the lively dipper follows the tumbling streams. The ring ouzel, the blackbird

CHANGING PLUMAGE
Male ptarmigan in summer (below) and winter (inset) plumage.

of the mountains, is also seen — as it breeds almost exclusively on high ground. The raven and the hooded crow (the northern race of the crow) are both Highland birds, although they also breed on lower ground elsewhere.

The magnificent golden eagle is the bird most associated with the Highlands. Much of the mischief laid at its door by gamekeepers and shepherds is probably the work of foxes, which are not uncommon in highland areas. Nevertheless, continuous persecution, not least by egg collectors, has forced the bird to take sanctuary in the deer forest. Sadly, increasing disturbance by tourists is a threat to its recently improved breeding success. Pairs require an immense area of largely undisturbed ground – up to 30 square miles – for their hunting territory.

LIFE AT THE TOP

High up the mountains, and indeed on the high plateau land too, there is another catalogue of wildlife. Here, far above the last heather, are found alpine plants which grow only or mainly on mountains. If they are also found to the north, in arctic Europe, they are known as arctic-alpines. Mountain azalea and snow gentian are two such species.

In parts of northern Scotland, some typical alpines are also seen down by the sea, but not between coast and mountain. Mountain avens is one such. Conversely, some familiar seashore flowers, such as thrift, are found growing high up in the mountains. Woodland flowers, such as bluebell, campion and violets, are also sometimes seen quite high up, in places where sheep or deer do not graze.

There is a logical explanation for these odd distributions. Capable of surviving a rigorously cold climate, the arctic-alpine and alpine flowers were among the first plants able to colonize the bare open ground at the end of the last Ice Age. Forests of trees later grew on the middle ground, shading them out. When the

YELLOW MOUNTAIN
SAXIFRAGE
(above) A bright perennial, this is one of numerous saxifrages found in the Highlands. It grows among rocks or by streams.

NESTING DOTTEREL
(above right) Less than 100 pairs of this charming and remarkably tame plover nest in Britain, mainly in the Highlands. Interestingly, the male incubates the eggs.

PINE MARTEN
(right) This beautiful hunter not only takes mountain hares and black grouse but also has a fondness for fruit. It is at home both on the open hillside and in the forests.

CLOUDBERRIES
(below) Related to the bramble, the attractive autumn fruits of cloudberry are just as edible as blackberries. The white flowered plant grows on peat bogs and moors.

trees were cleared, some of the woodland flowers survived in small pockets.

The tops are also home to some intriguing bird life. One breeding species is the ptarmigan, the grouse of the heights, which retreats to lower ground in winter. The male is unusual in having three coats, the brown of summer and white of winter being separated by a third greyish autumn plumage. The dotterel, a summer visitor, chooses land over 3000ft (900m) to nest, selecting rounded summits or plateaux where strong cross winds will sweep away any snow. The snow bunting, on the other hand, is never far from snow and ice, and tends to choose those craggy tops where snow lies late. Essentially an arctic bird, it is one of Britain's rarest breeding species. Probably fewer than 10 pairs nest each year – all in the Highlands. The fact that birds can flourish at this height shows that life can exist even in the most inhospitable conditions.

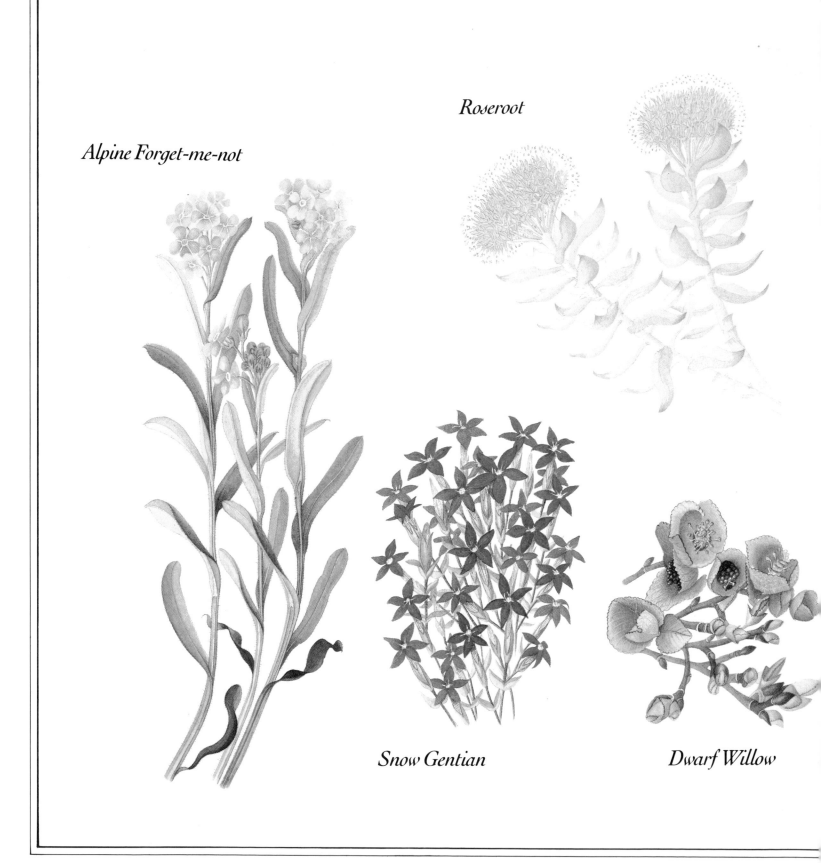

Alpine Forget-me-not

Roseroot

Snow Gentian

Dwarf Willow

ALPINE FORGET-ME-NOT (*Myosotis alpestris*) Up to 6″ (15cm) tall, stiff but elegant, this perennial has scented flowers in July and August, becoming tiny black fruit. A true alpine rarity in Britain – found only on limestone in Teesdale and Ben Lawers.

SNOW GENTIAN (*Gentiana nivalis*) An extremely rare annual alpine, found only on a few rocky ledges in the eastern Highlands. It flowers in July and August, producing single brilliant blue flowers on 4″ (10cm) unbranched stems above a tuft of leaves.

ROSEROOT (*Sedum rosea*) Also known as Midsummer-men, this succulent produces fleshy stems with terminal flower-heads from May to August, which become dense clusters of orange fruits. It is quite common on mountain ledges and sea cliffs from Wales northwards.

DWARF WILLOW (*Salix herbacea*) Also known as least willow, this shrub grows to barely more than 2″ (5cm) tall. It is a prostrate plant which creeps over the ground in large patches favouring sheltered mountain ledges in the north. The catkins appear in June.

Cloudberry

Mountain Avens

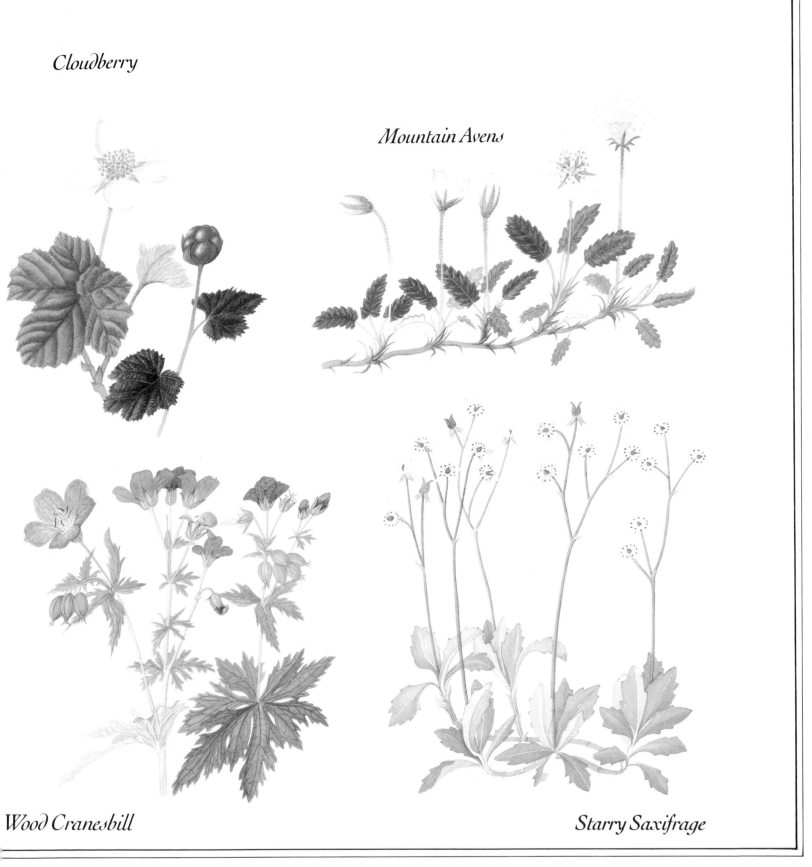

Wood Cranesbill

Starry Saxifrage

CLOUDBERRY (*Rubus chamaemorus*) Up to 7" (18cm) high, this perennial creeps in loose patches among heather in damp areas on moors and hills. It has solitary white flowers, and orange raspberry-like fruits. Found in the far north of Britain.

WOOD CRANESBILL (*Geranium sylvaticum*) A native of Scotland, where it embellishes meadows, damp woods and mountain ledges with its flowers from May to July, which become the characteristic long pointed fruit (hence cranesbill) on 28" (70cm) stems.

MOUNTAIN AVENS (*Dryas octopetala*) A 4" (10cm) creeping plant with 1" (2.5cm) flowers in May and June, which become feathery clematis-like seedheads. It grows on limestone, high up on rocky ledges from Snowdonia northwards, and in Ireland.

STARRY SAXIFRAGE (*Saxifraga stellaris*) One of the commonest highland saxifrages, this delicately formed 3" (7cm) plant flowers from June onwards in northern mountains, where it favours wet spots near streams and boggy places.

Golden Eagle

Dotterel

Male in winter

GOLDEN EAGLE *(Aquila chrysaetos)* Between 250 and 300 pairs of this magnificent bird inhabit the Scottish highlands. They are 34″ (85cm) long, with a 7′ (2m) wingspan, and feed on hares, grouse and even sick lambs. They lay 2 eggs in a large nest.

DOTTEREL *(Charadrius morinellus)* A rare breeding bird of Scottish mountains, which lays its 3 mottled eggs on the ground, on broad whaleback ridges and stony barren plateaux. It is a summer visitor, 8½″ (21cm) long, and feeds on insects.

PTARMIGAN *(Lagopus mutus)* An inhabitant of high mountaintops, mostly above the heather grouse moors, this 13″ (33cm) bird lays up to 12 eggs on the ground among short vegetation or stones. It eats shoots, leaves, berries and seeds. It turns white in winter.

Greenshank

Snow Bunting

Ptarmigan

Male in summer

SNOW BUNTING (*Plectrophenax nivalis*) A tame little 6½″ (16.5cm) bird which inhabits mountaintops in summer, and beaches in winter, searching for insects and seeds. It lays 4-6 blotched pale blue eggs in a cup-like nest of moss and grass in late May.

GREENSHANK (*Tringa nebularia*) An elegant 12″ (30cm) wader, which visits northern moors in summer to lay its 4 beautifully mottled eggs on the ground. In winter it frequents estuaries and marshland, where it feeds on worms, molluscs and fish, as well as insects.

The Scottish Wildcat

An unfriendly loner, the wildcat shuns man, and keeps aloof from its own kind, hunting
alone through the long hours of darkness in the cold and windy Highlands.

In the remnants of the ancient forests of Scots pine in the north west Highlands the shy and cunning wildcat shares a remote exile with other beleaguered species, like the otter, the pine marten and the golden eagle. In the rugged wilderness of the Cairngorms it has adapted to a world of headlong glens, cliffs and rocks, as well as mountain forests and high moors.

Despite a superficial resemblance to a large, home-loving tabby, the wildcat is not the ancestor of our domestic cats, whose line derives from an African cousin. *Felis silvestris grampia*, as the Scottish version of the European wildcat is known, has a compact, well-muscled body about two feet long excluding the tail. Its fur is a yellowish grey, with distinct vertical black stripes, and it weighs between 12 and 14lb, though much larger specimens have been recorded. Its feet and its skull are larger in proportion to its body than those of the domestic cat, as are its long upper fangs.

The wildcat takes great care to mark out its territory, both with urine and with faeces, which it deposits as a 'scat' in prominent places such as tussocks and stumps. Markers are also made by sharpening claws on trees, cutting through

the bark to the white sapwood beneath. The visual marker probably doubles as a scent marker, as the wildcat has sweat glands in its feet.

SHORT HONEYMOON

Solitary for most of the year, the male wild cat seeks out the female in March, uttering a noisy vocabulary of cries and yowls. The mating pair spend little time together, meeting up only occasionally over a period of two weeks, after which the male is sent packing by the female. The wildcat enjoys no cosy family life, and the toms are quite capable of killing and eating their own kittens.

After 65 or 66 days a litter of up to four kittens are born. They are light in colour, with markings that darken as they get older. The litter is born in a den, usually an inaccessible spot deep in the roots of a tree, among dense undergrowth, tumbled rocks, or excavated beneath a bank. Dens are also found in abandoned fox earths and badger setts. At about five weeks the kittens venture out for the first time to play in the open. As they become more mobile the mother may take them to other dens where hunting is easier and she can begin to teach

FEROCIOUS COUPLE
At first sight, the wildcat could be mistaken for a chunky fireside tabby. But such a mistake could be dangerous, since, when cornered, the wildcat is spring-loaded aggression incarnate, as it has had to be to survive at all in the pitiless northern outposts to which it is condemned. Adult males defend a personal territory of up to 300 acres in winter, but lead a more nomadic life at other times.

Scotland rabbits are the main item of diet, while in the west they eat more rodents such as voles and mice. They also take hares, game birds, smaller perching birds, and insects, according to terrain and availability. In times of shortage an adult wildcat will take a lamb or a young deer. This is not very common, but their enthusiasm for game-birds makes them unwelcome on grouse-moors, and up to 200 wildcats a year are still trapped or shot. More nocturnal than the fox, they hunt through the hours of darkness, but particularly at dusk and dawn. In the daytime they love to bask, half asleep, for hours in the sun. The wildcat can swim if it has to, and can catch fish, by standing on the bank or on a rock, and hooking with a paw. They are great climbers, and will use an abandoned bird's nest as a temporary den. Their method of descending a tree tail-first,

them the rudiments of survival. Hunting lessons start at about nine weeks, though the kittens are not completely weaned for four months. Yet one month later, still only half grown, they are independent. The mother abandons them, and may well drive them away. It is late autumn by this time, and the territory is only sufficient to provide one adult with the food necessary to build fat reserves for the winter months.

The kittens now must travel and hunt, and establish their own territories. They have few enemies, but golden eagles and foxes have been known to take youngsters and the harsh winter will thin their numbers. Those that survive the winter will reach adult size before the spring, though they are unlikely to mate until the following season. They will continue to put on bulk and muscle until they reach full weight at three years of age.

Their prey varies widely. In the east of

HUNTER AND PREY
A proficient hunter, the wildcat will stalk and pounce on rabbits and hares, small rodents and birds. Carcases are picked clean, and any remains are consumed later.

HARD FELINES
The serious process of training kittens for independent life begins when they are very young. But even kittens can never be tamed.

in an undignified scrabble, indicates that they are not truly suited to tree life.

It was the competition with man that first drove the wildcat north. From the Roman period onwards, forest clearance, enclosures, and the setting up of large hunting estates all contributed to the wildcat's decline. Hunters and gamekeepers persecuted it until by the middle of the 19th century it became virtually extinct south of the Scottish border. And although driven further and further north, the fortunes of the wildcat gradually improved as the great private estates broke up, the Forestry Commission established new woodlands, and the numbers of gamekeepers decreased. There is evidence now that wildcats are beginning to move southwards, recolonizing parts of the Southern Uplands in their search for food and new territories. One danger in this, however, is that they may begin to interbreed with domestic and feral cats to the point where their own gene bank is no longer pure. Furthermore, interbreeding would increase the number of litters produced each year, and lead to overpopulation of limited territories.

HUNTER OF THE HIGHLANDS

THE CANINE TEETH are ferocious, made for tearing prey and neatly picking the bones clean.

RETRACTABLE CLAWS hold struggling prey, until the cat kills it with a carefully placed bite. The wild cat marks its territory with scent glands in its paws.

THE COAT is always buff/grey clearly striped with black. It becomes much thicker in winter.

THE TAIL is bushy, with a characteristic blunt black tip.

The Cairngorms

Remote and desolate, the dark, undulating plateau of the Cairngorms is the largest expanse of untamed high ground in the British Isles. Its inhospitable, mist-shrouded summits are littered with rocky scree and pitted with snow-lined corries and isolated lochs which feed the swift torrents that tumble down to the valleys below. Deep, steep-sided glens slash their way through the mountain range – a legacy of the Ice Age, which sculpted the features of this dramatic landscape some 10,000 years ago.

THE
CAIRNGORMS

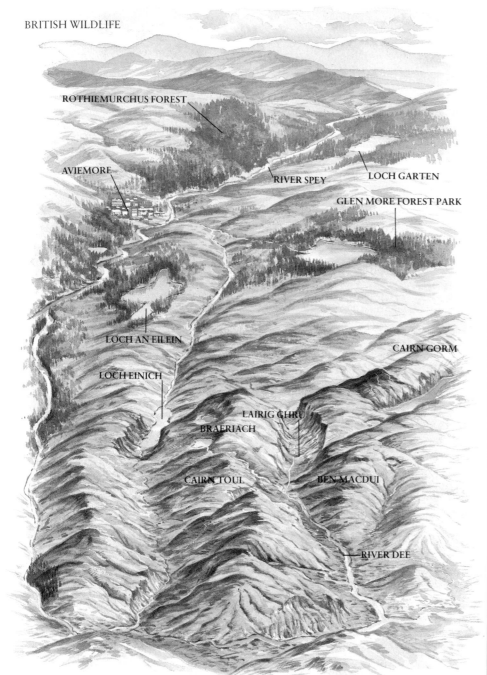

ROTHIEMURCHUS FOREST

AVIEMORE

RIVER SPEY   LOCH GARTEN

GLEN MORE FOREST PARK

LOCH AN EILEIN

CAIRN GORM

LOCH EINICH

LAIRIG GHRU

BRAERIACH

CAIRN TOUL   BEN MACDUI

RIVER DEE

HIGHLAND LANDSCAPE

At the heart of the Grampians the dark granite domes of the Cairngorm mountains rise to 4000 feet. Their broad, undulating summits were rounded by the same glacial action that gouged out the deep passes like Lairig Ghru, which cleaves the mountain range in two. Lochs and swift-flowing streams and rivers are a feature of the mountains and the surrounding country-side, where ancient pine woodland mixes with recent plantations in areas like the Glen More Forest Park and Rothiemurchus Forest. Where the forest has been cleared moorland and bogs now occur.

Covering 160 square miles between Aviemore in Strathspey and Braemar in Upper Deeside, the Cairngorm Mountains represent the greatest tract of high ground in Britain. Desolate and wind-swept, the 30-mile wide range is in fact a rolling plateau over 3000 feet (900m) high, dominated by four of the five highest summits in Britain, all over 4000 feet (1200m). Ben Macdui, 4296 feet (1310m) high, runs close second to distant Ben Nevis (4406 feet/1343m) as the highest mountain in Britain.

The rock of this mighty massif is hard granite. Pink felspar crystals often give it a pinkish tinge, which inspired the old Gaelic name of *Monadh Ruadh*, the 'Red Hills'. The name Cairngorm derives from the variously coloured smoky ornamental quartz found in the area. Indeed one of the summits in the range is named Cairn Gorm – meaning 'blue mountain'.

Although the shoulders of the high ground are smooth, the upper slopes are pitted with cauldron-like corries, scoured out of the rock as a huge ice-sheet moved north-eastwards across the mountains some 10,000 years ago. The steep-sided valleys which dissect the plateau were also deepened by glacial action. The most dramatic and best-known of these is Lairig Ghru – the 'gloomy pass' – cutting into the mountain block near Aviemore and separating the heights of Cairn Gorm and Ben Macdui to the east from Braeriach, Einich Cairn and Cairn Toul to the south-west.

On the mountain tops the climate is sub-arctic, with the average temperature remaining below freezing for seven months of the year. More snow falls here than anywhere else in the British Isles, drifting deepest at the end of April and melting steadily through the summer, to feed tumbling falls and torrents which become

famous rivers. One of the sources of the Dee lies in the bitingly cold Pools of Dee on Lairig Ghru, and the River Spey, counted among the fastest flowing rivers in Britain, obtains much of its force from tributaries running from the heights of the Cairngorms.

Up on the plateau, the melting snow reveals loose gravelly soils of fractured granite, which support only heathers and relic communities of plants and animals which were widespread during the last Ice Age, but which are now common only in the Alps and Arctic tundra.

This fierce mountain landscape has never been tamed. But the lower slopes and valleys present another face. Here the hummocky ground was once covered with a mixed forest of pine, birch and aspen, with oaks in some places. Most of this ancient forest has gone, cleared in centuries past, though the area is famous for its relic patches of native pine woodland, where some gnarled Scots pine trees may be two or three hundred years old. Today, though, vast plantations clothe many of the lower slopes, sometimes engulfing patches of relic forest.

INROADS INTO THE MOUNTAINS

The Cairngorms were first popularized as a focus for tourism by the Victorians, who tested themselves on the heights and stalked deer amongst the summits. But our own century has witnessed greater influxes of people. The long snow lie has encouraged the development of winter sports facilities, and the slopes of Cairn Gorm are now masked with chair lifts and ski tows. Fortunately, at the same time that the mountains were made more accessible to increasing numbers of visitors, the unique character of the Cairngorms and their plant and animal life was recognized and protected by the formation, in 1954, of the Cairngorms National Nature Reserve. This is now the largest reserve in Britain, covering 100 square miles, and protects both the best of the bleak heights and the more sheltered lower ground which falls within its boundaries.

LONELY LOCH
(left) The effects of the Ice Age are evident throughout the Cairngorms. Deep U-shaped valleys are a typical glacial feature and often form natural reservoirs for melt-water and rain running off the nearby summits.

CULTIVATED COUNTRYSIDE
(below) At the north-western edge of the mountains, forested slopes lead down to a fertile valley floor some 700 feet above sea level. Here the fast-flowing Spey meanders through a rich mosaic of forest and farmland.

Nature Walk

The Cairngorms region is rich in interesting natural and man-made features. Look out for:

RUTHREN BARRACKS which were put to the torch by the Jacobite army which disbanded there after the battle of Culloden.

CAIRNGORM STONE a smoky semi-precious quartz found in the Cairngorms and used in jewellery.

LAZY BEDS where crofters grew their vegetables. The ground was raised to improve drainage.

TREE LINE at Creag Fhiaclach – the only natural example of this in the British Isles.

Life of the High Tops

Sometimes called Scotland's Lapland, the Cairngorms are a magical wilderness holding birds of the heights, arctic flowers, a unique moth and even reindeer from the far north.

The high tops of the Cairngorms are one of the very special places in the British Isles for wildlife. Akin to the Scandinavian tundra, the extensive plateaux above 3000 feet are a rich wilderness of snowfields, screes, boulders and a short vegetation of hardy grasses, sedges and lichens. In summer the arctic-alpine grassland is enlivened by bright patches of flowering moss campion, trailing azalea and saxifrages.

On more sheltered slopes, carpets of woolly fringe moss grow, interspersed with cowberry and rigid sedge. In the snowy hollows grow the food plants of the ptarmigan – crowberry, bilberry and the stunted, 3-inch high least or dwarf willow.

LAND OF THE PTARMIGAN

Resident throughout the Cairngorms, ptarmigan are extremely hardy members of the grouse family which survive on the high mountain ridges even in winter. They are ideally adapted in their white winter plumage which changes to greys and browns in spring. Scotland's weather is unpredictable and the ptarmigan's camouflage breaks down if there is no snow cover in winter or fresh snow in June. Then, hunting golden eagles can pick them out easily. Below 3000 feet, where heather is growing well, ptarmigan are replaced by red grouse, one of the commoner birds of the moorland.

The Cairngorms are renowned for dotterel, one of several wading birds which return in spring to breed on the plateaux. They are beautiful birds and add greatly to a bird-watching trip to the mountains. Golden plover and dunlin occur in small numbers on grassy and mossy areas, while common sandpipers nest beside some of the lower level lochs such as Loch Avon, with the highest pair recorded at 3000 feet.

Small birds are scarce, which is not surprising considering the paucity of insects. Meadow pipits are well distributed, with smaller numbers of wheatears and skylarks. In winter time, small flocks of snow buntings search for seeds in short vegetation on the mountainside but some prefer easier pickings among the skiers and the car parks. A few remain to breed in the highest hills; their jangling song adding magic to the remote snowfields and rocks in summer. They often feed by catching daddy longlegs attracted

CRESTED TIT
Perched here with caterpillars for the chicks, the rare crested tit nests in old pine stumps. A few deers' hairs at the edge of the nest hole may give it away. When feeding the chicks they can be watched at close range, foraging in the pines. These birds are long-time residents of the old Speyside pines.

WILDLIFE ON THE CAIRNGORMS

Dotterel and ptarmigan nest on the high tops. The ptarmigan falls prey to two crag-nesting birds, the golden eagle and peregrine. Ravens, too, nest on crags, while the rarer snow bunting favours gullies. The dipper nests by swift flowing burns. Lower down, among the heather and pines, black grouse perform courtship displays. Here, too, red deer can be seen. Mountain hares feed on heather, least willow, grasses and rushes, keeping a look-out for predatory eagles. Wild cats take young hares, nesting grouse and occasionally fish. Bilberry and other shrubs produce berries.

KEY TO THE SPECIES

1 Ptarmigan
2 Golden eagle with hare
3 Dotterel
4 Peregrine
5 Ravens
6 Moss campion
7 Rose-root
8 Mountain sorrel
9 Scots pines
10 Red deer hinds
11 Bilberry
12 Three-leaved rush
13 Snow bunting
14 Northern hawkbit
15 Mountain hare
16 Cross-leaved heath
17 Mountain burnet
18 Bearberry
19 Wild cat
20 Blackcocks
21 Heather
22 Spiked wood-rush
23 Mountain ringlet
24 Lichen Ochrolechia parella
25 Wolf spider
26 Least willow
27 Trailing azalea
28 Dipper
29 Fescue

WILD AZALEA
(above) Also known as trailing azalea, this plant carpets areas of Scottish mountains. Bright mats of pink flowers enliven the slopes from May to July. Its leathery, evergreen leaves prevent dehydration.

MOSS CAMPION
(above right) Another pink flower of the mountains, moss campion has brighter green leaves than wild azalea and differently shaped flowers. It flowers from late June to August, growing in moss-like cushions.

to get to Perthshire pass south in autumn, sometimes in noisy terror at the glimpse of an eagle. Redwings and fieldfares feast on ripe berries in the mountains as they fly south in October, while migrating ospreys passing by from the northern lochs have thrilled bird-watchers for many years. Black-headed gulls and crows are commoner now than in the past, attracted by the sandwiches and waste of tourists. Unfortunately, these birds stay to prey upon the eggs and young of dotterel and ptarmigan.

GOLDEN EAGLE
(below) A female launches herself from the huge twiggy platform of her nest built on a rocky ledge. Eagles are scarcer in the Cairngorms than the western Highlands. Here, though, they prey on birds as large as the greylag geese, which migrate through in autumn.

to late lasting snowfields.

Ring ouzels frequent some of the corries and steeper hillsides and in late summer they take advantage of berry bearing plants such as bilberry (blaeberry), cloudberry and bearberry. Occasional dippers explore even the highest burns which well up from high-level springs.

Golden eagles and peregrines nest in the mountains and range over high tops, although most of their food is found on the lower slopes and moorland. Fortunately, eagles can still find safe nesting sites in crags and corries but at least one pair has been displaced by increasing numbers of tourists. Even in these high hills the eagles are resident and it is a superb sight to see a pair displaying above snowy cliffs on a crisp, sunlit day in February. Adult peregrines also remain in the hills in winter, except during the stormiest periods when they temporarily move to the coast. Peregrines are well distributed but most are in the lower glens.

The smaller merlins also favour lower ground but will make occasional forays to the plateaux. No owls nest on the high ground but short-eared owls sometimes stop off and occasionally the high tops are home for a vagrant snowy owl. Then the Cairngorms really are like Lapland, but they lack the lemmings which are so important for this huge white owl of the Arctic.

A variety of migrant and wandering birds visit the mountains. Skeins of grey geese eager

Though invertebrates are scarce on the tops, the Cairngorms are the only known British site of the Scotch or mountain burnet moth. Colonies occur above 2000 feet on the slopes and summit near Braemar. On sunny days in June and July the moths visit the flowers of mountain everlasting and bird's foot trefoil; their caterpillars feed mainly on crowberry.

Also flying only on sunny days, the mountain ringlet butterfly frequents boggy ground above 1000 feet, visiting flowers such as northern hawkbit. The Scotch argus is another sunloving butterfly of the slopes. The wolf spider *Lycosa amentata* can be found high up. It lives under stones, only venturing out in fine weather.

The most obvious mammal of the Cairngorms is the red deer. In summer, tormented by nostril flies and biting midges they move on to the high plateaux where the insects are fewer. Reindeer have grazed the Cairngorms since they were introduced from Scandinavia three decades ago.

SNOW BUNTING
(above) A female settles down into her nest lined with ptarmigan feathers. Many birds winter in the British Isles but few stay to breed. Males often mate with two or even three females. Five or more broods may be reared in the Cairngorms each year, their main British site.

MOUNTAIN HARE
(left) In its white winter coat this hare is well camouflaged from predators among the snow and frost which lie late into the year. The timing of their moult to brown is determined by the snow cover.

REINDEER BULL
(right) Reindeer are unusual in that both sexes have antlers, though those of the female are generally smaller. Males lose theirs in winter. The semi-wild Cairngorms' herd roams the Glen More forest area, mainly feeding on the grasses, sedges, lichens and mosses of the high ground. Females and young wander in herds but bulls are solitary, only joining the herd during the autumn rut.

Blue or mountain hares are present in low numbers at high altitudes but become commoner lower down and to the east. Beautifully white in winter, they moult to a distinctive greyish brown in summer. The occasional fox, stoat or wild cat visits the high mountains but life is easier at lower altitude for these animals.

The unique quality of these mountains is greatly enhanced by the nearby Caledonian pine forests in Strathspey and Deeside. These boast birds like Scottish crossbill, crested tits and capercaillie. Goshawks and buzzards now breed here, as do red squirrels and roe deer.

Sadly, the Cairngorms, like much of Scotland, have been badly overgrazed and burnt to encourage sheep, deer and game. Much of the original fringing forest is gone and the scrub of willow and birch is missing. With careful management it may return. We may then have blucthroats and Lapland buntings to make the Cairngorms even more like Scotland's Lapland.

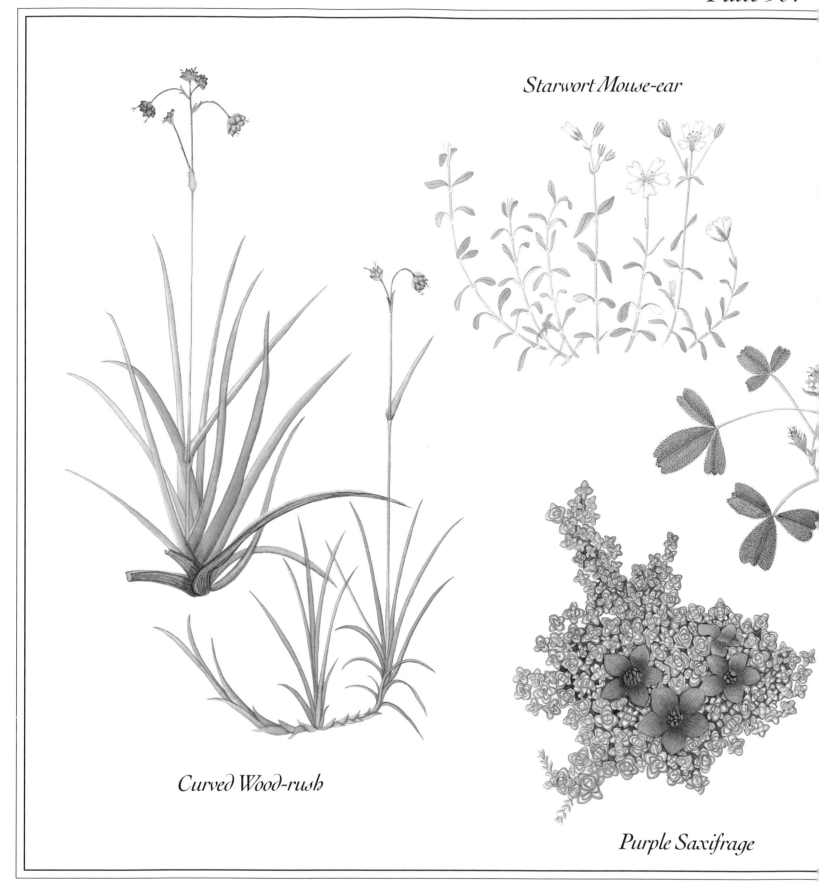

Starwort Mouse-ear

Curved Wood-rush

Purple Saxifrage

CURVED WOOD-RUSH (*Luzula arcuata*) A tiny, tufted perennial seen on nearly bare, stony mountain slopes above 3000' (914m) in north Scotland. Leaves are narrow and grooved, stems 1-3" (3-8cm) have curved branches with clusters of flowers in June and July.

STARWORT MOUSE-EAR (*Cerastium cerastoides*) A creeping perennial with branching stems and narrow leaves forming a loose mat. Semi-erect 2-4" (5-10cm) shoots bear flowers with deeply lobed petals, July-August. Found on acid soils high in the mountains of Scotland.

PURPLE SAXIFRAGE (*Saxifraga oppositifolia*) Restricted to limy rocks, this saxifrage is only found on the few limestone peaks of the otherwise granite Cairngorms. A mat of branching stems bears many tiny leaves, and flower stems to ¾" (2cm) have single blooms April to June.

SIBBALDIA (*Sibbaldia procumbens*) Tiny ¾" (2cm) tufts of this perennial grow from a woody base. Leaves are 3-lobed, each leaflet with a blunt, 3-toothed tip. Heads of small-petalled flowers open June-August. Widespread in Scottish Highlands, and Cumbria on high rocky ground.

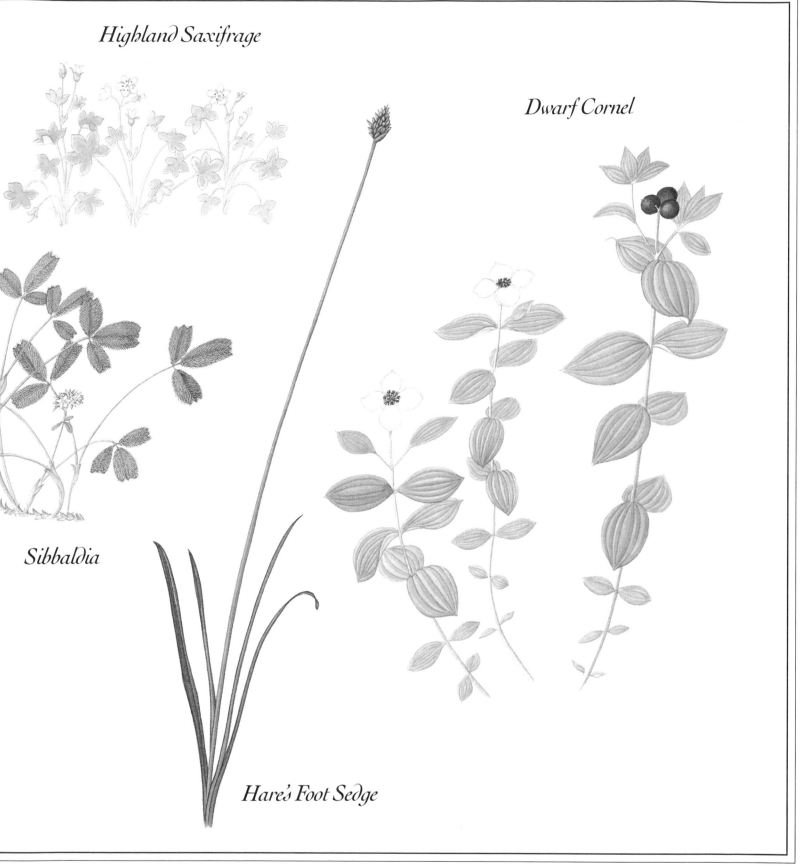

Highland Saxifrage

Dwarf Cornel

Sibbaldia

Hare's Foot Sedge

HIGHLAND SAXIFRAGE *(Saxifraga rivularis)* This tiny, rare plant occurs only in scattered localities in the Highlands of Scotland, on wet rocks above 3000′ (914m). Semi-erect weak stems up to 3″ (8cm) long bear 1-3 flowers, July and August, that are pollinated by small flies.

HARE'S FOOT SEDGE *(Carex lachenalii)* A rare sedge of bogs and wet rocks high up in mountains of north Scotland. It makes loose tufts of narrow leaves and 3-angled stems to 12″ (30cm). A head of dense single-sexed flowerspikes opens in July, male spikes at the bottom.

DWARF CORNEL *(Cornus suecica)* This creeping plant is found on acid soil on the mountains and moors of Scotland and north England, stems up to 8″ (20cm) support 3-5 veined leaves and bear heads of flowers cupped by white bracts, July and August. Fruits are round and red.

223

Peregrine

Juvenile

Twite

PEREGRINE *(Falco peregrinus)*
Since the population crash caused by pesticides in the 1960s, this 15-19″ (38-48cm) falcon is slowly recovering. A resident, it breeds mostly on the cliffs and mountains of the North and West, but needs protection from egg-collectors. It 'stoops' to catch and kill flying birds at great speed. The sexes are similar, females darker and larger than males. Their nest is a hollow scraped in debris on remote ledges. 3-4 heavily marked buff eggs are laid March-April. Both parents tend the young. Call is a 'kek-kek-kek'.

TWITE *(Acanthis flavirostris)*
A small 5¼″ (13cm) finch, sometimes mistaken for a linnet but the ochre throat of both sexes and pinkish rump of the male distinguish the twite. They are fairly common birds, frequenting scrub and upland moors of north Britain and Ireland

Juvenile

Juvenile

Osprey

during summer, seen more often near the coast in winter. Small groups of twite may nest socially. Females make deep grassy cups lined with wool in sites near the ground often in dense cover or holes in banks. 5-6 pale blue, speckled eggs are laid April-May. Call a nasal 'chweek'.

OSPREY *(Pandion haliaetus)*
A splendid sight as it glides over lochs and estuaries, plunging to catch fish, this 18-23″ (45-58cm) bird of prey returned to Britain in 1954 when the first pair for over 40 years bred in Speyside. Ospreys arrive there in spring – the breeding

pairs adding more material to large nests in treetops or ruins. 2-3 blotched, cream eggs are laid April-May. Hens do most incubating, while males bring fish. The young fly at about 8 weeks but are dependant until 3 months. Call is short, whistling *kewk-kewk-kewk*.

The Scotch Argus

As the sun breaks through the cloud on a summer's day, the
bare Scottish moors come alive with Scotch argus butterflies
darting and dancing from tussock to tussock.

The name, Argus, after the vigilant, all-seeing 100-eyed giant of Greek mythology is highly appropriate to the Scotch Argus butterfly, with the clear eye-spots on its wings and its watchful, alert behaviour.

These conspicuous eye-spots are located on the bold bands of orange which lie across the upperside of of its velvety brown fore and hindwings, while greyish or bluish white bands cross the pale brown undersides. The eye-spots are black with white centres, and it is these clear white centres that immediately distinguish it from the related, but smaller and rarer, mountain ringlet.

The male Scotch argus usually has three eye-spots on the forewing, while the female sports four. The male is generally smaller than the female, the wingspan ranging from 1½-2in,

(40-50mm), roughly the same size as the widespread small white.

Until the end of the 19th century, the Scotch argus was common in a few parts of northern England as well as in the Scottish highlands; but now, apart from a few localities in Cumbria, Scotland is the only part of the British Isles where you are likely to see this handsome butterfly. It is to be found on moorlands, on the damper patches of purple moor grass or on blue moor grass, especially in valleys surrounded by trees and where the grass grows in strong tussocks. It can be found up to 1500 feet (50m) but is not a true 'mountain' butterfly like its aplty named relative, the mountain ringlet. Beyond our shores it is common in eastern and central Europe, mainly in hilly country but, unusually for a butterfly that is found only in

WELL SPOTTED
*(above) The rows of false
eyes on the Scotch argus are
particularly prominent on
the female, which is also
lighter in colour and has a
much fatter abdomen than
the male. Both sexes love to
flit in the sunshine and dart
for cover as soon as the sun is
obscured, emerging only if
the air is very warm. Found
mostly on mountain slopes
and woodland edges, this
lively butterfly feeds from
most flowers in its habitat.*

SCENES FROM A LIFE

The Scotch argus caterpillar (below) feeds on grass at night and when threatened, it can fall suddenly to the ground and feign death. With a pointed head and tail, it is usually pale brown with a dark stripe down the back. The pupa (right) rests unattached in a flimsy, upright cocoon at the base of a food plant – often in leaf litter – to emerge as a full grown butterfly in about a fortnight.

spots which look like eyes and distract the stabbing beaks of their predators. But, although the Scotch argus has eye spots, its defence is to close its wings and rely on its well-camouflaged underside for protection.

At rest on the ground, the orange patterned uppersides are hidden as the Scotch argus folds its wings to resemble a dead leaf. This ploy is so successful that male butterflies flying over the grass tussocks searching for mates even stop to inspect dead leaves.

HIBERNATING CATERPILLARS

After mating, the female lays her white, ribbed eggs singly deep inside the tussocks of moor-grass in August and the pale brown caterpillars hatch in early September. They feed on moor-grass until the colder weather of October drives them to burrow deep inside the tussocks where they hibernate for the winter. They are active again by May and continue to feed, grow and moult until full size.

In June or early July, the caterpillars are ready to pupate. They stay at the base of the tussocks or even burrow just below the ground out of the sight of potential predators. The pupa or chrysalis takes at least a couple of weeks to complete the metamorphosis and the adult emerges in late July or early August. In good years, the numbers of caterpillars can be enormous and the subsequent butterfly population very large, but each one lives for only about three weeks. The whole life cycle of one generation of the Scotch Argus being completed within a year.

HELPFUL WINGS

(below) To camouflage itself from predators, the Scotch argus exposes the underside of its wings which can look remarkably like a dead leaf. So successful is the camouflage, that many an ardent male will inspect fallen leaves . . . just in case. A characteristic feature of the Scotch argus is the thickening of veins on the wings where they join the thorax.

the northern part of Britain, it is not present in Scandinavia.

Butterflies are often referred to as insects that fly only in sunshine. This is one species that closely adheres to this generalization – it has to be very warm indeed for a Scotch argus to fly on an overcast day. In sunny weather, however, the butterfly is restless and at its most active, constantly moving from flower to flower. It is particularly fond of grassy areas bordering woodlands and young open plantations which receive the early morning sunshine. Some butterflies become highly conspicuous when they show their strongly marked upper-sides, and so highly vulnerable to all kinds of predators, from wasps and birds to small mammals. As a defence, many brightly coloured butterflies – such as the peacock – protect themselves with

The Dotterel

High on the Cairngorms plateaux, small flocks of dotterel skim low over the rock-strewn ground. Once common throughout Britain, this summer visitor is now a rare sight, confined to the bleak, inaccessible highlands.

LITTLE WADER
One of the smaller waders, the tame and trusting dotterel has a very distinctive plumage during the breeding season, which once made it a popular target for marksmen, its feathers being used for fishing lures and decoration. A bright chestnut belly is separated from a grey breast by a narrow white chest band, and a black patch on the lower belly gives way to white beneath the tail. This colouring is stronger in the female, but lost during the winter months, when both sexes moult to a buff-grey. As a result of continued shooting, the dotterel is now rare and afforded special protection.

At the end of April or in early May, just as the snow begins to melt on the high wind-swept mountain tops of Scotland and the North of England, the first small 'trips' (or flocks) of dotterel arrive, flying in from the warmer climate of North Africa and the Middle East to breed.

Once common and widespread in Britain, the colourful dotterel is now rare and restricted to the desolate highland areas of the Cairngorms, West and Central Inverness, the Monadliaths, Cumbria and North Wales. The bird prefers rounded 'whale-back' massifs with short grass and tundra-type heath to sharper peaks. In a good year up to 100 pairs may breed.

In the Cairngorms – the stronghold of the dotterel in Britain – snow may linger until well into the summer months and the dotterel's breeding season is very much controlled by the weather, In favourable years egg-laying begins in May, but with a cold spring and snow lingering on the plateau the nest may not be made until June. Although this takes place at between 3000 and 4000 feet (900-1200m) above sea level in the Cairngorms, in the Arctic regions of Scandinavia and in the polders of the Netherlands, dotterels nest at sea level.

ROLE REVERSAL

Unusually, it is the female bird which is the more brightly coloured of the sexes, and at 8½ inches (21cm), she is slightly larger than the male. In a complete reversal of the usual roles, it is the male who incubates the eggs and rears the young, while the hen bird takes the lead in the rituals of courtship. She has the stronger sex drive and dominates the displays and dances.

After they have paired, both cock and hen

birds shuffle and scrape the ground in a number of places, as if to prepare nest sites. The hen usually makes the final choice, and a scrape is made among the rocky heath of the tundra and sparsely lined with mosses and lichens. On average three heavily blotched pale brown eggs are laid at intervals of about a day and a half, and are incubated by the male for 26 days before the chicks hatch.

The nests themselves are not easy to find, especially if they are made amongst mountain heather, and the cock bird sits so tight that he can go unnoticed from just a few feet away. When approached, the dotterel is so tame that it can even be stroked when sitting on the nest. This feature of the bird's character has, in the past, allowed it to be easily caught and killed for food and its decorative feathers, with drastic effects on the population.

While the male is incubating the eggs, the female joins up with other hens and together they may wander some distance from the nesting areas. A hen bird may even mate a second time while her first mate is brooding. This second mating allows the dotterel to produce twice as many young during the brief breeding season, giving the species a greater chance of survival.

All the chicks hatch within a few hours of each other and the cock flies off with the shattered egg shells to avoid attracting predators to the nest. The newly hatched young are small balls of fluffy down, speckled with brown and black, like the young of many other small waders. After just a day they are able to leave the nest and four weeks later are able to fly.

Many chicks die in their first few days of life, often from cold and damp. Predators also take their toll of young chicks. The hooded crow – a

ON THE ROCKS
(below) The dotterel makes its nest amongst the boulders of high stony plateaux, or in hollows in mossy ground. After the eggs are laid, the female takes no interest in her offspring. The male incubates and rears the young, driving away the female if she approaches. The chicks are fed on insects, spiders, earthworms and small snails prised from the rocks or the open ground.

A TALENTED ACTOR
(left) When the eggs or chicks are threatened the adult male lures the predator away from the nest using an elaborate distraction display. It attracts the intruder's attention by running along, crouched low over the ground, imitating a small mammal, then flies aggressively at the predator before finally flopping, apparently helpless, to the ground affecting a broken wing.

villainous scavenger and predator of the Highlands – frequently robs nests, and young and adult birds are also in danger from golden eagles, merlins and snowy owls as well as foxes. When the adult bird senses that the young may be in danger, it puts on an elaborate distraction display, feigning injury, to distract the predator from the nest.

During the first half of August dotterels band into small flocks, ready to begin their return journey south. It is at this time of year that they can be seen on open heathland and newly ploughed agricultural land where they stop to feed, often returning to the same fields year after year.

Despite legislation giving the bird special protection, the dotterel has never fully recovered from the severe decline in numbers caused by egg collecting and hunting at the end of the 19th century. Today, the dotterel's last strongholds are increasingly threatened as tourism expands in the Highlands and new access roads and ski-lifts bring visitors into the previously inaccessible areas where the dotterel makes its nest.

KEY FACTS

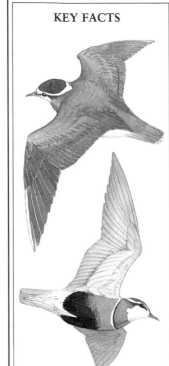

IN FLIGHT the summer plumage is clearly visible. In winter the belly and breast are white and grey, but the white breast band and eyebrow remain.

THE JUVENILE lacks the adults' chestnut belly, resembling them in their winter plumage.

THE EGGS are laid in May and June. Three heavily blotched buff-coloured eggs are the norm.

The Western Isles

On the far north-western fringes of the British Isles lies an archipelago of extremely ancient rocks – the Western Isles – which make up the islands of the Outer Hebrides and the many associated smaller ones, such as St Kilda and Rockall. Despite their remoteness from the mainland, these islands have long been populated, though sparsely, for life here has always been hard as the land gives little away and also bears the full brunt of the mighty Atlantic's fury. Nonetheless, the islands offer scenery of breathtaking beauty and support much interesting wildlife.

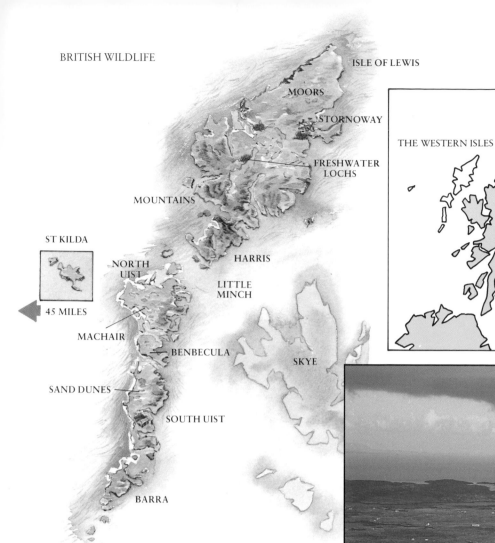

ISLE OF LEWIS

MOORS

STORNOWAY

FRESHWATER
LOCHS

MOUNTAINS

ST KILDA

NORTH
UIST

HARRIS

LITTLE
MINCH

45 MILES

MACHAIR

BENBECULA

SKYE

SAND DUNES

SOUTH UIST

BARRA

THE WESTERN ISLES

FRAGMENTS IN THE SEA
(left) A chain of fragmented islands in the North Atlantic, the Outer Hebrides present a desolate landscape of peaty, heather-covered moors, low-lying boggy ground strewn with freshwater lochs, rugged mountains and, in places, fertile machair. The coast is indented by numerous bays and inlets, clothed in the west with white shell sand and guarded in the east by towering cliffs. 45 miles further west lies the island group of St Kilda, inhabited only by birds and animals.

Nestling off the north-west coast of Scotland lie the Outer Hebrides – an archipelago of wild and watery islands which stretch for 150 miles (240km) from the Butt of Lewis in the north to Barra Head in the south. Known locally as 'the Long Island', this island group comprises Lewis, Harris, North and South Uist, Benbecula and Barra, as well as many smaller islets, and boasts the oldest rocks in Britain, with an age of over 2600 million years. This ancient and resistent rock is known as Lewisian gneiss, after Lewis, the largest of the Hebrides.

SCULPTED BY ICE

Originally shaped by faulting and uplifting, the present island landscape owes its contours to prolonged glaciation; ice sheets moving north-west from the mainland flowed over the Outer Hebrides and continued to beyond the Flannan Islands and North Rona, 45 miles (70km) to the north. The result is the rough, lake-strewn scenery, largely devoid of trees, so typical of these islands. Much of the land is less than 200 feet (60m) above sea level, but the sandstone mountains of Harris – deeply cut by their own local system of glaciers, long since vanished – rise unexpectedly from the desolate moorland of Lewis to reach 2600 feet (790m) on Clisham, the highest peak in the Western Isles.

The east and west coasts of the islands are dramatically different; while the east coast is bound by tall, rugged cliffs, the west coast is broad, flat and low-lying, with extensive beaches of white shell sand and frequent expanses of lush vegetated sandy plains called machair. The fertile lands of the west have been subsiding gradually since the end of the Ice Age, and masses of peat are often dragged up by the anchors of fishing vessels.

The islands were first settled in mesolithic times (10,000-4300 BC) and archaeological remains are abundant. Most famous is the Callanish Stone Circle of Lewis. Standing on an open moor overlooking Loch Roag, it is second only to Stonehenge amongst Britain's most significant megalithic sites. A few miles to

MORE WATER THAN LAND
(above) Much of Lewis, North and South Uist and Benbecula lies less than 200 feet (60m) above sea level. The flat landscape appears as a filigree pattern of freshwater lochs and rivers, which seem to merge with the maze of sea lochs and small islands of the nearby Atlantic waters. Many of the lochs are now stocked with fish, encouraging anglers to the islands.

the north is Dun Carloway, one of the finest brochs in Scotland, and North Uist is famous for its Iron Age wheel houses – circular dwellings with radial partitions reminiscent of the spokes of a wheel. By the dawn of the Christian era the islands' population contained a strong Celtic element, as many of the place names show, and missionaries of the Celtic Church have left their mark in the many remnants of chapel and monastery.

A LONELY SEAPORT

By the ninth century, however, the Norsemen had colonized the islands and established the port of Stornoway, which in their tongue means Anchor Bay. This was a staging post for galleys en route for the inner isles, Man and Ireland. In 1637 Stornoway was declared a Royal Burgh

THE CLIFFS OF
ST KILDA
(right) The remote islands of St Kilda provide some of Britain's most spectacular coastal scenery. The rocky remnants of an ancient volcano, they rise from the sea as sheer faces of rock, accompanied by towering stacks shaped by the fury of the Atlantic waves. The cliffs of Conachair on Hirta are the highest in Britain, rising to 1300 feet (394m), while those of Boreray soar to 1245 feet (380m) and provide perches for thousands of pairs of birds.

and to this day remains the only town in the Outer Isles.

This century has seen a decline in the long-established fishing industry, and crofting is now the chief occupation of the islanders. The principal crops are oats, potatoes, barley, turnips and cabbage, and cattle and sheep graze on the unenclosed pasture land. The main ancillary occupation is weaving.

50 miles west of Lewis lies the tiny island group of St Kilda, in many ways the most extraordinary of the Britannic Isles (and the most westerly apart from Rockall). Evacuated in 1930 because of its inability to support

the few remaining families, it is peopled only by staff of the National Trust and the military. The four main islands – Hirta, Soay, Boreray and Dun – represent the eroded remains of a huge Eocene volcano (dating from some 38-55 million years ago). Working along lines of weakness, the sea has excavated caves and natural arches and is in the process of reducing the islands to a series of isolated stacks. Huge granite cliffs and buttresses rise vertically from the sea; those of Conachair on Hirta are the highest in Britain at over 1300 feet (394m), while Stac an Armin is the highest sea stack in Britain – at 627 feet (190m) it is 200 feet (60m) higher than the Old Man of Hoy in the Orkneys. Equally fantastic are the caves, some of which reach a depth of 300 feet (90m).

Apart from a few dwarf willows, the deep glens and conical hills of the interior are devoid of trees. Heavy rains, mist and frequent gales characterize the St Kildan climate, and in winter severe frosts and snowfalls are common. However, the Gulf Stream has cast much unusual flotsam on to the beaches of all the outer islands, including coconuts, bamboo, shells and seeds from the West Indies and Sargassum weed from the Doldrums.

DIVERSE FATES

Whereas today St Kilda is managed by the National Trust, the Outer Hebrides are subject to all the pressure of supporting a human population. This has had profound effects on the landscape. Around the crofting communities and the interior of the islands, much of the 20-feet thick (6m) layer of peat has been 'skinned', exposing boulder clay and bare rock which is useless for planting or grazing. Offshore, the ever more efficient fishing of the Continental Shelf threatens the communities of sea birds and mammals as well as the economic livelihood of the islanders.

Nature Walk

Man's long presence in the islands is witnessed by many interesting remains, such as;

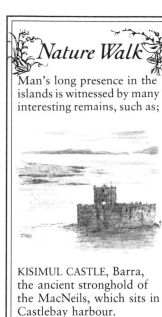

KISIMUL CASTLE, Barra, the ancient stronghold of the MacNeils, which sits in Castlebay harbour.

CALLANISH STONE CIRCLE, Lewis, erected on the moor by sun-worshippers some 3500-4000 years ago.

BLACK HOUSES, primitive thatched dwellings which originally had no chimney.

VILLAGE BAY, Hirta, once the only settlement in St Kilda, now being restored by the National Trust.

Wildlife of the Western Isles

Home to breeding waders and the disappearing corncrake, the flower-strewn machair is a riot of colour in summer; in winter exciting birds arrive from the north and whales appear offshore.

A tiny bird, almost lost in the dramatic sky over the flat machair, flickers its wings and slowly falls as it sings a thin, vibrant whistle. It seems a feeble sound, yet it carries far across the loch and the low landscape. It is the song of the dunlin, laying claim to its territory in the best wader breeding grounds in Britain. Stronger, yodelling calls come from boldly marked redshanks; a similar fluty song near the beach draws attention to a ringed plover, tilting this way and that in its low-level song flight above the dunes.

Lapwings rise from the wet grass to turn and twist back to earth in a frenzied display flight, broad wings ripping through the air with a sound like tearing cloth. High overhead, a tiny, eye-straining speck rises and falls with a constant rhythm, each dive accompanied by a wavering, bleating hum. This is a snipe drumming, using its outstretched tail-feathers to make the sound which says 'this is my patch – keep off'.

The Western Isles are full of breeding waders in summer. A pair or two of the rare and declining red-necked phalarope may still hang on here, but the islands are famous for the numbers of commoner species – the dunlin and snipe, golden plovers and redshanks.

CORNCRAKE STRONGHOLD

The corncrake is not a wader, but is a speciality of the Western Isles. Corncrakes are birds of mysterious habits that spend the winter in East Africa and return each spring to the damp, windswept fields of the Scottish islands. They need clumps of yellow flag in the spring for essential cover, before the hay has grown tall and dense enough to shelter them. All day and night the males call their monotonous ratchety *crek-crek*; *crek-crek*; *crek-crek*. The sound echoes from the dry stone walls and bounces around the little valleys at night, in a magical chorus that was once heard all over Britain but is now all too rare. Development grants to Hebridean farmers have lead to the early cutting of hay and the application of fertilizers. The change from rough tussocky fields to smooth, green swards with no cover, spells disaster for the corncrake. Even in these last strongholds, they are fast disappearing.

SOAY SHEEP
These multi-coloured sheep are found on Soay and Hirta in the St Kilda islands. They are primitive sheep, similar to Stone Age breeds, which now live wild since the last regular inhabitants left the islands in 1930. Without human interference the population builds up to a level that the grazing cannot sustain and, every three of four years, many die in the winter.

WILDLIFE ON A HEBRIDEAN ISLE

The waders of the machair and shore include oyster-catchers, ringed plover, dunlin, redshank and lapwing. The flowery hay fields are stalked by breeding corn-crakes that fly in for the summer from Africa. Wild greylag geese have long nested in the Western Isles on lochs adjoining the moors and machair, as do mute swans. The many flowers of the machair produce an aromatic hay when cut. Nectar-feeding butterflies visit the blooms and many lay their eggs among the grasses or flowers. The lesser yellow underwing lays her eggs on shrubs or heather. Marsh marigolds and holy grass grow in damper areas where the northern species of marsh orchid may be found. The field mouse is a staple food for several birds of prey.

KEY TO FEATURES AND SPECIES

1 St Kilda
2 Gannets
3 Fulmar
4 Skylark
5 Red deer
6 Oystercatchers
7 Grey seals
8 Kelp stack
9 Greylag geese
10 Mute swan
11 Lesser yellow
   water lily
12 Silverweed
13 Wild radish

14 Common blue
15 Dunlin
16 Yellow flag
17 Ringed plover
18 Wild carrot
19 Green-veined white
20 Nesting lapwing
21 Marsh marigold
22 Holy grass
23 Corncrake
24 Red clover
25 Nesting redshank
26 Northern marsh
   orchid

27 Tiger moth
28 Alkanet
29 Corn marigold
30 Lesser yellow
   underwing
31 Harebell
32 Viola curtisii
33 Storksbill
34 Xanthoria *lichen*
35 *Lichen* Lecanora
   rupicola
36 Anaptychia *lichen*
37 Long-tailed field
   mouse

RINGED PLOVER
(left) This dapper wader's neat nest and eggs are found on the shore, usually well camouflaged among the sand or shingle. Three to five eggs are laid from late April and are incubated by both adults. The ringed plover is a northerly breeding bird, used to sub-Arctic temperatures, and is quite at home on the exposed Western Isles.

HOODED CROW
(right) Hooded crows breed throughout the Western Isles and, where trees are absent, nest readily on cliff ledges, in deep heather or, as here, in gorse bushes. The large nest of sticks is roughly lined with wool and hair. The hooded crow is the northerly form of the European crow, and occurs in Ireland, the Isle of Man and Scotland. It is closely related to the all-black carrion crow and where the two populations meet they interbreed.

SPOTTED ORCHIDS
(below) Growing here on St Kilda are two moorland or heath spotted orchids, which are often found on boggy ground. Flowering from June to August, they are quite common in northern and western Britain. The cleitan in the background was used for storing eggs and salted seafowl.

In July, the machair is breathtakingly beautiful with a brilliant display of flowers and an abundance of common blue butterflies. The blue sea and sky, creamy-white shell-sand beaches and bright green grasses are set off by zigzag and red clover, cow parsnip, bright yellow ragwort, pink stars of storksbill, purple-blue tufted vetch, glorious yellow dandelions, buttercups, hawkweeds, and the delicate blue of harebells. Primroses sometimes grow in great profusion and other flowers include vivid little wild pansies, speedwells and eyebright, clumps of wild thyme and the purple-blue heads of self-heal. These flowers delight the eye on any patch of windblown sand that has become stabilized by permanent vegetation.

The grassland that borders the coast is rich in calcium from the crushed sea shells, so many snails are found here. By contrast, the nearby moors, where shell production is by no means easy, harbour a variety of slugs instead.

LIFE ON THE CLIFFS

The cliffs of the islands' headlands have their own characteristic flora. Dominant plants include a familiar array of colourful flowers such as sea campion, thrift and vernal squill, as well as roseroot, sea plantain and sheep's sorrel. A little earth ledge, surrounded by pink thrift and the nodding white blooms of sea campion, forms a typical nest site for a pair of fulmars; pink thrift and white scurvy grass make an attractive setting for a group of puffins; roseroot growing from a cliff ledge might frame the black and white form of an incubating razorbill – all, in their way, characteristic sights on the outer isles.

St Kilda, far out to the west of the island chain, is one of the world's most magnificent islands. It has been the headquarters of the fulmar in Britain for centuries and still has the world's greatest gannet colony. The breeding puffins are still spectacular, although there are fewer than in the past. At one time 89,000 puffins a year were killed by St Kildans in their annual cropping of sea birds – though this was not enough to cause any long-term change in their numbers. It was once estimated that three

million pairs of breeding puffins inhabited this island group, but numbers are now down to around 250,000. The reason for the decline is unclear, but is possibly related to their diet. Puffins depend to a great extent on sandeels to feed their young. In some years they resort to shrimps and other less nutritious fare, or, instead of bringing in one or two big, fat sandeels at a time, they come in with dozens of tiny fry – a sign of bad fishing. In those years their young are less healthy, less fat and heavy, and productivity is low.

In the winter months, when the cliff-nesting seabirds have dispersed, other birds arrive. In the sandy bays, where onshore winds drive abundant fish, great northern divers spend their winters. There may be 500, even more, in the coastal waters of these islands, a major propor-

RED CLOVER
(left) Widely cultivated by farmers, this attractive flower grows wild and is one of the colourful blooms of the herb-rich grassland, known as the machair. Cattle are fond of clover, and bees make a delectable honey from it. When cut it contributes to the aromatic hay. The flowers bloom from May to September.

HEBRIDEAN MOUSE
(below left) The long-tailed field mouse (also known as the wood mouse) of the Outer Hebrides, especially St Kilda, is larger than its mainland cousins. This is probably an adaptation to cope with the colder climate.

ST KILDA WREN
(below) Perched here with a caterpillar for its chicks, this wren belongs to a distinct geographical race confined to the St Kilda islands. They have been separated from their mainland cousins long enough to show subtle differences in size, song, plumage and habits.

tion of the British total and, apparently, too many to be simply Icelandic breeding birds. This suggests a movement from much further west, involving birds from Greenland and arctic Canada.

The shallow bays off the western coasts also draw in good numbers of our most attractive sea duck, the elegant and beautifully patterned long-tailed duck.

On land, buzzards are common and there is always the chance, even in the lowlands, of a memorable encounter with a golden eagle. There are no ptarmigan here, and few red grouse, so rabbits and dead sheep are important items in eagles' diets.

The machair holds other exciting birds in winter. Greylag geese fly in from the north and, here and there, an Icelandic whooper swan can be found on the little lochs, while spectacular barnacle geese from Greenland come to graze the rich green grass. Flocks of dainty snow buntings dance along like windblown snow-flakes ahead of the hardy birdwatcher.

The twite, an interesting little finch, finds the machair to its liking in winter. They nest here, too, as well as around coastal fields. The males sing like twangy linnets incorporating the *twaeet* call that gives the species its name. Twite are dependent on an abundance of small seeds, in much the same way as the linnet is in its southerly home. Linnets are absent from the outer isles in winter.

As frequent in winter as in summer, are striking black and grey hooded crows and aerobatic ravens. Other birds, often taken for granted in the south — woodpigeons, redwings, fieldfares and pied wagtails, for instance — are relatively scarce or absent altogether in the Hebridean winter.

MAMMALS OFFSHORE

One creature that must be mentioned in connection with the Outer Hebrides is the Atlantic grey seal. The smaller islands, especially Gasker, Haskeir and Shillay, are notable breeding places of this impressive animal. On Gasker as many as 1000 pups may be born annually, making it a very important colony. Hebridean seas are also very good for the would-be whale spotter, with killer whales, lesser and common rorquals and even the occasional blue or sperm whale to be seen.

The windswept shore, bleak moorlands, extensive areas of peat and the coastal cliffs present wildlife with a variety of challenges. Any visitor will soon find that the living world has responded to the challenge and Hebridean wildlife is indeed as rich, varied and exciting as the landscape.

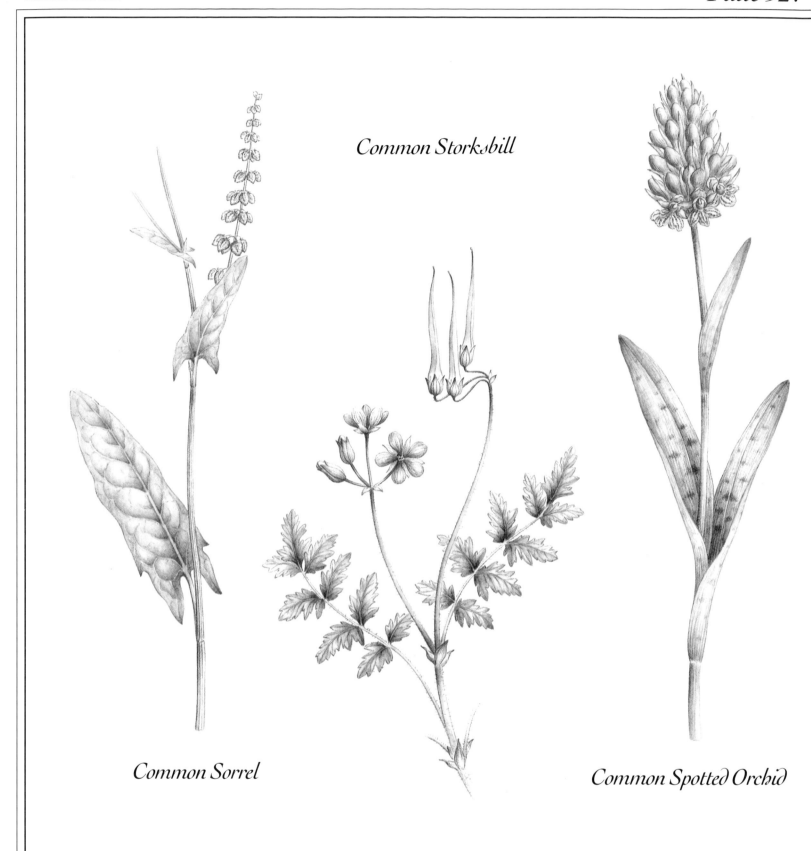

Common Storksbill

Common Sorrel

Common Spotted Orchid

COMMON SORREL *(Rumex acetosa)* Often abundant in grassy meadows, this perennial plant flowers throughout the summer producing bright red fruits. Variable in size up to 32″ (80cm) tall. The shiny leaves have a lemony taste and are sometimes used in salads.

COMMON STORKSBILL *(Erodium cicutarium)* A low, straggling annual or biennial which grows on bare, grassy places especially beside the sea. Its ½″ (1cm) flowers are produced from May until September and easily shed their petals. The leaves are often sticky.

COMMON SPOTTED ORCHID *(Dactylorhiza fuchsii* ssp. *hebridensis)* Much shorter than its mainland relative, this plant seldom exceeds 4″ (10cm). The flower spike is dense and the leaves are only finely marked. Flowers from June-August. Often frequent on the machair.

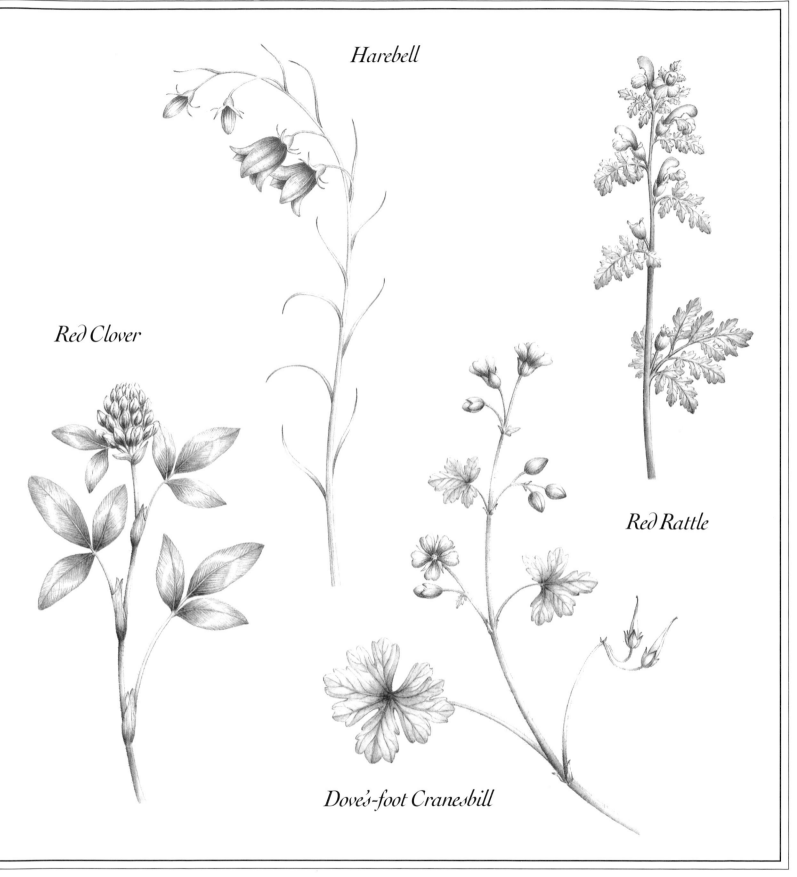

Harebell

Red Clover

Red Rattle

Dove's-foot Cranesbill

RED CLOVER (*Trifolium pratense*) Often forming large patches, this perennial produces globular flower heads 1″ (2.5cm) across from April until October. The flowers are variable in colour. Abundant in most grassy places, sometimes grown as a fodder crop.

HAREBELL (*Campanula rotundifolia*) Common on dry grassland often on dunes by the sea. Its delicate ½″ (1cm) nodding flowers are produced from July to September and are popular with insects. The plant itself is perennial and grows to 16″ (40cm).

DOVE'S-FOOT CRANESBILL (*Geranium molle*) Producing its ½″ (1cm) flowers from April until September, this low annual is sometimes common in bare, grassy places. Its stems are rather hairy and the leaves are dissected giving them rather the appearance of a bird's foot.

RED RATTLE (*Pedicularis palustris*) A semi-parasitic, upright biennial herb up to 2′ (60cm) tall. Prefers wet, grassy meadows and heathy places. The attractive flowers are produced from May to September. When dry, the seeds rattle giving the plant its name.

Greylag Goose

Common Gull

GREYLAG GOOSE *(Anser anser)*
Our only native, nesting goose, the greylag breeds near lochs which are close to moorland and machair, laying 5 or 6 creamy white eggs which are incubated for 27-28 days. Always wary, they are quick to take to the wing, uttering their characteristic honking and cackling calls. Their large size, 30″ (75cm), makes them easy to pick out both on the ground and in the air. They feed on grasses, seeds and other plant material. In winter they desert their nesting grounds in favour of coastal pastures to the south.

COMMON GULL *(Larus canus)*
This gull nests throughout the Hebrides both in small colonies and singly. Three mottled eggs are laid during May or June in a simple scrape amongst rocks and vegetation. The young gulls are fed on fish, insects and crustaceans until they are ready to fledge. In the winter, many common gulls move south and either scavenge or follow the plough. At 17″ (42cm), it is a medium-sized gull. Its flight is leisurely and relaxed and the black wing tips aid identification. It has a harsh alarm call uttered in flight.

St Kilda Wren

White-tailed Sea Eagle

WHITE-TAILED SEA EAGLE (*Haliaeetus albicilla*) Formerly extinct in this country, sea eagles have successfully been reintroduced into some of their former sites in the Hebrides. These majestic birds, with a wingspan of nearly 8' (240cm), can soar effortlessly for hours. The nest, often built on a sea cliff ledge, contains two eggs. The wedge-shaped white tail, broad wings and immense beak are good identification features. It catches fish, birds and mammals but will also take carrion. In winter, the young birds may wander over long distances.

ST KILDA WREN (*Troglodytes troglodytes hirtensis*) On the isolated island of St Kilda, the wrens have evolved into a separate race from those on the mainland. Although slightly larger, greyer and with a heavier bill, the St Kilda race is still only 3½" (9cm). The outer Hebridean race *hebridensis* is also considered different from mainland birds. Nests in holes in walls and banks and lays five to seven whitish eggs. Feeds on insects caught with its fine beak. The song is loud and vibrant and the alarm call is a harsh rattle.

The White-Tailed Sea Eagle

Soaring majestically over the remote island cliffs of the Hebrides,
the splendid white-tailed sea eagle has once again begun to breed
in Britain, after an absence of 70 years.

With slow, powerful strokes of its broad wings, a great bird of prey – larger than a golden eagle – turns into the wind. Cutting effortlessly through the billowing spray, the white-tailed sea eagle finally reaches its lonely eyrie and alights deftly on a cliff ledge. Then it reaches back to preen the snow-white feathers of its broad, wedge-shaped tail with its massive hooked yellow bill.

In the late 18th century, the sea eagle, or 'erne', as it was also known, bred in several parts of England, the Isle of Man, Ireland and Scotland. By the end of the 19th century, however, it had become virtually extinct, due almost entirely to ruthless persecution by landowners and shepherds. The sea eagle's supposed sin was that it killed lambs, an allegation that has since proved largely unfounded.

The island of Skye long remained one of the bird's traditional strongholds, but by the early 1900s it had the sad distinction of boasting what was probably the last pair of sea eagles to breed in Britain, and even these had disappeared by 1916.

THE EAGLE'S RETURN

Unlike ospreys, sea eagles are not wanderers so, only very occasionally does a lone bird ever turn up in Britain, driven from its northern European homeland by severe winter weather. Natural recolonization of Britain thus would be highly unlikely, so a programme of artificial reintroduction was proposed.

After an initial unsuccessful attempt on Fair Isle in the Shetlands in 1968, a second reintroduction programme was begun in 1976, initiated by the Nature Conservancy Council, with representatives from the RSPB and the Scottish Wildlife Trust. Each year a number of young Norwegian eagles were introduced to the island of Rhum in the Inner Hebrides. Although several of the eagles died, some from poisoning, 60 to 70 per cent survived.

Early attempts by the birds to breed failed, but in 1985 a pair of eagles successfully reared one young bird. By 1986, a total of 82 eagles had been introduced, and in that year two young eaglets were reared.

The sea eagles can now once more be seen along the island coastlines. They frequently

ADULT WHITE-TAILED SEA EAGLE
(left) Bulkier than a golden eagle, the white-tailed sea eagle has broader wings, a shorter snow-white tail and a more prominent bill.

JUVENILE IN FLIGHT
(left) Juvenile and immature white-tailed sea eagles have darker brown plumage than that of their parents, and also have greyish-black bills and brown tails. They do not acquire their splendid white tails until they are adult at five years old or more.

IN FLIGHT the white-tailed sea eagle has broad brown wings, widely stretched primary feathers and a fanned white tail.

THE FEET are bright yellow with strong, hooked talons and sharp spines on the undersides of the toes.

THE EGGS are produced in one clutch of two in April, are chalky white and hatch in 38-days.

hunt low over the ground or the water, taking a wide variety of fish, sea and shore birds, and mammals as large as roe deer calves or baby seals. Sea eagles are related more closely to kites than to the true eagles, and share the former's scavenging and piratical habits. When hunting for fish, the sea eagle often makes a spectacular plunge into the water, its talons reaching beneath the waves to grasp the slippery victim, its grip aided by sharp spines on the soles of its toes. Sea birds such as fulmars and gulls are also snatched from the rocks or water. Another tactic is for a pair of eagles to work together, forcing swimming seabirds to dive so often that they become exhausted and easy prey.

During their courtship period, sea eagles often indulge in flamboyant aerobatics. They soar high above the nest site, then the male suddenly dives at the female who turns over on her back, allowing him to grasp her talons firmly with his. Locked in this breathtaking embrace, they plunge towards the jagged rocks, whirling round in a spectacular series of cartwheels. They do not separate until it is almost too late, only a few feet above the ground, and then soar upwards again, sometimes to give a repeat performance.

The male and female, which pair for life, share the task of building several nests, although only one is finally selected to hold the eggs. Fashioned from stout branches, it is lined with dry grass and other plants. In April, the female lays two chalky white eggs, which hatch after she has incubated them for about 38 days. The male brings food for his offspring, which can fly at about 10 weeks old and remain near the nest for another five weeks.

The recent breeding successes of the introduced birds are likely to continue, so it is to be hoped that this magnificent predator – our largest bird of prey – will once again become a regular sight among the gaunt rocks and crashing breakers of its northern home.

NESTING SEA EAGLES
(left) White-tailed sea eagles generally build their nests on crags, cliff ledges or in tree forks, but rarely on the ground. The nest, built by both sexes, is a huge structure of branches, averaging 5' (1.5m) across and 2½' (75cm) high), and is lined with twigs, moss, heather, seaweed and grasses. The same nest is often returned to year after year, with fresh material being added, and mature nests often grow to an enormous size.

The Shetland Isles

Over 100 miles north-east of John O'Groats lie the lonely Shetland Isles, Britain's northernmost outpost. Wracked by the fierce Atlantic waves, the islands have some of the most spectacular coastal scenery in the British Isles: towering battle-scarred cliffs stand like island defences, while elsewhere the coastline is broken by winding inlets or voes. Inland, the scenery is green and gentle and dotted with freshwater lochs. But it is a bleak landscape, shaped by the earth's movement over millions of years and eroded by the relentless sea, which is gradually reclaiming the islands.

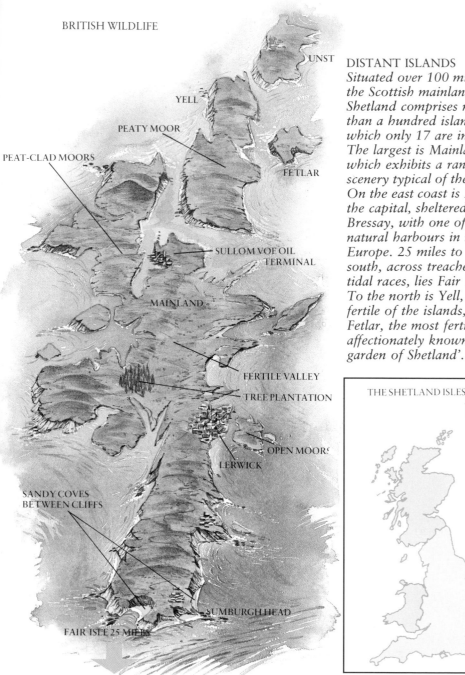

UNST

YELL

PEATY MOOR

PEAT-CLAD MOORS

FETLAR

SULLOM VOE OIL
TERMINAL

MAINLAND

FERTILE VALLEY

TREE PLANTATION

OPEN MOORS

LERWICK

SANDY COVES
BETWEEN CLIFFS

SUMBURGH HEAD

FAIR ISLE 25 MILES

DISTANT ISLANDS
Situated over 100 miles from the Scottish mainland, Shetland comprises more than a hundred islands, of which only 17 are inhabited. The largest is Mainland, which exhibits a range of scenery typical of the islands. On the east coast is Lerwick, the capital, sheltered by Bressay, with one of the best natural harbours in northern Europe. 25 miles to the south, across treacherous tidal races, lies Fair Isle. To the north is Yell, the least fertile of the islands, and Fetlar, the most fertile, affectionately known as 'the garden of Shetland'.

THE SHETLAND ISLES

Papa Stour. And at Ronas Hill in the north-west of Mainland, a red granite mass rises from the sea, forming cliffs which tower to 600 feet and culminating in a 1486 foot peak.

The Shetland landscape has been shaped over millions of years, with some rocks 2000 million years old. Most of the geological formations were laid down in the Devonian period (395-345 million years ago), when a folding action produced layers of sandstones, shales and limestones, with the intrusion of granite. Then one million years ago the North European ice sheet melted, the sea level rose, and Shetland became a group of islands, its valleys partially submerged to form the long narrow inlets known in Shetland as 'voes'.

A BARREN LANDSCAPE

Settling on the edge of the voes, small communities which have always relied heavily on fishing still nestle in the shelter provided by the landscape. Behind them the hills stretch out to the next voe or to the open sea. They are mainly gentle, but barren and treeless: upland peat bog and grasses mix with heath moorland and tiny freshwater lochs trapped by the surrounding hills.

The winters bring long nights and short days, but snow rarely lies for long and winter frosts are short-lived since the islands lie in the direct path of the Gulf Stream. Spring and autumn are short seasons, but summer lasts from mid May to the end of August. In June and July, the sun only sets for five hours and it is always bright enough to read.

S hetland is made up from over 100 islands comprising an area of only 550 square miles and yet boasting a magnificent 3000 mile coastline. The main islands are 110 miles from Caithness in Scotland and stretch over 70 miles from Sumburgh Head on the island of Mainland in the south to Muckle Flugga on the fertile island of Unst in the north. Outside this main cluster lies Foula to the west and Fair Isle to the south-west.

The sea makes its mark wherever you turn, and you are rarely more than 3 miles from it. To the west is the Atlantic Ocean, and to the east the North Sea. In a gale the coastline becomes the battlefield where the earth and water clash. The high cliffs are buffeted with sheets of spray as the sea meets the rocks below. Hollow drones can be heard as caves and crevices tunnel the surf inwards, only to die on the wall of beaten rock within.

Magnificent cliffs are a feature of all the islands, but especially of Foula, Bressay and

SHELTERED INLETS
(right) The bleak coastline of the Shetland islands is repeatedly indented by bays and long, winding inlets or voes, which once provided sheltered havens for the fishing fleets. These voes were once valleys in a range of ancient hills, but at the end of the Ice Age the valleys were engulfed by a rising sea, leaving only the hilltops above sea level to form the islands as we know them today.

AN ISOLATED PLANTATION
(above) The hills are green, but there is no natural woodland. Only at Kergord, on Mainland, have attempts at planting been made.

Early neolithic colonists arriving in Shetland around 4000 BC would have experienced a different place altogether. The climate was milder, enabling them to grow barley and wheat crops, and there was mixed woodland consisting mainly of birch and alder. By 3000 BC, however, a general increase in the wind speed had led to

plant damage, and coastal erosion had changed the islands. The trees had virtually been replaced by heath and the agricultural land by peat, formed during a prolonged period of extremely wet climatic conditions.

Today the islands still bear the legacy of successive invasions and occupations by different races. 95 defensive stone forts, known as 'brochs', dating back to the Iron Age stand on strategic headlands and sites along the shore. The Picts and Irish monks who arrived in the 6th century AD left little lasting impression on the landscape, but in the 9th century the Vikings invaded and 300 years of Norse rule began. Many place names come from Norse origins such as Sandwick (sandy bay), Lerwick (mud bay), Ness (headland), and Shetland itself is derived from 'Hjaltland' (high land).

MODERN PROSPERITY

Only in 1469 did the islands become Scottish, when they were given to James III of Scotland on his marriage to Margaret, daughter of the King of Denmark and Norway. Under Scottish rule Lerwick grew as an important fishing and trading port. This prosperity continued until the end of the vast herring fisheries in the early 20th century.

The islands today have discovered a new prosperity brought by the North Sea oil fields. Europe's largest oil terminal, dealing with about half the UK's oil, now stands on Sullom Voe. Fortunately, the fishing industry still continues, and when the oilmen have gone the islands will be able to fall back on traditional skills.

In the meantime there are some who hold their breath, waiting for an accident which could swamp the shoreline with oil, destroying the life that the islands have nurtured for thousands of years. The consequences of such a tragedy would be far more severe than those caused by the onslaught of the elements, and underlines the true fragility of this island community.

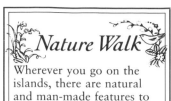

Nature Walk
Wherever you go on the islands, there are natural and man-made features to look out for, such as:

OLD GRAIN DRYING KILN Due to the damp climate, these were built to dry grain before threshing.

JARLSHOF An ancient site with the remains of three extensive village settlements from the Bronze Age to the Viking invasion.

MINERALS Gneiss (right, probably 2000 million years old), red sandstone (top) and talc (bottom) are present, together with serpentine and garnet.

Island Wildlife

The long Shetland coastline is noted for its flowery meadows
and for colonies of breeding seabirds, while otters,
seals and whales can be seen near the shore.

Lying midway between Norway and Scotland, Shetland adds a touch of the Arctic to British natural history. On the coast, colourful masses of flowers grow on the more established sand, and green, flowery meadows stretch behind the rocky shores. On the shell sands, marram grows where there are dunes, but in the hollows which flood in winter there may be bright patches of self-heal, dandelion, wild thyme and eyebright.

Coastal swards, often closely grazed, are dotted with the blue spikes of spring squill and the pink flowers of thrift. Northern fen and heath spotted orchids add extra colour. On offshore stacks, where rabbits and sheep are absent, the sward may belong to the puffins and grow a taller mixture of thrift and sea campion.

In the damp fens, usually grazed or mown for hay, there will be moor grass, common sedge and jointed rush, overtopped by clumps of soft rush and colourful yellow flag. Cotton grass and sundews appear in the poorer fens.

Up on the blanket bogs, mat grass and heath rush generally dominate, with scattered flowers of yellow tormentil and creamy-white heath bedstraw. Cotton grass, deer sedge, moor grass, crowberry, heather and bell heather are all common in varying mixtures. Where grazing is

RED-NECKED PHALAROPE

This dainty wader swims more readily than most waders and indeed spends much of the year at sea, where it may occasionally perch on a surfaced whale. The bird nests mainly in the Arctic but a few pairs breed in Shetland.

limited, the flora includes sheep's-bit, red campion and vetches which are not only luxuriant but produce notably large and intensely coloured flowers.

INTRODUCED MAMMALS

There are few land mammals in Shetland. Brown and blue hares were introduced, both much later than the 17th century introduction of the stoat. Rabbits were introduced long ago and house mice came in with early settlers on Viking ships. They now have the distinction of being the largest form of house mice in the world. Shetland's field mice are also larger than their mainland relatives, and are more brightly coloured. In the absence of competition from voles, they are common and found in a variety of habitats. Hedgehogs are widely distributed after being introduced in about 1850, and brown rats occur on most islands except Yell.

The other widespread mammal is the otter. There may be one otter for every three quarter mile of coastline in Shetland, the highest density in Britain. Though they take a few birds, most of their diet is sea fish, topped up with a variety of shellfish.

SHETLAND WILDLIFE FROM THE HILLS TO THE COAST
Trees grow where sheep cannot graze. Blue hares may be seen on the dry moorland where merlins nest and a pair of snowy owls nested until recently. Red-throated divers breed on lochans. On the damp moorland, among the peat hags, are nesting waders such as the dunlin, golden plover and the whimbrel which has its British stronghold on Shetland. Arctic and great skuas nest here, too, flying to the coast to harry seabirds. Puffins commandeer rabbit burrows in the cliff-top, while guillemots and fulmars nest on cliff ledges. Eider ducks nest around the coast but gannets prefer offshore stacks. Otters haunt the seashore, and seals breed on beaches, basking on offshore islets.

KEY TO THE FEATURES AND SPECIES

1 *Silver birch*	12 *Whimbrel*	20 *Hedgehog*
2 *Male merlin*	13 *Arctic skua*	21 *Rabbit*
3 *Snowy owl*	14 *Fulmar*	22 *Black guillemots*
4 *Kittiwake*	15 *Gannet*	23 *Red-throated diver*
5 *Shetland cattle*	16 *Porpoises*	24 *Marsh marigolds*
6 *Glaucous gulls*	17 *Blue hare*	25 *Golden plover at nest*
7 *Puffins*	18 *Cotton grass*	26 *Grey seals*
8 *Stack*	19 *Peat digging*	27 *Eider ducks*
9 *Creeping willow*		28 *Red campion*
10 *Heather*		29 *Dunlin at nest*
11 *Shetland sheep*		30 *Spring squill*
		31 *Long-tailed field mouse*
		32 *Thrift*
		33 *Otters*

PILOT WHALES
*(above) Schools of these
fish-eating whales can be
seen off the coast. Large
numbers were once driven
ashore in the traditional
caa' and slaughtered for
their blubber.*

In June, when the sky scarcely darkens at night, the common seals give birth on some rocky skerry or on a smooth slab beneath a cliff. The grey seal, by contrast, hauls out on to stony beaches or into caves to give birth in the wildest weather of the late autumn. It breeds mainly on the west side of the islands but there is a large group on Fetlar. Common seals are more widespread and, after a decline under heavy persecution, are now steadily increasing. There are about 3,800 common seals and 3,500 greys in Shetland, about 20 per cent and 5 per cent of the British population respectively (though the British grey seals comprise over half of the world total).

Both species eat fish, the common taking flatfish and fast-swimming species such as herring, whiting and haddock. The grey seal

COASTAL GUILLEMOTS
*(above) Numerous guillemots
and two shags gather on
coastal rocks close to the
cliff-ledge breeding sites.*

RARE FLOWER
*(right) Shetland mouse-ear
chickweed grows on screes
alongside other rarities like
Arctic sandwort and
northern rock cress.*

BLOOD-DROP EMLETS
*(below) This striking flower,
introduced from Chile, grows
with the related monkey
flower in wet meadows.*

prefers cod, skate and saithe and will more frequently vary its diet with squid and octopus. Both take a few salmon and sea trout and cause occasional damage to lobster pots and nets.

WHALES, DOLPHINS AND SHARKS

The commonest of the baleen whales off Shetland is the minke, or lesser rorqual; the fin and sei whales remain far offshore. Sperm whales visit occasionally and have, rarely, been stranded. The whale most likely to be seen is certainly the killer whale, especially between April and October and often in fast tidal streams around headlands – a suitably exciting and awesome setting for this dramatic creature. Risso's and white-sided dolphins are also quite frequent in Shetland waters, but other dolphins are rather rare.

The largest fish in Shetland waters is the harmless, plankton-eating basking shark. This huge and impressive animal is fairly common. Inshore, sprats and mackerel are pursued both by marine mammals and by fishermen but it is the abundant shoals of sand-eels which are most important to the seabird colonies.

The visitor to Shetland will inevitably notice

ARCTIC SKUA

GREAT SKUA

PIRATICAL SKUAS
*Both species harry seabirds.
The Arctic skua chases terns,
kittiwakes and puffins,
while the great skua takes
on auks and gannets.*

GREY SEAL COW
*Grey seals lose many young
in their exposed breeding
sites and seals from Orkney
probably help to maintain
the Shetland population.*

the birds. As the boat approaches Lerwick there will be flocks of gulls attended by great skuas and even the odd gannet. In the bays are buoyant black guillemots and groups of comfortable-looking eiders. Shags and cormorants sit on rocks, while offshore the constant comings and goings of fulmars, kittiwakes, puffins and guillemots provide endless enjoyment.

the cliffs, defending only the area around the nest from intruders. They attack sheep, humans and any other trespassers and provide great excitement for the birdwatching visitor.

Not all of the important birds are seabirds, however. Shetland has a large proportion of the British breeding populations of such species as dunlin and golden plover and almost all the nesting whimbrels. On the small lochans, but feeding in the sea, there is a large population of red-throated divers and some special pools still have a few pairs of red-necked phalaropes.

BIRDWATCHER'S MECCA

Shetland has a great variety of seabirds and waders, but relatively few breeding landbirds. It nevertheless has a listing of visiting birds second to none. It is a great focus for migrants and every spring and autumn a remarkable number of rare birds turn up, blown off course from eastern Siberia, south-east Europe and North America. On Shetland, the extraordinary becomes almost the norm and rare birds, almost unknown elsewhere in Britain, are only to be expected.

LONG-TAILED DUCKS
Breeding in Scandinavia, Greenland and other Arctic regions, small flocks of these sea ducks winter off northern coasts.

Shetland's sea-cliff bird communities are some of the best in the eastern Atlantic. There are dramatic gannet colonies at Hermaness and Noss – the former has for many years hosted a single, lost, black-browed albatross, a vagrant from southern oceans which lives with the birds which most resemble its own kind. Islands like Fetlar also have the mysterious storm petrels and Manx shearwaters, coming to land only on dark nights for fear of the gulls and skuas to which they might fall easy prey.

Shetland has long been a stronghold of the powerful great skua and smaller numbers of the more elegant Arctic skua. Both chase seabirds and make them drop food. Because of this they are able to nest in colonies on the moors above

Red Campion

Frog Orchid

Shetland Mouse-ear Chickweed

FROG ORCHID *(Coeloglossum viride)* Growing among short grass on damp chalky soil or sandy soils throughout Britain, this orchid is frequent by Shetland shores. Slim, 2-10″ (6-25cm) spires of flowers appear June-August. Unspotted leaves clasp the stem.

RED CAMPION *(Silene dioica zetlandica)* Common on Shetland and Orkney, this 12-35″ (30-90cm) perennial is mostly coastal. It differs from the mainland red campion by its thicker stems, narrower, hairier leaves, larger seed pods and more densely clustered flowers May-June.

SHETLAND MOUSE-EAR CHICKWEED *(Cerastium arcticum edmonstonii)* Only found on low serpentine rocks on Unst, this is a closely tufted perennial of just 2″ (5cm). The whole plant is densely hairy, dark and purplish, with tiny round leaves. Flowers June-August.

Trailing Azalea

Blood-drop-emlets

Purging Flax

BLOOD-DROP EMLETS *(Mimulus luteus)* A garden escape, this is a sprawling, uncommon perennial to 16″ (40cm), growing by water and in ditches, north England and Scotland. Flowers, seen June to September, are heavily marked with red spots. It is hairless, with toothed leaves.

TRAILING AZALEA *(Loiseleuria procumbens)* A low-growing shrub which is abundant on the high slopes of the Highlands of Scotland though rare in Shetland. The sprawling, much-branched stems bear clusters of tiny blooms May-July and leathery, evergreen leaves.

PURGING FLAX *(Linum catharticum)* Most common on chalky soils, this small, slender annual 5-10″ (5-25cm) can be seen on grazed turf, cliffs and dunes throughout Britain. Well-spaced leaves are borne on the wiry stems and tiny flowers open from June-September.

Snowy Owl

Male

Whimbrel

Female

SNOWY OWL (*Nyctea scandiaca*)
Shetlanders call this large, 21-26"
(53-66cm) owl the catyogle. Rarely
found elsewhere in Britain, it is a
scarce resident here but despite
success in the 1960s and 1970s, there
have been no breeding pairs since
1975. Females are larger and more
heavily flecked brown-black than
males – which can be almost pure
white. They hunt by day, over open
country and take animals as large as
rabbits and hooded crows. The hen
lays 4-10 white eggs in a scrape on an
exposed site on the ground and the
male brings her food as she broods.

WHIMBREL (*Numenius phaeopus*)
A small but steady population of
these 16" (41cm) waders breeds on
the moors of the Outer Hebrides
and Shetland Islands. Both sexes
have mottled, barred plumage, with
a white rump patch seen clearly in
flight. Whimbrel pick insects and
molluscs from soft mud and seaweed
with their long thin bills and will also
eat berries. The call is a high trill.
Single-brooded, 4 olive, speckled
eggs are laid in a scrape on the
ground, May and June. Both parents
tend the eggs and short-billed
young. In winter they fly to Africa.

King Eider

Female

Male

White Wagtail

Summer

Winter

KING EIDER (*Somateria spectabilis*) Adult males of this 22" (56cm) duck are a splendid and unmistakable sight – but females are a more sober mottled red-brown. Breeding in the Arctic, these hardy seaducks migrate southwards in winter to keep clear of ice, a few regularly reaching the coasts of Shetland. Rarely, a non-breeding bird may remain all summer, keeping company with common eider around rocky shores. King eiders feed in deeper waters than other eiders, eating molluscs and crustaceans. Drakes make a loud but soft call, ducks have harsher notes.

WHITE WAGTAIL (*Motacilla alba alba*) A rare summer visitor to Shetland, where only a few pairs breed. It is distinguished from the pied wagtail, which is very common on mainland Britain, by its greyer back. The female bird is similar to the male in winter plumage. Slim, 7" (18cm) birds with a constantly flicking tail, they feed on insects caught near water or on open ground with short vegetation. A hair-lined nest of stems and moss is built by the female in holes in walls, rocks or trees. 5-6 greyish, speckled eggs are laid in April or May.

The Snowy Owl

A regular visitor to northern parts of the British Isles, the
spectacular snowy owl made history in 1967 when it bred here for
the first time on the Shetland island of Fetlar.

The snowy owl is one of the world's largest
and most powerful owls. Bigger and
thicker set than a buzzard, it may grow to
21-26 inches (53-66cm) long with a wingspan of
around 5 feet (152cm). It is a bird of the treeless,
barren tundras of the Arctic, living as far
north as there is ground free of snow in
summer, and flying southwards, occasionally to
the Outer Hebrides, Orkneys, Shetlands and
northern parts of Scotland and Ireland, to avoid
the worst of the weather in winter.

For many years, the snowy owl's status in the
British Isles remained as a rare winter visitor to
northern parts. Then, on 7 June 1967, the first
ever British snowy owl nest was discovered on
an open hill on Fetlar, the 'green island' of the
Shetlands. The pair of owls was closely watched,
protected, and their activities monitored. Five
young, from the clutch of seven eggs, survived
to their first winter. For the next eight breeding
seasons, until 1975, the pair continued to nest,
hatching out 44 eggs in all with 20 young
surviving to their first winter. Between 1973
and 1975 another female also nested on Fetlar

but the one male was unable to supply enough
food for the two owls. No chicks hatched out
from the eggs laid in this second nest.

Subsequently, snowy owls have been seen
regularly on Fetlar. Unfortunately, though, no
breeding has taken place on the island since
1975. The simple reason for this is that the old
male owl disappeared in the late autumn of
that year. He never tolerated other males on
Fetlar, so even the young males that hatched
out from the nine breeding seasons were forced
to leave the island and have never returned.
Often, the females born there come back, each
being recognizable to wardens on the island.

AN INTREPID HUNTER

The snowy owls of the Arctic and sub-Arctic
feed on lemmings and voles and the occasional
ptarmigan or duck. In Fetlar, where there are
no lemmings, rabbits form the major part of
their diet. The owls hunt mostly by day, con-
tending with long hours of darkness in winter
and continuous light in summer. They perch on
a rocky vantage point, and from here make long

WHITE HUNTER
*(above) Rather larger than
the male, the female snowy
owl is distinguishable from
her almost pure white mate
by the dark brown barring
on her breast, back and
wings. These markings make
her less conspicuous as she
sits on her ground nest
among the lichens and
grasses of the tundra,
keeping a look out with her
startling bright yellow eyes.
Snowy owls' plumage is thick
and downy to combat the
sub-zero conditions of the
arctic wastes which they
usually inhabit.*

A MALE IN FLIGHT (*right*) *One of the world's largest owls, the snowy owl is an impressive bird in flight, with a wingspan of about 5 feet. It has a distinctive gliding flight very similar to that of the buzzard, and even hovers occasionally, before swooping down on its unsuspecting prey which it kills with powerful talons.*

IN FLIGHT the wings have a huge span which enable the owl to make long glides. The male is almost pure white; the female has brown markings on the top of its wings and on its belly.

TALONS Dense white feathers cover the owl's legs, feet, and claws, providing good insulation.

EGGS are smooth and white. Pellets contain undigested fur, feathers and bones.

glides over the ground in pursuit of prey, even hovering occasionally. The hunting territory of a snowy owl is usually a vast area of 3½-4 square miles which is defended with loud 'krow-ow' calls and harsh shrieks. In Fetlar it was just 1½ square miles and the owls tended to hunt at night.

Like all other owls, the snowy owl staggers her egg laying. She starts incubating the first egg straight away, with the result that the hatching times are also staggered. This ensures that in the event of a food shortage the older, stronger chicks survive: they will take most of the food brought to the nest and may even eat their younger, weaker siblings. The size of the clutches varies according to availability of prey, and may be as many as 10-12 eggs in a good lemming year in the Arctic, or 3 or 4 eggs in a bad season after a lemming migration.

The chicks hatch out after 32-33 days incubation by the female. The young owlets are able to sit and stand up at an early age and will lie on their wings to avoid contact with the cold ground. For a while the male hunts for the food for the family. He gives his catch to his mate, who carefully prepares pieces of meat for the young birds. Only later does she give them bones, fur and feathers. The owlets leave the nest when their true plumage is developing and huddle against nearby rocks waiting to be fed by both parents. The young birds usually make their first flights when they are about 50 days old.

VULNERABLE YOUNG

Despite the vigilance of their parents, in the Arctic the young often fall victim to Arctic foxes and skuas. On Fetlar the reasons for the chick mortality were not always apparent. The very nature of the Shetland climate could have been one contributing factor. Mist and rain occur frequently and for long periods. This must have made it very difficult for the male to bring sufficient food back to the nest.

UNDER THREAT
The female makes a nest, or 'scrape' on a small hill or mound, scratching a hollow in the ground which she may line with moss, grass or feathers. She lays her large, white eggs at intervals during May or early June, and the chicks hatch after an incubation of 32-33 days. Here a female adopts a defensive posture, shielding her young chicks under the mantle of her wings.

The Shetland Pony

The strongest horse in the world in relation to its size, this endearing miniature shaggy-haired pony still roams the wild, treeless hills of the Shetland Isles, its home for centuries.

Herds of diminutive, shaggy Shetland ponies still graze on the windswept hills and moors of the Shetland Isles, just as they have done for thousands of years. The smallest native British pony – standing not more than 42 inches (106cm) at the shoulder – yet strong enough to carry a full-grown man – the Shetland can thrive on the poorest of grass and in the harshest of weather. Long a vital part of the Shetland economy, only relatively recently in its history has it become one of the most popular children's riding ponies.

The first Shetland ponies – which closely resemble a native Norwegian breed – may have arrived on the islands by crossing an ice bridge linking Norway and Britain during the Ice Age. And from the earliest times islanders relied on their Shetland ponies as a robust and sure-footed means of transport over rough ground. For until well into the 19th century there were no roads in the Shetland islands, and little wheeled transport for many years after the few roads were built. The immensely sturdy little ponies also made superb pack-horses, carting enormous loads of peat for fuel – necessary as there were no trees – and seaweed for fertilizing the land.

PIT PONIES

In the mid-19th century mine-owners in north-east England began importing the plucky Shetland to replace children forbidden by law to haul tubs of coal along low seams. Other ponies were sent to all parts of Britain for driving, farmwork and general riding, and they started to become a popular first mount for children.

Bred for quantity, the Shetland became thick-necked, straight-shouldered and tubby, with large feet. But in 1870, the Marquis of London-derry established a stud on the islands of Bressay and Moss, and through careful selective breeding helped to recreate the true Shetland stock from which the best Shetlands of today have descended. In 1890 the Shetland was the first native pony to have its own society.

PACK PONIES

Any colour, except spotted, the Shetland pony has a short head, powerful deep body, short muscular legs and long, thick mane and tail. Intelligent, hardy and sure-footed, it is easily handled – though capable of showing wilful spirit – and makes an excellent pack or riding pony. Even if bred in less hostile conditions, a Shetland pony will grow no bigger than 42" (106cm) at the shoulder.

After a slump in demand during the World Wars, the Shetland Stud Book Society and the Department of Agriculture for Scotland sent fresh infusions of pedigree stallions to the Shetlands in 1948 and 1956 to improve the stock and encourage breeders to start up again. Today, up to 18 stallions a year are released on scattalds (common grazing land) throughout the islands.

MANAGED HERDS

The 'wild' herds roaming the Shetlands today are all privately owned. Some run on the hills all year round, roaming many miles and surviving on poor moorland grasses and, if necessary, heather. Their bellies are large and swollen because they must eat large amounts to obtain sufficient nutrients. In winter, especially in very deep snow, crofters put out a supplementary feed of hay and other grains. Ponies by the coast may feast on seaweeds, which provide valuable traces of minerals to boost a poor winter diet.

The smooth, short summer coat is shed in September for a distinctive, double-thick winter coat, which not only keeps the Shetland pony warm, but keeps out rain and snow.

Stallions are turned out only for the breeding season from May until August, and each herds about 30 mares. In autumn, stallions leave their harem, and, in contrast to other native breeds, adjacent herds mix together. Pregnant mares – some of which are brought in to convenient enclosures during the winter – give birth after 11 months. Most foals are born without difficulty but if the new-born foal is struggling to free itself from the enveloping membranes a stallion may help its release by biting through them. A healthy youngster can then look forward to a lifespan of up to 40 years.

'WILD' HERDS
(above) Although privately owned, herds are free to wander the grassy hills of the Shetland Isles as they have done for nearly 2000 years.

THE DIMINUTIVE SHETLAND
(left) Not much taller than an Irish wolfhound, the Shetland is our only native pony to be measured in inches, not hands. Although a foot shorter than the smallest horse – it is much stronger for its size.

SHETLAND PONY   HORSE

WINTER SURVIVOR
(right) Able to cope with the harshest of winters the hardy Shetland scrapes away the snow to reach the moorland grasses beneath. Its dense winter coat keeps it both warm and dry. A fine undercoat is overlain by a coarse, greasy outer layer of long hairs which group in downward-pointing triangles so that rain runs off without wetting the inner layer.

The Orkney Islands

Across the Pentland Firth, just eight miles or so from the north-eastern tip of mainland Britain, lie the fragmented islands of Orkney. Low-lying for the most part, with an open landscape of peat moorland and green fields, broken only by the occasional croft and the steel-blue waters of inland lochs, to the west they are bordered by spectacular sea cliffs which rise like stalwart defences against the fierce pounding of the Atlantic waves. Today only the larger islands are inhabited, but the remote holms and skerries provide undisturbed havens for thousands of birds.

NORTH RONALDSAY

WESTRAY

SANDAY

ROUSAY

EDAY

STRONSAY

MAINLAND

MOORS

SHAPINSAY

KIRKWALL

CLIFFS

LOCH OF STENNESS

SCAPA FLOW

MOORS

OLD MAN
OF HOY

FLOTTA

HOY

SOUTH RONALDSAY

THE ORKNEY
ISLANDS

ON THE WILD SIDE
(right) The coastline of the
Orkneys varies from
towering vertical cliffs in the
west, to the sandy beaches of
islands like Stronsay and
Sanday in the east. The white
shell sand gives rise to light
fertile soils which are easily
cultivated and provide
excellent grazing.

THE ORKNEY GROUP
(left) The scattered islands
and islets of the Orkneys
stretch like stepping stones
between the Scottish
mainland and the Shetland
Isles, covering some 50 miles
from Brough Ness on South
Ronaldsay to the northernmost point of North
Ronaldsay – an island noted
for its stone wall which
encloses the low-lying land
and keeps the native sheep
on the shore, where they
feed on seaweed. Although
the landscape is varied, most
of the interior is gentle,
undulating and fertile. Only
21 of the 70 islands are now
inhabited, with the majority
of the population living on
Mainland – the largest island
– where the only two towns,
Stromness and the capital
Kirkwall, are found.

Between the north coast of Scotland and the remote Shetland Isles lies a cluster of some 70 islands surrounded by turbulent and unpredictable waters. The sea has played a large part in the shaping of the Orkneys, and water is a dominant feature of the landscape: innumerable sounds and bays indent the 500 miles (800km) of coastline, and lochs and lochans echo the sea inland.

Most of Orkney is built from Old Red Sandstone which was laid down under shallow primeval seas more than 300 million years ago. The sandstone is intensely layered and, where exposed on the coast, has weathered into unusual, highly stratified forms. The gently undulating landscape which is so characteristic of the islands was shaped in the last Ice Age when ice sheets from Scandinavia scoured their way across northern Europe. As the ice retreated, boulder clay and fertile mud was deposited, leaving a country rich in agricultural potential.

On the western extremity of the island group, the sea has cut the hills into dramatic vertical cliffs which afford some of the most important

seabird sanctuaries in Britain. The cliffs on the west coast of Hoy are without parallel, rising to 1100 feet (335m) at St John's Head. Spectacular waterfalls cascade off the cliffs where streams drain the interior, and caves and stacks have been eroded by continual wave action. The most startling feature of this coastline is the Old Man of Hoy, which appeared in the last century when an arch collapsed leaving a 450 foot (137m) pillar of rock standing in precarious isolation.

Hoy also boasts the highest ground in Orkney. Ward Hill is over 1500 feet (450m) high and commands a view over all the islands. The hill tops have a tundra-like vegetation and the intervening valleys are reminiscent of the highland landscapes of Scotland. One of these – a little gorge called Berriedale Glen – is the site of the only remaining natural woodland on Orkney, and consists of birch, rowan, willow, aspen and hazel. Elsewhere on the islands trees are generally conspicuous by their absence.

The islands to the east are flat and low-lying. Sanday and North Ronaldsay rise so little above the sea – just 50 feet (15m) above sea

The Orkneys are a treasure house of archaeological remains. Look for:

BROCHS like the Broch of Gurness on Evie. There are 102 defensive brochs in Orkney, some of which may date from as early as 5BC.

EARTH HOUSE at Rennibister on Mainland – an underground dwelling which probably dates from the Iron Age. It also served as a burial chamber – ancestral sculls were left when the family moved on.

level in the highest areas – that they are a danger to shipping. Long beaches of white shell sand fringe many of the islands of the north and east and give rise to 'machair' soils which provide rich pasture for beef and dairy cattle – the mainstay of Orkney agriculture.

EARLY REMAINS

The islands have been inhabited since the Stone Age, and the Orkney landscape is rich in archaeological remains, with more prehistoric monuments for its area than any other part of Britain. There are many chambered tombs and brochs, as well as more recent Norse, Pictish and early Christian remains. These archaeological sites are of crucial importance to the development of tourism in the islands – one of the most important sectors of the economy.

To the traditional activities of whisky distilla-tion and fishing for herring – which has suffered a decline in recent years due to the overfishing of Orkney waters by the fleets of EEC nations – has been added the oil industry. The island of Flotta now harbours a large oil terminal which receives oil from the Piper Field in the North Sea. All the planning was done in close consultation with the county authorities and the site was developed so that the environ-ment and the traditional patterns of life were affected as little as possible. Orkney is fortunate that such developments are occurring in an age when the importance of environmental concerns is beginning to be appreciated. In the past, its isolated position has ensured that the pressure on its natural ecosystems has been less intense than elsewhere in Britain, and the pastoral landscape and way of life has changed little over the centuries.

SYMBOL STONES like the enigmatic Brough of Birsay stone – an example of Pictish artistry. Although there are several such stones in Orkney, their meaning remains a mystery.

GREEN FIELDS (left) Orkney is largely a pastoral landscape. Although it has a long agricultural tradition, the small farms dotted throughout the islands now concentrate on producing good quality grassland for the beef cattle which are the mainstay of the islands' agricultural economy. As a consequence, Orkney is much greener than it used to be – only 10 per cent or so of farmland is given over to oats, barley and rootcrops.

Orcadian Profusion

What Orkney wildlife lacks in variety it makes up for with sheer numbers; there are cliffs teeming with seabirds, huge seal colonies, expansive carpets of flowers and massed choirs of displaying waders.

Reach John O'Groats, at mainland Britain's north-eastern extremity, and peer out to sea. There, a few miles off-shore, are the islands of Orkney, lying, in the words of Orcadian author, George Mackay Brown, 'like sleeping whales'. Islands have always exerted an almost magnetic attraction to mankind and to naturalists in particular. Those who respond to that irrepressible urge to cross the turbulent waters of the Pentland Firth will not be disappointed, for, although the number of species is rather restricted, the sheer abundance of those that are present will live in the memory.

The waters of the Pentland Firth rose before most of the land mammals, following the retreating Pleistocene ice, reached northern Scotland. This water barrier has resulted in Orkney having very few native mammals. Consequently, almost all those species present now are believed to have been introduced – even the famous Orkney vole – although some of these introductions may have occurred as long as 4000 years ago. Some

mammals, however, are not deterred by water barriers. Both grey and common seals are abundant. Greys, which number some 20,000, come ashore to give birth in October in huge noisy colonies. 3500 of the less gregarious common seals also gather to give birth to their pups in June and July.

Porpoises are relatively numerous in Orkney waters; their breeding areas are unknown but the occurrence of very tiny calves close to the islands suggests they may not be far away. Other cetaceans regularly sighted include white-beaked dolphin, pilot whale and killer whale.

ORCADIAN PLANTS

Orkney once boasted a cover of mixed scrub woodland but, due to the activities of man, this is today confined to one valley, Berriedale on Hoy. Heather and cotton grasses have replaced woodland over much of the islands.

On the exposed island of Hoy, a number of alpine species can be found at low altitudes:

EIDER DUCK ON EGGS
(left) The female's dull plumage and her habit of sitting tight until almost stood upon are good defence policies. On hatching, the ducklings are led to the sea by the most direct route, even though this may entail a drop over a 30' cliff.

WILDLIFE ON AN ORKNEY ISLAND

Hen harriers and short-eared owls quarter the moorland in search of Orkney voles or the chicks of waders, such as snipe or curlews. Moorland nesting Arctic skuas come to the coast where they force terns and kittiwakes to disgorge captured fish. Kittiwakes, fulmars and guillemots all nest on the cliff ledges. The heather of dry moorland gives way to cotton grass and grass of Parnassus in damp areas. Thrift, sea aster and sea plantain grow in saltmarshes and on the headlands and cliffs.

KEY TO FEATURES AND SPECIES

1 Male hen harrier
2 Arctic skua
3 Arctic tern
4 Dyke system
5 Old woodland
6 Whale
7 Kittiwake
8 Nesting cliff
9 Fulmar

10 Snipe
11 Lochan
12 Saltmarsh
13 Grey seals
14 Short-eared owl
15 Heather
16 Dunes
17 Ronaldsay sheep
18 Shag

19 Curlew
20 Thrift
21 Sea plantain
22 Sea aster
23 Cotton grass
24 Grass of Parnassus
25 Scottish primrose
26 Orkney vole
27 Skylark

BLACK GUILLEMOT
(left) The guillemot nests on cliff ledges but its rarer cousin, the black guillemot – known locally as the tystie – prefers boulder-strewn coasts. It usually nests in holes or crevices, or a cave if one is available. Because it is more vulnerable to mammal predators it tends to nest on rat-free islets. One holm holds 150 pairs, the largest British colony of this northern species.

GREY SEAL COLONY
(right) Seal colonies are usually associated with rocky or sandy beaches. Here, however, on Muckle Green Holm, the breeding seals have hauled out onto the grassy sward. Numerous white seal pups can be seen.

BOTTLE-NOSED DOLPHIN
Although less commonly seen than white-beaked and white-sided dolphins, the familiar bottle-nosed dolphin occasionally makes a playful appearance off Orkney during the summer months.

holly fern, moss campion, alpine saw-wort and purple, starry and yellow mountain saxifrages can all be located in the ice-hewn corries. On the exposed western cliff tops, especially of Papa Westray, Westray and Rousay, a special community of plants known as maritime heath occurs. Here dwarf shrubs, such as crowberry and creeping willow, grow in close association with sedges and flowering herbs, among which are numbered the frog orchid and the beautiful Scottish primrose.

A striking feature of the Orkney landscape is the number of lochs and marshes, although many wetlands have been drained in the past to create more grazing pasture. In spring the marshes are a blaze of colour, the profusion of golden-yellow marsh marigolds beautifully offset by the pale mauve of lady's smock and ranks of deep purple northern marsh orchid mingle with the delicate white blooms of bogbean. Even the agricultural ground puts on a fine show, acre upon acre blooming with meadow buttercups.

BIRDS OF THE ISLANDS

Of all Orkney's wildlife, it is the birds which most capture the imagination. The moors may hold as many as a hundred hen harrier nests – nests not pairs, as cock harriers frequently have three, four and, on occasion, as many as six mates! Other birds of prey include peregrines, merlins, kestrels, and short-eared owls.

Red-throated divers – known locally as rain geese – nest on moorland lochans. They lay their two large eggs close to the water's edge and fly to the sea to feed, with wild, goose-like cries. The sound of the moors, however, is the bubbling call

of the curlew. Found here at greater breeding densities than elsewhere in Britain, the curlew has a strong claim to being Orkney's 'national' bird.

Colonies of common gulls are numerous, meadow pipits and skylarks abundant, so that the moors are a source of food for various scavenging predators, Ravens patrol the hills; great black-backed gulls, from their large colonies on Hoy, Stronsay and the Calf of Eday, do likewise; and great and arctic skuas – both common breeders – are ever on the look-out for an unattended nest.

On the maritime heaths, birds are even more abundant. Here are Orkney's major Arctic tern colonies, that on Papa Westray sometimes holding as many as 10,000 pairs. Wintering on the edge of the Antarctic pack ice, the 'pickie-ternos', as they are known, arrive back in the islands in mid-May at the end of an 8000 mile flight. Their return is looked forward to with as much anticipation as is that of the cuckoo or swallow in the South – one Arctic tern usually *does* mean that Orkney's short, sharp summer has arrived at last! Many Arctic skuas nest in close association with the terns. Oystercatchers, too, are abundant on maritime heath.

The cliffs themselves, especially on Orkney's western seaboard, are packed with breeding seabirds. Here is to be found one of the largest concentrations of fulmars, guillemots and kittiwakes in Britain. The rock strata forms ideal ledges for nesting, while the mixing of the waters of the Atlantic and the North Sea provides an abundance of food. The largest of the colonies is on Westray where as many as 70,000 guillemots and 50,000 kittiwakes may breed. It is the fulmar, however, whose story must rank as the success of the 20th century. Not recorded as a breeding bird in Orkney prior to 1900, its population now totals almost 100,000 pairs.

Not all seabirds are confined to high, inaccessible cliffs, however. There are several cormorant colonies on low, rocky skerries; and puffins prefer to burrow their way beneath sea-washed turf. Their Orkney metropolis is on tiny remote Sule Skerry, forty miles out into the wild Atlantic, where some 45,000 pairs have honeycombed the surface. Tinier, more remote and decidedly less accessible even than Sule Skerry, is the dark glowering rock of Sule Stack. Some 6000 pairs of gannets nest here, at their only Orkney site.

DUCKS AND WADERS

Back on dry land, bird-watchers will be drawn to the loch margins and marshes. Here nest no fewer than ten species of duck and nine species of wader. The ducks include wigeon, shoveler, the scarce gadwall and the nationally rare pintail – Orkney may hold 50% of the British population of this immaculate duck.

A few pairs of corncrakes, driven out of farmland by modern, intensive methods, may find refuge in the long vegetation of the wetland fringes. But summer nights no longer guarantee a chance to hear this master of throat-rasping ventriloquism. The 'sound' experience of Orkney is now undoubtedly provided by the waders. A fine spring dawn with displaying lapwing, curlew, redshank and oystercatcher, interspersed with drumming snipe and the occasional thrilling dunlin, is one of the pleasures of a bird-watching holiday in the islands.

FROG ORCHID
(left) Small specimens of this orchid occur among the dwarf shrubs and other flowers which make up maritime heath.

SCOTTISH PRIMROSE
(below) Another species of maritime heath, the Scottish primrose is confined to Orkney and to similar habitats on the northern coasts of Scotland. It occurs nowhere else in the world.

Yellow Mountain Saxifrage

Thale Cress

Hoary Whitlow-grass

THALE CRESS *(Arabidopsis thaliana)* Wiry stems 2-12″(5-30cm) high arise from a rosette of grey-green leaves. An annual with a short life-span, flowers may be found spring-autumn, followed by spreading seedpods. Widespread, seen especially in dry, stony places.

YELLOW MOUNTAIN SAXIFRAGE *(Saxifraga aizoides)* This perennial forms a cushion from which 2-8″(5-20cm) erect stems arise, bearing 1-10 flowers, June to August. Locally common by streams and on wet, gravelly slopes in the North and Ireland.

HOARY WHITLOW-GRASS *(Draba incana)* Flowering June-July, the 2-20″ (5-50cm) flowerstem and toothed leaves, bear star-shaped hairs. A rare, alpine perennial, it grows on limy mountain slopes in the North, at sea level in the extreme North.

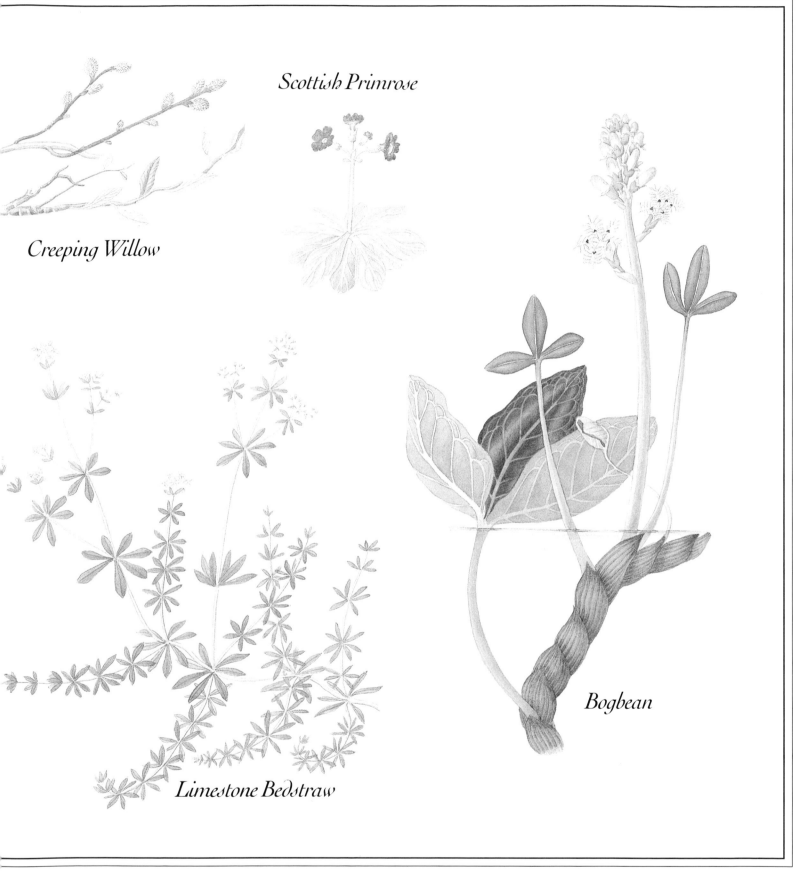

Scottish Primrose

Creeping Willow

Bogbean

Limestone Bedstraw

CREEPING WILLOW (*Salix repens*) A dense thicket of woody stems to 60″(150cm) grows from creeping roots. Leaves vary in shape, young ones are covered in silky hairs. Male and female catkins open on separate plants April-May. Common on wet, sandy heaths.

LIMESTONE BEDSTRAW (*Galium sterneri*) Common on grassy pastures on limy soils in the North and west Ireland, this perennial makes a tangled mat of stems. Flowers are borne on shoots to 10″ (25cm) June-August, leaves have tiny prickles along the edge.

SCOTTISH PRIMROSE (*Primula scotica*) Seen in scattered colonies on wet, coastal pastures of Orkney, Sutherland and Caithness, this is a species that grows nowhere else in the world. From a rosette of 'mealy' leaves, a stem 1-4″(3-10cm) bears a head of flowers, May-September.

BOGBEAN (*Menyanthes trifoliata*) This aquatic perennial is widely distributed but most often seen in bog pools and acid lakes of the North and West. Fringed flowers and leaves divided into 3 leaflets are borne above the water on a 5-12″ (12-30cm) stem May-July.

Juvenile Second Year

Cormorant

Adult

Juvenile

CORMORANT *(Phalacrocorax carbo)* A bronze-black, 36″ (90cm) bird, distinguished from the similar shag by its slightly larger size, white cheeks and lack of crest. Commonly seen around our shores, and on waterways and inland lakes. They swim low in the water, diving to catch small fish. After swimming, they stand erect on rocks with wings held open to dry. Colonies frequently nest on rocky ledges but may also choose bushes or the ground. 3 blue eggs are laid in a weedy nest from March. Mostly silent, with a few moaning croaks.

GANNET *(Sula bassana)* Our largest seabird, the 36″ (90cm) gannet has a 6′ (1.8m) wingspan. It breeds in colonies on steep cliffs and rocky islands mostly in the North and West with scattered sites elsewhere. Out of the breeding season they occur offshore, and far

Birds

Gannet

Juvenile

Adult

Corncrake

out to sea. They dive for fish from up to 100′(30m) above the sea, catching their prey with a spectacular vertical plunge. Bulky nests are made high on ledges. 1 egg is laid April-May – the chick is fed for up to 13 weeks, then deserted, when it takes to the sea.

CORNCRAKE *(Crex crex)* Now sadly diminished, the 11″(28cm) corncrake is a rare summer migrant found largely on some Scottish islands and in west Ireland. Here it lives among tall herbage in meadows and fields. Extremely well camouflaged, it is betrayed by

the loud, distinctive *krrx krrx* call of the male in search of a mate. Nests are built in tussocks at ground level, and 8-12 greyish eggs are laid May-June. Young leave the nest a few hours after hatching and are soon independent, leaving their parents to forage for invertebrates.

The Great Skua

Until comparatively recently, the great skua was almost unknown as a breeding bird in Britain. Today it has large colonies in Orkney and Shetland where it terrorizes the local population of seabirds.

It is a spring afternoon, and the desolate moors of Hoy are bathed in bright sunshine. Nearby, the sea reverberates with reflected light as gentle waves move almost imperceptibly towards the foot of the cliffs. Suddenly the peace is shattered by the angry call of a great skua – *piah piah piah*. A sheep has strayed into its territory and the bird plunges from the sky with wings and feet outstretched, uttering its menacing call. Time after time it swoops at the sheep, brushing its head and battering it with its wings, until the sheep is driven out of its territory. This large seabird of northern Britain is renowned for its vigorous defence of both territory and young, as many a birdwatcher can testify.

Bulky and rather ungainly on the ground, the great skua – or 'bonxie' as it is known locally – is masterful in the air, its broad wings allowing an easy flight. Slightly larger than a herring gull, it is easily distinguished from juvenile gulls with similar brown plumage by its conspicuous white wing patches. These are used to good effect in its territorial display, when the wings are raised over the body. Unlike most of the gulls, it has jet-black legs which are rather short in relation to the size of its body and are set well back, making it look unbalanced. The bill is also black and is heavy, with a slightly hooked tip which helps when feeding.

PIRATE OF THE SEAS

Skuas are well-known for their piratical and predatory life-style. They often chase other birds and harass them until they disgorge their last meal, which is promptly caught and eaten by the skua. The great skua is, however, rather less dependant on other birds than its relatives. Its large size and powerful bill enable it to catch its own prey, including puffins and young kittiwakes, and it will also resort to cannibalism when an injured young skua presents an easy meal. More often, it catches surface shoaling fish or follows fishing boats and feeds on the offal and undersized fish thrown overboard.

Nevertheless, the great skua still indulges in piratical behaviour, and its nesting colonies are seldom far from the breeding areas of other seabirds. Gannets are a particular target despite their large size and fierce bill. The skua relentlessly pursues its victim, pulling at its wing feathers until it either regurgitates or alights on the water. If the latter happens, the skua continues its attacks until the gannet's last meal is brought up. The only sea-bird the bonxie seems reluctant to tackle is the fulmar, whose habit of spitting a foul-smelling oil at any aggressor is sufficient deterrent.

Great skuas arrive at their nesting colonies in March or April, flying in from the open waters of the Atlantic, where they spend the winter. Most British colonies are on moorland sites in northern Scotland and the Orkneys. Skuas return to the same territory each year, generally pairing for life. On arrival at the colony, the male vigorously defends his territory from rivals, throwing his head forwards, lifting his wings, and voicing short nasal calls. He selects several prospective nest sites for the female to choose from, and once one is chosen, both birds make a simple scrape, turning and pressing the ground with chest and belly, and mate.

The female lays two grey-brown eggs in May and incubates them for one month. When the chicks hatch they are particularly vulnerable and are defended by their parents for the six to eight weeks it takes them to fledge. The downy young usually leave the nest scrape soon after hatching and crouch quietly in the vegetation until their parents appear with food. Those that stray too far are likely to be attacked and eaten by adults

MAKING A STAND
The largest of the skuas, the great skua is a heavily built bird, well-known for its bullying tactics and for its fierce defence of its territory and young. The aggressive display posture (above) is adopted whenever an intruder strays into the bird's territory. It also occurs when male and female birds initially meet up on the nesting site.

in another territory, or by the many non-breeding birds associated with these colonies, which together with off-duty parents spend a lot of time in 'gangs' loafing around near pools of fresh water.

From the number of birds in a skua colony, it may appear that they are a numerous bird, but in reality they are quite scarce and Britain holds a significant proportion of the world's population. Even here, there are probably no more than 6000 or so pairs, and this after a recent expansion in their numbers and range. In fact the first colonization of Orkney took place as recently as 1915 when the main colony on Hoy was founded. At the last count – taken in 1977 – there were some 500 pairs on Orkney, and more than 5000 pairs on the Shetlands. In August and September the great skuas leave their nesting colonies to head out to sea for the winter, and the moors become quiet again, lashed only by the wind and the rain.

ON GUARD
(above) The downy chicks leave the nest scrape soon after hatching and nestle separately amongst nearby vegetation. Most of the time they are guarded by the female; the male usually brings food to the nest, regurgitating it so that it can be fed to the young by the female. Chicks which venture beyond their home territory are easy prey for other hungry skuas.

FLIGHT is agile and fast, despite the bird's size, and the white wing patch is prominent. Angry swoops are accompanied by pecking and blows from the feet.

COMMUNAL MEAL
(left) Fish forms the mainstay of the great skua's diet, and the sea is the bird's main hunting ground. Food may be gained by bringing down other seabirds and forcing them to drop or disgorge their catch; by feeding from fish shoaling at the surface; or by taking offal and undersized fish discarded by fishing vessels. Here, unusually, a particularly bold skua competes for food with a group of fulmars.

PREDATION habits vary in different areas, but young kittiwakes are often taken during the breeding season, as well as other seabirds.

EGGS A clutch of two eggs is generally laid in May. Colouring varies from brown, grey and olive to pale blue, with dark markings.

Lough Neagh

A vast expanse of open water located almost at the centre of Northern Ireland, Lough Neagh is the largest freshwater lake in Britain. Its rich, shallow waters are fed by eight rivers from five of the six counties which make up Ulster, and surrounded by flat, marshy fenland and tranquil green pastures. Sandy bays and small harbours used by local fishermen indent the lake's gentle shoreline, which is overlooked on three sides by distant mountains – the shadowy reminders of ancient upheavals which created this quiet inland sea some 38 million years ago.

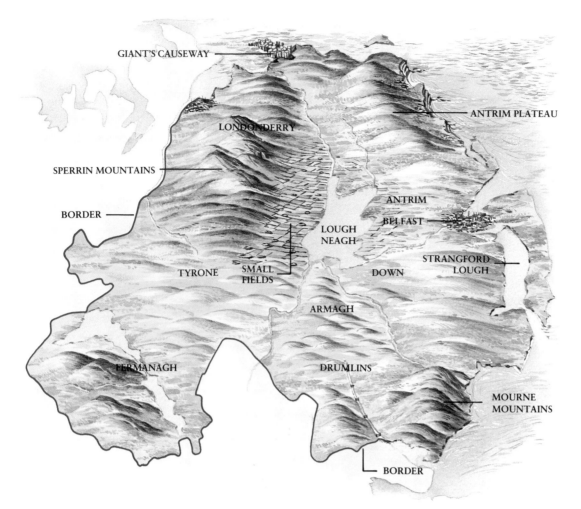

GIANT'S CAUSEWAY

LONDONDERRY

SPERRIN MOUNTAINS

BORDER

TYRONE

SMALL
FIELDS

FERMANAGH

ANTRIM PLATEAU

ANTRIM

BELFAST

LOUGH
NEAGH

STRANGFORD
LOUGH

DOWN

ARMAGH

DRUMLINS

MOURNE
MOUNTAINS

BORDER

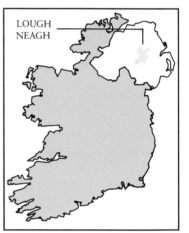

LOUGH
NEAGH

Lough Neagh, the largest lake in the British Isles, occupies a great depression in the land, just east of centre of the heart of Northern Ireland. Its dimensions are impressive – some 150 square miles of water, a fairly regular shoreline 15 miles long and 10 miles wide, with a 65 mile circumference taking in many sandy beaches and small harbours.

Despite its size, this large inland 'sea' is curiously monotonous – there are no large islands on its surface covered in ancient woodland, as with so many other Irish lakes, nor are there any reflections cast in its waters from nearby landmarks. There are, however, distant highlands on three sides of the Lough Neagh basin: to the north-east, the Antrim Plateau rises to its highest point of 1846 feet (563m); to the north-west the Sperrin Mountains peak at 2240 feet (683m); and in the south-east the Mountains of Mourne sweep down to the sea from a height of 2796 feet (852m).

Lough Neagh was formed after the tumultuous period of volcanic activity in north-eastern Ireland during the pre-glacial Tertiary period, some 60 million years ago. The massive dark basalts, so characteristic of this region, were extruded from the depths of the earth at that time, to become the youngest rocks in the island. They once covered a much more extensive area than the present 1550 square miles, but earth movements lifted them up and exposed them to the erosive forces of wind and water, which, in the prevailing tropical humid climate, planed them to the Antrim Plateau we know today.

Accompanying this uplift were complementary sinking forces, along great fault lines. By Oligocene times, some 38 million years ago, the Lough Neagh basin was in existence, but was occupied by a much larger lake than that of today, set at a far lower level beneath the basaltic plateau. Over the years, rivers have brought tons of sediment into the lake, filling it up, so that today Lough Neagh is relatively shallow, on average about 40 to 50 feet (12-15m) deep.

EXTENSIVE FENLAND

These sediments, over 1000 feet (305m) thick and consisting of a variety of rocks (sand, limestone, acid granites, chalk) derived from many areas, solidified into the Lough Neagh 'clays'. Today, they cover some 200 square miles, mainly on the eastern and south-western shores of the lake. Pale grey, heavy and muddy, these clays are generally poorly drained and infertile, supporting only marshy fenland growth. Where the clays have been lightened and fertilized, crops such as potatoes and oats are grown, and good quality pastureland for cattle is maintained.

It was the last glaciation, which first affected Ireland some 200,000 years ago, that had the greatest effect on Lough Neagh and its environs, changing the scenery and land use of the whole area. When the ice sheet melted, thick deposits of glacial drift were left, often piled into low hillocks called drumlins, which are abundant to the north and south of Lough Neagh. These glacial hills, made of sand, gravel and boulder

A CHANGING LANDSCAPE
Over the last hundred years drainage schemes have dramatically altered the shape of the lake; the water level has dropped 10 feet, exposing silt banks like these on Derrywarragh Island.

The richest farming area in the Lough Neagh basin is south of the lake in Co. Armagh. Here, beyond the infertile clays, is the 'Garden of Ulster', a productive market-gardening area of some 25 square miles. The light, well drained soil of the drumlins supports rich orchards, especially apples.

Lough Neagh receives a massive 40 per cent of Northern Ireland's drainage. Eight rivers flow into the lake, but only one leaves. This is the Bann, which rises in the Mournes to the south, flows through Lough Neagh and out the northern side, along a wide valley filled with glacial drift, to the sea on the north Antrim coast.

THE FIRST SETTLERS

The earliest record of man in Ireland comes from Mountsandel, on the Lower Bann River near Coleraine. Here, Mesolithic remains, dating from about 7000 BC, have been found. Another younger settlement, from about 6000 BC, is found on the north-western shores of Lough Neagh and provides tantalizing clues to Mesolithic man's semi-nomadic lifestyle, of hunting in the dense forests of the day for animals now long extinct in Ireland – wild boars, bears, wolves, elks – and fishing in the rich waters of the vast freshwater lake that lay at his doorstep.

clay, are blessed with good drainage, and it is on their slopes that much of the lake counties' farming takes place. The peaty marshland in between the drumlins is often left undrained and used as poor quality grazing land. As in the rest of the country, the persistent moist climate makes drainage an expensive and ongoing task. The Lough Neagh area receives an average annual rainfall of 33 inches (84cm), spread over some 150 to 175 'wet' days a year.

RECLAIMED PASTURES
This pastoral scene is typical of much of the land surrounding Lough Neagh. Here, to the south-east of the lake, in Co. Down, the clays have been lightened to make good-quality grazing land. Elsewhere there has been no reclamation, and the original marshy land remains – one of the most extensive areas of fenland left in the British Isles.

Nature Walk

Man-made features around Lough Neagh give insight into local customs.

NAVAN FORT, near Armagh, was the main residence of the Kings of Ulster.

GRANITE PILLAR STONES with Irish inscriptions mark early Christian burial sites dating from 700 AD.

EEL TRAPS at Toome, part of a major industry in and around the lough.

THATCHED COTTAGES with the thatch tied with rope in the local tradition.

Around the Lough

Lough Neagh is a prime feeding ground for thousands of wintering ducks and swans and, in summer, the shores are ringed by marsh flowers among which fly bright damselflies and butterflies.

In the cold light of a November morning the lough shore is shrouded by rain, slanting down before a searching, north-westerly wind. A flock of tree sparrows swoops into the shelter of a deserted farmhouse. Over the sodden fields, a solitary wader runs a few yards then turns to see if it is still followed. It seems reluctant to fly but raises a wing to reveal the distinctive blackish armpit of a grey plover. They are usually seen at the coast but this is a late migrant on its way to warmer winter quarters.

From a gorse covered promontory an unseen wildfowler shoots at wigeon and for a few moments the air is filled with the whistles of a thousand frightened duck. A mixture of wigeon, pintail and teal circle round before landing, necks outstretched, in the rushes in front of Church Island. Hundreds more, still wary – or less hungry – join a vast concourse of seemingly grey duck far out on the open water. No sooner have they settled than up they spring again; this time at the menacing shape of a peregrine falcon, emerging out of the gloom.

The wildfowl population usually peaks in January, when more pochard, tufted duck, scaup and goldeneye are present than on any other lake in the British Isles. Large flocks of wild swans – whoopers from Iceland and Bewick's from Siberia – join resident mute swans in the fields around the lough.

BELOW THE SURFACE

Lough Neagh is shallow and rich in nutrients. Beneath the surface of its vast waters there is an equally vast bed of algae, on which live countless millions of tiny animals, such as chironomid larvae, waterfleas, mussels and snails. This animal community and the algae and other abundant plantlife provide a plentiful source of food for the birds.

Early in March, salmon begin to hatch in the rivers and streams flowing into Lough Neagh, the Moyola, Ballinderry, Main and Six-mile Water. Out in the lough lurk pike, millions of eels and the Lough Neagh trout, or dollaghan. Here, too, are bream and pollan but the arctic char died out some 150 years ago. Mystery

A GRASSHOPPER WARBLER
Ireland has fewer species of breeding warbler than Britain. The reed warbler and lesser whitethroat, for instance, are both absent. Grasshopper warblers, though, can be found in good numbers around Lough Neagh, often sharing their breeding habitat with sedge warblers. Both will nest in waterside vegetation or in drier areas of tangled grass or bramble.

WILDLIFE AROUND LOUGH NEAGH

Lough Neagh is renowned for its birds. Teal, herons, grebes and grasshopper warblers all breed there. In winter, thousands of ducks and hundreds of swans and geese fly in. Buzzards and golden plovers may be seen in the Antrim Hills to the north. Ireland has fewer mammals, reptiles and butterflies than the rest of Britain, and though there are no snakes, common lizards are present. The pollan, a whitefish similar to the vendace, is found in several Irish loughs. **NB** *The maritime species listed here – 18, 22 & 32 were last noted in 1959, before they were lost following a drop in the lough's water level. There is a chance though, that they may become re-established as the level rises again.*

KEY TO THE SPECIES

1 Buzzard
2 Antrim Hills
3 Pipistrelle bat
4 Great crested grebe
5 Conifer plantation
6 Grey heron
7 Heronry
8 Green-veined white
9 Golden plover
10 Fallow deer
11 Common blue damselfly

12 Teal
13 Greylag geese
14 Scots pine
15 Sika deer
16 Pintail
17 Grasshopper warbler
18 Sea club-rush
19 Bewick's swans
20 Red squirrel
21 Ringlet butterfly
22 Sea plantain

23 Four-spotted libellula
24 Irish stoat
25 Holy grass
26 Common lizard
27 Irish hare
28 Pollan
29 Waterwort
30 Pygmy shrew
31 Rock sea spurrey
32 Irish lady's tresses
33 Wood mouse

279

surrounds the introduction of the roach some time in the 1970s. Already it is unpopular among fishermen; with no commercial value it is not welcome in their nets and is time-consuming to remove.

Before drainage schemes lowered the lough's water level, flooding was regular and there were extensive marshes. Nowadays, plants like the marsh cinquefoil, marsh violet and marsh marigold are confined to wet margins. Some, like the marsh pea, grow in just a few locations, while the marsh fern is now extinct in the Lough Neagh basin. Marsh ragwort and both yellow and purple loosestrife occur on damp grassland ungrazed by cattle.

Before the end of March, hordes of wading birds gather on the shores and flat farmland around nearby Lough Beg. One that appears in some numbers at this time of year is the Icelandic black-tailed godwit which, in summer plumage, is a deeper chestnut than the continental race breeding in a few parts of England. After reaching a peak in early April the godwits tail-off gradually, giving way to lesser numbers of whimbrel.

Recent surveys of breeding waders have shown that the damp grassland on the west and south shores of both Lough Neagh and Lough Beg

IRISH STOAT
(above) Sometimes known locally as the weasel – there are no weasels in Ireland – the Irish stoat differs slightly from its British cousin. It tends to be smaller with a dark upper lip and dark edges to its ears.

POCHARD
(below) Concentrations of over 20,000 pochard have been counted on Lough Neagh in winter, forming a large proportion of the visiting wildfowl.

PYGMY SHREW
(above) Ireland has only one species of shrew but this delightful little animal is widely distributed.

SEA CLUB-RUSH
(right) This is one of several maritime plants which grow around the lough, suggesting that the sea once had access to Lough Neagh.

holds important populations of lapwing, snipe, redshank and curlew. In Northern Ireland only the wetlands of Upper Lough Erne in County Fermanagh hold more of these birds.

Many species of duck stay to nest on the islands in the lough, including one thousand pairs of tufted duck. These islands are often shared with noisy black-headed gulls and a few pairs of common terns. Perhaps the most impressive breeding bird is the great crested grebe which nests here in huge colonies.

Less visible are the corncrakes which nest around the south-eastern corner of the lough. Their rasping voices can be heard in late April and early May. Though really nocturnal in habits, the males at this time of year are so obsessed by nuptial instincts that they call by day and night. Even when calling they keep well hidden in the long grass. Where there are tussocks of grass and patches of thick vegetation near the lough shore another bird of retiring habits, the grasshopper warbler, might be encountered.

INSECTS ON THE WING

Some twelve months after hatching, the larvae of non-biting midges emerge from their watery birth-place to begin life as Lough Neagh flies. On windless days in May and June vast swarms hug the lough shore.

In the few remaining pockets of fen other insects are on the wing, including marsh fritillary butterflies, an assortment of dragonflies, and, in the month of July, the diminutive Irish damselfly. Only recently discovered in Ireland, this damselfly can be separated from others with pale-blue abdomens which are found around Lough Neagh by the 'half-moon' on its second segment.

Along the woodland rides of Randalstown Forest and Shane's Castle estate, butterflies such as the stunning silver-washed fritillary and fluttering wood white – a different race to that found in southern England – might be glimpsed in high summer.

Wandering through these woods at night can be rewarding. What sounds like a rusty sign, creaking in the wind, might lead to the appropriated nest of a wood pigeon or a jay. The 'creaking sign' turns out to be a vocal brood of long-eared owl chicks, calling impatiently for their next meal of field mouse, rat or roosting songbird. In the absence of the tawny owl, the long-eared owl is Ireland's only brown owl. The only other breeding owl – the barn owl – has become scarce in Northern Ireland.

Rarest of all Ireland's mammals, the pine marten has occasionally been caught in traps set for troublesome mink. Around the lough badgers and foxes are widespread but the red squirrel is restricted to the small amount of mature woodland in the north-eastern sector. A hedgerow tangle, old stone wall or bramble thicket is all that is needed by a family of Irish stoats. This small subspecies cannot be mistaken for a weasel because the weasel, like the mole and the field vole, and a few other British mammals, is not part of the Irish fauna.

The hares around the lough are different, too. Not the brown hares of lowland Britain, but a distinct race of the mountain or blue hare. This is normally the first mammal to greet the visitor landing at nearby Aldergrove Airport.

IRISH LADY'S TRESSES
This rare flower, which has probably always been very local in its distribution, is a small orchid which flowers towards the end of summer. It occurs elsewhere in Ireland and is found in North America but has recently become extinct in England.

NESTING GREBES
(right) These handsome great crested grebes nest in colonies on Lough Neagh. In one reedbed, 60 yards long, 104 nests were found with up to 11 eggs in each nest. The birds' dramatic courtship displays can best be seen from the Oxford Island National Nature Reserve. This is not an island but a peninsular jutting out from the south-eastern shore. Stripey chicks can be seen on the back of the sitting bird.

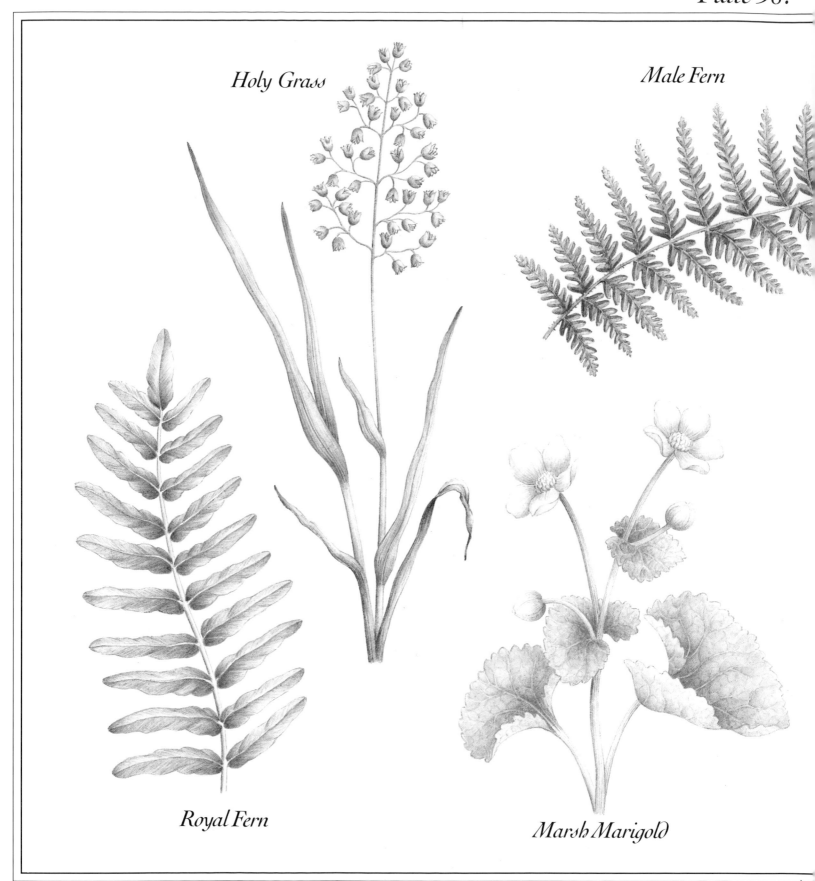

Holy Grass

Male Fern

Royal Fern

Marsh Marigold

ROYAL FERN *(Osmunda regalis)*
A large fern with sterile fronds to
100″ (250cm) long, often planted
by ponds in gardens and found
locally on wet peat, western Britain
and Ireland. Erect fertile parts turn
orange when the spore-cases ripen
and shed spores, June to August.

HOLY GRASS *(Hierochloe odorata)*
Restricted to the wet grassy banks
of Lough Neagh and a few Scottish
localities, this very rare grass is a
sweet-scented perennial. It grows in
close tufts, with rough-edged leaves.
Stems of 8-20″ (20-50cm) have
open flowerheads, March-May.

MALE FERN *(Dryopteris filix-mas)*
Widespread and common in shady,
damp habitats throughout Britain,
arching fronds with scaly stems
reach 35″ (90cm). The small, flat
leaflets are toothed, fertile ones
bearing 6-12 round spore-cases.
Ripe spores are shed July to August.

MARSH MARIGOLD *(Caltha
palustris)* A handsome perennial
with large golden flowers and dark
glossy leaves, growing in 12-24″
(30-60cm) clumps on riverbanks and
in marshes. Common in Britain and
Ireland and a sure sign of spring,
blooming from March to May.

Waterside Plants

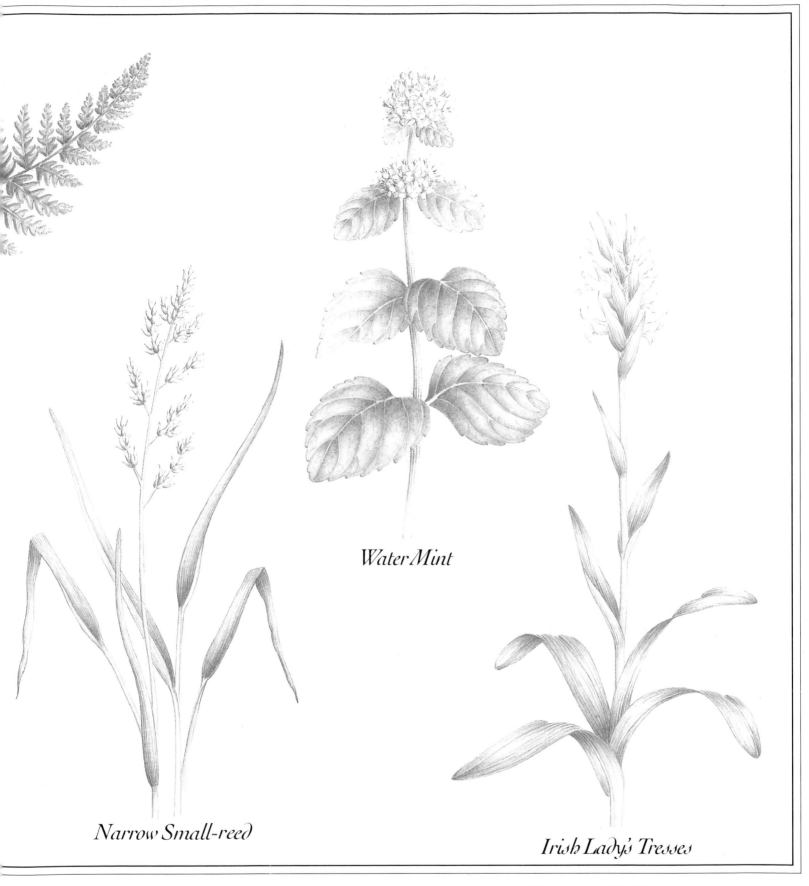

Water Mint

Narrow Small-reed

Irish Lady's Tresses

NARROW SMALL-REED
(Calamagrostis stricta) Erect tufts
of this rare grass grow only in a few
marshes and bogs in England,
Scotland and Ireland. Stems to 40″
(100cm) bear narrow, dense heads
of flowers June-August. Leaf
margins are rough to the touch.

WATER MINT *(Mentha aquatica)*
When bruised, this 6-35″ (15-90cm),
hairy perennial has a fresh, minty
smell. Widespread and common by
streams and in ditches throughout
Britain, the upright square stems
have oval, toothed leaves and tight
whorls of flowers July to October.

IRISH LADY'S TRESSES
(Spiranthes romanzoffiana) A rare
orchid of peat cuttings and marshy
grassland in scattered localities of
west Scotland and Ireland. Lance-
shaped leaves clasp the base of a 5-
10″ (12-25cm) stem with spirally
arranged flowers, July to August.

Redshank

Chicks

Chicks

REDSHANK *(Tringa totanus)*
A common 11″ (28cm) wader with long, bright red legs. In flight, a white rump and wing-bar are clearly seen. The speckled and barred plumage is greyish in winter. Found on grassy marshland, swamps and saltings, they are nervous birds,

quick to take flight, with a shrill high-pitched call. They feed on crustaceans and insects. Nests are concealed in tufts of grass and a single clutch of 4 speckled, buff eggs is laid in May. Both parents incubate and care for young, leading them to water when only a few hours old.

RINGED PLOVER *(Charadrius hiaticula)* A chubby 7½″ (19cm) bird, its black-tipped yellow bill and bright orange legs distinguish it from other plovers. Resident in Britain and Ireland, its numbers are swollen in winter by migrants from further north. They breed on pebbly shores

Chicks

Water Rail

Ringed Plover

and shingly riverbanks, where a sketchy nest of shell fragments or small pebbles is made. Clutches of usually 4 heavily spotted eggs are laid March onwards and the parents will feign injury to distract predators. They feed on small invertebrates and their call is a mellow trill.

WATER RAIL *(Rallus aquaticus)* Though the wide range of grunts, croaks and wheezes produced by this bird are often heard in reedbeds and marshes, it is secretive and seldom seen until flushed at close range. 11½" (29cm), with attractively marked plumage and a long red bill,

the sexes are alike. Their diet is varied – mostly aquatic invertebrates and tadpoles, but also berries and seeds. A large, bulky nest is made in dense cover on or near water and 2 clutches of 6-10 sparsely spotted buff eggs are laid April to June. Resident, some winter migrants.

Winter Swans

Two species of wild swans come as winter visitors to Britain, migrating southwards in large flocks from their summer breeding grounds in the Arctic tundra, to pass the winter on our warmer waters.

Across the grey skies of November, rushing before cold easterly winds, come flocks of huge white birds, honking and trumpeting in wild clarion as they drop down on to the choppy waters of a large lake. It is the arrival of two species of swans—birds from cold distant lands, escaping the chill of the far north. For the grey cygnets accompanying the adults it is the first time they have seen their winter home; but the parents are regulars and have returned faithfully every season for many years.

The winter swans are two species of wild swan – whooper and Bewick's. From early September they begin their exodus from their breeding grounds in the Arctic tundra regions – where their stay is limited to about 130 ice-free days in late-spring and summer – to spend the winter in the more temperate climates of western Europe. On reaching their wintering grounds, they head for the quiet waters of loughs, reservoirs, rivers and coastal estuaries, which are accompanied by suitable undisturbed grazing areas. In Britain, these winter visitors are found mainly in Ireland, Scotland and northern England, with the Bewick's ranging further south than the whooper swans.

By day many feed on the succulent pasture and waste crops of farmland near to their home water, flying out in the morning in yelping flocks. Before taking off, they perform elaborate pre-flight displays, to give warning of their intention to fly. These consist of head and neck-bobbing and loud, trumpet-like calls. The swans take off with a considerable clatter, pattering over the surface, beating their great wings, labouring to lift off their heavy bodies.

Some swans stay behind, remaining on the water all day, feeding on submerged plants by thrusting their graceful necks under water, or sometimes up-ending and dipping to reach down to the bottom. They feed on vegetable matter such as water plants and grasses.

Although they gather in large flocks, each family will not allow neighbours to invade its 'private' territory and will threaten any outsider that comes too close. Intruders may be met with a series of threat-displays by family parties, such as stretching the neck out at 45°, pumping

WINTER ARRIVALS *(above) Bewick's and whooper swans migrate southwards for the winter when their food supplies in the tundra regions become locked in snow and ice. The general movement towards the more temperate climates of western Europe begins in early September and the firstcomers may start arriving by mid October. Wild swans form large flocks outside the breeding season, with whole families travelling together.*

the head up and down, quivering or spreading the wings and a shrill calling. Sometimes a tussle may ensue, the birds hacking at each other with beaks and wings. The victor generally rears up, quivering its partly unfurled wings, and gives a satisfied wag of the tail.

Of the two species of winter swan, the whooper can be distinguished by the larger, more pointed yellow patch on its bill – that of the Bewick's is smaller and more rounded. The whooper also has a longer neck and a more triangular-shaped head. At 60 inches (152cm), the whooper is the larger swan, being almost as big as the more common and resident mute swan; Bewick's swan is the smallest of the three, averaging 48 inches (120cm). The pattern on the bills of the Bewicks are unique to each swan – like human fingerprints – and individuals can be recognized by this distinctive patterning.

The biggest difference between the mute and winter swans lies in their voices. The wide vocabulary of hisses and grunts of the mute swan is quite different from that of the shrill vocal migratory swans that call to their kith and kin across the skies. The whooper is even named after its wild trumpeting yell.

As spring kisses the land, the swans become restless, and with the first warm days and favourable westerly tail winds of March they begin to depart. The imperative call to return home and breed cannot be denied. The whooper swans head off in their non-stop flight to Iceland, parts of Scandinavia and northern Asia. Meanwhile the Bewick's swans leave for Siberia. Over the next two months they travel northeast, stopping off periodically to feed, and gathering in large flocks on the shores of the Elbe estuary. Often they return to find the barren landscape of the treeless tundra still covered with snow. But they must be there to begin nesting as soon as the snow clears to take full advantage of the brief arctic summer.

Sadly, the survival of these wild swans is at risk. Oil and mineral exploration in the Arctic wastes are increasingly intruding into their once undisturbed breeding grounds, and wetland drainage schemes are disrupting many of their regular wintering sites. Should such habitat destruction be allowed to continue, and no alternative nesting and wintering sites provided, then the sight of these beautiful birds brightening our winter skies may be lost forever.

WHOOPER

BEWICK'S

BILL DIFFERENCES
The easiest way to distinguish between the Bewick's and whooper swans is by looking at their bills. The whooper has a larger, more pointed patch of yellow – the Bewick's bill has a smaller yellow area which is curved in shape.

FAMILY PARTY
(above left) A strong bond is built up by the male and female of both species, although they may not nest for 4-6 years after. Breeding and rearing of young has to be timed carefully so that at the end of the short Arctic summer the cygnets are old enough and strong enough to accompany their parents on the long journey southwards.

REGULAR VISITORS
(left) Both whooper and Bewick's swans frequently return to the same wintering sites year after year. They prefer undisturbed reed-fringed lakes, rivers and swampy wetlands, where there is good, accessible grazing. Their diet consists mainly of vegetable matter.

The Republic of Ireland

An outpost of Europe, the emerald isle of Erin – as Ireland has long been affectionately known – has been settled and farmed for nearly 6000 years and still presents a gentle rural landscape, its verdant face greened by high rainfall. A country of many contrasts, the patchwork farmland of the central plains is flanked by the ice-cut hills and dramatic mountains of Donegal, Cork and Kerry, the extensive lake systems of Killarney and the River Shannon, the blanket bogs of the West, and a diverse coastline of high, rugged cliffs and scenic bays.

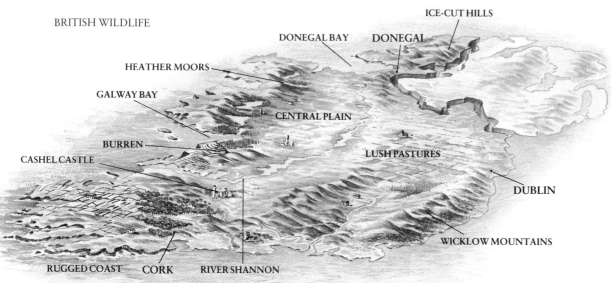

THE REPUBLIC
OF IRELAND

The Republic of Ireland occupies about five-sixths of the entire island, stretching for 300 miles from north to south and 160 miles from east to west. It is essentially a rural landscape of infinitely varied and largely unspoiled beauty, with a central low-lying plain bordered by high ground around the periphery. Nowhere does the land rise to more than 3500 feet (1066m), the highest peak – Carrantoohill in Kerry – reaching 3414 feet (1040m) above sea level.

For its size, the Republic has a remarkable range of rock types and geological structures. In the north-west, the mountains of Donegal replicate – though on a lesser scale – the highlands of Scotland; ridges and peaks of granite, gneiss and quartzite have been carved out by erosion in a north-east/south-west trend. In the south-west, in Cork and Kerry, east/west ridges of Devonian sandstone rise up like the Brecon Beacons in Wales, while the western ends of the intervening valleys have been flooded by the Atlantic, creating narrow scenic bays. The south-east corner, Carnsore Point, is a low granite boss, similar to the higher bosses of the West Country, such as Dartmoor. The rocks into which the granite intruded are the oldest known in Ireland, dating from some 2400 million years ago.

A KARST LANDSCAPE

Much of the low-lying centre is occupied by Carboniferous limestone. Younger deposits with coal seams probably once buried the limestone, as they still do in many parts of Britain, but in Ireland long continued erosion has removed the overlying layers, together with large quantities of the limestone itself. Solution by acid rain-water was the chief agent and has produced a karst landscape, with closed hollows, or *dolines*, pitting the limestone surface. Such features are well developed around Lough Gill in Sligo,

SNOW-CAPPED PEAKS
(right) At the heart of Kerry, in the south-west corner of Ireland, Devonian sandstone rises up in foreboding peaks. Amongst these mountains lies Carrantoohill – Ireland's highest peak.

though in many places they have been buried by later glacial deposits.

Glacial conditions probably became established in the British Isles about two million years ago, and great ice-masses covered most of Ireland. After their last retreat, 10,000 years ago, they left a much modified landscape. The moving ice had eroded and carried away the rock and soil beneath it, and this material was deposited more or less at random when it melted. As a result the agricultural soils of much of Ireland owe their quality more to the mixing action of the ice than to the underlying solid rock. Many are heavy, clayey soils which

IRISH OVERVIEW
(above left) The landscape of the Republic of Ireland presents many different faces – ice-cut hills and majestic mountains contrasting with lush pastures, small patchwork fields and a filigree pattern of rivers and lakes. Prehistoric remains are scattered throughout the island, together with early Christian sites and medieval castles.

THE WEST COAST (*right*) *In places Ireland's coast is steep and rugged, and the heavy Atlantic seas crash against the towering cliffs. But there are also quiet, scenic bays dotted with small islands, as here in Mayo, on the west coast, where the Nephin Beg range of mountains rise hazily in the distance.*

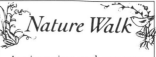

waterlog easily, a problem exacerbated by the high humidity of the Irish climate.

The cold, damp climate also inhibits plant decay, and over the centuries plant debris has accumulated into thick layers of peat, forming bog. All along the very wet western Atlantic coast, except where slopes are steep, the ground is blanketed by peat – the so-called blanket-bog.

Bogs also occur in low-lying central Ireland, where numerous hollows in the glacial deposits originally held open-water lakes. These were gradually choked by fen plants which formed fen peat. Low in nutrient, the peat was invaded by mosses and heathers which built up into a great dome of peat – the raised bog. Today the peat is harvested mechanically on a large scale for peat-fired power stations, and the bogs are vanishing rapidly.

At the end of the Ice Age the open grasslands typical of much of the country were soon replaced by woodland; broad-leaved trees such as oak, elm and hazel colonized the east of the country, while a broad band of pinewoods stretched down the west coast. Man first came to Ireland to hunt and fish as the climate warmed some 9000 years ago. 3000 years later the first farmers settled and began clearing away woodland to make fields for their crops and flocks. Woodland clearance continued until the 17th century, when trees acquired a cash value, and many woods were sold to provide timber for ships or charcoal for iron-smelting.

IRELAND'S CHANGING FACE

The beginning of the 18th century witnessed dramatic changes to the Irish landscape. Land-owners profited from the Agricultural Revolution and stately houses and exotic trees sprang up on large estates. The potato was beginning to enter the diet of the poorer classes, and the ease with which it grew and its high nutrient value combined in the early 19th century to produce a disastrous increase in population and a severe lowering of living standards. Fuel as well as food was sought more and more desperately, and excepting the large estates, trees and hedgerows vanished from the Irish scene. Famine and emigration reduced the population, but 100 years later, Ireland has not yet regained its trees. Afforestation with conifers is redressing the balance, but the percentage of land covered by trees in the Irish Republic is the lowest in Europe. Ireland's greatest natural resource is its pasture, which accounts for 80 per cent of all agricultural land and is the basis of a thriving economy based on sheep and cattle.

Nature Walk

Ancient sites and customs testify to Ireland's long heritage. Look out for:

EARLY BUILDINGS built in the shape of an upturned boat, once common on the west coast.

BEN BULBEN, Sligo, a spectacular cliffed block of Carboniferous limestone, covered with blanket bog.

BLARNEY CASTLE, Co. Cork, where the Blarney Stone is believed to confer eloquence on all who kiss it.

THE CURRAGH, a boat of ancient design made from hide stretched over a wooden frame.

Life in the Emerald Isle

Ireland's early isolation at the end of the last Ice Age, combined with a climate strongly influenced by the North Atlantic Drift, have resulted in a flora and fauna quite different to that of mainland Britain.

From the air, the Emerald Isle appears aptly named. The lush green fields of the central plain stretch on and on until finally ended by coastal hills and mountains and, beyond these, the sea. But this apparent verdant uniformity hides a mixture of wildlife that is intriguingly different from that of Britain.

Ireland's principal treasure is a unique flora, nurtured by a warm, moist Atlantic climate. In winter, there are no prolonged periods of frost, and in the South-west snow is rare. Cossetted by the North Atlantic Drift (the Gulf Stream), the seasons are not strongly marked and the mile upon mile of fuchsia hedges glow purple until deep into winter, accompanied by the deep orange of montbretia, while the hills are bright all year round with the yellow of European and Irish gorse.

Though it has fewer species than Britain or the Continent, Ireland boasts 20 species of plant not found in Britain. Ten of these come from the Iberian peninsular – members of the so-called Lusitanian flora – including the Irish orchid, St Patrick's cabbage, strawberry tree, and St Dabeoc's heath. Many of these fascinating plants are found huddled in the South-west, where the influence of the North Atlantic Drift is greatest.

Providing a contrast to these Mediterranean plants are species of North American origin, such as blue-eyed grass and the rare slender naiad and pipewort. This unique combination of flora is typical of much of Ireland, but in the mountains of the north further surprises lie in store for the botanist. For the uplands of Donegal support many interesting alpine species such as purple saxifrage which adorns the north face of Slieve League, one of Ireland's highest mountains. Mountain avens, spring gentian, alpine clubmoss, alpine meadow-rue and viviparous fescue may also be found in Ireland's highland habitats. Viviparous fescue is so-called because instead of producing seeds, it generates tiny new plants which break off and root themselves. Another prize of Donegal is Hart's saxifrage. Discovered over a century ago, this white-flowered mossy saxifrage is unique to the region.

The midlands, often only glimpsed from cars by tourists on their way to the more spectacular west, have their own charm. The lordly Shannon, the longest river in the British Isles, winds its way through a number of lakes and great reed beds. Islands in two of the largest loughs, Lough Ree and Lough Derg, are covered in vegetation undisturbed for generations and are

LARGE-FLOWERED BUTTERWORT
Identified by its large, purple, streaked blooms, this carnivorous plant has sticky glands on its leaves which trap and digest small insects.

WILDLIFE OF IRELAND

This picture draws together species from many parts of Ireland. Buzzards nest in Donegal and Monaghan; hen harriers and merlins, though not common, are widespread birds of prey in the uplands; red grouse breed on the heather moors; ravens nest inland and on sea cliffs; and both white-fronted geese and Bewick's swans are winter visitors, found in strength on Wexford Slobs. St Patrick's cabbage and kidney saxifrage grow in rocky mountain areas; the butterworts are bog plants; and blue-eyed grass favours damp, hillside meadows.

KEY TO THE SPECIES

1 White-fronted geese
2 Gannets
3 Buzzard
4 Red deer
5 Ravens
6 Grey seals
7 Male hen harrier
8 Sessile oak
9 Raft of pochard
10 Bewick's swans
11 Red grouse
12 Strawberry tree

13 Irish hare
14 Honey bees
15 Male merlin
16 Heather
17 Blue-eyed grass
18 Grey heron
19 Sphagnum moss
20 Bilberry
21 Wood mouse
22 St Patrick's cabbage
23 Large-flowered
  butterwort

24 Large heath butterfly
25 Pale butterwort
26 Parsley fern
27 Kidney saxifrage
28 Marsh spider
29 Common frog
30 Kerry slug

and Scandinavia.

In spring there are still corncrakes to be heard, and quite recently the first pair of black-tailed godwits nested by the Shannon. In Donegal, Ireland's most northerly and least known county, endless blanketbogs cover a vast landscape. Breeding here are a few pairs of red-throated divers, ravens, peregrine falcons, merlins and the Irish red grouse.

carpeted in spring with ramsons, bluebells and early purple orchids which brighten the hazel and alder jungle.

In winter, the flooded watermeadows, or callows, of the Shannon basin hold great numbers of wildfowl, notably whooper swans from Iceland and a large part of the European populations of lapwing and golden plover which find sustenance in the flooded fields while most of the rest of Europe is under snow. Ireland is at the end of two important flyways of Arctic and sub-Arctic birds. One from Arctic Canada, Greenland and Iceland, the other from Siberia

BARNACLE GEESE
(above) Throughout the winter huge flocks of barnacle geese from East Greenland can be seen grazing on islands such as the Inishkeys and Blaskets, with a smaller number near Sligo.

KERRY SLUG
(top right) Common on the Iberian peninsular, in the British Isles this spotted slug occurs only in Cork and Kerry.

PURPLE SEA URCHINS
(above right) Warmed by the North Atlantic Drift, this Mediterranean sea urchin can be found in the tidal zone off the west coast of Ireland.

ST DABEOC'S HEATH
(left) This heath-like shrub to 18", with purple or white flowers, is found in the counties of Galway and Mayo.

STRAWBERRY TREE
(right) Famous throughout Killarney, this unusual shrubby little tree sports strawberry-like – but inedible – fruit. Native to the South-west and West, it is uncommon in the rest of Ireland and rare in most of Britain. It is an evergreen with distinctive red flaking bark.

of summer to provide Irish ornithologists with plenty of surprises.

In comparatively undisturbed and unpolluted Ireland, birds and mammals that have become scarce in the rest of Europe are still holding their own. Choughs along the west and south coast; otters along all coasts and rivers; and pine martens in several districts, notably in the Burren where they don't live in pines but in the open. Ireland, however, has a relatively impoverished fauna, having separated from mainland Europe much earlier than Britain at the end of the Ice Age. Badgers, foxes, rabbits and red deer are all found but there are no roe deer, though introduced sika and fallow deer are quite common. The seven rodent species include red and grey squirrels, black and brown rats, wood and house mice and the recently discovered bank vole. Ireland's only shrew is the pygmy shrew.

Some species have become uniquely Irish. The Irish hare now is a different animal from the Continental one; it does not turn white in winter and, as there is no competition from other hares, it populates mountains and lowland alike. The Irish stoat has become smaller and does not turn white in winter.

Ireland has only one reptile – the common lizard – and few amphibians – the common frog, natterjack toad and smooth newt.

RED DEER STAG
Red deer once roamed all over Ireland, but the main herds are now confined to Glenveagh National Park, in Co. Donegal, Killarney, the Wicklows and Donerail Park in Co. Cork.

CALLING CORNCRAKE
A secretive bird, fond of skulking in wet meadows, the corncrake is a summer migrant from Africa which sojourns in Ireland to breed.

In the South-east, on an area of reclaimed mudflats in Wexford harbour, called the Slobs, about half the world population of the Greenland race of the white-fronted goose now winter. Dublin's Bull Island, another man-made landscape, sees the arrival during October and November of flocks of brent geese that come from Arctic Canada.

A special feature of the Irish landscape is the bogs. Many, if not most of them, have been exploited for energy production, but a few totally unique ones still remain, such as Mongan bog along the Shannon.

With its feet bathed in a relatively unpolluted Atlantic, Ireland is a haven for seabirds, including fulmar, gannet and most European species of auk, shearwater and petrel. Little Skellig, ten miles off the Kerry coast, houses some 22,000 gannet pairs and the colony is still growing.

In the south-west corner of Ireland, with its wild Atlantic coast and countless islands, many a lost American bird makes a landfall at the end

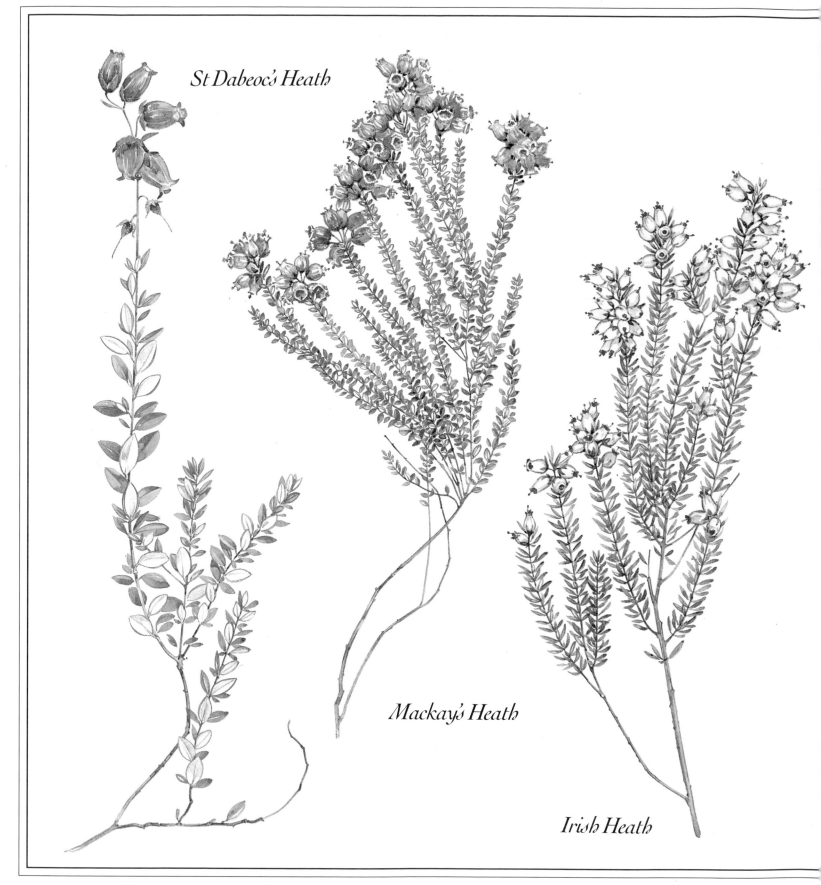

St Dabeoc's Heath

Mackay's Heath

Irish Heath

ST DABEOC'S HEATH (*Daboecia cantabrica*) Found only in Connemara moorland, this is an untidy shrub reaching 24" (60cm) tall and bearing large, globular flowers of bright purple from May through the summer. The narrow leaves have inrolled edges, white beneath.

MACKAY'S HEATH (*Erica mackaiana*) On a few wet moors in Galway and Donegal, the small, deep pink flowers of this dark, thickly leaved heath, bloom in tight clusters from July onwards. The plant hybridizes with the common cross-leaved heath.

IRISH HEATH (*Erica erigena*) An attractive bushy heather, up to 7ft (2m) high, with large, pale purple flowers in leafy spikes appearing in spring. It is found in a few spots on wet moors in western Ireland, where it is sometimes quite common.

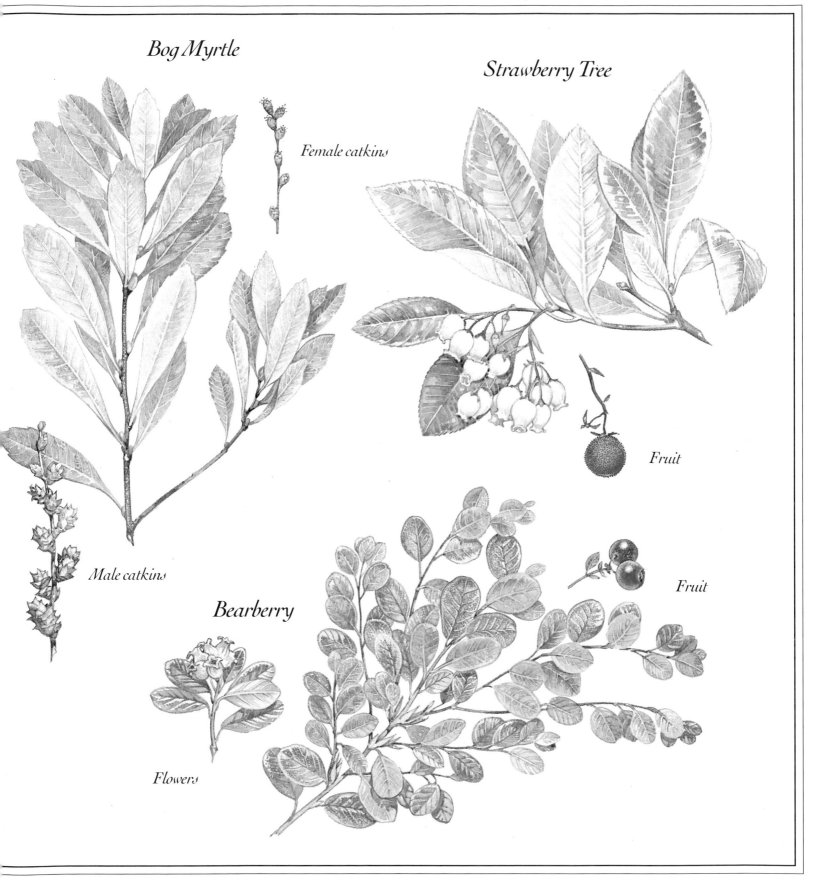

Bog Myrtle

Female catkins

Male catkins

Strawberry Tree

Fruit

Fruit

Bearberry

Flowers

BOG MYRTLE (*Myrica gale*) A small, 3ft (1m) shrub of bogs and wet heaths, making large patches of grey-green with a characteristic, fragrance, rather like pine-resin. It has orange (male) and red (female) catkins before the leaves appear, in April.

BEARBERRY (*Arctostaphylos uva-ursi*) Sprawling mats of thick, dark green leaves similar to cowberry may be found on moors over much of north and west Britain. Pinkish or white flowers appear in May, in small bunches, making shiny red berries.

STRAWBERRY TREE (*Arbutus unedo*) A rare evergreen in Cork and Kerry, making a large, red-brown shrub with thick, dark green, shiny leaves. In late summer, droopy clusters of creamy flowers appear which produce ¾" (2cm) berries that begin to turn red a year later.

Fulmar

FULMAR *(Fulmarus glacialis)* This 18″ (45cm) stocky seabird has stiff, often straight wings with an obscure pale area just inside the dusky grey wingtips. The pale grey tail is broad and the distinctive, thick beak has prominent tubular nostrils that indicate its relation to shearwaters, petrels and albatrosses. In flight it glides like a miniature albatross; at home over the ocean it comes to land only to nest, laying one white egg on a cliff ledge on the coast. Fulmars defend themselves with a pungent oil which they squirt at attackers.

Buff-breasted Sandpiper

Baird's Sandpiper

BUFF-BREASTED SANDPIPER (*Tryngites subruficollis*) A rounded, 8″ (20cm) wader which prefers dry, grassy places and dried mud near lake shores. It breeds in the Canadian Arctic, migrating through the American prairies to spend the winter on South American plains.

A very rare stray in Europe, it is sometimes seen in south-west Britain and along the Irish coasts in September. It has a plumage pattern like a young ruff, but is a cleaner, brighter buff colour and has pale, yellow legs. The call is a low trilled *pret* and a sharp *tick*.

BAIRD'S SANDPIPER (*Calidris bairdii*) A 7″ (18cm) wading bird from arctic America, normally migrating south to spend the winter in South America. It only rarely reaches European shores after being driven off course by storms – some Irish loughs and coastal flats have

regular visits from such American strays. A short, black bill, short dark legs, long wings, tapered body and rather buff-brown colour are characteristics of this rarity. Juveniles have darker feathers above bordered with cream. Call is a mellow *preet-preet*.

The Hen Harrier

Now a bird of remote rolling moorland and bracken-covered hillsides,
the graceful hen harrier gets its name from the days when it was a
common sight in the countryside and preyed on domestic poultry.

A BARRED HEN
(left) *Still a threatened species in Britain, the
hen harrier breeds on moorland, marsh, in
young forests and even on peat bogs.*

With long, pale wings held in a shallow V, a large, graceful bird glides low over the heather-covered moor, its eyes fixed on the ground below. Suddenly it swoops, pouncing on its prey, and with powerful wing beats climbs slowly back into the sky, a small mammal held firmly in its talons.

It is the male hen harrier – one of three harriers seen in Britain, all of which are quite rare and now protected by law. Once widespread, by the early 1900s the hen harrier had become very rare and was virtually confined to Orkney, the Outer Hebrides and Ireland as a result of direct persecution and the loss of nesting sites to intensive farming. Today, numbers are on the increase again and breeding sites are spreading back through England, Ireland and Wales.

Male and female hen harriers are very different in colour and markings. At 17 inches (43cm), the male is significantly smaller than the 19 inch (48cm) female. He is pale grey above with dark grey wingtips. The grey on his throat and breast pales to white below the belly and around the long legs, but reappears in the tail feathers. The 'owlish' face shows bright yellow irises and sports a black hooked bill. The female is drab by comparison. Dark brown above and paler brown beneath, she has darker markings forming broken lines around the head and along the breast. The characteristic tail is marked with broad dark bars giving rise to the name 'ring-tail' which is also applied to other harriers. Both birds have yellow legs and feet.

RITUAL FLIGHTS

In March or April pairs of hen harriers may be seen circling over possible nest sites. Display and pre-nesting flights are a delight to watch – time after time the male soars upwards and dives towards the ground. And when the female begins to build the nest, the male brings her food, passing it to her on the wing. The 'food pass' takes place near the nest, the hen rising to meet the cock bird as he flies low over the ground with the prey in his lowered claw.

The nest is invariably on the ground, either among heather or on a site trodden by the birds, among thick vegetation. The nest is a 'soup-plate' structure built of heather and old bracken stalks and lined with soft grasses. The materials are collected from within a couple of hundred

CONSTANT PROVISIONS
(above) Once the chicks hatch both parents bring food – mainly small rodents and birds – to the nest, but it is the female who feeds them.

SITTING PRETTY
(below) Pairing lasts for just one season. After mating, the male's task is to supply the incubating female with food, although he sometimes covers the eggs himself.

yards of the site and a number of pairs may nest in the same area, building their nests within 100 yards (90m) of each other in a loose colony.

Four to six eggs are laid in April and May, depending on the spring weather. A failed clutch laid early may be replaced in June. An interval of 48 hours is usual between the eggs, and over a week may elapse before the clutch is complete. When they are first laid the eggs are a delicate pale blue, but this soon fades to white. The female incubates the eggs for about 30 days before the chicks hatch, which takes place over a number of days, and feeds the small downy chicks with food brought in by the male. Brooding lasts for at least two weeks after hatching, especially in cold wet weather, and the chicks fledge about three weeks later.

The hen harrier remains in Britain all year round, but from September onwards many birds fly south. Males especially appear to prefer the easier conditions in the south, while females can survive farther north. This may be due to the female's ability to catch larger prey, even when the ground is covered with snow.

During the winter, hen harriers are sociable birds and roost in groups among tall reeds and grasses in low-lying marshy regions. Over 40 birds have been observed arriving at a roost site in the hour before sunset. The birds leave the roosts each day within about an hour of sunrise and disperse until the evening. The exact reasons for this fascinating aspect of their behaviour is not fully understood. There may be an element of defence in numbers against predators, but there is probably a social function as well. Mature and inexperienced birds come into close contact, and pair bonds may be formed ready for the coming breeding season.

PLUMAGE of the male (top) is grey above and white below – markedly different from the female (below) which is brown above with a pale brown barred underside. Display flights include the spectacular 'food pass'.

EGGS are pale blue turning white. 4-6 are laid in April and are brooded by the female for 30 days.

The Burren

The Burren – a Gaelic name meaning 'Great Rock' – is a massive, cracked crust of naked limestone which scars the countryside of north-west Clare in Ireland. The heart of this mysterious landscape is a plateau, built up under the sea from the skeletons of tropical sea creatures millions of years ago. Later, when the land rose under huge geological forces, it was scoured by Ice-Age glaciers, resulting in one of the strangest landscapes to be found in the British Isles – with unnatural-looking 'pavement' rock formations, and lakes which appear or disappear overnight.

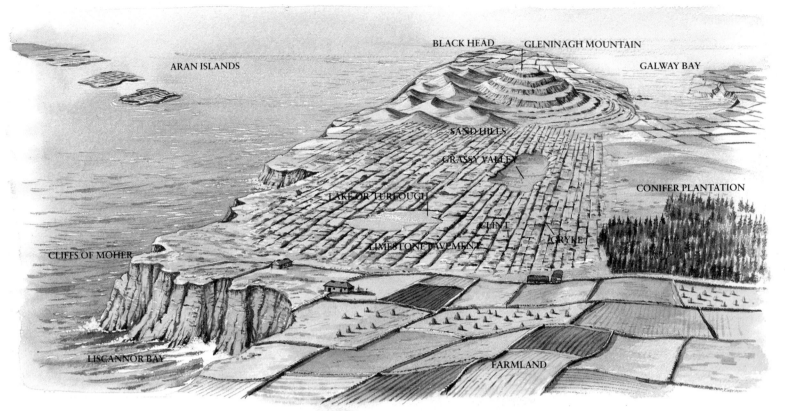

PAVED WILDERNESS

The Burren, which covers an area of about 100 square miles in north-west Clare, is a mixture of strange elements, making up a unique landscape. From Black Head southwards there is a trio of bare rounded mountains, shelving gently down to the sea via a series of vast sand-hills, and to the bare limestone pavement in the south. Here lie the mysterious disappearing lakes or turloughs, and pockets of lush green grass. The southern half of the Burren is composed of impermeable shale, erupting at the coast as the massive dark cliffs of Moher.

THE BURREN

A country in which 'there is not water enough to drown a man, wood enough to hang him, nor earth enough to bury him'. So one of Cromwell's men described the Burren in 1651. The passing of time has changed little – the Burren is still a wild and rocky land, where great pavements of treeless limestone run in orderly fashion from north to south, or shattered blocks strew the ground in savage chaos. Looking at first sight like a lunar landscape, seemingly barren and devoid of life, the Burren hides between its fissured blocks a botanical wonderland. It presents a strange landscape of compelling beauty, stretching grey into the distance, bathed in a soft pearly light.

LIMESTONE PAVEMENTS

The massive limestone crust – 3000ft thick in places – was built up 320 million years ago from layer upon layer of sea creatures which lived in the warm subtropical seas of the time. Later the sea bed was thrust up by crumpling of the earth's surface, and water erosion stripped away the softer rock. Later still, great ice-sheets scoured the surface, planing away the last vestiges of soil to leave the landscape we see today, with its pavements (clints), crevices (grykes) and rounded terraced hills.

The plateau dips gently, from the High Burren in the north (over 1000ft) down to Liscannor Bay in the south. Here, the limestone disappears under the more recent shales of southern Clare. These are the remnants of a pre-glacial covering layer of shale which was eroded away and remains only in isolated pockets of resistance, such as Slieve Elva, the highest peak in the north-west (1134ft), and Poulacapple to its east.

The junction of these two rock types is revealed by the differing behaviour of the plentiful waterways of the region. The impermeable shales are networked on the surface by streams, which, on meeting the pervious limestone, abruptly disappear down sluggas – the local name for swallow-holes. They may spring up again elsewhere, only to plunge underground once more. There is only one permanent river in the Burren – the Caher – which rises east of Slieve Elva.

The apparently parched limestone is honeycombed with underground streams. Over 30 miles of 'active' tunnels (with rivers) have been charted by experienced cavers and potholers, but there are many more yet to be explored. Typical features of the Burren's caves include stalactites and stalagmites, dripstone formations of fantastic shapes, the purple mineral fluorspar, the gemstone amethyst, both set in cavities in the calcite walls, which are coloured by traces of iron and manganese. The largest stalactite recorded in western Europe is found in a cave near Elva – it is over 25ft long, massively thick, and has been growing for thousands of years.

DISAPPEARING LAKES

The Burren's complex underground drainage system also produces another characteristic and mysterious feature – turloughs or 'dry lakes'. These are depressions hollowed out of the limestone and deepened by glacial erosion, sometimes extending over several acres. The apparently contradictory name comes from their capacity to fill and empty within a matter of hours. This is due to the fact that they are fed by the underground watertable which rises after periods of heavy rain – which are frequent on

BARE CLIFFS
(right) The coast of Inishmore – the most remote of the Aran islands – exhibits the same pitiless bleakness as the mainland cliffs of Moher. The islands are a continuation of the Burren rock strata, and are covered by a web of low walls constructed from the limestone blocks with which the Burren is littered.

GREEN ROAD
(below) The Burren is not all bare and bleak. As one of Cromwell's generals remarked in 1651, the grass between the rocks 'is very sweet and nourishing', and the grazing animals can grow fat. These green roads have their place in history, as military routes linking forts, and lanes to chapels and shebeens (illicit drinking places).

the Atlantic coast. Water seeps up through the pervious rocks and fills the turloughs. When the watertable drops, the turlough empties through a swallow-hole in its floor, like bathwater through a plug-hole.

Surprisingly, this realm of haunting desolation bears signs of human habitation going back 5000 years – the area is littered with megalithic tombs, huge dolmens weighing hundreds of tons, Mesolithic middens in the Atlantic dunes, Bronze Age communal graves and Iron Age burial barrows. Stone forts grow out of the rock, of which the most spectacular example is the prehistoric fort of Dun Aenghus on the Aran Islands – just off the coast of the Burren.

It is possible that human determination to inhabit this remote corner of Ireland contributed to its present-day bleakness – there is evidence that ancient forests of yew, pine and hazel once clothed the rock. But the combined forces of nature and man – glaciers, and Stone Age farmers – stripped the fragile land of its forest cover, and thereby hastened the erosion of the thin soil. But as a result of the mild and moist climate, warmed by the Gulf Stream, and the excellent drainage of the pervious rock which stores summer heat, this unique, apparently barren land, shelters an extraordinary diversity of plants and creatures.

Nature Walk

Man has inhabited the Burren for many millennia, leaving stone memorials such as:

HIGH CROSSES dating from the 12th century, which display rich and intricate symbolism.

DOLMENS or Neolithic and early Bronze Age tombs. Built to face the setting sun, they may bear capstones weighing over 100 tons.

CYLINDRICAL TOWERS in strategic positions, mostly built in the 16th century to repel raiders.

OLD COTTAGES roofed with the plentiful raw stone of the Burren. Many are deserted or used as animal byres.

Wildlife of the Burren

**Amid the rocky, windswept landscape of the Burren grow many
rare and beautiful wild flowers, and the deep crevices provide
a home for all kinds of small insects and mammals.**

From afar, the Burren looks a barren, desolate place, where the Atlantic gales seem to have blasted the very soil from the hills, leaving just acres of bare, grey rock and a few stunted trees. In winter, it is bleak indeed. Yet small pockets of soil between the rocks harbour a range of flora unmatched anywhere in the British Isles. The Burren is a natural rock garden of rare and beautiful wild flowers and, come summer, it bursts into glorious, colourful life.

On the hilltops in June, scrambling over bare limestone and boulders left behind by retreating glaciers long ago, are delicate clusters of pure white, yellow-centred mountain avens. Rare elsewhere, it grows here in profusion, a survivor from the bleak arctic days. In the crevices in the bare rock, the delicate heads of myriad other flowers are tossed in the wind that constantly sweeps the Burren. Even in the crevices the soil is thin – or non-existent – but many flowers have gained a foothold, benefiting from the Burren's unique combination of dry, well-drained ground and warm, moist air.

Out from the deepest fissures peep vivid magenta sprays of bloody cranesbill, so bright and bold that they seem almost like garden hybrids. Yellow blooms of bird's foot trefoil flourish in thin dishes of soil on the rock surface, barely protected from the wind. And the rare dark red helleborine orchid seems to require hardly any soil at all, for its tall stem and dark red star-like blooms creep up from almost lifeless scree.

Over the rocks and down into the valleys straggle all kinds of trailing plants and flowers. On many days the fragrant scent of wild thyme can be detected in the air throughout the Burren, while the hoary rock rose makes the most of patches of thin soil where grass cannot gain a hold. Like the mountain avens, the hoary rock rose is an arctic relic, and it takes strong sunshine to cajole its bright yellow blooms into opening fully.

Remarkably, alongside the arctic relics, many plants and flowers of Mediterranean origin flourish, and it is this mixture that makes the Burren so cherished by botanists. No one is quite sure why the Burren provides a home to such apparently incompatible flora, but it may be the combination of moist, cool summers and

ROCK RESIDENT
*(left) Like many insectivores
the little pygmy shrew finds
a comfortable home among
the rocks of the Burren. The
scailps and the shrubs
provide good ground cover,
while the abundant insect
life affords a healthy diet.*

THE WILDLIFE OF THE BURREN

*In the narrow scailps or crevices in the bare limestone of the Burren grows
a profusion of wild flowers – delicate mountain avens, vivid blue spring
gentian, bright magenta bloody cranesbill, spiky Burren orchid, and many
more. Fragile maidenhair and hart's tongue ferns are nurtured in the
shadiest crevices, while the more hardy shrubs, hazel and hawthorn, poke
spiky branches into the air, only to be pruned by the wind that sweeps
constantly over the Burren. Butterflies flit among the abundant blooms,
while slugs, snails and spiders feed among the plants. Wrens, skylarks and other
insect eaters make the most of the invertebrate feast. Herbivores, such as
the Irish hare, rabbits and voles, crop grasses and other vegetation. The Irish
stoat and the pine marten hunt stealthily for the many rodents that hide
among the rocks while, in the distance, gulls of all kinds wheel over the lonely
west coast of Ireland.*

KEY TO FEATURES AND SPECIES

1 Golden plover	13 Mountain avens
2 Skylark	14 Bird's foot trefoil
3 Cave	15 Fragrant orchid
4 Great black- backed gull	16 Dingy skipper
	17 Fescue grass
5 Herring gull	18 Bloody cranesbill
6 Bothy	19 Striped snail
7 Ash and hazel	20 Spring gentian
8 Hawthorn	21 Wren
9 Irish hare	22 Maidenhair fern
10 Common blue	23 Kerry slug
11 Shrubby cinquefoil	24 Zebra spider
12 Irish stoat	25 Hoary rockrose

the extraordinarily warm winters here. Even on the hilltops, bright green fronds of maidenhair and hart's tongue ferns from southern Europe shelter from the Atlantic gales and the sun in deep fissures in the rock, while all over the Burren there is a rich variety of rare orchids.

The white blooms of the Irish or Burren orchid, fairly common near the Mediterranean, are rarely found elsewhere in the British Isles, but here they can often be seen growing singly on gravelly ridges where the soil is thick enough to support grass. Much less rare, but equally attractive, early purple and clove-scented fragrant orchids are scattered throughout the Burren, while those remarkable mimics, the bee and fly orchids, grow here on dry grassy banks and damper slopes respectively. The bee orchid so closely resembles a female bee that male bees try to mate with it, picking up pollen which then rubs off when they try to mate with other bee orchids, thus ensuring fertilization.

In the north of the Burren, where the bony fingers of Black Head project into Galway Bay, the variety of wild flowers is especially profuse, for here a thin layer of peaty soil allows fine

LIFELESS ROCK?
(above) The bare limestone pavement seems at first to offer little to flora, but many plants have colonized the deep fissures in the rock, where they find both soil and shelter.

FLOWERING HAWTHORN
(above) Although full-sized trees are rare on the Burren, cut down by the constant wind, shrubs like hazel, juniper and hawthorn flourish in the shelter of the deep crevices in the rock.

turf and grasses to flourish around the islands of bare rock. Amid the grass, the tiny spring gentian raises its vivid blue blooms. Though popular as a garden flower, the spring gentian, like the mountain avens, is a protected plant very rare outside the Burren – yet it grows here by the thousand. Broad yellow carpets of shrubby cinquefoil turn the landscape golden in places, while up the hillslope scramble tangled mats of pink-flowering bearberry and crowberry.

Oddly, even heather and gorse grow in patches on the lower slopes, especially near the sea. Over most of the Burren, the calcareous soil on the limestone keeps the acid-loving heather at bay, but here and there it gains a foothold where a humus of rotting moss provides an acidic bed. Pallid, leafless parasites such as broomrape and lesser dodder, find their sustenance in the roots of other plants, notably lady's bedstraw and wild thyme.

Despite the huge variety of flowers and shrubs in the Burren, there are few trees here. It is the deep, moist crevices that provide the kind of shelter that the woodland plants such as ferns need. Trees cannot grow in the shallow soil. Nor can they withstand the fierce winds that cut any over-ambitious bush down to size. Such woody shrubs that do grow are low and stunted, their stems often at right angles to the ground and twisted like natural Bonsai trees. A few oak, ash and hazel thickets do grow in the deeper glacial drifts of the more sheltered valleys, but on the pavements of the high hills, only a few stunted specimens of yew, juniper, hazel and hawthorn emerge from the deep crevices.

Yet, though there are few trees, the abundance of flowers draws all kinds of bees and butterflies here like a honeypot. Out of Ireland's 33 species of butterfly, 26 are found in the Burren. The

WIDGEON PAIR
(above) Among the many birds that frequent the Burren widgeon are sometimes seen by the Burren's ephemeral lakes, or 'turloughs' in winter.

BLOODY CRANESBILL
(below) So-called because it was once used to staunch the flow of blood from wounds, the bloody cranesbill is a vividly coloured flower.

wood white butterfly can often be seen flitting among the hazel scrub and alighting to feed on the sweet yellow flowers of bird's foot trefoil, while occasionally the pearl-bordered fritillary – found nowhere else in Ireland – alights on bugle or little violets.

The insects, of course, draw all kinds of birds to the Burren. Throughout the summer, meadow pipits can be seen climbing steeply on their song-flight, then parachuting down over the rocks and shrubs to land with a little trill. The piercing song of the skylark, too, often echoes across the landscape, while twites, yellow-hammers and wagtails make the most of the abundant insect life – keeping a wary eye for predators such as kestrels, sparrowhawks and the rare peregrine falcon.

Many mammals, too, live in this rocky land, finding abundant food and shelter in the caves, crevices and pockets of woodland. The largest mammals in the area are the feral goats that roam the high hills. They are not a threat to the delicate plant community because they eat the ever-invasive hazel scrub and thereby perform a valuable ecological service. Badgers, foxes and stoats hunt the open pavements for mice, young rabbits and hares. The shy pine marten has its Irish stronghold here, remote from human disturbance. Despite its woodland origins, it has adapted readily to the rocky terrain of the Burren – finding its mixed diet here.

Another rare mammal, found only in the western counties, is the lesser horseshoe bat. Great colonies of these bats are found roosting in the Burren's caves. Because of the mild, frost-free climate, the flowering season, and so the insect season, is long. The bats find plenty of spiders, beetles and moths to eat.

The Burren's ephemeral lakes, the turloughs, have a natural history all their own. The plants and animals must adapt to the alternate periods of flooding and drying out as the watertable fluctuates with the rainfall. As on the seashore, the plants are zoned on a turlough's slopes. Aquatic and marsh plants grow on the damp floor, such as floating sweet grass, fool's watercress and marsh marigolds. Species typical of grassland grow on the slopes, such as creeping buttercup and silverweed, but these can survive the flooding. Pale-blue turlough violets (fen violets of UK) cover the middle slopes in summer.

When the waters recede, a lush grassy sward grows during the summer for grazing hares, rabbits, cattle and horses. Their faeces encourage planktonic growth which feeds a multitude of water fleas, winged water bugs and beetles, the nymphs of dragonflies, and the fairy shrimp which is found nowhere else.

GLACIAL RELIC
(above) In the delicate mountain avens, the Burren harbours a relic from the arctic climate of the last Ice Age. Nowhere else in the British Isles but Upper Teesdale in the North of England is this rare flower commonly found.

BURREN ORCHID
(below) Alongside arctic relics like the mountain avens grow fugitives from the warm south of Europe like the rare Burren Orchid, found in few other places in the British Isles.

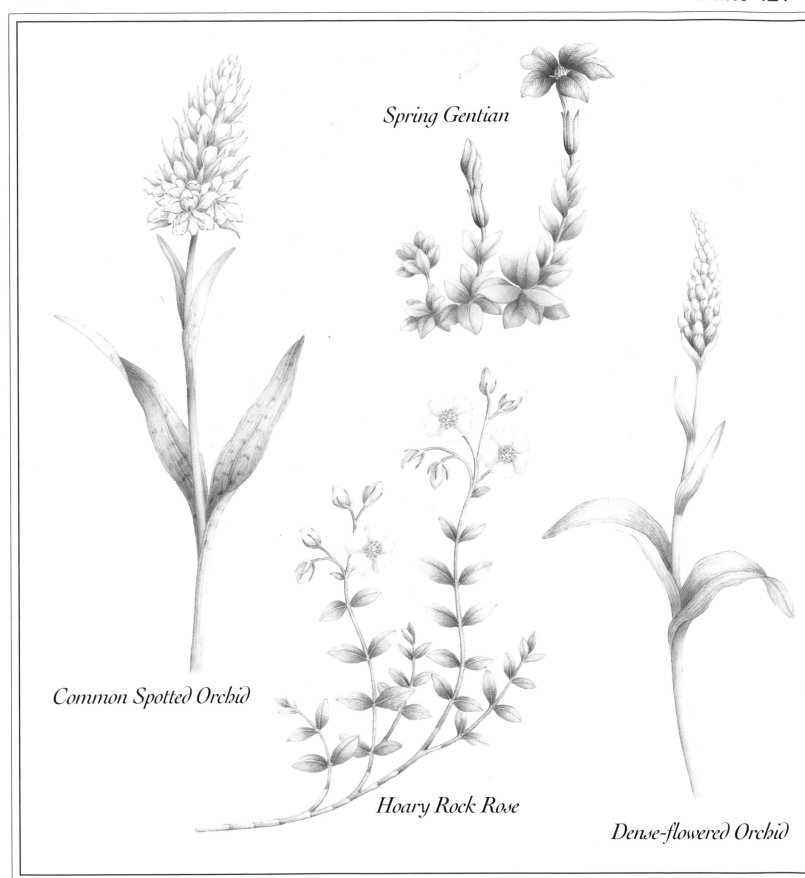

Spring Gentian

Common Spotted Orchid

Hoary Rock Rose

Dense-flowered Orchid

COMMON SPOTTED ORCHID (*Dactylorhiza fuchsii*) A common but variable orchid, with intermediate subspecies forms. Reaching 20″ (50cm) the flowerspike has white to rose-purple blooms, June-August. Leaves are mostly spotted. It grows on wet chalky soils in the U.K.

SPRING GENTIAN (*Gentiana verna*) Now protected, this lovely alpine is a rarity of peaty limestone in northern England but more abundant in western Ireland. Rosettes of basal leaves are seen all year; the 1-2″ (3-5cm) stalks bear a single flower from April to June.

HOARY ROCK ROSE (*Helianthemum canum*) A rare, spreading, shrubby plant 1½-8″ (4-20cm), with many wiry stems. Tiny oval leaves are cottony-white below and short-stalked flowers are seen May-July. Found on rocky, limestone grassland – widespread but rare.

DENSE-FLOWERED ORCHID (*Neotinea maculata*) This orchid has a crowded spike of hooded, greenish flowers, May-June and twisted seed pods. Stems reach 12″ (30cm) and leaves may be spotted. A lowland plant of limestone grassland and dunes near Galway Bay, Ireland.

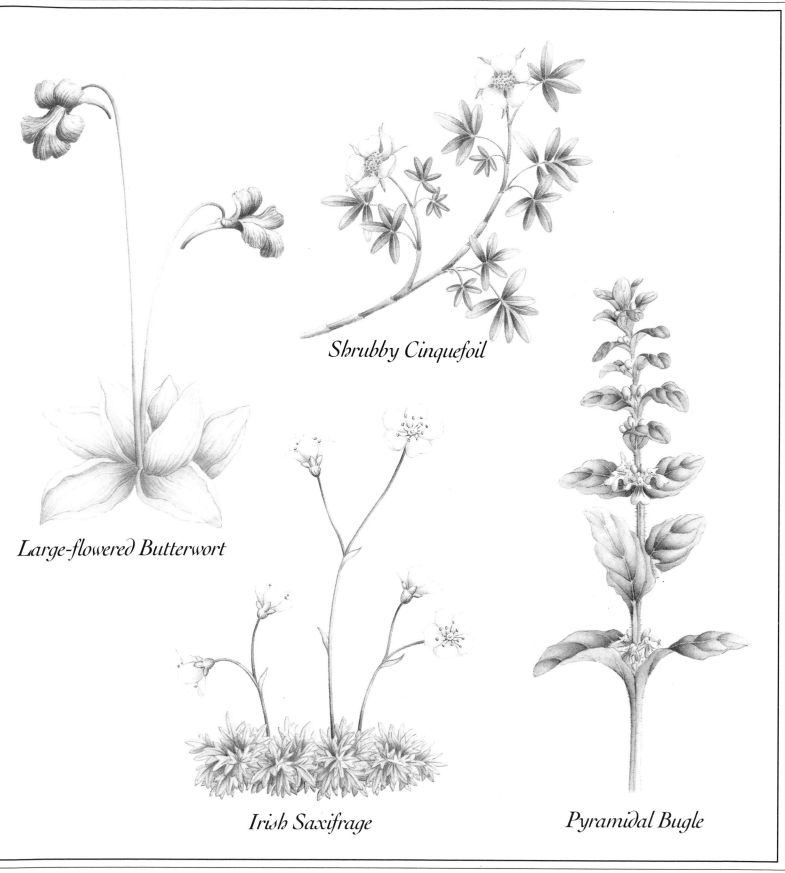

Shrubby Cinquefoil

Large-flowered Butterwort

Irish Saxifrage

Pyramidal Bugle

LARGE-FLOWERED
BUTTERWORT (*Pinguicula
grandiflora*) Sticky glands on the leaf
surface trap and digest small insects,
to provide nutrients missing from the
peaty bogs in south-west Ireland.
Large single flowers are seen May-
June on leafless 3-8″ (8-20cm) stems.

IRISH SAXIFRAGE (*Saxifraga
decipiens*) Locally abundant in west
Ireland, tufted patches with stems
to 8″ (20cm) grow on wet limestone
rocks and by streams. Glandular
hairs are scattered on lobed leaves
and stems. Heads of 1-8 flowers can
be seen June to August.

SHRUBBY CINQUEFOIL (*Potentilla fruticosa*) An upright, branched
shrub reaching 39″ (100cm), with
softly hairy stems and divided leaves.
Male and female flowers are found
on separate plants, June-July. Locally
plentiful in western Ireland, very
rare in northern England.

PYRAMIDAL BUGLE (*Ajuga
pyramidalis*) This 4-12″ (10-30cm)
plant has leaves, bracts and stems
that are hairy all round. Pale
blooms appear May-July. It is a rare
perennial of calcareous rocks in
northern England, Scotland and
western Ireland.

Greenland Whitefront

Black Guillemot

Long-billed Dowitcher

GREENLAND WHITEFRONT
(*Anser albifrons flavirostris*)
Almost all these dark, 26-30″ (66-76cm) geese overwinter in Ireland, Scotland and Wales. They arrive in autumn to graze on waterlogged grasslands. Their habitats are threatened by drainage schemes.

BLACK GUILLEMOT (*Cepphus grylle*) Seen in groups close to the shore, this 13″ (33cm) resident breeds along the rocky coasts of Ireland and north-west Britain. Plumage is black with white wing patches in summer and white with a mottled grey back in winter.

LONG-BILLED DOWITCHER
(*Limnodromus scolopaceus*) Most likely to be seen in waterlogged fields and freshwater ponds, this extremely rare vagrant sometimes arrives in Britain or Ireland, storm-assisted from North America. It is a stocky wader with a long bill.

Least Sandpiper

Lesser Yellowlegs

Greater Yellowlegs

LEAST SANDPIPER *(Calidris minutilla)* No more than 4¾″ (12cm), this neat wader has a short, very slender black beak and pale yellowy legs. Native to North America, it is seen close to fresh and salt water only very rarely in Britain and Ireland. The call is high and thin.

GREATER YELLOWLEGS *(Tringa melanoleuca)* This 14″ (36cm) wader is a very rare vagrant, blown off course from North America by autumn storms and seen on boggy lakes and marshes. It has sturdy yellow legs and a beak curved slightly upwards. The call is clear and ringing.

LESSER YELLOWLEGS *(Tringa flavipes)* This is a rare autumn vagrant from North America, seen rarely on coastal marshlands and heaths of Britain and Ireland. A slim, 10″ (25cm), wader with long, yellow legs, a white rump and a thin beak. The call is a soft whistle.

The Corncrake

A shy summer visitor, the corncrake now only nests in the more peaceful meadowlands of the rural North and West – driven from its former range by increasingly mechanized farming.

On warm summer evenings at the turn of the century, the monotonous, rasping *crek crek* of the elusive corncrake was a familiar, even irritating, sound to country folk, so numerous were these birds. Large numbers of this shy visitor from Africa would arrive to make their summer home among thick stands of grass and rough vegetation throughout Britain. But during the last 70 years or so the corncrake has slowly and dramatically disappeared from most of its breeding haunts and is now only regularly heard in the west of Scotland, the Scottish Isles, north-west Wales and, above all, in rural Ireland, where about 1500 pairs still nest each year.

Despite its name, the corncrake prefers damp meadows with plenty of nettles and other tall weeds, to fields of ripe corn. Here it spends most of the day skulking among the vegetation, perfectly camouflaged by its brown, black-streaked plumage. About the size of a moorhen and resembling a slim, short-necked gamebird, it is, like other members of the rail family, more commonly heard than seen. Shy and secretive by nature, the corncrake cranes its neck above the grass stems to reconnoitre the scene before emerging from cover. If approached, it quickly vanishes, creeping stealthily from one patch of cover to another. Only as a last resort will it take to the air to escape danger, as its flight is fluttering, weak and ungainly. Aloft, its bright chestnut wing patches, and dangling legs trailing behind its short tail, clearly identify the bird. Under cover of failing light, though, at dusk it becomes bolder and more active, searching among the grass for beetles, grasshoppers, slugs, snails, earthworms, leaves and seeds.

NIGHT CRYER

It is the male corncrake which is responsible for the far-carrying, rasping call. He uses it to advertise his claim to territory – all night, for

CALLING CRAKE
(above) Neck stretched skywards, wings drooped and stumpy tail fanned out, a male corncrake rasps out his harsh 'crek crek' song in the hope of enticing a female into his territory. The call is often the only clue to the presence of this rare, secretive bird among the thick grass of its summer home.

SITTING TARGET
The corncrake's nest is a simple pad of grass hidden among rough vegetation or in hay meadows. By pulling surrounding grass stems towards her the female makes a loose roof that helps disguise her nest from crows and other potential predators.

weeks on end, from the same field. The sound has a peculiarly ventriloqual quality, which makes this elusive bird even more difficult to locate.

However, one way of luring it into view is to mimic its call by rubbing a wooden ruler across the teeth of a comb, for a calling male often finds it hard to resist investigating what it takes to be a rival.

If two rival males do meet, they puff out their body feathers, open their wings wide to show

SKULKING RAIL
(below) The corncrake – sometimes known as the landrail – arrives in Britain around mid-April from its African winter home and returns in October. Despite being a reluctant flyer, it makes the 8000 mile round-trip each year.

off their chestnut patches, and stretch their heads and necks out at each other. If particularly incensed, they may stab out with their short, sharp, pinkish bills.

The corncrake's nest is a shallow scrape, on which the female fashions a sparse pad of dry grass. It is usually well hidden deep in lush meadow vegetation or among hay crops. The female lays between 6-14 eggs and incubates them for about a fortnight. Three or four days after hatching the fluffy black chicks are able to leave the nest and find food for themselves. After 4 or 5 weeks, they can fly, and in September set off with the adults on their southward migration across the Mediterranean and Sahara to the grasslands of East Africa. Though apparently weak in flight, they are able to make a 4000 mile (6500km) journey to their winter quarters.

DRASTIC DECLINE

Many of them, however, never complete their journey. The thousands of miles of overhead cables, that spread across the countryside like giant spiders' webs take a large toll of low flying migrating corncrakes. But the greatest hazards to the corncrake population in the British Isles since the early 1900s have been the changes in farming methods. Where once the birds and nests in the hay meadows were generally spared by the leisurely and discerning hand on the scythe, they are now mown down, unnoticed by the mechanical harvester. The development and use of new varieties of grass which mature earlier also means that harvesting time often coincides with the corncrake's incubation of its eggs and so causes maximum damage to the breeding population.

By the early 1960s, there were very few places in the British Isles where corncrakes could find sanctuary and the birds were increasingly restricted to the less intensively farmed areas of the country. Today, the Burren and other parts of Ireland form the last major stronghold of the ever-decreasing corncrake population.

Index

Page numbers in italics refer to illustrations

A

agrimony
    hemp 115, 119, *119*
alkanet, green *235*
Anglesey 184–191
apple
    Japanese crab 16, *16*
ash 129, *129*
aspen *175*, 177
avens, mountain 207, 209, *209*, *309*
azalea
    mountain 207
    trailing 253, *253*

B

badger 58, *147*
balsam
    Himalayan *15*
    touch-me-not 164, *164*
barbel *see* Fish
bat, Daubenton's 12
bearberry 297, *297*
bedstraw
    limestone 269, *269*
    northern 179, *179*
beet 125
beetle, stag 28, *29*
bellflower, clustered *43*
betony 46, *46*
bilberry *57*, *175*, 176, 206
bindweed, sea *191*
birdsfoot, orange 90, *90*
bird's nest, yellow 193, *193*
bistort, alpine 149, *149*
bittern 114, *115*, 120, *120*, 122–123, *122–123*
blackthorn 43
bleak *see* Fish
blood-drop emlets *250*, 253, *253*
bluebell 207
bogbean 269, *269*
bog myrtle 297, *297*
bracken 144, 162, 174
    see also Fern
Breckland 96–103
Broads, Norfolk 110–117
broomrape, thyme 77, *77*
bugle *176*
    pyramidal 311, *311*
bunting
    cirl 62, *62*
    Lapland 87
    rustic 93, *93*
    snow 207, 211, *211*, 218, 221
Burren, The 302–309
butcher's broom *31*, 33, *33*
butterbur, white 164, *164*
buttercup, Bermuda 91, *91*
butterfly
    argus, brown 144, *145*

Scotch 206, 226
blue, adonis 43
    common 87, *235*
    silver-studded 189
    small 43, *43*
brimstone 174
brown, meadow 13, 87
clouded yellow 43
    Berger's 44
copper, small 146
fritillary, dark green 43, 189
    Glanville 42, *42*, 50–51, *50–51*
    marsh 189
    silver-washed 29
grayling 29
hairstreak, green 57
heath, large 177
orange tip 174
ringlet, mountain 161, 162, 206, 221, 226
swallowtail 114, *115*, *116*
white admiral 29
white, green-veined *235*, 279
butterwort, large-flowered 292, 311, *311*
buzzard 56, 64–65, *64–65*, 160, *161*, 177, *293*
    honey 35, *35*, 36–37, *36–37*

C

cabbage 125
caddis fly 14
Cairngorms, The 214–221
calamint, wood 46, *46*
campion 207
    moss *175*
    red 252, *252*
carp *see* Fish
cat, Scottish wild 206, 212–213, *212–213*
catchfly
    Nottingham 133, *133*
    Spanish 107, *107*
celandine, lesser 174
centaury, yellow 33, *33*
chickweed, Shetland mouse-ear 250, 252, *252*
chough 181, *181*, 188, *189*, 198–199, *198–199*
cicada, New Forest 28, *31*
cinquefoil
    alpine 178, *178*
    shrubby 311, *311*
cliffs and quarries 246, 251
cloudberry 209, *209*
clover
    large Lizard 77, *77*
    red 237, 239, *239*
    sea 46, *46*
    twin-headed 77, *77*
    upright 76, *76*
club rush, sea 279, *280*
columbine 61, *61*
coot *115*
cormorant 75, 270, *270*
corncrake 234, 267, 271, *271*, 281, 295, 314–315, *314–315*
cornel, dwarf 223, *223*
cow-wheat, field 46, *46*
cowbane 118, *118*
cowberry 206
cowslip 174
coypu *115*, 117

cranberry 206
cranesbill
    bloody 133, *133*, 308
    dove's-foot 239, *239*
    meadow 146
    wood 209, *209*
cress, thale 268, *268*
    see also Rockcress
cricket
    conehead 191
    great green bush 75, 89
    wood 28
    see also Cicada, Grasshopper
crossbill *102*
crow, hooded 207, *236*
crowberry 179, *179*
crowfoot, three-lobed water 77, *77*
cuckoo flower *see* Lady's smock
curlew *see* Waders

D

damselfly 281
    banded agrion 13
    common blue 279
    Irish 281
    scarce blue-tailed 29
    see also Dragonfly
Dartmoor 52–59
deer
    fallow 30
    red 206, 221, 295
    rein 206, 221, *221*
dipper 174, 206
diver
    great northern 236
    red-throated 266
dock, shore 193, *193*
dodder 61, *61*
dolphin, bottle-nosed 266
dotterel *see* Waders
dove
    collared 18, *18*
    turtle 34, *34*
dowitcher, long-billed *see* Waders
dragonfly
    brown hawker or aeshna 13
    four-spotted chaser or libellula 73, 279
    Norfolk aeshna 115, 117, *117*
    see also Damselfly
duck
    eider 264
    king 255, *255*
    goldeneye 197, *197*
    goosander 161
    long-tailed 251
    mallard *13*, *115*, 116, *161*, 163
    merganser, red-breasted *161*, 163, *163*, 190, 196, *196*
    pintail 279
    pochard 116, *280*
    scoter, common *15*, 196, *196*
    shelduck 197, *197*
    teal 161
    tufted 116
    widgeon *308*
dunlin *see* Waders

E

eagle
    golden *206*, 207, 210, *210*, 213, 220, *220*

white-tailed sea 241, *241*, 242–243,
    242–243
eel *see* Fish

F
fern 116, 174, *175*, *176*
    adder's tongue *13*
    male 282, *282*
    polypody *147*
    royal 74, 162, 282, *282*
    see also Bracken, Spleenwort
fieldfare 131
fig, hottentot *74*, *89*
figwort, balm-leaved 90, *90*
firecrest 62, *62*
fish
    barbel *14*
    bleak *13*, 14
    carp 22–23
        common *22*
        mirror *23*
    eel *161*, *162* 163
    pike 116, *125*
    roach 116, 280
    salmon 182–183, *182–183*
    schelly 163
    tench *13*
    trout 163
        rainbow *128*
    vendace 163
    see also Shark
flax, purging 253, *253*
fleabane, lesser 32, *32*
fleawort, field 195, *195*
flowering rush *13*
fly, horse *147*
flycatcher
    pied 56, 161, 163
    red-breasted 93, *93*
Forest, The New 24–31
forget-me-not
    alpine 208, *208*
    early 105, *105*
fowl *see* Duck, Goose
fox 125, 160, *161*, *162*, 213
fritillary, snake's head 12, *15*
frog *175*
fulmar 267, 298, *298*

G
gallinule, American purple 94, *95*
gannet 267, 270, *270*
gentian
    snow 207, 208, *208*
    spring *307*, 308, 310, *310*
gladiolus, wild 30, 31, 33, *33*
globe flower *131*, 132, *132*
goat *175*, *177*
godwit *see* Waders
goldcrest 34, *34*
goosander *see* Duck
goose
    barnacle *294*
    bean 116
    Canada 114, *115*
    greylag 114, 240, *240*
    white-fronted 116, 292
        Greenland 312, *312*
gorse 72
goshawk 151, *151*
grape hyacinth 105, *105*

grass
    bent, bristle-leaved 61, *61*
    blue-eyed *293*
    cat's tail, purple-stalked 107, *107*
    cotton *130*, *144*
    deer 60, *60*
    fescue, viviparcus *292*
    grass of Parnassus 165, *165*
    holy 282, *282*
    scurvy 194, *194*
    small-reed, narrow 283, *283*
    whitlow, hoary 268, *268*
grasshopper
    marsh, large 29
    meadow 13
    see also Cicada, Cricket
grebe, great crested 114, *115*, *279*, *281*
greenshank *see* Waders
greenweed
    dyer's 74, 76, *76*
    hairy 74, 76, *76*
grouse
    black 130, 150, *150*
    red *146*, 150, *150*, 206
guillemot *254*
    black 266, 312, *312*
gull
    black-headed 161
    common 240, *240*
    great black-backed *43*, *45*, 80–81,
        80–81
    lesser black-backed 80
    little 49, *49*
    ring-billed 95

H
hare
    Irish *279*, *281*, 295
    mountain (blue) *130*, 206, 221, *221*, 279
harebell *235*, 239, *239*
harrier
    hen 56, 116, *265*, 266, 300–301,
        300–301
    marsh 114, 115
hawthorn 176, 308
heath
    Cornish 72, *72*
    Irish 296, *296*
    Mackay's 296, *296*
    St Dabeoc's 294, 296, *296*
heather 174, 176, 206
Hebrides, Outer *see* Western Isles
hellerborine
    dark red 132, *132*
    dune 189, 193, *193*
    marsh 189
heron, grey 12, 56, *115*, *145*, *279*, *293*
Highlands, Scottish 200–207
hobby 30
hottentot fig *74*, *89*
hutchinsia 148, *148*

I
Ireland, Republic of 288–295
iris, stinking *44*, 45
Isle of Wight 38–45
Isles of Scilly 82–89

J
jackdaw *73*, 117
jacob's ladder 133, *133*

jay *43*
juniper 174, *175*

K
kingfisher *13*
kite, red *175*, 177, 181, *181*
kittiwake *189*
knawel, perennial 105, *105*

L
lady's mantle, alpine 165, *165*
lady's smock 174
lady's tresses
    autumn 32, *32*
    Irish *281*, 283, *283*
lake 188
    lochan 251
    turlough 304, 309
Lake District, The 156–163
lapwing *see* Waders
lark, sky 177
leek
    Babington's 90, *90*
    three-cornered 91, *91*
lichen *175*
    Parmelia 30
lily
    Snowdon 178, *178*
    water 112, *115*
limestone 142, *143*
    pavement 304–308
lizard
    common 73, 74, *190*, *191*
    sand 29
    wall 44, *45*
Lizard Peninsula 68–75
lochan 251
loosestrife
    purple 114, *115*
    yellow 114, *164*, *164*
Loddon lily *see* Snowflake
Lough Neagh 274–281
lungwort, long-leaved 32, *32*

M
madder, wild *43*
magnolia, southern 17, *17*
mallard *see* Duck
mallow
    tree 194, *194*
        smaller 91, *91*
marigold
    corn *235*
    marsh 282, *282*
marten, pine *161*, *162*, 176, *207*
meadow-rue, alpine 174
meadowsweet *115*
medick, bur 107, *107*
merganser *see* Duck
merlin 144, 174, *175*, 176, 177, 180, *180*
milkwort, dwarf 149, *149*
mint
    pennyroyal 33, *33*
    water 283, *283*
moneywort, Cornish 60, *60*
monkey flower *129*
moorhen *115*
moss, sphagnum 61, *61*
moth
    burnet
        five-spot *189*

317

mountain 221
chimney sweeper 135, *135*
Chinese character 134, *134*
fox 57, *59*
hawk, elephant 12
mullein *102*
shoulder stripe 134, *134*
streamer 135, *135*
tiger
    garden *235*
    wood *131*
underwing, lesser *235*
yellow-tail 135, *135*
mountain 171, 174
see also Cairngorms, Scottish Highlands
mountain ash *see* Rowan
mountain everlasting 148, *148*
mouse 213
    field 249
    long-tailed field *see* Mouse, wood
    wood *237*
    see also Vole
mouse-ear, starwort 222, *222*

N
New Forest, The 24–31
nightingale *74*
night jar *103*
nightshade, alpine enchanter's 164, *164*, 174
Norfolk Broads, The 110–117

O
orchid
    Burren 308, *309*
    bog 60, *60*
    common spotted 238, *238*, 310, *310*
    dense-flowered 310, *310*
    early marsh 116, 119, *119*
    early purple *43*, 174
    frog 252, *252*, 267
    green-winged *13*
    heath spotted *236*
    pyramidal *43*
    soldier *101*
    southern marsh 115, 119, *119*
    Welsh marsh 192, *192*
    see also Helleborine, Lady's tresses
oriole, golden 94, *94*
Orkney Islands 260–267
osprey 225, *225*
otter *115*, 116, 249
Outer Hebrides *see* Western Isles
ouzel, ring *145*, 151, *151*, 152–153, *152–153*
owl
    barn 117
    long-eared 176, 281
    short-eared 15, 117, 176, *265*
    snowy 254, *254*, 256–257, *256–257*
oystercatcher *see* Waders

P, Q
pansy
    dwarf *86*
    mountain *145*, 148, *148*
    seaside 193, *193*
    wild *189*
parsley, milk 114, *115*, 118, *118*
pea, marsh 119, *119*
Peak District, The 124–131

peat 112, 246
pennyroyal mint 33, *33*
peregrine falcon 147, *176*, 177, *190*, 220, 224, *224*
pillwort 31
pike *see* Fish
pine, Scots 102
pink
    maiden 192, *192*
    sea *see* Thrift
pipit
    meadow 174, *175*, 177, 206
    red-throated 92, *92*
pittosporum *88*
plaintain
    hoary 133, *133*
    ribwort *43*, 50
plover *see* Waders
polecat *175*, *176*, *177*
pollution 113, 123
pondweed 117
pony
    Dartmoor 59
    New Forest *30*
    Shetland 258–259, *258–259*
poplar, white 17, *17*
poppy *177*
    yellow horned *43*, 195, *195*
porpoise, common 264
primrose 174
    birdseye 149, *149*
    Scottish *265*, 267, 269, *269*
ptarmigan 207, 210–211, *210–211*, 218, *218*
puffin 80, *191*, 236, 267
purslane, Hampshire 32, *32*
quartz 216, *217*

R
rabbit 99, 103, 213
rail, water *see* Waders
rare birds 94–95, *94–95*
rattle, red 239, *239*
raven 56, *145*, 160, *161*, 168–169, *168–169*, 174, *175*, 177, 180, *180*
razor bill 87
redshank *see* Waders
redstart 28
    American 79, *79*
reed *112*, 114
    bur 125
reedmace 114
    great 125
Republic of Ireland 288–295
ring ouzel 56, *145*, 151, *151*, 152–153, *152–153*, *175*, *176*, 206
roach *see* Fish
rockcress, northern 178, *178*
rock rose
    annual *190*
      spotted 194, *194*
    common 132, *132*, 145
    hoary 310, *310*
rook 117
roseroot 208, *208*
rowan 59, *175*, 177
rue, lesser meadow 165, *165*
rupture-wort, smooth 106, *106*
rush
    wood, curved 222, *222*

S
St Kilda *see* Western Isles
salmon *see* Fish
saltmarsh 191
sand dunes 187, 190, 191
saw-wort, alpine 165, *165*
saxifrage 174, *175*
    golden, opposite-leaved 47, *47*
    highland 223, *223*
    Irish 311, *311*
    mossy 178, *178*
    purple 222, *222*
    starry 209, *209*
    yellow mountain 268, *268*
scabious, sheep's bit *189*
schelly *see* Fish
Scilly Isles 82–89
Scottish Highlands 200–207
sea holly *87*, 189
sea urchin, purple heart *294*
seal
    common 250, 264
    grey (atlantic) 75, 88, 237, 250, 264, 266
sedge 112, 116, 206
    hare's foot 223, *223*
    slender tufted *13*
shag 74, *250*
shark, basking 75
shearwater, manx 80, 89
sheep 99, 154–155, *154–155*, *175*, 203
    Dalesbred 167, *167*
    Herdwick 166, *166*
    Lonk 166, *166*
    Rough Fell 167, *167*
    Scottish blackface 166, *166*
    Soay *234*
    Swaledale *155*, 167, *167*
Shetland Isles 244–251
shoreweed 31
shrew
    pygmy *280*, 306
    water 12
    white-toothed, lesser 88
shrike
    red-backed *102*
    woodchat 92, *92*
sibbaldia 222, *222*
skua
    arctic 251, *251*
    great 251, *251*, 272–273, *272–273*
skylark 177
sloe *see* Blackthorn
slug, Kerry *294*
snail
    banded *189*
    two-lipped door 14
snake
    adder 57, *58*, 72, *73*, 75, *189*
    grass 66–67, *66–67*
snipe *see* Waders
snowflake, summer (Loddon lily) 13
Solomon's seal, angular 132, *132*
sorrel 176
    common 238, *238*
    mountain 179, *179*
sow-thistle, marsh 118, *118*
sparrow 20–21
    house *20*, 21
    tree *21*
speedwell
    Breckland 105, *105*

fingered 104, *104*
spiked *103*, 104, *104*
spring 104, *104*
spider *175*
   Argiope bruennichi 44, *44*
   wolf 221
spikenard, ploughman's 192, *192*
spleenwort, sea 195, *195*
spoonbill 114
spring beauty 90, *90*
squill, autumn 74, *74*
squirrel, red 45, *103*, 161, 163, *163*, *279*
star-of-Bethlehem 107, *107*
starfish
   common 87
   featherstar 88
starling, rose-coloured 93, *93*
stoat, Irish *279*, *280*
stock, hoary 47, *47*
stonechat *57*, 72, *75*
storksbill, common 238, *238*
strawberry tree 294, 297, *297*
swan
   Bewick's *116*, 286–287, *286–287*
   mute 12, *12*
   whooper 286–287, *287*
swift 177

T
tamarisk 47, *47*
tonager, scarlet *95*
teal *see* Duck
tench *see* Fish
tern 190
   arctic 267
   Sandwich *188*
Thames Valley, The 8–15
thistle, marsh sow 118, *118*
thrift 207, *265*
thyme
   Breckland 106, *106*
   wild *189*
tit
   bearded 114, *114*, 120, *120*
   crested *218*

toad, South African clawed 44
trout *see* Fish
tulip tree 16, *16*
turlough 304, 309
twite 224, *224*, 237
tussock, pale 134, *134*

V
vagrant birds 94–95, *94–95*
vendace *see* Fish
vetch, kidney *43*
violet 207
   water 117
viper's bugloss 192, *192*
vole 117, 213
   field (short-tailed) *175*, 176
   Orkney *265*
   water 12, *115*

W
waders
   curlew 136–137, *136–137*, 267
     stone 102, 108–109, *108–109*
   dotterel *177*, *207*, 210, *210*, 219,
     228–229, *228–229*
   dowitcher, long-billed 312, *312*
   dunlin 235
   godwit, black-tailed *42*, 280
   greenshank 206, 211, *211*
   lapwing 144, *145*, 189
   oystercatcher *189*
   plover 117, 177
     golden 56, *59*, 130, 279, *307*
     lesser 94
     ringed *236*, 284, *284*
   redshank 284, *284*
     spotted 48, *48*
   sandpiper
     Baird's 299, *299*
     broad-billed 117
     buff-breasted 299, *299*
     common 174, 218
     curlew 49, *49*
     least 313, *313*
   snipe 117, 131
     jack 19, *19*

water rail 285, *285*
whimbrel 254, *254*
yellowlegs
   greater 313, *313*
   lesser 313, *313*
wagtail
   grey 174
   white 255, *255*
   yellow *13*, 151, *151*
wallaby, red-necked 138–139, *138–139*
warbler
   black and white 78, *78*
   Cetti's 114, 121, *121*
   Dartford *31*
   grasshopper 176, *278*, 279
   marsh 18, *18*
   orphean 78, *78*
   Pallas's 92, *92*
   parula 79, *79*
   reed 114, 116, 121, *121*
   sedge 114, *115*, 116, 121, *121*
   spectacled 79, *79*
water lily *see* Lily
water mint, 283, *283*
water soldier 117
weasel 125, *145*
Welsh Hills 170–177
Western Isles 230–237
whale 250
   pilot 250
wheatear 56, *57*, *175*, 176, 177
whimbrel *see* Waders
whinchat *63*, *63*, *174*, 176, 177
widgeon *see* Duck
willow
   creeping 189, 269, *269*
   dwarf 208, *208*
wormwood, field 106, *106*
wren 72, *307*
   St Kilda 237, 241, *241*

Y
yellowlegs *see* Waders
yellow wort *43*
Yorkshire Dales, The 140–147